INDIGENOUS VANGUARDS

Modernist Latitudes

Modernist Latitudes

JESSICA BERMAN AND PAUL SAINT-AMOUR, EDITORS

Modernist Latitudes aims to capture the energy and ferment of modernist studies by continuing to open up the range of forms, locations, temporalities, and theoretical approaches encompassed by the field. The series celebrates the growing latitude ("scope for freedom of action or thought") that this broadening affords scholars of modernism, whether they are investigating little-known works or revisiting canonical ones. Modernist Latitudes will pay particular attention to the texts and contexts of those latitudes (Africa, Latin America, Australia, Asia, Southern Europe, and even the rural United States) that have long been misrecognized as ancillary to the canonical modernisms of the global North.

For the list of titles in this series, see page 373.

INDIGENOUS VANGUARDS

Education, National Liberation, and the Limits of Modernism

BEN CONISBEE BAER

Columbia University Press

New York

Columbia University Press
Publishers Since 1893
New York   Chichester, West Sussex
cup.columbia.edu

Copyright © 2019 Columbia University Press
All rights reserved

Library of Congress Cataloging-in-Publication Data
Names: Baer, Ben Conisbee, author.
Title: Indigenous vanguards : education, national liberation, and the limits
    of modernism / Ben Conisbee Baer.
Description: New York : Columbia University Press, 2019. | Series: Modernist
    latitudes | Includes bibliographical references and index.
Identifiers: LCCN 2018029913 | ISBN 9780231163729 (cloth : alk. paper) |
    ISBN 9780231548960 (e-book)
Subjects: LCSH: Education, Colonial—History—20th century. | Indigenous
    peoples—Education—History—20th cenetury. | Modernism (Aesthetics) |
    National liberation movements. | Decolonization. | Postcolonialism.
Classification: LCC LC2605 .B28 2019 | DDC 370.89—dc23
LC record available at https://lccn.loc.gov/2018029913

Columbia University Press books are printed on permanent and durable
acid-free paper.
Printed in the United States of America

Cover design: Elliott S. Cairns
Cover image: Winold Reiss, *Two Public School Teachers*, 31½" x 23¼", pastel
on Whatman board, 1925. Fisk University Galleries, Nashville, Tennessee.

To my grandparents, Bernhard Baer and Ann Baer

CONTENTS

ACKNOWLEDGMENTS

This book would not have been possible without the friendship, conversation, encouragement, critical commentary, advice, and laughter of the following people, and I thank them all:

Gayatri Chakravorty Spivak, Partha Chatterjee, Jonathan Arac, Beth Povinelli, David Damrosch, Simon Gikandi, Eduardo Cadava, Hal Foster, Sandy Tait, Sangeeta Ray, Emily Apter, Gyan Prakash, Isabelle Clark-Decès, Jonathan Gold, Hosam Abou-Ela, Subramanian Shankar, Ania Loomba, Nicole Rizzuto, Zahid Chaudhary, Susana Draper, Devin Fore, Natasha Lee, Sarah Whiting, Ron Witte, Meredith Martin, Dermot Ryan, Alex Neel, Eric Glatt, Joseph Slaughter, Jennifer Wenzel, Nergis Ertürk, Brian Lennon, Emma Bianchi, Mrs. Gouri Bandopadhyay, Amal Shankar Bandopadhyay, Himadri Banerjee, Anjan Sen, Subha Chakraborty Dasgupta, Pradip Basu, Anirban Das, Aditi Sen, Mandira Bhaduri, Sandra Bermann, Eileen Reeves, Daniel Heller-Roazen, Lital Levy, Jesse Knutson, Sonali Perera, Jill Jarvis, Cate Reilly, Gavin Arnall, Moira Fradinger, Katy Clark, Katie Trumpener, Carol Jacobs, Dudley Andrew, Shivi Sivaramakrishnan, Souleymane Bachir Diagne, Ritwik Ranjan, Surya Parekh.

Special thanks are due to Susan Wragg, Molly Conisbee, and Faya Causey.

I am extremely grateful to the series editors, Jessica Berman and Paul Saint-Amour, as well as Columbia editor Philip Leventhal, for their patience and gentle-but-firm encouragement.

I am indebted to the following institutions for their support:

Le Musée National de l'Éducation, Rouen, France; La Bibliothèque Diderot de Lyon, France; the Moorland-Spingarn Research Center, Howard University; the Princeton University Committee on Research in the Humanities and Social Sciences; the Princeton Institute for International and Regional Studies; Princeton University Department of Comparative Literature; Yale University Department of Comparative Literature; New York University Department of Comparative Literature.

I thank Siona Wilson, who traveled the road with me in love and companionship.

INTRODUCTION

Thus we believe we have solid reasons for thinking that, behind the "theatre" of the political struggles which the bourgeoisie has offered the popular masses as a spectacle, or imposed on them as an ordeal, what it has established as its number-one, that is its *dominant*, Ideological State Apparatus is *the scholastic apparatus* [Appareil scolaire].

    —Louis Althusser, *On the Reproduction of Capitalism*

Comrade, dear friend, help, save us! Already there is no school. No new school, no old school, nothing.

    I have taught for twenty years and I cannot take it in, cannot comprehend it.

    For we can only build the future on the education of the people. What will an illiterate generation say to us?

    —Anonymous schoolteacher from Gomel (Soviet Union)

I wonder sometimes if school inspectors and department heads are conscious of their role in the colonies. For twenty years in their school programs, they desperately try to make a White man out of the black man. In the end, they give up and tell him: you have undeniably a dependency complex regarding the White man. . . .

    But I am a man, and in this sense the Peloponnesian War is as much mine as the invention of the compass.

    —Frantz Fanon, *Black Skin, White Masks*

School is the instrument through which intellectuals of various levels are elaborated.

    —Antonio Gramsci, *Prison Notebooks*

The question of schooling as a decisive process for the formation of "modern" subjects is the theoretical lever of this book. I read the interwar period as an epoch of worldwide struggles for the expansion of common schooling linked to an unprecedented emergence of new anticolonial movements in Africa, Asia, and the Americas. Beyond mere mobilization of a "mass" into a "people," vanguard intellectuals of this epoch were preoccupied with a more elaborate educative formation of future citizens able to think independently and participate in making a nonimperial world. These two sides of the problem form a double bind. On the one hand, a necessarily long term and painstaking labor of preparation, at the level of mind and spirit, for the practice of freedom as citizen of a new State. On the other hand, a demand and desire—a great collective dreamwork—of immediate liberation and enfranchisement that short-circuits the deferral seemingly entailed by the former. It is not a matter of choosing between one knot or the other of this double bind; the field of their disjunctive and supplementary relationship defines the situations and dilemmas I read in the chapters that follow.

Dreams of immediate freedom and concerns with institutions and methods for the making of future citizens also took hold of such contemporary interwar revolutionary formations as the Soviet Union, Austrian Socialism, and German Social Democracy, connected by fragile threads to emergent national liberation struggles in Africa, Asia, and the Americas.[1] In this epoch, national liberation and revolution are not identical phenomena. The latter aims systemically to transform bourgeois State and society, altering their relation to capital, and this is not necessarily the aim of *national* liberation. Yet the historical affinity between national liberation and revolution is symbolically and aesthetically marked by the fact that Frantz Fanon named his urgent prognosis of national liberation after a quotation of the first line of the "Internationale," the anthem of the Socialist International: "Debout, les damnés de la terre."[2] The question of the relation between intellectual and worker in socialism undergoes displacements in colonial situations even as the Soviet Union was itself a postimperial conjuncture and initially a new (and arguably benevolent) empire-form.[3] (It was also in the 1920s a conjuncture that was obliged to think a *workers'* State that comprised mainly peasants and the rural poor, with a miniscule industrial working class.) In an overlapping way, the problem of common education was acutely prevalent in modern colonial societies because great numbers of their populations were positioned in the massively heterogeneous diversity of subalternity, "removed from all lines of social mobility."[4] Antonio Gramsci wrote about these problems of social difference in the 1930s. In his terms, subalternity is a place at "the margins of history," thus liminal to the historical unity that is represented by the State. This means an artificially mute exteriority to the State: variegated groupings, "disaggregated and episodic," that periodically stake political claims on State and society, but that are in the normal unfolding of things instrumentalized and "subject to the initiative of ruling groups."[5]

This book is about moments where the emancipatory *and* pedagogical dreams of the vanguard, dreams crisscrossed with literary desires and ambitions, meet the epistemological and practical limits of subalternity in the task of national liberation. Evoking limits in this way, I draw from Michel Foucault's formulation that the experience of the limit is also the incalculable experience of its transgression.[6] The subaltern "limit" is neither an absolute barrier, nor a blank slate, nor a realm of plenitude on the far side of a determinate line: "Transgression, then, is not related to the limit as black to white, the prohibited to the lawful, the outside to the inside, or as the open area of a building to its enclosed spaces. Rather, their relationship takes the form of a spiral which no simple infraction can exhaust."[7] For the present study, this figure of the spiral is a way of representing the interface between vanguard intellectuals and subaltern spaces: a relation of supplementarity without guarantees.

This is a book of literary criticism and theory. It argues that the problem of affecting and being affected by the subaltern, primarily educatively, in the work of national liberation and a projected democratic future, can be managed neither by modernist aesthetic practices themselves nor by the kinds of disciplinary research (constative literary criticism) they generate. Work done by the protagonists of the present study in the 1920s, 1930s, and 1940s encounters and discloses limits of modernist aesthetic practice that cause some of these protagonists to change course and others to retrench. Such changing course takes different directions, at tangents from benevolent primitivisms that seek to draw aesthetic "practices of negation" from subaltern spaces.[8] Practices of negation shelter the subaltern in subalternity as the negations unfold elsewhere, this side of the limit, for whatever benefit experimental art has left to tap. Disciplinary limits for constative literary criticism, which are another kind of "modernist latitude," recur in this book as a persistent question about the desire to incorporate an ever-expanding body of works into a "global" picture of modernism. As with artistic negations, such incorporation is valuable in its own terms as a correction or augmentation of an existing disciplinary archive. Yet it leaves room for other kinds of work that fall outside of modernist studies—a limit this book can only gesture toward.

Definite and original kinds of cultural activism and modern writing emerged from the connections between anticolonial work, literary experimentation, and practices of teaching and learning from the 1920s to the 1940s. I discuss these through figures that form the pivots of the following chapters: Alain Locke represents Harlem's "New Negro" generation by translating German Enlightenment educational philosophies of spiritual upbringing, maturity, and emancipation from colonial conditions, thereby subverting and renewing the lexicon of race in the United States. Léopold Senghor negotiates the colonial pattern of "Africanizing" education for the French West African subaltern, making a critically intimate revision of French education a condition of elaborating the modernist Négritude experiment in social and political terms. Aimé Césaire retraces the elementary French schoolbooks of the Caribbean classroom, poetically experimenting with a programmed curriculum and pedagogical techniques so as to turn them toward nonimperial meanings. Both Senghor and Césaire later became leaders of State, and their early fixation on educational problems is undoubtedly a factor in this development. D. H. Lawrence fantasizes about the coercive reeducation of the Mexican subaltern below the lines of the modern State and its social pedagogy—laying bare the articulation of authoritarian desire. Finally, Rabindranath Tagore and Mahatma Gandhi intervene in the massive and sedimented complex of educational experiments and institutions in colonial India. Addressing the impact of colonial education and cultural epistemology, they posit a revised elementary instruction in the mother tongue to offset cultural alienation (Tagore); and a radical short circuit of the political rationality they entail (Gandhi). I conclude with discussion of a modern Indian novel's dramatization of subaltern demands for infrastructural access to the State. This singular instance is imagined through the grammatized formalism of a teaching drill, challenging the "educated reader" to work through the question of engaging with subaltern desires and languages as the condition for future solidarity.

❖ ❖ ❖

As perhaps the most general noneconomic social institution of modernity during a certain epoch, the schooling system's environment, institutional forms, and technologies have determined incalculable subjective, epistemic, and experiential transformations of the lifeworld. The establishment of common public schooling unfolded in an uneven wave across the nation-states of the modern world from the mid-nineteenth to the mid-twentieth centuries, as both condition and effect of the nation-state itself. The wave is still breaking. It is therefore a comparatively recent—and increasingly fragile—development, but its accumulated social and ideological force is reflected in the fact that the right to a free and compulsory elementary education is enshrined in the Universal Declaration of Human Rights of 1948 and in other subsequent international treaties such as the United Nations' International Covenant on Economic, Social and Cultural Rights of 1966 and the UN Convention on the Rights of the Child in 1989.[9] Public schooling was a constituent aspect of the development of nation-states, which are the "signatories" of international declarations. Almost every "postcolonial" State became, at least nominally, a democratic nation-state or democratic republic—entailing some sort of imaginative and institutional negotiation with principles and practices of education that were formalized in the European Enlightenment. The latter's formula of elementary schooling may be expressed in rarefied and idealized terms as "an educational structure based on literacy, numeracy, reading skills [la littération], and familiarity with 'universal ideas'; [a] version of what German educators called Bildung, a 'formation' in which there is also the projection of an image (Bild). This national(ized) literary [littérale] projection is a synchronization constituting the unity of the democratic industrial We."[10] The constitution of such a "We"—in space and time, projected and synchronized—is precisely the question opened up in this book. In spite of the tremendous class-dividedness of actual modern common education systems as machines for the perpetuation of prevailing social differences, the conditions of modernizing societies have nevertheless necessitated the development of specific kinds of capabilities, knowledges, and habits across a far more general social body than in prior historical conjunctures (i.e., *public* education). Bernard Stiegler calls this the social requirement of "an elevated level of both individual and collective responsibility" and links it to the Enlightenment imperative to construct a condition of "maturity" for a citizen-public.[11] I shall return to this abstract educative schema later.

In a radio discussion of the late 1960s, Theodor Adorno said that "the demand for independent maturity [*Mündigkeit*] seems self-explanatory in a democracy. . . . Democracy rests on the educative formation of will [*Willensbildung*] in each individual, as conjoined in the institution of the representative vote. If this is not to result in irrationality, the capacity and courage of each individual to use their understanding must be presupposed."[12] Adorno poses the faculty of understanding (*Verstand*) against irrationality (*Unvernunft*) here, recapitulating a Kantian thematics of preparation for *Mündigkeit* that I examine in detail in chapter 1. In this presupposition is contained the need for an education (*Bildung*) of the "will" (and thus something of the desiring-part of the subject). Adorno highlights not just courage to use the faculty of understanding, but a *capacity to use an education* in terms of desire as well as understanding, which is an ever-ramifying problem.[13] This goes for teacher and student alike. In a nutshell, it tells us that *education itself needs education*, and this problem is at the center of *Indigenous Vanguards*. Its institutional and sociopolitical ramifications are as significant as its representational articulations are complex.

Modern, mandatory public education contains the historically unprecedented possibility of preparation for a socially general practice (or "savoir-faire") of citizenship, and a sharable, public, democratic cultural politics, in principle open to anyone. The production of desire for this kind of civil society in colonial space—which is an aspect of the making of the "colonial subject"—has been covered in detail by others.[14] What this book adds is an account of how some of the "enlightened" educators approached the problem of (re)educating themselves from within the presuppositions of the exceptional humanistic training they had received. Furthermore, I seek to show how they sought to imagine and represent, often in experimental literary ways, the millions not trained into the thought and presuppositions of democratic practices that were nevertheless projected as the goals of (their) national liberation. "Democratic practices" are by definition fundamentally ambiguous and open-ended. In what ways was the "anyone" imagined and represented, welcomed, excluded, or put off until later, during and after the great scenographies of national liberation? Rather than consider such questions from the angle of political science, which I am not qualified to do, I address them in terms of literary representations and interfaces between literature and institutional teaching and learning.

At an early phase of the uneven wave of general public education, variants of modern colonial states also deployed schooling at several levels to produce strata of indigenous colonial subjects who occupied an ambiguous managerial position in relation to the vast populations of the European empires. An unforeseen effect was that these strata also supplied almost all the leaders of anticolonial nationalist movements (the named founders and leaders of nation-states that later would sign formal international declarations of the right to education). If common schooling constituted in principle an intellectual, ethical, and technical preparation to enter the structures of citizenship and practical participation in metropolitan States, the systematic denial of democratic structures in colonies engendered countermovements in imaginative upper- and middle-class intellectuals trained in the former's presuppositions. Such intellectuals inhabited the scholastic apparatus to the point that they were able to "read" it and to use it, write with it, as training toward other ends where democratic participation was blocked. It is not by chance that a vivid and early example of this unfolds in an educational institution. As Partha Chatterjee tells us, in 1843 an English teacher of literature at Calcutta's Hindu College sought to close down a meeting of the Indian Society for the Acquisition of General Knowledge, which had been founded by some former students, because the meeting was critical of the very government that had founded Hindu College for Indians' benefit in the first place.[15] The society members were exercising what they thought to be their "democratic" right to criticize the limits of colonial freedom. What Chatterjee calls the possibility of "our modernity" emerges in such circumstances, precisely at the point where Enlightenment universalism encounters a limit because it cannot include a particular group within its framework of a public domain of free discourse. Enlightenment betrays itself in the deferral or limits built into the colonial relation. "The same historical process that has taught us the value of modernity has also made us the victims of modernity," writes Chatterjee ("Modernity" 210). "At this founding moment of modernity

[1840s] we did genuinely want to believe that in the new public domain of free discourse there were no bars of color or of the political status of one's nationality, that if one could produce proof of one's competence in the subjects under discussion one had an unrestricted right to voice one's opinions" (205). Colonial blockage of access to a promised universality then engenders a claim to the universal from the other side—one now marked by an emergent "national" signifier. A "distinctly *national* modernity" emerges (207, my emphasis). If modernity now takes on an Indian face, "our" modernity is ironic, "ambiguous," because the very logic under which colonialism was supposed to civilize and enlighten India is that by which Indian nationalists made a case for emancipation from colonial rule (210).

Inhabiting the equivocality and torsion of this space, the small "progressive bourgeoisies" that led struggles for national liberation came to produce versions of the nation on the basis of broadly "orientalist" images of a national past.[16] Therefore, their active, supplementary repurposing of Enlightenment instruments may not always seem felicitous today. It should be examined case by case, however, because, I shall argue, in practice not all (national, public) education inevitably entails an orientalist outcome. It is varieties of such ambiguous currents within and alongside national liberation that I have gathered in this book under the heading of "indigenous vanguards." This bizarre title reflects the complex and often paradoxical struggles, writings, and representations of schooling the minds and spirits of the young for the future in situations that, like all nationalisms, also assert self-indigenizing and self-ethnicizing methods of soul-making and subject-formation.

❖ ❖ ❖

What are the broad outlines of soul-making and subject-formation as they are—in principle—inculcated by modern systems of common education?

Every educative program is one of "soul-making" to the extent that it establishes itself as the humanization of a not-yet or not-quite human other.[17] This classically appears as the humanization of the undifferentiated animal. In Kant's most programmatic writing on education, for example, he says that "the human is the only creature that needs to be educated [*erzogen*]." Kant states that discipline and rearing, *Disziplin* and *Zucht*, are two of the essential components of education in general. Their application "changes animality into humanity."[18] Further, "discipline prevents the human being turned away by its animal drives from humanity, [which is] its determination [*Bestimmung*]" (*Education* 3/698). Gramsci later reflects this concession when he writes that "the history of industrialism has always been a continuing struggle . . . against the element of 'animality' in man. It has been an uninterrupted, often painful and bloody process of subjugating natural (i.e. animal and primitive) instincts to new, more complex and rigid norms and habits of order, exactitude and precision which can make possible the increasingly complex forms of collective life which are the necessary consequence of industrial development."[19] For Kant, the line of development is couched in terms of humanity's "perfectibility" or the "end of its being" (*Vollkommenheit* or *Zweck seines Daseins*), though as we shall see he introduces a profound epistemological problem regarding the knowability of this end (and thus regarding the practice of an education toward it) (*Education* 7–10/700–702). Initially, we are faced with the paradox of a seemingly "inhuman," cruel, and systematized ordeal of disciplinarization to make human animals human (oriented toward a determined end), and, more specifically, to make them capable of internalizing and assuming the knowledges and habits required for an increasingly complex and demanding social existence.

The indiscipline of *Wildheit*—wildness or "savagery"—is in the Kantian passages the name for "independence from laws."[20] It can appear in any poorly reared child. "Discipline subjects humans to the laws of humanity," getting them into the correct habits and mental attitudes to learn. Any human can remain in a state of lawless indiscipline, but to illustrate this Kant specifically introduces the figure of "savage nations" (*wilden Nationen*) that stand outside the laws of humanity. These nations can simulate the functions (*Dienstetun*) of Europeans, even for long periods, but cannot sustain a European way of living. They are not noble savages à la Rousseau (with a "noble disposition to freedom") but embody "rather a certain rawness [*Rohigkeit*] inasmuch as the animal has, in a sense, not yet here developed humanity in itself" (4/698). Kant is not specifically interested in the *wilden Nationen* as such; he is using their example as a foil to illustrate the claim that to humanize the animal means to subject it to the prescriptions and discipline of reason early on lest it preserve its *Wildheit* (its nonsubjection to law) for its entire life and thus remain outside the determination of a human end. This has a relationship with the fact that, as Gramsci observed in the 1930s, "for a social élite, the members [glielementi] of subaltern groups always have something of a barbaric or a pathological nature about them."[21]

Elementary education in particular touches the subaltern positionality of every human. To the extent that the human organism is, as Lacan once put it, subject to a "veritable specific prematurity of birth," and is for a time "still sunk in motor impotence and nursling dependence . . . at the *infans* stage," its individual access to lines of social mobility and agency is absent.[22] Each individual passes through a certain subalternity in its own way, but whether subalternity is systemically prolonged and normalized, or developed out of itself, is a matter of long circuits of social history and social difference. This is why for the Enlightenment and beyond, the capacity for validated independent thinking and agential public responsibility would authoritatively be theorized in terms of a "maturity" (*Mündigkeit*) inculcated by family and school.[23] The well-reared infant is evidently swept up in a wave of (preparation for) its maturity, a life of agency, institutional recognition, and validated speech almost as soon as it is born. Drawing on the Lacanian schema, Althusser will claim that the always-already structure of ideological interpellation is even at work before each child's birth, that "it is certain *in advance* that it will bear its Father's Name, and will therefore have an identity and be irreplaceable."[24] Yet the social structuring of these practices of recognizing the subject is determined in vastly differentiated ways and according to different cultural scripts. Please note that this line of argument does not mean I think that actually existing adult subalterns are more immature or childlike or indeed "outside" ideology than anyone else; it is rather that subalternity resides in the systemic denial of institutional frameworks in which individual or group speech and action can be recognized or take hold. I therefore point to what Adorno called "artificial stupification" (*synthetische Verdummung*), modes of *systemic* infantilization that sustain subalternity by ensuring that "subaltern groups are always subject to the initiative of dominant groups" in increasingly ramified and complex ways.[25] "Artificial stupification" can, of course, apply across all social strata depending upon the specific situation.

Each individual must undergo a process of development to the extent that it comes into the world "raw" (*roh*), to use Kant's word (*Education* 2/697). Others are charged with developing its humanity in an intergenerational structure of responsibility. These others, then, are already-educated older generations, not necessarily the child's biological parents. Each human can only be educated by humans who have themselves been educated—a recurring paradox for education in theory and practice that I have already underlined and to which we shall return (6/699). Already in Kant, however, this institution of the more developed rearing the less developed can describe the outlines of the imperial "civilizing mission" of his epoch (and ours), a point that Spivak has made regarding the Categorical Imperative and the appearance of the "raw man" in the *Critique of Judgment*.[26] The pedagogical text is far more empirical and lightweight than Kant's foundational philosophy of Reason, having been compiled from notes for an occasional lecture course Kant had to deliver as part of his professional obligations at Königsberg University between 1776 and 1787. Nevertheless, its account of education raises important questions that transgress the limits of philosophical correctness at the same time that it anticipates or repeats the gestures analyzed by Spivak in *A Critique of Postcolonial Reason*.[27]

Opening a supplementary passage from the high points of Kantian philosophy, Spivak elaborates "soul-making" as the "imperialist project cathected as civil-society-through-social-mission": that is, a desire-filled assumption of the responsibility of making humans out of heathens that are child-like in their immaturity or proximateness to animality (CPR 116). The "raw man"—the aboriginal named by Kant in the *Critique of Judgment*—represents the systemic limit to thinking Reason and the human philosophically (Man, the reasoning human, the "subject of speech or judgment"). The raw man's perspective is strictly impossible within the system: it is foreclosed rather than expelled.[28] The project of imperial soul-making is thus a kind of "travesty" of the Kantian schema in an oddly benevolent guise (CPR 123). Rather than foreclose the "raw man" as an absolutized structural limit, imperialism, when it is not genocidal colonization, manifests as a project of *development* of the "raw man." It is a generalized pedagogy that, as imperial ideology, may be formularized in Kantian terms as "make the heathen into a human so that he can be treated as an end in himself; in the interest of admitting the raw man into the noumenon" (as subject of philosophy) (26, 123–24). Thus, in the civilizing mission, the raw man *may* appear, may even be promised enfranchisement, but only once he is being properly educated.

As we have seen, according to Kant's pedagogical writings *all* humans are born "raw" and should be subject to a disciplinary and educative rearing that, as it were, cooks them into maturity. But, by way of illustrative foil, some "wild nations" remain "not yet" (*noch nicht*) autodeveloped into (European) humanity (*Education* 4/698). Empiricized into the liberal scheme of the colonial civilizing mission, such developmental logic projects an ever-receding horizon of the heathen/child/primitive's readiness for the independence and responsibility that come with the maturity conferred by successful passage through an education of the mind and spirit. Dipesh Chakrabarty has characterized this unattainable horizon as the "not-yet" of a historicist developmentalism: the position that "Indians or Africans," for example, "were *not yet* civilized enough to rule themselves," that consequently they must wait on an endlessly deferred point of arrival for the maturity that would permit suffrage and political independence.[29] This problem produces a terrible paradox for national independence movements, but a paradox they short-circuit by counterposing a "now" to the "not yet": a " 'now' that marks all popular movements toward democracy. . . . In their search for a mass base, anticolonial nationalist movements introduced classes and groups into the sphere of the political that, by the standards of nineteenth-century European liberalism, could only look ever so unprepared to assume the political responsibility of self-government" (PE 8). The "now" of the claim to immediate enfranchisement would make a citizen of the subaltern "long before he or she could be formally educated into the doctrinal or conceptual aspects of citizenship" (9). The studies in this book examine some of the difficulties of what the practice of education means and does "when the peasant or the subaltern emerges in the modern sphere of politics, in his or her own right, as a member of the nationalist movement . . . or as a full-fledged member of the body politic, without having had to do any 'preparatory' work in order to qualify as the 'bourgeois-citizen' " (10–11).

It is possible, however, that Chakrabarty is too romantic about the ways in which "the 'nation' and the political are also *performed* in the carnivalesque aspects of democracy: in rebellions, protest marches, sporting events, and in universal adult franchise" (10). This thought of performance does make a salutary point: that the pedagogical practices of (national, public) education are necessarily structured according to a more or less standardized matrix that positions other modes of acting and knowing as anachronistic, immature, or worse. Chakrabarty argues that the subaltern might find its own ways of practicing democratic citizenship and doing politics (by rebelling, protesting, or taking part in sporting or religious rituals) that question an education that can appear as a kind of top-down imposition of an often painful and pointless-seeming discipline. The idiomaticity of the world's variegated democratic practices and languages is a vital corrective to a one-size-fits-all modular checklist of "democratic" behavior.

On the other hand, the existence of colorful and heterodox practices of political performance can easily remain the alibi of manipulative and demagogic politics "from above" (and not just in ex-colonial States), where popular movements are ceaselessly coopted by the top. "Sports" can translate into zero-sum violent competition between political parties seen as competing clubs with enforced "team loyalty" or worse coercions during elections, and the mediatic channeling of the hero or the celebrity figure can take on a direct or tangential dictatorial function. To celebrate such "demotic" activity as anti-Power, anti-State, anti-Discipline breaches of the standardized time and space of the Nation is the privilege of the posttertiary educated intellectual who has other resources with which to build. In this context Fanon remains a counterpoint, a premonitory sentinel of what was announcing itself as colonialism unraveled, warning of the worst so as to try to avert it: the haunting return of persistent precolonial structures of the *longue durée* such as "the tribalization of power" that seems to "reprise the old laws of endogamy" for a ruling clan within the independent nation-state (*Wretched* 126). *Indigenous Vanguards* is not an investigation of these realities in today's divided world, but it does touch on aspects of their prefiguration in a period during which democracy not only was a watchword for the lifting of colonial domination, but also named a turn toward an incalculable future for new generations.

As Chakrabarty indicates, the systemic infantilization I indicated earlier does not preclude modalities of political action on the part of subaltern groups and individuals. There is by now a long bibliography of work in the subaltern studies tradition that documents and theorizes subaltern initiatives; but this documentation itself recognizes the recurrent problem that such action is systematically misread by those to whom it is addressed. The political delegations and protests of tribal and poor rural groups in colonial India were, for example, understood by colonial authorities as so many arbitrary acts of "criminal behavior."[30] Subaltern initiative is a sign of subalternity "brought to crisis" as militancy, and thereby as a possible emergence that can "burst the outlines of subalternity."[31] Because crisis signifies that subalternity may be on the way to something else, it must also be recognized as the exception to a subaltern normality that has barely been documented and is in any case not susceptible to generalization.

Fanon did not address the detail of formal, common education in his writings about the future of Africa and the colonized world, but its role is presupposed in almost everything he wrote about culture in *The Wretched of the Earth*. "Being responsible," he writes, "in an underdeveloped country is knowing that everything rests definitively on the education of the masses, on the elevation of thinking [*pensée*], and on what is too quickly called civic instruction [*la politisation*]."[32] Fanon continues, "civic instruction [*politiser*] is opening the mind [*esprit*], awakening the mind [*esprit*], putting the mind [*esprit*] in the world. It is, as Césaire said, 'inventing souls'" (*Wretched* 138). He reiterates the Enlightenment figure of maturity: "The civic instruction [*la politisation*] of the masses does not aim to infantilize them but to make them adults" (124).

The true wound of colonialism, for Fanon, is precisely the destruction of *esprits* (minds and spirits), souls, and thought among the colonized, a violence that he even elsewhere calls a "form of Nazism."[33] As a trained psychiatrist, Fanon was ideally placed to recognize the mind-, spirit-, and soul-destroying phenomena of colonial conditions, the fact that extreme violence is the only thinkable and acceptable course for such damaged spirits (children even murdering one another).[34]

The Wretched of the Earth confronts this terrible dilemma with Fanon's account of how the only response to mental destruction through extreme disenfranchisement-without-remedy appears as a zero-sum logic of lethal violence. In extraordinary passages illustrating the ethical residue within extreme violence, Fanon writes that the definition of decolonization can be contained in the biblical eschatological phrase "the last shall be first." "Decolonization is the verification of this phrase," he says.[35] It is an example of the limit-performance of an equalizing tabula rasa in colonial conflict. The biblical parable of the vineyard suggests that God works within neither human temporality nor economy nor proportion. The "last" workers of the day will receive the same as the "first," even though they come late and have not done any work. God's measure is not "fair" in one set of human calculations of equality (it is not an equivalent commensurate with effort, not a proportional and differential equality). It represents absolute equality regardless of individual quality, difference, or effort. Unconditional democracy? The "compartmentalized world" of colonial society is definitively unequal and disproportionate: "lights and paved roads" versus "no space," sated versus hungry, white versus black, the few versus the many (*Wretched* 4–5). The calculus of colonialism reckons a radical inequality of human lives in which a single European life is infinitely precious and native life is massively expendable (43). Death here is the limit case (the "absolute praxis") wherein equality may be claimed by the oppressed. First, the act of deadly violence instantiates a seal and pact of equality among the insurgent group: "the group requires that each individual commits an irreversible act. . . . The Mau-Mau required every member of the group to strike the victim. Everyone thus became personally responsible for the death of this victim" (44). The ethical structure inhabiting the logic of the "last shall be first" works two ways: by symbolically doing one killing we make ourselves the same, we are all equally condemned by this shared murder or the killing each of us has performed. Lethal specular violence—and thus equality with the colonizer in death—is the only way of razing disproportion into equality. This is a radical leveling that puts us all on the same plane, a tabula rasa, and the ethical structure of a postcoloniality that would hope to begin again from a shared zero. A lesson in unconditional democracy for the day after liberation: the killers are equal to everyone else in the postcolonial State, no matter how dissimilar they may seem or feel.

I believe that Fanon's effort here is to work on this violent desire to equalize not by a simple moral condemnation of its horror, but by entering into the logic of the wish it articulates (the "dreams of the indigenes") and staging a kind of "teaching" of its possible reorientation (5, 15). Fanon develops the outlines of a way to try to understand this ethical extremity and to work with it so as to begin to undo its specular bond of cycles of violence ("the circle of hatred") and heal its damaged souls with organizational and epistemological means (47). He warns repeatedly that the self-same immediate liberation and enfranchisement that he also unrelentingly worked for and advocated, if achieved without such healing, risk two things in a displaced manner and within a worldwide Cold War frame: (1) repeating the violence of colonialism; and (2) recharging persistent precolonial chauvinisms whose long historical circuits colonialism did not undo, or even exacerbated (a passage from "nation to ethnic group, from State to tribe") (97).

One *sees* that decolonization is a "program of absolute disorder," a "tabula rasa" "without transition," an absolute reversal of polarities. Fanon is describing its mode of appearance, the immediate, nakedly *visible* phenomenon whose logic is fatal substitution. To begin to undo this, knowledge is required. The work is epistemological. Thus, in a parallel construction, we move from sight to knowledge: "*La décolonisation . . . on le voit . . . on le sait*" (*Damnés* 39–40). One *sees* decolonization as a transitionless (*sans transition*) reversal, the phenomenon of violence itself, the (dream of the) other killed so that I may live; but one *knows* decolonization as "a historical process," and in this knowing reside the rudiments of an epistemological change that can be used to work through the "dream." The impoverished imaginary that is structured in relation to the fantasmatic "immediacy of his muscles" images the subject as "being able to pass without transition from the state of the colonized to the state of sovereign citizen of an independent nation," but this imaginary blocks "real progress on the path of knowledge [*connaissance*]" (*Wretched* 88). All Fanon can do in a book is articulate the unfolding of struggle itself as an educational process and tell us (again revisiting with frankness the Enlightenment and vanguard figures of adulthood and maturity) that in practice the process is "extremely difficult" and dependent on "organization" and "ideological level" in those who lead (95). *Who* will come to know is the question here, and I would argue that although Fanon tends to write in terms of phenomenological general types ("the colonist," "the leader," "the peasant"), he is trying to give his readers a sense of how damaged psyches and mental machineries have become: for singularities, go to the case studies. The rest describes an affective and epistemological field—made by the "generalization of inhuman practices"—in which the task of mending souls and minds cannot presuppose that those souls and minds are immediately the *semblables* of the enlightened but must enter into their dehumanized space nevertheless (183).

Fanon was scathing about colonial education and Europe's betrayal of the best side of its Enlightenment heritage. As we know, he also claimed a new Enlightenment "Spirit" in the name of the "brain mass of all humanity, whose connections must be multiplied" rather than "obliterate and derail" the brain (*le cerveau*) once more.[36] Yet he was also interested in turning (colonial) poison into medicine—a medical doctor who knew the value of pharmacology.

This pharmakontic approach, then, is a major reason educational activism became important for other figures in the present study. The mind-bending poison of an educative relation, in which the entire colonized society becomes a cruel schoolroom spawning nightmares, retains a rare potential to be used medicinally to help heal the wounds it has participated in inflicting. We know that colonies denied infrastructural access and political representation to indigenous elites, too; and though I necessarily center discussion on such figures—highly educated literary producers—I consider how their interest and involvement reflects on the elementary levels of schooling as the most general (because often mandatory and in principle directed toward *all* children in a society, not just the well-born) and most formative (because acting on the development of the youngest minds, the physiological infant).[37] As with literature, the aforementioned generality does not imply a one-size-fits-all approach; rather it brings us to the problem for modern societies of training *all* of the different and individual children who will become their citizens into readiness for the abstract generality of that status and the "maturity" to act in it. This is a daunting, difficult prospect in practice, especially if the basis of such formation is understood neither as the unmodified extension of European-type schooling to everywhere else in the world, nor as the revival and generalization of indigenous modes of knowing and teaching—phantasmatically depicted in the orientalist imaginary as having been merely temporarily disrupted by colonialism.

❖ ❖ ❖

Soul-making is necessarily systematized, up to a point, in instituted education through curricula, standardized examination systems, and so on. As Althusser and his students have shown, this is also the recipe for the "reproduction" of social divisions in a class-stratified society.[38] For Étienne Balibar, following in the wake of Althusser, "universal schooling" is an integral element in the complex and artifactual process of a modern "nationalization of society" that is in principle endless (not only because it must be a part of the rearing of every future generation and the integration of immigrants, but also because national unity is constitutively a future projected on the basis of a factitious past).[39] As with Stiegler, Balibar's account of the "nation-form" generalizes from the French example, but he rightly observes that varieties of the nation-form have been the dominant configuration for almost all the States that emerged with the formal ending of colonialism. The question of varieties is important here to the extent that not all modern nation-states replicate the logics and institutions of power manifest in the secular-rational organization of a modern France. As we saw, it was colonial practices of exclusion from the democratic norms and institutions enjoyed in the metropoles that occasioned the emergence of anticolonial nationalisms and the invention of ways of making States and doing nationhood differently. The question then becomes: What happens in this doing-differently, when the majorities of postcolonial nations are not formed according to metropolitan presuppositions and norms?[40]

Within a normative argument concerning schooling and the nation-form, Balibar argues that subjectivation should be understood not as the transmission of a set of sociopolitical values as content, but rather as constituting a "primary process" of "fixation of the affects of love and hate and representation of the 'self'" ("Nation Form" 94). The individual comes to recognize itself as a national subject in terms of a conjuncture of affect and consciousness of being "at home" in a place with others. These others are like me, *semblables*, not because they are identical in every way, but because our differences are relative to the great "symbolic difference between 'ourselves' and 'foreigners.'"[41] This interpellation invests the relatively empty and formal positionality of the constitutional *citizen* with imaginary content, yoking State to nation.

Subjects nationalized in this way invest a "sense of the sacred and the affects of love, respect, sacrifice and fear" in the proper name of the nation-state (and its flag and associated symbolizations, as well as the imaginary institution of a community composed of a national "we" that historically preexists every individual). This mobilization of affect and ethical formation is the mark of soul-making work underlying and constituting a subject capable of the ritualized performance of specular (self-)recognition that is the proper sphere of the interpellated subject. Thus, "one can be interpellated as an individual *in the name of* the collectivity whose name one bears" ("Nation Form" 96). What specific role does schooling play here? For Balibar, the main function of the school is the task of orienting each child to the (national) collectivity, a collectivity that preexists each child in the form of material representations of a past. This orientation also necessarily involves instruction in the practical capabilities, knowledges, habits, and attitudes commensurate with a specific social formation. Not just history and geography, but arithmetic, geometry, grammar.

In the space-time of the modern nation-form, collectivity appears as a "fictive ethnicity" shared by national subjects. It is fictive not because it is consciously made up, but because the represented "past" appears in the form of a transcendental unity of all the prior generations of peoples constituting a historically continuous community. This is *structurally* fictional (it posits a never-present past on a continuum to a destined future) and is organized representationally by a surface narrative continuity articulating a desiring investment in the education of children and young people ("Nation Form" 102). In the course of a lot of educational work, the child assumes or adopts a nationally oriented "identity of origins, culture and interests" in several ways. Balibar argues that the inculcation of "a common code and even a common norm" is instantiated in school, primarily through instruction in a national language, such that social differences *within* the national formation are always encoded upon the *shared* ground of a national(ized) language: "Schooling is the principal institution which produces [national] ethnicity as linguistic community."[42] However, this is not true of many multilingual postcolonial States for which a plurality of languages can be both a source of conflict and the chance for the invention of new kinds of democratic cohabitation. And in any case, a language is an "open" collectivity, universalizable and in principle habitable by anyone capable of learning it, not the exclusive property of members already marked as belonging to a particular national collectivity. Monolingual or not, the national formation therefore requires a "supplement of particularity, or a principle of closure, of exclusion" ("Nation Form" 99). The linguistic community is closed by the ethnoracial community—a symbolic structure of genealogical continuity in the transmission of a biospiritual "substance." This permits, for example, the representation of the nation as a sometimes diverse "family" and all the "biopolitical" structures of intervention that this entails in which a specific kind of national burden is historically placed upon women ("Nation Form" 100). The general argument clarifies how and why common public education is coemergent with the nation-form as well as being an element of its sustained reproduction and performance.

Stiegler adds an important pharmakontic twist to the baleful story of "fictive ethnicity." Once captured and closed by the symbolic structure of ethnoracial particularity, the necessarily factitious past undoubtedly provides material for all manner of nationally defined exclusions and distinctions as well as identifications, i.e., national*isms*. Stiegler offers a more elaborated account of the value of (1) intervening in the epistemological capability of imagining "nation" as an ideal object, as a past that was never present, and (2) teaching and learning the competencies to abstract the rules for the production of such representations (imagination). In a condensed formula he writes, "public instruction provided by national Education is the national(ized) [*nationale*] organizing of the interiorization (and naturalization) of the 'a priori' prosthetic synthesis."[43] Simplifying the philosophical richness of Stiegler's argument rather, I will say that "'a priori' prosthetic synthesis" is his name for the already-there-ness of a materially sedimented "past" into which each child is born. No one lived or experienced that past: it is a past made of "tertiary retentions," a term for externalized memory-aids, recordings that are "written" in the general sense of material bearing a trace of a past.[44] "Trace" because it is a past that has never been present and thus subsists in the *promise* of a sign and thus the promise of meaning, and hence remains oriented to a future. In a general sense, this "tertiary retention is . . . the prosthesis of consciousness without which there would be no mind [*esprit*], no recall, no memory of a non-experienced past, no culture" (TT3 39). Prior to any individual consciousness, a *"spatializing of the time of consciousness beyond consciousness"* (CPE 8, original emphasis).

In the Kantian framework assumed by Stiegler, the a priori synthetic judgment of consciousness is produced in the absence of evidence: it is transcendentally deduced. But this synthesis of consciousness, he writes, is the *après-coup* of a prosthetic synthesis because the prosthesis is precedent in time to consciousness and therefore empirical. However, the a priori synthetic judgment of consciousness cannot be retroactively *derived* from its empirical precedents as from a determinate origin (this would take us back to Kant vs. Locke).[45] The prosthetic synthesis "inherits at the same stroke the apriority of the synthesis of judgment it makes possible—in an *après-coup* that is somehow fictive [*fabulaire*], performative, and grounding [*fondateur*]" (TT3 141). This fabulary or factitious prosthetic condition of experience is existent only on condition of the a-posterior "history of technical inventions," but the latter "history" is only a *history* on the condition that its structure as *trace* (indeterminate cultural thread) has been turned into the meaningful *sign* of a specific historical script (141). It is not that one is at liberty simply to choose the signs of a particular history and thus construct whatever historical narrative one likes. But the politics and epistemology of history-writing and indeed cultural identifications and transformations are precisely about the struggles over making trace into the sign of a past-present.

While "prosthesis" usually designates a secondary and artificial *replacement* for something lacking or lost (a limb, for example), Stiegler underlines its character as "originary," not as a locatable origin. Its supplanting exteriority makes up for something that was not there on the "inside" all along. This supplementary logic means that "human reason and understanding *begin* in the possibility of this process of delegation onto prostheses and into a technical medium," the originary organization of the subject's self-consciousness in terms of space and time (its originary access to the transcendental) (TT3 79).

This argument enriches and clarifies the Marxist position on the "materiality of consciousness." The child's consciousness and its access to the transcendental are nested in this prosthetic "world" of "tertiary retentions" that in fact make it possible for the subject to have a world in some way sharable with others:

> the I is not simply itself *in itself*, but originarily *outside itself*. The I is *surrounded by* [au milieu de] "itself," which is to say by its objects and prostheses, a milieu that is at once not just itself, but its other.
>
> And it is a matter of an other that precedes it, an *already-there*, a past it has not experienced and is not its past except on condition of becoming its future. This structure of *pros-thetic precedence* is the *projective support* of consciousness.
>
> (49, original emphases)

The proposition of a determining agency-in-alterity outside the conscious self is also therefore the pharmakontic space in which education works. It makes possible both chauvinistic indoctrination and intuition of the ethics of justice. Artifactual memory, the "artificial already-there," the "tertiary retentions, technical traces constructing this artificial past that is not 'one's own' but that must become one's own, must be 'inherited' as one's own history" (36–37). While the subject cannot not inherit, a national public education is, for Stiegler, the (nonexclusive) institutionalized guiding of this process, out of which the "phantasmatic inheritor can desire a common future with those who share equally phantasmatically this [factitious] past by adoption" (TT3 90). The methodological formalization of this other-directedness holds the potential of promoting the sense of a "we" that is not just ethnocentric but acknowledges the equality of the non*semblable* in the space constructed as "national."

The factitious past can of course remain a completely ethnocentric and nationalistic fetish. But the originary prosthesis of the materiality of consciousness also leaves the space open for both questioning and detranscendentalizing transcendentalized cultural fetishes in an educational setting: "The education system retraces the paths of access to the plane of these nonexistent objects, these consistencies that are idealities, and this tracing is a method: it is the reconstitution of a course (*methodos*) that was traced by ancestors, that is *re-traced* by descendants" (TC 68). This opens the door to training the imagination as the othering of the self, as my "time" is always the time of the other. Learning to *know* this is an epistemological lesson that leads us back to the empirical. Not necessarily to immediately fill it out with a specific content, but first, at the elementary level, formally: to come to *know*, through attention-formation or formal exercises, that this is the case for me and others. This is an idealized and rarefied formula, of course, but the child's intellectual capacity is set in place by its conditioning externality-to-self. This also means that access to its thinking-machine is also conditional on the teacher's self-insertion into the space of the determining "mnemotechnical" cultural script: a language or languages, a milieu, history, geography, gendering, all without final guarantees. How does the "transcendental," thus desiring and ethical as well as sensorial, system work for *this* one? The stake of education is in the relation between the way the "transcendental" (because nonevidentiary, "believed") modes of judgment and desire play with epistemological functions. Thus my guiding question in this book is precisely how literary intellectuals involved in processes of national liberation have approached the question of access to a determining cultural script when the subject of a common education does not share their own formation. This is also a question of the education of education, as I have already outlined.

I would argue that this is the reason that Fanon is able to say that "national consciousness . . . is not nationalism."[46]

❖ ❖ ❖

Jules Ferry's educational reforms in nineteenth-century France, which became a global model for the standardization of mandatory common schooling, were organized around the formulaic trinity of "compulsory, secular, and free" in the context of a postrevolutionary nation-building struggle against the power of the church. The Ferry Laws on education fought to transform, in Stiegler's words, "socio-*ethnic* programs into socio-*political* programs" aiming, at least in principle, at the "formation of a secular and responsible maturity [*majorité*] beyond the inheritance of a tradition or the transmission of a dogma of revelation."[47] That is, to institute a structure of nontheological instruction to prepare for independent existence as national citizen ("socio-political") rather than religious-communal ("socio-ethnic") existence. One must question the ultimate stability of such a distinction and at the same time not collapse all discourses of "reason" and its pedagogy into the coercive extension of European (protestant) epistemology and ethics. Different colonial formations had different emphases and practices when it came to schooling, and the institutions and techniques of modern teaching had everywhere unforeseen effects that undid or attenuated such "secularizing" (or indeed Christianizing) aims school may have carried. The role of missionaries and religious reformers in modernizing and spreading educational structures in colonies is central to this paradox.

Correspondingly, the fact that for the epoch of Ferry "the nation" is the newly invested collective social object is a paradox that entails immense conceptual and practical dilemmas. As we have seen from Balibar's argument, the nation-form itself was already turning out to be a "socio-*ethnic* program" of a new type in spite of the arguably felicitous abstraction of constitutional citizenship that typically accompanied it. Yet sacralized "fictive ethnicity" is a point at which questioning ceases and national identity becomes a "phantasm" in Stiegler's words, which overwrites the actual relations and processes that produce, and also break up, social units (TC 61). If "powerful lineal or tribal solidarities" are, in addition to religious affiliations, examples of the socioethnic program preexisting a "complete" national formation, then, as Balibar points out, nationalism should not be considered a "regression to archaic forms of community" but rather "the substitution of one imaginary of kinship for another" ("Nation Form" 102). The sociopolitical is in a struggle with the socioethnic in a situation where the mere spread of educational institutions, literacy, and the like, desirable though they are, cannot guarantee that socioethnic affinities will not prevail. Educational institutions, or even general social pedagogy, are not sufficient to close this gap.

Ferry's reforms thus remained productively entangled in the conflictual interdependence between nation and State, between "socio-*ethnic* programs [and] socio-*political* programs" so called. On this basis, Ferry's educational reforms are compatible with his role as the modernizer and expander of French imperialism: the civilizing mission hand in hand with the institutional and technical development of the colonies as a national project of a "greater France." As Stiegler reminds us, however, the importance of Ferry's intervention cannot be underestimated. It sought to institute changes in the cognitive, epistemic, and technical capabilities of an entire population against both residual theological power and the manifest intellectual and spiritual destructiveness of unregulated industrial capitalism.[48] It was "effectively the legal and even mandatory suspension of the necessity [that children] dedicate their lives to subsistence work," which in its time was an extraordinary matter.[49] Finally, it sought to make possible the transformation of collective desire: citizens who would *want* to live in a society consistent with modern notions of liberty and equality (to inhabit the tense aporia between them). In the case of Ferry, this cathexis or desiring-investment is in principle channeled toward the collective "ideal object" called "the nation," representative placeholder for such a society and ideological means of managing the democratic double bind of liberty and equality. But as we have seen, "the nation" need not be the only such object, and the radical openness and daunting difficulty of educational reform—and also its double-edged potential—thereby disclose themselves. Modernized public education is a pharmakon—both poison and medicine for the social body, "a base upon which both elitism and critique can be built."[50]

In spite of their restricted latitudes, different efforts to introduce common education in colonial settings transformed significant strata of the colonial lifeworld, scrambling indigenous codes and practices. Such scrambling and institution-building had correspondingly dual and interwoven effects. Laws and institutions of compulsory and missionary education played a role in the destruction or drastic modification of indigenous or long-established patterns of social hierarchy, knowledge and organization, and epistemological and epistemic formation. Even when "native" institutions were left in place, their function and meaning were often transformed by colonial intervention. I seek neither to condemn nor to condone this history, but to read different ways of entry into it as a learning process, for better and worse. My epigraph from Fanon points to the cultural alienation unknowingly (at best) propagated by colonial education. Yet Fanon also lays claim to an unmarked human history accessible through the same medium.

❖ ❖ ❖

Developing the discussion of common education as collective, unguaranteed pharmakon, I now return to the question of the education of education.

"Man can only become man through education" (*Der Mensch kann nur Mensch werden durch Erziehung*) (*Education* 6/699).[51] This heterotautological proposition tells us that, according to Kant, man, or humanity, can only become *what it is* by making up the gap or lack in itself by means of education. This is perhaps the most rarefied way of stating the supplementarity of education: the felicitous supplementation of the lack at the origin, the lack in "human nature," may be supplied by humanity's autoeducation toward the determination that is its own perfection, i.e., the "perfectibility of humanity" (*Vervollkommnung der Menschheit*). Thus, "behind education hides the great secret of the perfection of human nature" (7/700). The use of the word "secret" (*Geheimnis*) is not fortuitous: Kant must argue that the ends of man (*der Mensch*) are, if not indeterminate, then unknowable even by the reasoning individual. His philosophy posits a *Bestimmung*, a determination, for humans, which is humanity itself (*Menschheit*), but it is impossible for any individual to attain this determination. Only the human species collectively can reach that determined end, and education thereby becomes the task of "developing" the species' "natural capabilities" toward it (*Naturanlagen*, the program-like capacities given by nature) (10/701–2). "In humans, development of the natural capacities [*Naturanlagen*] does not happen of itself," and it follows that the human individual, unlike the animal, is not able to bring itself to its determination by its own efforts (the animal does this automatically, without the ability to know what it is doing) (13/703, 9–10/701). However, the structure of education leaves the extent of humanity's *Naturanlagen* themselves unknowable because education simultaneously "develops" the given *Naturanlagen* and "teaches" specific and contingent techniques (*Geschicklichkeiten*, such as reading and writing) (6/699, 19/706). These two interwoven but apparently distinct supplements confuse the ability to discern the exact measure of human capacities as naturally given, but since the development of the *Naturanlagen* is supposed to be the condition of moving toward humanity's determination and its perfectibility, the work of education is thus necessarily an exercise in trial and error. In other words, education is effectively a kind of experiment or, as Kant puts it, an "art" (*Kunst*) (10/702).

It is structurally and logically impossible to uncover and quantify humanity's *Naturanlagen* by beginning from a tabula rasa that would be the imposition of an absolute uniformity (*Gleichförmigkeit*). A uniformity of ground could in principle make visible the outlines of humanity's naturally programmed capacities. But if it were possible to impose such uniformity, this would involve the construction of an artificial "second nature" (*andern Natur*) established by each human's acting according to exactly the same grounding principles (*Grundsätzen*) (9/701). This simulated "other nature" would displace the very natural programs it was supposed to reveal, and the question of who or what could possibly impose this pre-educational grounding principle can moreover only lead to the idea of a suprahuman agent: "Were some being of a higher kind to undertake our education we would then see what the human could become" (6/699). The fact that this cannot occur makes of education a complex, empirical, generational two-step operation, each generation necessarily modifying and supplementing the "experiences and knowledges" it has acquired before passing them on without any guarantee that the developments make the right step toward the (unknown) end. "For insight depends on education, and education depends in turn upon insight" (11/702). This figure of codependence, an expanding circle in which insight and education supplement each other, is an extraordinarily equivocal one, leading to the possibility of fissures and discontinuities as much as to an image of unbroken progress toward perfection. In this situation, a "correct concept" of education could "only emerge belatedly," and in fact has not yet been clarified (12/702–3). The bettering of education subsists under a "perhaps" (*vielleicht*) that shakes confidence in the thought that "every following generation will be one step closer to the perfection of human nature" (7/700). Kant reluctantly acknowledges that education is persistently subject to the very conditions that it must overcome.

Kant's fragile and hedged-in account of educative progression insists once more on drawing a line. While the philosopher acknowledges both double binds and the limping forward gait of education, he will insist that the theory and practice of the development of *Anlagen* should not begin with the "raw" state of society. The latter cannot be successfully developed because its civilizational progress has proved repeatedly reversible: the sinusoidal wave shape of its history describes an irregularly rhythmic "fall back into primitiveness [*Rohigkeit*]" and a hauling back up out of it. Real development should begin beyond a certain limit of civilization, beyond the limit of an ever-recurring *Rohigkeit*: "looking back on civilized peoples, the beginning of the art of writing could be called the beginning of the world—a strong border with *Rohigkeit*." "For how much culture is there already in writing? [*und wieviel Kultur gehört nicht schon zum Schreiben?*]" (12–13/703). Kant may be correct to assert that a certain human "world" is only possible on the basis of a kind of "writing"—a technical and objective means of retention and reconstruction that permits transmission and selective transformation from generation to generation. But he is also obliged to cleave to a well-known line that holds certain peoples, those in the state of *Rohigkeit*, to be without writing (because without alphabetic or phonetic writing) and thus unable to access a fully human, historical world.[52]

Within the enclosure of techno-literate civilization, the *Naturanlagen* to be developed are differentially distributed among all individuals. The uniformity of an artificial tabula rasa would render humanity's *Naturanlagen* invisible. Thus, education must work backward from the manifest diversity of human modes of being ("in what different ways men live!") such that the end and determination of humanity are a *species* project inaccessible to the individual as such. Bringing out most clearly here the metaphorical seam in educative terminology that relates to rearing, stockbreeding, and cultivation (*Erziehung, Zucht, Zögling, Wartung*), Kant analogizes from a local species of flower, the auricula:

> You see for example with the auricula that if one raises [*zieht*] them from the root, one only gets flowers of a sole and single color; if, however, one sows their seed one gets them in the most unlike [*andern*] and diverse colors. Nature has thus set out [*anlegt*] the germs [*die Keime*] in them, and their development is only a matter of the proper sowing and transplanting [*Verpflanzen*]. So it is with man! [I remark here the interest of Kant's use of the metaphor *trans*plantation. If there is a proper sowing or semination (*gehörige Säen*), the figure of a trans-plant questions the idea that there is only one proper soil or territoriality for the ensuing development. Semination thus opens onto *dis*semination.]
>
> There are many germs in humanity, and now it is our task to develop the *Naturanlagen* proportionally and to unfold humanity out of its germs and to see that man reaches his determination (*Bestimmung*).
>
> (9/701)

Thus, the point is to go so far back in the human programming that you work from the genetic setup. The *Keime*—the germ-programs within the seed—are not uniformly distributed in all human beings. Rather, their collective development will be the realization of humanity's determination, not producing uniformity across individuals but a differentiated whole. Kant wants to get behind the roots, get to the root of the roots, to the preroot, the seed and its inner *Keim*, bringing out the efflorescence of a diversity in the service of human development toward a species-end that cannot be assumed by any one individual.[53]

We see here the outlines of a cosmopolitan liberal philosophy of education—even including a rationale for the cultivation of diversity—that travels a long way after Kant. It is still with us. At the same time, running interference with this attractive picture, the structural programming in the human remains a *mere* structural program (*blosse Anlagen*), a possible framework that is not ready-programmed for any particular development, not ready-set-up for the "good" (*seine Anlagen zum Guten . . . [ist] nicht schon fertig in ihm gelegt*) (11/702). The autodevelopment of humanity remains open-ended and without guarantees, and this produces two related ambiguities. First, the epistemological problem that humanity cannot know in advance either the aim, results, or reliable methods of its development. If, in this part-blind predicament, the ultimate outlook for the good (the perfection of humanity in its attainment of its determination) is both unknown and unattainable for any individual, then why would any individual elect to strive for the realization of this collective end? Why would the individual choose to work for what can only appear to it as a "*possibly* improved future condition of the human race [*menschlichen Geschlechts*]" when the individual's programming inclines it in other directions? Why not just let it all hang out, exercise my nature-given "great bent for freedom [*Hang zur Freiheit*]" for which, if left to myself, I will "sacrifice" everything (14/704, 4/699). The categorical imperative begs the question of a solution to this ethical problem of the creation of a will or inclination to work for the benefit of a distant collective future. As Étienne Balibar has observed, the "primary objective" of Kant's theory of pedagogy "is to confront the problems posed by the 'pathological' aspects of subjectivity—that is, those aspects which, at the heart of freedom, turn the will away from obedience to the categorical imperative and subject it to egoistic and thus non-universalizable interests."[54] A disciplinary supplement to freedom is required, and this is the first step in education. And in the first instance, education is training attention: "Thus, for example, one first sends children to school not with the intention that they should learn something there but so that they will be able to get used to sitting still and being quick to attend to [*beobachten*, "observe"] what is prescribed to them; such that in future they will not want to put whatever occurs to them actually and instantly into practice" (*Education* 3–4/698). "Discipline" here is precisely not mindless obedience but the cultivation of the ability to undertake intellectual work, which, as Stiegler has written in a comment on the passage, necessitates an "observational apprenticeship" that includes provisional "neutralization of motor-functions [*motricité*] (by the capture of attention)."[55] Prior to the transmission of "content," teaching children in this way is an elementary mode of instruction in the moves necessary to carry out epistemological work. For Stiegler it counts as "the ground [*base*] of the constitution of an object (attention) that here becomes an object of knowledge, that is to say a constructed object" (65/123). Construction of an object of knowledge in and as *the child's own attention* is therefore a preliminary exercise in epistemological capability, the premises of which the child can share in through this psychophysical work as it learns to learn.[56] "Discipline ... trains the way to think [*bildet die Denkungsart*]" (*Education* 83/740).

Kant does not take this side of the argument very much further. Yet he had seen the development of the earliest general public education system in Prussia and is thus reflecting on the social implications of wider epistemological change.[57] In keeping with the atmosphere of late-eighteenth-century Prussia, Kant advocates public education not as a right, but as the correct preparation of socially responsible and effective citizens of State, of the "character of a citizen [*Bürger*]" (25/710). "Public education ... is the best preparation [*Vorbild*, with the strong sense of a prefigure or preprojection] for future citizens" (29/212). In the mixed public school, the compulsory encounter with the limit imposed by the "rights" of others opens the space in which "one of the biggest problems" for education plays out: not how to attain freedom, but how to "use" freedom as responsibility toward self and others (27–29/711–12).[58]

No matter how explicitly or implicitly instrumentalized national institutions of public education are (and for Prussia they certainly became a machinery of State centralization and control), the account Kant provides for a general education of the citizen does not have to remain restricted to the outlines of the State or the fostering of nationalist identifications.[59] Stiegler develops this position in an updated and systemic framework. The training of children's epistemological capacity on a social scale potentializes practices of citizenship and democracy that may overflow the ability of States to control them, and this is one reason why Althusser once wrote that "the Ideological State Apparatuses," the educational apparatus foremost among them, "may not only be the *stake* but also the *site* of class struggle."[60] Accordingly, in the struggles for national liberation no less than in revolutionary conjunctures, education is one of the foremost considerations in imagining their future.

Mass application, as must be the case in a nationally controlled system, still faces the double bind of social stratification. It therefore depends on *which* children and *how* they are taught. The Soviet education commissar Nadezhda Krupskaya would observe as early as 1918 that "in a bourgeois state—whether a monarchy or a republic—the school serves as an instrument for the spiritual enslavement of the popular masses [*narodnye massy*]" because it is organized for the exclusive intellectual development and spiritual enrichment of one part of society.[61] Every "bourgeois" public/ national school system taken as a *system*, that is, a differentially articulated whole, is constrained by the reproduction of social division under a hegemonic appearance of national unity.[62] Stiegler's faith in the systemic power of common education, even if it is now being destroyed by digital capitalism, occludes this double bind because he does not address the different bases from which children enter into the system and thus the methodological care that must be expended *on* and *by* the educators themselves. His systemic picture is indeed only possible on the basis of a highly centralized system such as that of France (an attractive but naive-seeming ideal that all the "new generations" in the system can "go over the totality of rational knowledge in a few short years" [TT3 150]).

Division can be lived out in different ways, as Paul Willis's classic qualitative anthropology has shown in its depiction of an anti-intellectual or antielite cultural formation among working-class children, a culture that nevertheless embodies a neutralizing imaginary relation to, and compensation for, a specific social reality.[63] At the other end of the spectrum, it can be lived out in formations of highly educated literary avant-gardes whose subsequent distance from the responsibilities and practicalities of the classroom engenders a phantasmatic politics of the artistic short circuit (where art itself will speak directly to, "inspire," or activate the latent but replete voices of the oppressed). Finally, bad education can of course be more ruinous, or worse, than no (formal) education under the right circumstances. Recall Fanon's epigraph to this introduction, and see, in particular, examples discussed in this book's second, third, fourth, and fifth chapters. If the "normality" of bad schooling for the poorest in an underdeveloped country (in spite, perhaps, of the remarkable efforts of individual teachers) can result at best in a general "worship for power . . . obedience and respect for their superiors . . . rivalry among pupils," then consider also, among very many possible examples, the curricularized militarism and hatred of German "war pedagogy," down to elementary level, in the period from 1914 to 1918.[64]

❖ ❖ ❖

I have sketched the outlines of imagining education as a socially general program. The second ambiguity that I draw from Kant's pedagogical lectures subsists in the structural (here, generational) difference between educator and learner, which must assume the prior development of the educator and its ability to develop the young in turn: if the "(hu)man can only become (hu)man through education," then "it is noticeable that man can only be educated by men, by men who likewise have been educated" (6/699). This gap, unclosable by the assumption of mere generational progression, remains an open and persistent question, a tormenting figure of thought and representation for the case studies of *Indigenous Vanguards*. Who will educate the educators? Kant's paradox anticipates Marx's third "thesis" on Feuerbach (1845), which precisely raises a question of the educative relation as a general social process:

> The materialist teaching on the alteration of circumstances and education forgets that circumstances are altered by humans and the educator must himself be educated. It must therefore split society into two parts—one superior to the other.
>
> The coincidence of the alteration of circumstances and human activity or self-change can only be framed and rationally understood as *revolutionary praxis*.

> [Die materialistische Lehre von der Veränderung der Umstände und der Erziehung vergißt, daß die Umstände von den Menschen verändert und der Erzieher selbst erzogen werden muß. Sie muß daher die Gesellschaft in zwei Teile—von denen der eine über ihr erhaben ist—sondieren.
>
> Das Zusammenfallen des Ändern(s) der Umstände und der menschlichen Tätigkeit oder Selbstveränderung kann nur als *revolutionäre Praxis* gefaßt und rationell verstanden werden.][65]

The "materialist" position Marx refers to is one that sees the educative process as a unidirectional top-down operation.[66] If humans are the product of their "circumstances," a kind of blank slate that calculably changes according to changes in the environment, then a formative rearing or education (*Erziehung*) that adjusts circumstances in the appropriate ways will likewise form human subjects. This is an argument for enlightened despotism as biopolitical social engineering that can nevertheless accommodate a notion of basic human equality and thus even appear democratic. All humans are born with equal capacities. To transform those humans and spread Enlightenment, the benevolent and already-enlightened ruling agency—State or sovereign—must shoulder the responsibility of managing "circumstances" in such a way as to form enlightened human minds and souls, a transcendent power of assigning benign laws. It must presuppose a social division in which a pedagogical directive power, knowing itself "better" than those whom it helps, is above and exterior to the individuals being formed and re-formed by development policies altering their environment. Social structure, divided into "teacher" and "learner," is itself one big teaching machine, and the social fissure remains an absolute power gap. Moreover, where government gets its theory from is left unthought: it is just doing good. This fantasy of a philosopher-king (State or development organization) forgets from where the ruling agency (the "educator") got its education, and this forgetting determines innumerable subsequent problems around the questions of "uplifting the people," consciousness raising, and the role of vanguard or Party, as well as colonial and postcolonial practices of development and aid.

As we have seen, the vicious circle was formulated by Kant: "man can only be educated by men, by men who likewise have been educated" (*Education* 6/699). It is politicized by Marx, who in his own way risks short-circuiting it. When Marx names a *Zusammenfallen*, a coincidence of changing circumstances and active self-change, he is indicating that the educating agency—the one that desires to program human change by altering individuals' surroundings—is implicated in the social process it seeks to shape. It is not a legislative power external to, and acting upon, a collection of individuals. Rather, it is part of a *social* process (*Gesellschaft*) defined by a falling-together, a conjuncture or "coincidence" of human education—as an *activity*—that crosses both sides of the fissure. While this does not deny the inevitable space between teacher and learner, the space may now appear as an active interface, such that "self-change" reframed as "revolutionary praxis" rewrites the vicious circle with a different figure of the turn (re-volution). The exact meaning of "revolutionary praxis" here is unclear. If it posited a continuous process of autotransformation as autoeducation as autoemancipation leading to the revolutionary transformation of society, this would level out *Erziehung* as such. Marx does not deny a fissure between educator and educated and thus the place of a directive agency; he poses the question of how the educating agency may be educated, which is only through an active interface within the very society that it seeks to educate. In this sense, it will itself be changed and turned around, an unstable ferment that cannot (without socially and intellectually damaging consequences) be permitted to freeze into a transcendent power of assistance and legislation, a head above the social body.

Gramsci reflects the intricacy of these problems when he writes about a projected "common school" (*scuola unitaria*) that will prepare the ground for subaltern and proletarian children to become a "new type of intellectual," which is a new kind of citizen. To some degree, this means using and opening up the existing practices of the "traditional school" (schools for the upper classes) on a wider social scale rather than perpetuating a system of class-divided schooling that makes one school for those who have the right to do intellectual labor and another for those consigned to manual labor. "The entire function of educating and forming the new generations ceases to be private and becomes public." For this work, "it is necessary ... to stress with some energy the duty of the adult generations, i.e. of the State, to 'mold' [*conformare*] the new generations."[67] The crucial point at which Gramsci modifies and supplements Marx's "thesis" is where he indicates the "active and reciprocal" relation between student and teacher, such that "every teacher is always a pupil and every pupil a teacher." Gramsci will write in the same passage, underlining his augmentation of the Marxian thesis's motif of the *Umstand*, that "the *environment* reacts back on the philosopher [the new intellectual] and imposes on him a continual process of self-criticism. It is his 'teacher' " (SPN 350, my emphasis). As with Marx, we move up to the social scale as follows: "This form of relationship exists throughout society as a whole and for every individual relative to other individuals. It exists between intellectual and non-intellectual sections of the population, between the rulers and the ruled, *élites* and their followers, leaders [*dirigenti*] and led, the vanguard and the body of the army. Every relationship of 'hegemony' is necessarily an educational relationship" (SPN 350).

In his incomplete drafts of a political theory in the *Prison Notebooks*, Gramsci writes a passage on the "primary elements [*primielementi*]" that will become the "pillars of politics and of any collective action whatsoever" (SPN 144). He is, in other words, trying to define irreducible, minimal (and supporting) constituents, and setting a contemporary debate about vanguardism into a much longer stream of political-philosophical discussions of leadership and sovereignty that emerged from classical antiquity and the early modern era:

The first element is that there really do exist rulers and ruled [*governati e governanti*], leaders and led [*dirigenti e diretti*]. The entire science and art of politics are based on this primordial and (given certain general conditions) irreducible fact. . . . One could and should study how to minimize this fact and eliminate it [*attenuare e far sparire*] . . . In the formation of leaders [*dirigenti*], one premise is fundamental: is it the intention that there should always be rulers and ruled [*governati e governanti*], or is the objective to create the conditions in which this division is no longer necessary?

(SPN 144)

The final question is key here, raising the problem of the kind of work (cultural and epistemological as well as practically political) needed to "create the conditions in which this division is no longer necessary." A self-change required of "leaders" as well as "led" that is not simply a reversal of positions. The practical and philosophical stakes of this question are abyssal, and I can only gesture toward their monitory shadow over the entirety of the present study. The question extends beyond the limits of both citizenship and the human.[68] However, its narrower shape for the present study is determined by practices and representations that concerned the involvement and proximity of subaltern groups to struggles for national liberation, and the forms of imagining and preparing for the enigmatic event of emancipation and its day after. The morning when figures unlike the prevailing leaders or ruling groups or vanguards, their non-*semblables*, not only are "mobilized" in struggle but appear formally independent and enfranchised.[69]

Enfranchisement puts each citizen, in principle but also with real effects, in the legislative position, as having the capacity to govern, even if only with the ability to vote. Thus, Gramsci, summarizing what is in fact a long tradition of thought about democracy: "democracy, by definition, cannot mean merely that the unskilled worker can become skilled. It must mean that every 'citizen' can 'govern' and that society places him, even if only abstractly, in a general condition to achieve this." Public education is in principle if not necessarily in practice "for each non-ruler a free training in the skills and general technical preparation for this end" (SPN 40–41).

Gramsci reprises an aspect of one of the most important modern (revolutionary) philosophies of education, that of Condorcet (1743–94), who set out a framework for the institutionalization of a French public education system. This is an education in which the right to work the mind is recognized and, in principle, instituted for all, so as to begin dismantling the destructive effects of a rigid division of labor that keeps "Enlightenment" the preserve of the *Gelehrter*, the rich, or the upper-class. In the latter case, the consequent persistence of "a master people and a slave people" produces "danger and deadly effects" that will not be preventable by mere law enforcement even if there are "wise laws." Education *supplements* law, because the mere granting of legal "rights" is useless without an understanding of their exercise and a nonprogrammed (unguaranteed) free capacity to work them: "Laws pronounce equality of rights, institutions for public education alone can make this equality real. . . . It is necessary, therefore, that one level of common instruction makes even men of ordinary capacity capable of fulfilling all public functions."[70]

Enfranchisement without an advance "preparation" for all followed revolutions and decolonization. Almost every ex-colony that gained national independence after the Second World War instituted constitutional democratic forms and granted enfranchisement to a population without "the skills and general technical preparation," or the rituals and habits, of modern citizenship in its prevailing models, massive groups for whom thinking and learning had often been immemorially taboo.[71] Postcolonial States are a great and unfinished experiment in the invention of new modes of modern citizenship. This situation brings into focus both the opportunities and the tremendous problems faced in the postcolony precisely because of the gift of this open-endedly experimental conjuncture.

In the turmoil of Russia's revolution, Lenin made a political intervention countering contemporary objections to the idea that a working-class organization would be capable of developing a new State apparatus from the ruins of the old one. He visited the question of the *who* of governing:

> We are not utopians. We know that an unskilled laborer or a cook cannot immediately get on with the job of state administration. . . . [But] we demand an immediate break with the prejudiced view that only the rich, or officials chosen from rich families, are capable of administering the state, of performing the ordinary, everyday work of administration. We demand that training in the work of state administration be conducted

by class-conscious workers and soldiers and that this training be begun at once, i.e., that a beginning be made at once in training all the working people, all the poor, for this work.[72]

Yet during the 1920s, Lenin's "anguished concern to revolutionize the educational Ideological State Apparatus" simply so as to attempt to "secure the future of the dictatorship of the proletariat and the transition to socialism" met with almost insuperable and unforeseen difficulties.[73] In one of her many interventions addressing such problems, Krupskaya in 1927 cited children's letters she had received from the *Pioneer* journal in which the children described their imagination of socialism.[74] While the letters describe a technoscientific world of machines doing all the work, comfortable housing, and the end of material poverty, "not a single child wrote that relations between people will be quite different under socialism," that thinking, feeling, and pleasure will be otherwise (294–95). Krupskaya argues that this area is the hole in soviet education. While there is nothing intrinsically wrong with wanting technoscientific and material development, for there to be socialism an intellectual and affective change must accompany it, the imagining of other kinds of human relations. And this will not happen without struggle across the entire area of epistemology and episteme (school and home). "It is now necessary for the vanguard section of teachers and the population to fight attempts to quietly put the school back on the old path," she writes, and she concludes by quoting from Lenin's old speeches that evoke the problem of developing "communist ethics" (*morali* and *nrávstvennost'*) and the slow task of working away from residual and persistent "capitalist psychology."[75]

   None of this is to idealize what was actually made of Soviet elementary (or higher) education over the short life span of the Union.[76] Following Althusser's remark, I would even venture that, in the context of perhaps genuinely being at a loss as to what to do with the intellectual and spiritual development of tens of millions of rural poor, the Soviet Union programmed the extremely short life span of the Bolshevik experiment. The subsequent rigid standardization of "socialist ethics" in terms of social hygiene, clean living, and superficially civilized and egalitarian behavior was at best a tiny "cultural," "everyday" Band-Aid over a huge historical wound. Stalin himself was only one generation removed from serfdom. In this connection, Gramsci's enigmatic comment about the weakness of "immanentist philosophies" in forging a relation between "the 'simple' and the intellectuals" might allegorize the history of the unraveling of Bolshevik socialism. By analogy with "the rapid collapse of the Renaissance . . . their weakness is demonstrated in the educational field, in that the immanentist philosophies have not even attempted to construct a conception which could take the place of religion in the education of children."[77]

Beyond the terrible contingencies of war communism and the New Economic Policy (NEP), in 1923 the disturbing and uncanny persistence of the past haunts and menaces the future, further corroding the figure of peasant and worker as citizen-legislator, agent in 1917's dreamed-of "democracy from below" (*demokratii snizu*).[78] Thus in 1923 Lenin recognizes that impatient haste to insert workers and peasants immediately into the running of the State has produced the opposite of democratic practices because no one knew how to *do* democracy. The radically democratic short circuit is undermined by functionaries who do not (cannot) run the State in a socialist way. There is a "cultural," and especially an educational, gap that Soviet society was not in a condition to supplement. Lars Lih has called this Lenin's thesis of a "cultural deficit."[79] Because the *longue durée* structures of the past grip both the Russian poor and the spirit in which the soviets are run, the old structures and habits may have been turned around (*perevernuto*) but are not yet defunct.[80] This sense of the difficulty of struggling from within the old frameworks becomes decidedly more emphatic in Lenin's later writing. Revolutionary inversion has left an undisplaced afterimage of the social structures and practices of the past (not just capitalism, but "bureaucratic culture or serf culture"), and it "would be better to proceed more slowly" even to the point of acknowledging that "it would be enough to start with a real bourgeois culture" rather than to keep spinning the vanguard dream of an actualized "proletarian culture."[81]

As Lih points out, this final Lenin came to the conclusion that a slower, more careful and painstaking "cultural" preparation was the prerequisite for the future viability of socialism as a new kind of State made to regulate capital. In a number of his last writings from 1923, Lenin acknowledges that while certain "political prerequisites" (*politicheskiye predposylki*) for socialism have been established in the Soviet Union, there is a lack of the "civilization" or "culture" that would foster the desire and the means to practice socialism.[82] Lenin seems to use the words *culture* (*kul'tura*) and *civilization* (*tsivilizatsiya*) interrelatedly in this context, wherein culture would perhaps be the molecular arrays of representations, mind-sets, and practices that can be organized and articulated into larger civilizational units. The cultural or civilizational "prerequisites" or "premises" for the subject of socialism are only minimally defined as "culture, everyday life, and habits" (*kul'turu . . . byt . . . privychki*) (238 / 390).[83] And the groundwork for these cultural premises has to be a genuine educational structure for the poorest, those previously not permitted to develop their intellectual capacities. Otherwise, their materially determined thought and action will continue to run interference with the ability to *use* emancipation and enfranchisement and freedom within the soviets.

In these telegraphic and desperate writings, Lenin tacitly recognizes that his (revolutionist's) sense of how to create a will for social justice that could sustain the everyday habits for a socialist organization of society had been absorbed from his family and class environment and his humanistic absorption of literary culture. ("It would be enough to start with a real bourgeois culture.") Spivak has brilliantly observed that "Marx was able to think the social as pharmakon because he himself understood the social as consensual welfare of the class-diversified collective through his own humanistic education."[84] Like Marx, Lenin too was able to think and imagine epistemological and desiring subjective readiness for this on the basis of his own prior educative and circumstantial formation—the son of two trained elementary school teachers whose father was also a school inspector with a special interest in rural education and development for the poorest. Lenin came to recognize that inspired and imaginative consciousness-raising, as once imagined in the "dream" (*mechtat'*) of *What Is to Be Done?*, had yet to begin its real work, otherwise.[85]

❖ ❖ ❖

The Trinidadian activist and writer George Padmore had seen firsthand the miscarriage of the Soviet experiment in peoples' democracy during the 1930s. He brought an acute awareness of the problems of the long term—between past and future—to his subsequent work in colonial Africa during the 1940s and 1950s, on African independence struggles and the thinking of what would come afterward: "It is only with changes in thought and customs and approach that it will be possible to create the social mechanism and human means which socialism and its building call for . . . you cannot build socialism without socialists."[86] While Padmore assumes socialism as a normative goal of development after national liberation (as Ferry-type reform assumes bourgeois democratic civil society), the fact that one needs socialists to make socialism—or democrats to make democracy—remains the site of a productive and more general dilemma. How are democrats and socialists made, minds changed? "Social customs are stubborn things," he writes to Du Bois in 1955, "and cannot be just brushed aside without arousing violent opposition among a nearly 100 per cent illiterate population."[87] In the manuscript from 1959 on African socialism, Padmore writes that "the new education must be geared to producing a different kind of citizen" (AS 233). Not only to fight tribalism, at one end, but to manipulate the capital necessary to run a society at the other: "There must be capital," he writes. "Socialists are, in effect, the manipulators of capital free of capitalist aims. . . . They *want* to invest capital for social aims rather than for private profit" (AS 234, my emphasis). How does the making of socialists in Africa or elsewhere proceed from the existing kinds of "thought and customs and approach" in the vanguard and subaltern if not by working with and through what is happening in them? These are the areas where the vanguard's cutting edge begins to blur.

❖ ❖ ❖

Althusser suggested that a structural connection between literary culture and educational institutions becomes visible

> during great political and ideological crises in which, for example, educational reforms are openly recognized as revolutions in the methods of ideological action deployed against the masses. At such times it can be clearly seen that education is directly related to the dominant ideology and it is apparent that its conception, its orientation and control are an important stake in the class struggle. Some examples: the Convention's educational reform, Jules Ferry's educational reforms, the educational reforms that so preoccupied Lenin and Krupskaya, the educational reforms of the Cultural Revolution, etc.[88]

Crises and contestations of educational reforms disclose the otherwise unperceived "norming" function of humanistic literary culture.[89] In other words, they make visible the points at which the necessarily standardizing, grammatizing programs of humanistic cultural training are disciplinary, regularizing functions of subject-formation. Analysis of such disciplinarization would be taken further by Michel Foucault in *Discipline and Punish* (1975). His work on "docile bodies," in particular, analyzes ways the body is made susceptible to instruction and control in a continuum of institutions from prison to barracks to hospital to factory to school.[90] But whereas Foucault is almost exclusively focused on the corporeal aspects of disciplinary subject-formation (that translate in unaccounted ways into mental habits of obedience), Althusser's emphasis on the ideological/epistemological realm is more pertinent to the wider questions of schooling that I raise here. As Althusser indicates, crises reveal points at which "normalizing" programs devolve to the incalculable because it becomes apparent that the prevailing norms can be altered. The fact that education can be an object of reform shows that its program is open-ended and without guarantees. Such open-endedness is an immanent factor for schooling, even of the supposedly normalizing type, making of it the model of the "dangerous supplement."[91] "Grammatization," writes Stiegler, "constitutes a connector [*agencement*], altogether extraordinary in human history, between *logos* and its other" (TC 143/256). Human beings can certainly be turned into robots through instruction, but the systematizing or "disciplinary" (grammatized) aspects of learning are also means by which norming methods develop the capability of their own transgression. Disciplinarity (in Foucault's sense) in education is especially visible at elementary levels where learning is organized more formally (more drills, memorization, and so on). Even there, however, the larger pedagogical task is to teach the child to reassemble the knowledge-bits dissociated and broken up by the rationalizing and standardizing process of grammatization, to develop a mode of attention that can interiorize the grammatized parts and rewrite and reconnect them independently. This can, as per Foucault, involve the corporeal regulation of sitting, listening, copying, and so forth. Yet as I have already underlined, the standardized, grammatized systems of general public education are more than cynical or unwitting fictions for guaranteeing obedience or reproducing social division. Even at their most mundane they may make possible, as Gramsci recognized, practices of critical thought for an unrestricted collection of citizens (and in principle for the "anyones" who do not enter the category of citizen). There are no guarantees here. Thinking about the subaltern child's potential formation as a democratic subject in the 1930s, Gramsci, echoing Kant, had already laid out this line of argument, defending superficially "traditional" or conservative pedagogies of historical grammar, formal logic, and the painful training of attention:

> Formal logic is like grammar: it is assimilated in a "living" way even if the actual learning process has been necessarily schematic and abstract. For the learner is not a passive and mechanical recipient, a gramophone record—even if the liturgical conformity of examinations sometimes makes him appear so. . . . The child who sweats at *Barbara, Baralipton* is certainly performing a tiring task, and it is important that he does only what is absolutely necessary and no more. But it is also true that it will always be an effort to learn physical self-discipline and self-control; the pupil has, in effect, to undergo a psycho-physical training. Many people have to be persuaded that studying too is a job, and a very tiring one, with its own particular apprenticeship—involving muscles and nerves as well as intellect. It is a process of adaptation, a habit acquired with effort, tedium and even suffering. . . . If our aim is to produce a new stratum of intellectuals, including those capable of the highest degree of specialization, from a social group which has not traditionally developed the appropriate attitudes, then we have unprecedented difficulties to overcome.
>
> (SPN 42–43)

"Unprecedented difficulties": there are no unequivocal answers in this area. It should be clear that in such terms, the Gramscian-Althusserian frame of analysis is pertinent to the status of educational reforms in colonial situations as well as revolutionary ones. This book takes criticism in such directions in terms of Althusser's crucial qualification that common education is a "stake" in the class struggle, and according to a later Althusserian formulation we have already encountered, also a "site" of struggle ("Ideology" 147). In the context and practice of "reform," it must therefore also operate as the locus of an opening, a chance, and not simply a one-dimensional episode in a baleful history of governmental institutions of State, or capillary networks of disciplinarization. I must therefore repeat that common education is a pharmakon: it is *both* poison and medicine (poison *as* medicine). This double and pharmakontic aspect of the "disciplinary," which opens to the incalculable rather than only the docile, is too often glossed over by studies of colonial surveillance, classification, and control. And it is in the work of modernist literary experimenters, who put themselves and their work as close to developing educational institutions as possible, that this duality becomes clear, along with the "unprecedented difficulties" it carried for colonial and postcolonial societies.

Why literary experimenters here rather than ordinary teachers? Because beside evident disciplinary constraints, I am interested in the uncanny affinity between literary work and teaching processes. In the elements of surrender, but also uncompromising demand, violence, and coercion they sometimes involve. And the relation between these things and their possibility to produce the unexpected. Educative structure is immanent to literature to the extent that the dream or desire of the literary work is to train, instruct, or educate its reader in a singular curriculum of previously unthought-of competencies. (The learning concerned can be as subtle as the ability to recognize a variation or innovation within the patterns of an established genre.) Derrida puts it as follows: the "work then becomes an institution forming its own readers, giving them a competence which they did not possess before: a university, a seminar, a colloquium, a curriculum, a *course*." Each work dreams of rewriting the "reading" curriculum anew and both succeeds and fails to do so. It " 'betrays' the dream of a new institution of literature. It betrays it first by revealing it: each work is unique and is a unique institution unto itself. But it also betrays it in causing it to fail: insofar as it is unique, it appears in an institutional field designed so that it cuts itself up and abducts itself there."[92] It is of the first importance that Derrida places this aspect of the work under the heading of "dream," signaling both that it is a desiring-structure and that it is a text to be read and interpreted, not taken as the actual fulfillment of the represented project.

❖ ❖ ❖

A final word on the limits of modernism. *Indigenous Vanguards* aims to enrich yet also to question recent understandings of "geomodernism," "global modernism," "planetary modernism," and world and global literature.[93] These latter perspectives are variously based on models of World Systems Theory, the idea of "great literary monuments," and a multicentric diversity of national or regional examples (many modernities and therefore many modernisms). Much of this new work, and especially the multicentric model, has promisingly moved scholarship away from a diffusion/derivation model of modernism and world literature. Yet this development has also sometimes led to unexamined geographical and temporal expansiveness that sidelines the epistemic and social conditions of a modernist aesthetic practice. That is to say that counterexamples are selected on the basis of their recognizability in terms of metropolitan instances, a continuity that is probably inevitable. Traversal of this limit perhaps demands the learning or invention of new ways of working. It is therefore time to read again Raymond Williams's opening chapters in *The Politics of Modernism*, especially his remarks that point to the problem of "the metropolitan interpretation of its own processes as universals."[94] In spite of diversities of place and multicentric appearances, it is largely continuities of class-specific perception and structures of feeling that are universalized in the scramble for global examples. *Indigenous Vanguards* examines the limits to the expansiveness of the modernist aesthetic paradigm, not in terms of timelines or spatial extension, but in terms of social stratification: class and subalternity, heterogeneous layerings in contemporaneity. The book's focus on common education and its relation to modernist literary art raises the question of thinking socially conditioned access to validated cultural expression, both in aesthetic terms and in terms of the legitimated performance of active citizenship. *Indigenous Vanguards* asks us to consider anew where the limits of modernist latitudes lie.

1

HARLEM/BERLIN

Shadows of Vanguards Between Prussia and Afro-America

À propos of the German habit of greeting all the time Gutentag, Gutentag—I have fallen into the habit myself—and every time I go to the W.C. I say Good morning, dear old ass—or Grüss Gott, heilige Petrus.

—Alain Locke, undated handwritten fragment from Berlin, 1910 or 1911

An unexpected burst of laughter resounds in the archive as I trawl through the modest collection of fragments preserved from Alain Locke's graduate student days at Berlin University. As I search for evidence of Locke's reading in modern German philosophy, especially of his engagement with J. G. Fichte, this account of a private, comic subversion of Wilhelmine Germanic gentility focuses anew the act Locke was performing with Fichte, among others. As we shall see, Locke does not flush Fichte down the toilet; but he does seek to change the destination of the Germanic address. Locke's treatment of Fichte remains private inasmuch as the proper name Fichte does not appear in his intervention into the culture of American modernity. You'd perhaps never know, perhaps never need to know. Yet beyond the water closet of a cryptic rendezvous, the public and transformative force of an unmarked exercise in translation unfolds, and the problems of a vanguard address take on a new mode of appearance.

❖ ❖ ❖

The New Negro: An Interpretation, a collection edited by Alain Locke and published in 1925, became the symbolic manifesto of American black modernism and modernity in the interwar period.[1] While its status did not remain uncontested during the 1920s and 1930s, the *New Negro* anthology can still be described as the most generally significant and influential attempt of that moment to announce and disclose the theory and practice of an American black cultural modernism.[2] Reverberations of the "Red Summer" of 1919 may be read between the lines of The New Negro, even as it seeks, as Barbara Foley has argued, to manage that political crisis of African American radicalization.[3] Thus, she writes, did "the arms-bearing, anticapitalist New Negro of 1919 get transmuted into the culture hero of The New Negro (1925)."[4] It would be imprudent to argue that the subsequent folding of the American Left into a mode of nationalism was determined by the mere appearance of an avant-garde anthology; and Foley correspondingly argues that the Lockean New Negro should rather be read as both condition and effect of that more general folding.[5] Complicity, then, rather than a simplified opposition between a homogenously radical Left New Negro and a politically compromised Lockean one. And hence, according to Foley, the power and persistence of the Lockean New Negro: this collection articulated nationalistic currents already at work within and beyond the Left itself, in a representational apparatus that could, for a while, smooth out the tensions and complexities of a contested ideological terrain.

Alain Locke was trained as a philosopher, but he worked at undoing the opposition between philosophy (as theory) and cultural activism (as practice). The New Negro attempts to interpret, so as to shape, the narrative of a historical African American becoming. If, as Jacques Derrida has proposed, every nationalism is in some irreducible way philosophical (and vice versa), this assigns a new task of reading the Locke of The New Negro as a philosopher as well as a cultural impresario. Nationalism and philosophy are structurally coimplicated because each presents itself as "both particular and potentially universal."[6] Each is a discourse in or of a particular idiom and locus that must yet claim a universal relevance or truth. Cosmopolitanism is the dominant modern expression of this coimplication of philosophy and nationalism. The implicit—and sometimes explicit—avowal is that this particular (national) concretion or instance can exemplify the universal. It is a short step from here to this, our, nation (or philosophy) is the best, because the most universal, and therefore instantiates the leading edge, the vanguard of the rest of the world. The linkage of philosophy and nationalism persistently recurs—and is not a moral failing—and must equally persistently be negotiated with. In the present case, although Locke's theorizations of the emergence and function of a black cultural vanguard are not written in a way that underlines their disciplinary philosophicalness, they are nonetheless written by a philosopher. They set to work philosophical positions of a vanguard nationalism in ways that are both instructive and cautionary, exemplified in representational questions about the complex national location of the enlightened African American's cultural self.

The New Negro is an anthology of artistic achievements and a heralding of those to come, an intervention into an emerging cultural trend and a comment upon it. The subtitle, *An Interpretation*, must be read in all its dimensions, as the book enters and redirects a stream of existing debate about what the "New Negro" is or will be.[7] The philosopher Locke announces to his readers that the New Negro is one facet of a worldwide "resurgence of a people," of a progressive national spirit also exemplified by contemporary Zionism and movements in India, China, Egypt, Ireland, Russia, Bohemia, and Mexico (xxvii). Smoothing out their differences, he understands these endeavors as popular and national "movements of folk-expression and self-determination," and places the New Negro within global nationalist currents of his day, a day in which nationalism could still function as a signifier of emancipation from the tutelage (and worse) of imperial or absolutist systems (xxv, xxvii, 7, 14). It is evident that the deep intellectual background for Locke's imaginative figuration of the spiritual "renaissance" of American blacks took shape as an interpretation of the political and philosophical struggles of the early-nineteenth-century Prussian intelligentsia for a unified and independent German nationality.[8] That struggle was intimately linked to the Germanic declarations of Enlightenment of the period, and its exemplary text is Fichte's *Addresses to the German Nation* of 1807–08. In a diagnostic essay on black art published in *The Nation* in 1928, Locke draws a more overt analogy than he permits himself in *The New Negro*, suggesting that the contemporary American "race temperament" (exemplified by what he calls the "folk temperament" as the key element in black art's potential to become authentically national) "stands today . . . in the position of the German temperament in Herder's day."[9] Herder's day is not identical with Fichte's day, of course; but of the two I will show that Fichte is Locke's more compelling philosophical interlocutor for the questions raised by *The New Negro*.

Nationalism, indeed philosophical nationalism, had, as Locke underlines, come into its own in his time. The entrance of a certain Fichte into, for example, the political discourses of Zionism, Chinese nationalism, and Arab nationalism during the period has been documented; and these movements, as well as the ones that interested Locke in India, Mexico, central Europe, and Russia, were not without their own vanguard philosophers.[10] The Zionism of this period, which is one of Locke's favorite analogies for the New Negro movement, was as much a philosophical as a practical, political current. One need only recall that the philosopher Martin Buber, one of the main intellectuals of Zionism, was working in Berlin during the period Locke studied there. Not only did Buber engage with Fichte, but he also published several articles in the early 1900s that discussed the question of a "Jewish Renaissance" (jüdische Renaissance) in the context of a broader discourse on Zionism.[11] While renaissances were everywhere in the air during the nineteenth and early twentieth centuries, the German/Zionist environment is important inasmuch as Locke makes Zionism a special point of comparison for the cultural movement he heralds as a negro renaissance.[12] It is also important to note that Buber's notion of Zionism emphasized its cultural activism, something that we shall also see mediated by Fichte in Locke's version of a nonseparatist black American nationalism.[13] There is scant evidence for how much or little Locke knew about the specificities of Zionism in the various forms it took in the 1910s and 1920s.[14] Nevertheless, it is an analogy he returns to regularly in his writings on race.[15]

Referring to a related but later conjuncture of the era after World War II, Pheng Cheah has argued that "Fichte's views about the living nation are also exemplary for subsequent nationalist discourse, especially in decolonizing and postcolonial Africa and Asia."[16] Cheah's argument for the more general (and perhaps empirically undocumentable) place of Fichte's Addresses to the German Nation in yet broader currents of anticolonial nationalism after 1945 is important; yet it tends to identify those movements with an untransformed Fichteanism. Thus Cheah claims that Frantz Fanon and Amilcar Cabral "make identical arguments [to Fichte's] about the importance of national culture to political liberation" and that Ngũgĩ wa Th'iong'o also reprises almost unchanged Fichtean thematics.[17] It is also necessary to ask, however, about the extent to which these writer-activists, including a previous generation's Alain Locke, détourne in translating, rather than simply reiterate, Fichte and the current of Enlightenment-as-nationalism that he represents.

Locke first aligns the sociocultural struggles of African Americans with the variegated (and often anticolonial) nationalisms of his own times, a question of interest to both postcolonial studies and African American studies. More substantially, at the same time as suggesting that this movement is part of a more general wave of cultural, racial, national efflorescence happening in many other places, he puts metropolitan American blacks into a reterritorialized site of the Fichtean national subject.

What does this mean? Most generally, it means that Locke assumes the structure of feeling of an embattled German Enlightenment story of self-emancipation. It is not here necessarily a matter of a conscious decision by Locke to adapt a story and its figured structure of feeling to the circumstances of contemporary black life in the United States. To the extent that he translates its terms and borrows its resources, Locke is equally transfixed and taken by this (German) nexus—just as that German nexus itself translates and borrows historical and current impulses for self-emancipation among black Americans and is at the same time caught by them.

The story of Enlightenment, which is also a theory, did not announce a punctual event in either Kant's or Fichte's account of it (Fichte both amended and readdressed Kant's version of the story). If the task of Enlightenment had announced itself as the emergence of humanity from dependency and tutelage (as a narrateme of growing up into adult maturity, for short), then Fichte's lament is that the Germans have collectively allowed themselves to be infantilized by being ruled over by another nation. He would relaunch Enlightenment in a truly national system of education or rearing (*Erziehung*), revising the class and gender limits of Kant's version and at the same time imagining an epistemology and pedagogy of patriotic ethical programming. At this general level, it is Fichte's expression of the structure of feeling of a subjected intellectual vanguard that catches Locke and indeed the many other metropolitan intellectuals and activists for whom Fichte's vision was compelling. Fichte claims to disclose the way in which the philosopher's voice can activate a project of national, social, cultural renewal for precisely those subjects who feel unjustly marginalized by a colonial-type situation.[18] If my account so far can be reproached for possibilizing, psychologizing, or empiricizing Fichte's philosophical moves, I would add that the Fichtean text itself opens the door to such "mistaken" gestures. It presents itself from the first words to the last as an activist philosophy.

In the *Addresses to the German Nation*, Fichte speaks to an audience that he defines as Germans presently subjected to the occupying rule of a foreign power (*fremde Gewalt*), a people under conditions that appear colonial in a sense more general than the Prussians' recent defeat by Napoleon's army.[19] It is precisely the fact of being "subject [*unterworfen*] to an alien power" that occasions the possibility of bringing about a "new age" (*neue Zeitalter*) (AG 10/12). Fichte thus reasons the march of history dialectically: the "selfishness" (*Selbstsucht*) of the Germans has "negated itself" (*sich selbst vernichtet*) though its own "complete development" (9/11). This self-negation defines the present—"this negation would thus be our own present"—by making possible the foreign takeover that "destroyed the realm of selfishness," thereby opening the passage to the *Aufhebung*, negation of the negation, in a creation of a "new self and a new age" (14/17, 10). The scene Fichte seems to have in mind is one of a ruling class so corrupt and self-interested that it has weakened the internal and external bonds of State to the extent that the State itself became vulnerable to foreign takeover.[20] While the construction of a genuinely popular national subject should guarantee that self-interest will not prevail in the future, we are now in the negation, says Fichte, and a "new life in a new world" would have to be "unmediatedly tied [*unmittelbar angeknüpft*]" to it. The negation thus constitutes the "proper starting point [*Ausgangspunkt*]" of the addresses, which seek to catalyze by the power of philosophical exhortation the reemergence of a Germanity that nonetheless already exists (14/17).

The motif of a subjected people struggling for independence and freedom is, to be sure, unique to neither Fichte nor Locke. As I will show, Locke negotiates these aspects of the modern black American situation by also echoing Kant's motif of Enlightenment as maturity: coming of age and coming into step with the present as an exit from dependence. Fichte's own proposed project of national upbringing or education (*Nationalerziehung*) is an attempt to account for how Kant's "maturity" can be brought about as a universal social program rather than as a class privilege. Fichte's *Addresses* is thus an important critique of the class-fixity of Kant's account of an Enlightenment occurring among the lucky few who already have social advantages: for Fichte, the education that will bring about enlightened independence must be equally available to all social strata and must mold them all in the same kind of way.[21] It is precisely this, however, that leads Fichte into formulating its specifically national character: to educate equally all social classes of the Germans is to create a national education that will give shape to a unified and consistently patriotic national subject.

Fichte can be read in this broad sense as giving philosophical expression in his time and place to a structure of feeling common to many groups facing territorial occupation or deracination. His is an exemplary philosophical articulation of the mind-set of a frustrated colonized metropolitan intelligentsia, opening the way to so many subsequent identifications, expansions, translations, and appropriations, including those of Locke. This may help explain why Fichte's account of nationality and resistance has proven so powerful and lasting a resource among those far-flung metropolitan intellectual elites that have attempted to theorize their own predicaments of national identity in colonial, colony-like, or diasporic conditions. It may also account for comparable "nationalist" formulations in situations where this particular Fichtean text was not read. Fichte is not the sole source of all philosophical nationalism; he is exemplary, one among many originary translations of it. In his account, as physical space is invaded or occupied, and territorial borders are crossed or abolished, the subjects of occupation or displacement, progressively detached from a place they can feel as homely, come to desire the preservation of a virtual "internal" border, a border, in Fichte's language, of spirit, so as to forestall an experience of complete annihilation.[22] In Prussia in 1807, where spirit/mind (*der Geist*) is the object of the highest philosophico-cultural stakes, this structure is expressed in the German philosopher's well-known concept of the "inner frontier, drawn by man's spiritual nature itself" (*innern, durch die geistige Natur des Menschen selbst gezogenen Grenze*) (166/211).[23] Étienne Balibar has detected a significant "equivocation" in this concept of the internal border: it can designate a site of resistance, the moral, spiritual, intellectual precondition of the reconquest of the external borders of the occupied territory, or it can designate a site of refuge, the place where a moral, spiritual, intellectual world can be preserved and developed indefinitely under (colonial) conditions of external defeat. I am not sure that these options are mutually exclusive; and in any case they give rarefied outlines of different permutations of nationalism.[24] Fichte seems to suggest that a long-term (philosophical) process of retreat and spiritual retrenchment will eventually be manifest as political resistance. The "German love of fatherland" engendered over generations by national upbringing "shall entrench and steel itself in quiet concealment, in order, at the proper time, to burst forth with youthful vigor [*Kraft*] and restore even to the state [*dem Staate*] its lost independence" (117/148).

❖ ❖ ❖

We know that Locke studied Fichte in Georg Simmel's class on modern German philosophy during 1910–11, his year in Berlin. The class is listed in Berlin University's 1910–11 *Verzeichnis der Vorlesungen* as "Philosophie des letzten Jahrhunderts (von Fichte bis Nietzsche und Bergson)."[25] In view of the other classes Locke took that year in Berlin, he would have received an intensive grounding in German post-Kantian philosophy in what was at that time probably the best place in the world to do so. The class notes from Simmel's "Philosophie des letzten Jahrhunderts" that have been reproduced in the *Georg Simmel Gesamtausgabe* indicate that Simmel's main line of teaching Fichte examined the breakthrough arguments of the *Wissenchaftslehre* (1794). Simmel explicates the "Ich" of Fichte, the "I" or "Ego," in the wake of Kantian epistemology, as an absolute, impersonal, logical category, the self-positing that engenders World and, later on, through its negative determination by the necessarily coposited "nonself," the things we call phenomenal or existential selves.[26] The absolute I as activity engenders the world precisely because it needs an object for its action; the I requires "the formation, penetration and mastery of an object—in order to become real," as Simmel puts it elsewhere.[27]

Simmel is among the first to suggest that Fichte's position is a socialist one. This is an important link for the discussion of Locke, as it discloses a relay from the philosophical logic of the "I" to the sociocultural activity of a self and the ultimately national character of that sociality/socialism. At least as recorded in his lecture series, Simmel proposes Fichte as the first German socialist not for his economic arguments, but because Fichte argues that rational thought, and hence the thinking "I," should be sovereign (*Herr*) over the contingency and randomness of being or existence.[28] Socialism appears here as the projection of rational control over contingency. The socialism (as a universal sociality) of the Fichtean "I" was further developed by the neo-Kantian Hermann Cohen in 1915, revising Simmel's account of Fichte's necessarily world-creating "I."[29] For Cohen, Fichte makes explicit the socialism that remains latent in Kant's ethics. This is because, writes Cohen, Fichte "has discovered that the social I is a national I"; "the national I of his Germany is the truly ethico-social realization of the idealism of humanity."[30] In Cohen's account, Fichte's national I is the supraempirical ground (*Begründung*) of the I; and that I is not, as in Kant, only formal, but, as Derrida puts it, "manifests itself to itself originally in its national determination, as belonging to a spirit, a history, a language. I—the Self—signs first in its spiritual language."[31] In the Fichtean system, the I posits (*setzt*) its own being in an act of language (a speech act or performative, as Paul de Man has pointed out).[32] The move made in the *Addresses* and pointed to by Cohen is the acknowledgment that this takes place not in language as such, but in *a* language, German, which for Fichte has a particular value of nation-defining living primordiality. If, at the level of positing, the I is an empty form, the fact that its positing happens in a specific language makes this national I a supraempirical (*überempirische*) ground, because the I originally posited on that same (national) ground logically precedes any empirical entity. That I can only appear to itself as such in relation to this national and social other.

As I have already underlined, I am not here trying to trace some exactly determinable "influence" of Simmel's teaching of philosophy (and of Fichte in particular) upon Locke, as if to say that the truth of Locke was there all along in Fichte/Simmel/Berlin. No amount of empirical work on Locke's reading list and library will produce guaranteed results in the—in any case unreliable—endeavor of tracing influences and reducing the writer to them. Our task is, however, to think through what work these German words may have done on Locke, how Fichte's idiom haunted him and acted upon him as he wrote on the social and cultural text of his own conjuncture but without evidently trying to analyze it in a legibly "Fichtean" or even a "German" way. Locke's idiom is, at least superficially, always closer to that of the American pragmatism he was immersed in at Harvard.[33] While it may be Fichte's example that allows Locke to move between the philosophical and the socio-cultural in the way he does, the how of that movement must be discerned in the unverifiable play of near-invisible translations. Similarly, Locke's cultural cosmopolitanism parallels Cohen's philosophical extension of Fichtean logic into the social, but it does so through the contorted knots of a translation that we can only begin to unravel here.

◆ ◆ ◆

Locke both inhabits the protocols and botches the performance of key Fichtean passages and terms. This intimate botching, enacted sometimes as translation of the untranslatables of Fichte's lexicon, enables him to imagine in national terms relays between philosophy, the social, and cultural practice. These moves open for Locke a space in which a new national subject, illegitimate in Fichte's terms, can be posited. Couched in ways that both echo and translate into new conditions Locke's philosophical training in Berlin, and to some extent Harvard and Oxford, the foreword and Locke's other introductory contributions to *The New Negro* conceptualize this protagonist in terms of spirit, folk, enlightenment, escape from dependence, and race and generation. Term for term, but not at all synonymously, it may be possible to decipher the labor of translation in his framing of the Harlem scene: *Geist, Volk, Aufklärung, Abhängigkeit, Geschlecht*. As with Du Bois's reading in German philosophy, Locke's language of cultural formation, development (*Bildung*), and emancipation invites additional consideration as designating a complex philosophical passage into the conditions of twentieth-century Harlem. This work of translation or adaptation has been hinted at by Locke's biographers.[34] However, these possible translations of terms from the modern German philosophical lexicon stand as problems or question marks for the reader of Locke; in *The New Negro* he neither uses the German words nor mentions the names Fichte or Herder.[35] Locke's translation—if it is indeed that—is not the simple deployment of a series of terms that could appear as unproblematic English synonyms; nor are the key words of a Germanic politicophilosophic lexicon "applied" untransformed to the American scene. In his own idiom, Fichte would not have resonated with a broad section of the black American intelligentsia, let alone the grassroots, though it is possible to imagine the appeal of Fichte's apocalyptic tone and his biblical allusions both to a people in internal exile and to the making-flesh once more of the valley of dry bones that is the present.[36]

We must actively read the effects of Locke's own reading and education as he makes the proleptic Fichtean assertion of a German national subject—reared or trained or educated (*erzogen*) into independent maturity—define the unanticipated "approach to maturity" or "Coming of Age" of a stratum of American blacks (NN, xxvi, 16). Working within a key precept of Enlightenment, Locke tells us that American blacks, who have not historically been allowed to grow up, have done so, or at least that their vanguard has led the way in so doing. Fichte's class and gender corrective to Kant remained merely theoretical because the content of his proposed national education was cognitively and ethically shallow. It could not provide a grounding for general, let alone universal, emancipation; something rather narrower than that happened.[37] Locke revisits the quasi-mythic narratives of Enlightenment so as to activate them once more in the realm of a practice of a cultural politics of race, among subjects absolutely unimaginable as "national" in the modern sense to Kant and Fichte.

Fichte's national subject has to be "German" (*deutsche*), but in a peculiar way. He expands on and mysteriously derails Herder's famous equation of nation, people, and (a) language by, in Derrida's words, decoupling the "German" from "any German naturality or factuality," but without reducing nationality to a contingent discursive construction.[38] Thus, in a key passage of the *Addresses*, Fichte writes that "whatever [*was*] believes in spirituality [*Geistigkeit*] and in the freedom of this spirituality, that desires the eternal progress of this spirituality through freedom—*wherever it is born and whichever language it speaks*—is of our race [*Geschlecht*], it belongs to us and it will join with us."[39] While on the other hand anything else, legally German or not, "wherever it is born and whichever language it speaks," is, if it believes in "stagnation, retrogression and circularity, . . . un-German and alien to us [*undeutsch und fremd für uns*]."[40] David Farrell Krell has commented on the oddity of the impersonal pronouns here. It is as if Fichte momentarily opens up the *Geschlecht* beyond the visible or empiricizable "who"s that may be part of an "us," to welcome a seemingly unconditional "what" or "whatever" (*was*).[41]

If this moment of unconditional welcome is narrowed to the conditionality of national subjects, Fichte still opens the possibility of there being both un-German German-speaking German citizens and non-German-speaking noncitizens who are nevertheless "German" in the important way: they are "of our *Geschlecht*." Both will prove highly appealing to Locke: the unconditional opening to "whatever," and a collectivity of spirit and common belief expressed in terms of racial and generational conditionality.

In a context in which other thinkers had sought to bring the word's multivalence under control, Fichte exploits the polysemy of *Geschlecht* in a way that maximizes the flexibility of assigning both belonging and not-belonging.[42] *Geschlecht* can signify race, kinship, lineage, stock, community, generation, gender, sex; it is a term that gathers a sense of community with a sense of lineage and generational belonging, and thus conveys a kind of belonging that is dependent on reproduction and sexual difference. How many "we" are—we, "us," as the German *Geschlecht*—is determined finally for Fichte as a *belief* entered somehow into a genealogical code that is more than the arbitrary affirmation of a solidarity. It can be avowed as shared spirit, but not empirically demonstrated in merely shared language or citizenship.

Fichte gets to his rarefied determination of national belonging as *Geschlecht* through a series of complicated moves and passages of reduction between the fourth and seventh discourses. Though it passes by way of language, the national bond is not narrowly linguistic, natal, territorial, or racial. The national "we" can persist in spite of territorial dispersion, for example. "The change of native soil [*Veränderung der Heimat*] is insignificant" when it comes to determining the "essential character" (*Grundzuge*) of the *Deutschen* and the bond or circle that defines their collectivity (AG 49). As long as the relation to an originary language is not lost, diaspora or invasion does not fundamentally alter the structure of the "we." By originary language (*ursprüngliche Sprache*) Fichte means one in which conceptual abstractions, its means of expressing the suprasensible, sustain an uninterrupted analogical link to the "living root" of language in general (55). This root is the nonarbitrary phonemes used by human beings to express sensible objects and concepts. What is thereby set in place is a distinction between, on the one hand, a dead, deracinated language cut off from its originary set of intuitions, applied to new and alien ones, unable thereby ever to return to its "living root," and, on the other hand, a living language that maintains an essential genealogical relation to the sounds of originary speech that designated the objects of unmediated sense perception. Language and life and people thus have a mutually reinforcing and stimulating dynamic structure:

> The words of such a language . . . are life and create life in turn. . . . A language that has continued to develop without interruption according to this law also has the power [*Kraft*] to intervene directly [*unmittelbar einzugreifen*] in life and to stimulate it. . . . [This language] has developed uninterruptedly out of the actual common life of that people [*wirklichen gemeinsamen Leben dieses Volks*] . . . [to express] . . . an intuition actually experienced by this people, an intuition that coheres with all the others in an interlocking system [*allseitig eingreifenden Zusammenhang*].
>
> (53)

Fichte's Fourth Address offers an example; and one that is clearly there to make a point. The humanity of the human is at stake (though because this is a matter of rooted idiom, for Fichte it cannot be truly spoken in these Latinate words). The German *Menschlichkeit* says something radically different from the Latinized *Humanität* because the lexicalized Latinate word has lost any connection to an indigenous intuition and thus to an "immediate sensuous perception" (51). To be understood, the meaning of *Humanität*, at first a "wholly empty noise" to the German, must receive a merely historical, antiquarian exposition; its *Sinnbildlichkeit*, or ability to construct sensible symbolization, is, for Fichte, thereby dead, because the word is an interruptive superimposition, a "foreign symbol of Roman origin" (54–55). This goes for all the Latinate peoples, who erroneously believe that their lexicon belongs to their mother tongue whereas it is in fact a historically instituted power of cultural death that has severed them collectively from their primordiality or originality. "Humans are formed by language," writes Fichte, "far more than language is by humans" (49, translation altered). An originary (*ursprüngliche*) language retains a primordial connection to nature, to life, because its relation to a collective intuition remains unbroken in spite of historical transformations. Living language is the portal of spirit, indeed of spiritual culture (*Geistesbildung*) as it "intervenes in life" (59). Foreignism (*Ausländerei*) is the harbinger of the limit, and therefore of death.

This initiates the relay by which the Germans come to represent "the people as such" (*das Volk schlechtweg*), humanity in general, carrying a universalizing charge of infinite development, progress, perfectibility (85). The Germans, *die Deutschen*, are the people that has a relation to life, not death. As the ultimate predication of this relation to life has an increasingly ambiguous reference to any specific language, so Fichte's definition of the national subject becomes progressively rarefied until we reach the special *Geschlecht* that would appear to both represent and lead the *Menschengeschlecht*, the human race. What "believes" (*glaubt*) in spirituality and its freedom is "of our *Geschlecht*," and it is in the living speech of the philosopher that the proposal is made to the German nation to "renew the bond [*Bund*] and close its circle" (97, translation altered). The circular alliance with its own origin—which thereby becomes its destination—is installed or renewed by the philosopher's discourse itself. "He that hath ears to hear, let him hear," says Fichte evoking the Gospel of Matthew (97).

Thus, the auditors of Fichte's lectures are interpellated by him as the vanguard of the vanguard: "let us make ourselves the pre-figuration [*Vorbilde*], the prophecy, the pledge of what after us shall become reality. . . . We must become on the spot what we ought to be in any case: Germans" (155); and this circular bond of the "we" touches its own originarity and destination in freedom and "infinite improvability" of spirit. Further, Fichte, lecturing "in the room in which you visibly breathe," asked his hearers to work for the systematic cultivation, in children, of the capacity to actively project these imaginative prefigurations (*Vorbilder*) of a future social order for the "German nation" (183). Such prefigurations are the condition of the realization of this social order inasmuch as their subject's will is developed through this education to (want to) actualize the images it has the power now to prefigure. Within the logic of the circular bond of its alliance with itself, humanity "fashions itself with freedom into that which it really and originally is" (42).

Such a Fichtean "German" subject is named by the dense knot of *Geschlecht*, allying race, sex, generation, reproduction, and community. The exemplarity of *Geschlecht* appears plastic yet remains rooted in a national proper name—but it is precisely the overloaded and untranslatable tangle of *Geschlecht* that permits Locke's botched use. The *Geschlecht*, finally so rarefied as to be defined as shared "belief" in Fichte, is suddenly fleshed out in manifestly racial terms, given a face, visibilized, empiricized, phenomenalized. It is a black face, the face of "the race" (which is one way to translate *das Geschlecht*). *The New Negro* is full of images of black faces and masks, metonymizing as national subject a group that is not linked by the symbolism of deep unbroken genealogy to the national territory of the United States or its European tributaries. Taking up the untranslatability and polysemy of *Geschlecht* as the name of a national subject, Locke proposes the deracinated descendants of a slave diaspora, lacking civil rights, as the felicitous U.S. national subject with a universalizing mission.[43] This in a context in which "the ideal [U.S.] national subject has actually been a highly specific person whose universality has been fashioned from a succession of those who have designated his antithesis, those irreducibly *non-national* subjects who appeared in the different guises of slave, Indian, and, at times, immigrant."[44] If multiple modes of "racial demarcation" have "historically been a central measure of the inner constitution of modern, civic identity" in the United States, paradoxically signifying

the "universality and inclusion" of the polity, then the Lockean identification of a newly felicitous black American cultural subject may be read
as diagnosing an ongoing practical critique of an exclusionary universalism.[45] Yet it cuts two ways, this announcement of a "new race-spirit," a
"new generation," and a new national subject.[46]

For Locke, those who have been historically denied the chance to "grow
up," to exercise their freedom, have taken it. The vanguard of spirit exemplifies an incalculable self-emancipation and a widening, infinitizing, universalizing movement. As we saw, Fichte's term for the German national
subject waiting to renew its bond with itself is "our *Geschlecht*." It will form
a circular alliance, make a collectivity, in its relation to an *Ursprache* that
is in principle disconnected from place and birth, yet finally determined
in the present moment of the address. Locke will preserve the value of
speech as constituting the bond with itself of the newly emergent community, but will also propose that the "race" of deracinated blacks has itself
been the forming ground of the American spirit, an American *Volk*.

The place of formation of the new subject's spirit in Fichte is *Nationalerziehung*, "national education" or "upbringing." The new spirit must be
consciously forged by a vanguard, a leading edge. "Who should put themselves at the leading point [*Spitze*] in the execution [*Ausführung*] of this
plan?" he asks (AG 141, translation altered). The first answer is the State
and the German states. Yet if the State is unable to fulfill this role, it will
be left to "private individuals" and will inevitably proceed at a slower rate
(151). After a great series of "ifs," establishing the ever more adverse conditions under which *Nationalerziehung* could begin even without State support, Fichte imagines the most marginal possible figure with which it
could start: parentless, homeless children. These deparented children
would be both remainder and symbol of the now abject German *Geschlecht*.
"Let us," writes Fichte under the sign of the conditional, "turn to the poor
orphans, to those who lie about in misery on the streets, to all those whom
the adult world has cast out and thrown away!" (151). "For all of posterity
it will be a warning and a testament to our age, if precisely those whom it
cast out earn, by dint of their expulsion alone, the privilege of inaugurating a better race [*ein besseres Geschlecht*]" (152).

"Those whom the adult world [*erwachsene Menschheit*] has cast out and
thrown away" (Fichte) are also those not permitted to grow up in the normal way, to accede to the recognizable "maturity" of Enlightenment. Locke

here does something bizarre with Fichte's already bizarre setup. Assigning the rising new race not as our homeless orphans but as those hitherto marginalized in racial terms, he silently translates once more the very term Fichte would use as that definitive of the national collectivity. It is as if there *is* no future American *Geschlecht* without "the race." That is to say, without blacks, without what Locke calls the "racialism of the Negro" and without the "Younger Generation . . . bringing its gifts" (NN 12, 47). Making the central *Geschlecht* of his argument deliberately narrower in translation ("race" as referring to the community of black Americans and from there outward the world population of "people of African descent"), Locke borrows the resources of Fichtean nationalism to claim as *Geschlecht* precisely that which had been the negative condition of modernity's previous cosmopolitanisms or universalisms. The national spirit can arise from the contingencies of unpredictable historical processes: slavery, diaspora, struggle against exploitation.

Fichte calls for the training of the spirit in a systematic national education system for all. Locke leaves the process of re-formation of the race more obscure and less calculable. Groundwork for the emergence of this subject takes place primarily beyond the specifics of political organization or instituted education. It happens rather "in the internal world of the Negro mind and spirit," manifest at the level of aesthetic culture where this "spirit"—the "folk-spirit" becoming the "race-spirit"—are the truly active "essential forces" (NN xxv, xxvii). This level is for Locke more originary than political organization ("social change and progress . . . establishing new contacts and founding new centers") because it is the site of independent self-activity as such, of "positive self-direction" in Locke's own words (xxv, xxvii, 8). The transformation of the state, politics, institutions will derive from the cultural transformation that "positive self-direction" engenders. Outwardly—in the sphere of the sociopolitical—New Negroes already share "the ideals of American institutions and democracy" (10). The remaking of American nationality will authentically proceed from the domain of spiritual expression—itself reflective of the affective realm of an "inner life"—as a renewed subject/spirit appropriates and inhabits the "outer" institutions of American democracy (10).

Hence the "new spirit" as a cultural entity is an unaccountable surprise for observers concerned with social externalities, a monstrous birth or "changeling" in the eyes of "the Sociologist, the Philanthropist, the

Race-Leader" (3). Energized by a primordial folk-spirit from which it is nevertheless detached in important ways, this new cultural "race-spirit" does an inside job on "American culture and institutions" contaminated by a racism not true to their own "American ideals" (12). Locke calls upon the spirit to enact a general transformation of American society from within, beginning from the cultural sphere, rather than to install a permanent "negro problem" as a "benign foreign body in the body politic" (12). Consequently, the stakes of Locke's specifically *national* claim for the New Negro are condensed in the following sentence: "we cannot be undone without America's undoing" (12).[47]

This insurgent nationalism, staking a claim for inclusion in or even proprietorship of "America," communicates immediately with types of internationalism, cosmopolitanism, and universalism. Following a logic that we can provisionally call Fichtean, the relay from a new national collectivity to a cosmopolitan, universal mission passes precisely by way of philosophy (no accident that the orchestrator and midwife of *The New Negro* was a philosopher). Fichte locates the philosophy of a new spirit and a creative freedom in a Germanness that is so originary and essential that its singular example is destined to become universal (AG 104, 195). Germany will become the indigenous vanguard of the world; *as essentially German*, it will lead humanity in the movement toward an infinite perfectibility.

Addressing the Germans at the conclusion of his allocution, Fichte writes that "If you rouse yourselves and make a stand . . . you will see in this nation the regenerator and restorer of the world. . . . Of all modern peoples it is you in whom the seed of human perfection [*menschlichen Vervollkommnung*] most decidedly lies and to whom the lead in its development is assigned. If you perish *in your essentiality* [*eurer Wesenheit*], then all hopes of the entire human race . . . perish with you."[48] Locke's notion that American blacks would act "as the advance-guard of the African peoples in their contact with Twentieth Century civilization" is immediately followed by his applause for the "cosmopolitan scale" of their multilingual media, the recognition of the "race question as a world problem," and the evocation of a "new internationalism" (NN 14–15).[49] Yet to take part in the universalizing movement of American democracy is also to run the risk of expanding its imperializing reach. What does it mean to claim that the New Negro is an inevitable and constitutive part of the infinite perfectibility of American democracy? On what is precisely a world scale, there is nothing more politically equivocal in Locke's *New Negro* writings than the following: "the possible rôle of the American Negro in the future development of Africa is one of the most constructive and universally helpful missions that any modern people can lay claim to" (NN 15). It is an uncannily reversed foreshadowing of the apprehension Antonio Gramsci voiced in 1932 that "American expansionism should use American negroes as its agents in the conquest of the African market and the extension of American civilization."[50] Locke's suggestion is so vague that it could of course be filled out in several directions; but it is precisely this equivocal universalism (helping the "future development of Africa") that is structured by the logic of a systematically national principle of benevolent patronage sanctioning the aesthetic primitivization of "Africa" elsewhere in *The New Negro*.[51] In being cast as the "past" of the African American, monolithic "Africa" is denied modernity, differentiation, and contemporaneity, as well as the capacity for self-emancipation claimed by the New Negro and his predecessors. Thus, in spite of the "new internationalism" that Locke asserts, *The New Negro* reterritorializes Africa and the international in the name of "African descent," making of them a story of an American national becoming. *The New Negro*'s desires for internationality are recaptured as they are stated, by figures of nationality and indigeneity.

❖ ❖ ❖

"So far as he is culturally articulate," writes Locke in his foreword to *The New Negro*, "we shall let the Negro speak for himself" (xxv). It is a complex, far-reaching assertion. Deploying the manifesto-form's characteristic insistence on voice, it contests the type of primitivism that sees black cultural production in terms of the "savage, . . . the peasant or the child," those who must be spoken for; and it opposes the benevolent "sympathetic curiosity" that patronizes the benighted efforts of the "darkened Ghetto" (xxvi).[52] Locke's second introductory essay in the collection, "Negro Youth Speaks," is crowded with figures of voice:

> Youth speaks, and the voice of the New Negro is heard. What stirs inarticulately in the masses is already vocal upon the lips of the talented few, and the future listens, however the present may shut its ears. . . . Negro youth . . . [foretells] in new notes and accents the maturing speech of

full racial utterance. . . . But it is a presumption to speak further for those who in the selections of their work in the succeeding sections speak so adequately for themselves.

(47, 53)

Intimately linked to the primitivist impulse by its wish to return to the beginning so as to herald the new, the manifesto-form lays claim to the voicing of a naked speech. Yet it is a "convention-laden, ideologically inflected genre" whose generic character comprises the performative paradox of a denial of its own mediations, its own conventionality.[53] If the manifesto-form can be said generally to stage a desire, then that desire is for "transparent public expressions of pure will," direct and unmediated plain speech.[54] This paradox is not an error to be denounced; I seek rather to follow the discursive and formal possibilities it opens up and the dilemmas it discloses. While it is admittedly necessary for Locke to introduce his *New Negro* collection, he comes to a certain limit point indicated by the "further" in the final sentence just quoted. I will not speak further, he writes, because the New Negroes I am speaking for here "speak so adequately for themselves" (NN 53). Key discursive articulations of Locke's manifesto occur between his announcement of the unprecedented birth of the New Negro (the staging of his own declaration) and his multiple introductions to the voices of the New Negroes themselves. Locke *must* stop speaking for them, because his entire argument is that the New Negroes have attained a "spiritual Coming of Age" and liberated themselves in advance from the very type of dependency that an introductory representation would exemplify (16).

The position Locke defines for himself thus clarifies the paradox of his later self-representation as "midwife" of the new, developed by David Marriott and others. It also suggests that if not the name, then the subject position Locke would retrospectively call "mid-wifery" was in place as early as *The New Negro*.[55] As Marriott points out, while the midwife is part of the process of generational reproduction, (s)he does not belong to the emergent generation. Instrumental as a facilitator of the birth of the new *Geschlecht* (its renaissance, the rebirth of art and spirit), the midwife necessarily stands apart from that new generation; is both ahead of it and in the rear; is a lone figure beside a nascent community.[56] The figure of the midwife is another condensation point at which Locke can make a limited translation of the immense problematic of *Geschlecht* into American English. Although it will overspill this limit, it solves, rhetorically speaking, the problem of representational leadership on the one hand (the midwife must be there to facilitate the birth but by definition cannot represent the new generation); and on the other hand it locates the agency of the rebirth of American spirit in an almost impersonal (black, male, queer) self-emancipating and procreative desire—beyond the limits imposed by historical racialization. Thus can the creative black (man) become the felicitous national subject.

Is it any wonder, therefore, that the frontispiece for *The New Negro* is a remarkable *Brown Madonna* by Winold Reiss? The pose is generic, though a model for the painting may be Giovanni Bellini's *Madonna and Child in a Landscape* (ca. 1480/1485), currently in the National Gallery of Art. The Bellini was exhibited at the Metropolitan Museum in 1923, and subsequently hung in the Detroit Institute of Arts until its transfer to Washington, DC, in 1947.[57] A figuration of a virgin birth preserves the presence of the (black) woman while minimizing her role and in fact leaving a more important agential and symbolic space for the midwife to bring forth the new generation. The trim, controlled lines of Reiss's female figure and her phallic modernist haircut echoing the veil worn by the Virgin are almost banally illustrative of Kristeva's "fantasy of the so-called 'Phallic' Mother" (*phantasme de la mère dite phallique*).[58] Reiss modernizes, phallicizes, and domesticates a less normative version of African American motherhood, one that is rather different from the tradition of representations understood by Kristeva. Unsurprisingly then, most readings of Reiss's image (and its strategic positioning in the *New Negro* collection) frame it along the lines of "an image of conservative black motherhood," devoid of sexuality or productive agency.[59] Such readings are broadly compatible with the thesis of the phallic mother, a symbolizing female body needed to make the impersonal emergence of a new *Geschlecht* correlatively symbolize as the formation of a newborn spiritual subject able fully to speak for itself. Yet such readings downplay the ideological effort of producing the screen. Are there fault lines not entirely occluded by it? I leave this question to future iconographers of the New(er) Negro.

As a rhetorical structure, the pattern engendered between *Brown Madonna* and Locke's introductory moves is consequently more than a matter of the etiquette and genre of the introductory speech: Locke is laying

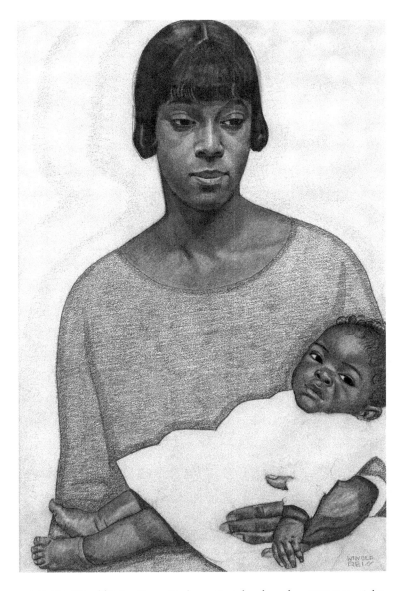

FIGURE 1.1 Winold Reiss, *Brown Madonna.* Pastel on board, c. 1925. Copyright © Fisk University Galleries, Nashville, Tennessee.

FIGURE 1.2 Giovanni Bellini, *Madonna and Child in a Landscape*. Oil on panel, c. 1480/1485. Ralph and Mary Booth Collection, National Gallery of Art.

claim to a seismic transformation of the shape of American culture, a "resurgence of a people" that has world-historical significance comparable to the revolutions, national revivals, and anticolonial insurgencies taking place across the globe (NN xxvii). He deploys an implicit sign of negation (I will not speak further) that seems retroactively to cancel all the prefatory and introductory discourse he has laid out so carefully in heralding the coming of the New Negro. At the same time, the midwife's work appears compulsively repetitive, with Locke contributing no fewer than four prefatory essays to the parts of the collection, and an additional critical analysis of Afro-Americans' relation to the formal possibilities harbored by African art ("The Legacy of the Ancestral Arts").

Locke's is the dilemma of a cultural rather than a political vanguard, true; but he regards culture as the leading site at which important social and political transformations become generally legible. He speaks of and for a group that has been culturally coded as at best unready for modernity (immature, primitive, like the "savage, . . . the peasant or the child") and as having no valid cultural mode of self-expression (xxvi). This problematic is revealed by both the negative sign (I shall not speak further) and the conditional sign ("so far as he is culturally articulate, we shall let the Negro speak for himself") under which Locke permits the New Negro to appear on the cultural stage of a "New America" (xxv). The figure of the midwife asks us to read such gestures as other than an exercise in bad faith or a simple self-contradiction that would enable a dismissive criticism of Locke for failing to do what he says he will do, or for being a controlling micromanager of how the New Negro will appear in a contested and competitive avant-garde field. This structure of paradox or "performative contradiction" is rather the mode of appearance of a genuine vanguard predicament; and midwifery is the rhetorical figure that allows for a solution of the problem of being the vanguard's vanguard: the leading figure becomes rather the attendant at the self-birth of the new *Geschlecht*.

Locke heralds something new, the happening of an incalculable event, "beyond the watch and guard of statistics," in the "changeling" birth of the New Negro on the scene of the modern (3). Returning us to the scene of the *Brown Madonna*, the "changeling" motif once more displaces or downplays the role of the woman (but not necessarily the importance of *Geschlecht* as generation and sexual difference). The changeling is a substitute, not necessarily the child of a woman's body, but something else put into the newborn infant's crib in place of the purportedly rightful heir or line. The subversive suggestion of this metaphor is clear: the felicitous subject position, the inheritor, is now not necessarily white; and the agent of substitution is, at least by implication, the midwife, Locke, who swaps out the child at birth and places a new *Geschlecht* into the cradle of modernity. Vanguard work of transformation is recast as the short circuit of a magical sleight of hand.

Locke's presentation of *The New Negro* conducts a new figure into that cultural cradle, a figure no longer "caricatured" but "seriously portrayed and painted" (9). This different mode of formalization and visibilization finds its enabling condition in the "social and economic freedom" of the "northern city centers" (6). Locke is careful to stress the agency of the migrating southern blacks by adducing their "vision of opportunity" and "spirit" to grasp the "more democratic chance" as the primary reason for the migration and its effects, rather than socioeconomic determinants such as industrial demand, the boll-weevil epidemic, and "social terrorism" in the South (6). Thus, neither economic interest nor social oppression fundamentally animates the migrating southern blacks; rather, their movement is ascribed to a self-emancipating spirit. In this way, the liberation of southern blacks in metropolitan migration allows the image of the automodernized black, the New Negro, to appear as a genuinely new modernist cultural current whose manifesto now proclaims its advent.

Locke's is thus a key instance in its time of a vanguard claim to an alternative modernism that would give a new face to modernity, that would be "its truest social portraiture, . . . a new figure on the national canvas, . . . the enlightenment of self-portraiture" (xxv). *The New Negro* aims to "document" and "register" (xxv) something hitherto unseen and unheard, to bring it both into the light of visibility (but also to disclose its own self-determined autoillumination, its enlightenment) and into the realm of audibility (by letting it speak for itself). Let the face and voice of modernity be black, Locke writes, in "stepping alignment with contemporary artistic thought, mood and style. They [its practitioners] are thoroughly modern" (50). Synchronize with modernity, says Locke, so as to re-form it. Locke, speaking from a minoritized, marginalized place, trying to establish sufficient cultural continuity with the "modern" to change its racist face, lays claim to a vanguard function and simultaneously occludes its ventriloquist's work.

Locke's collection inhabits this predicament. It counterposes to racist primitivism or invertedly racist benevolence the visibility and audibility of modern/modernist Afro-American cultural production as a "document" of the resurgence of a racial and nation-like "folk" (xxv, xxvii). This "*spiritual* Coming of Age" prefigures political enfranchisement and civil rights, a "full initiation into American democracy" as yet not attained (16, my emphasis). The vanguard of the spirit leads the way to political emancipation, and Locke's anxious representation of that vanguard simultaneously discloses a limit to the cultural activism of the spirit.

◆ ◆ ◆

Locke lays claim to a counterpublic voice, a collective formation—the New Negro—whose audibility is structured and given a place in the manifesto called *The New Negro*. The circle—the *Bund* of collectivity—is rhetorically delineated in this figure by which the New Negro will find itself in *The New Negro*.

If Locke gestures toward his own occlusion by refusing to speak for others, it is because the New Negro does not need a spokesman: conditions now exist in which black Americans can speak for themselves. What are these conditions? Locke is painfully aware that the "portals of the thinking Negro's mind" have been "protectively closed" (NN 9) by history; that hundreds of years of internment in the American slave system have led to lasting epistemic and cognitive damage for the mass in postslavery society, because to think and speak for oneself was to incur punishment. Denied the right to intellectual labor, defined in terms of body labor, they have been *made* "inarticulate"; inarticulacy was part of a structural denial of access to knowledge and authorized expression.[60] As Frederick Douglass put it in *Narrative of the Life of Frederick Douglass*, a slave maxim was "that a still tongue makes a wise head."[61] A glance at the early chapters of Douglass's account is sufficient to confirm Locke's point regarding slave punishments for learning, thinking, and speaking: "By far the larger part of the slaves know as little of their ages as horses know of theirs, and it is the wish of most masters within my knowledge to keep their slaves thus ignorant. . . . I was not allowed to make any inquiries of my master concerning it. He deemed all such inquiries on the part of a slave improper and impertinent, and evidence of a restless spirit" (47). Douglass quotes one of his masters, Mr. Auld, saying, "Learning would *spoil* the best nigger in the world" (78, original emphasis). In the majority of cases, we must assume that the policy was effective. It spurs the exceptional Douglass to learn more, however he can. Now, contends Locke, African Americans are entering into continuity with a modern mind-set and the public sphere: with the "large industrial and social problems of our present-day democracy, . . . initiation into American democracy, . . . stepping alignment with contemporary artistic thought, . . . thoroughly modern, . . . ultra-modern, . . . Negro thoughts now wear the uniform of the age" (NN 5, 16, 50).

In his two opening essays for *The New Negro*, "The New Negro" and "Negro Youth Speaks," Locke thus revisits a certain story of Enlightenment and reterritorializes it in twentieth-century Harlem. By 1925 Locke was a professor of philosophy at Howard University. As we have already seen, his work in ethics, values, and aesthetics situates him firmly in a post-Kantian tradition working out the implications of the broad framework of Enlightenment thought. While Kant's newspaper article "An Answer to the Question: What Is Enlightenment?" (1784) is not Kant's most extensive treatment of the problems of Enlightenment, it is surely his best known.[62] It is also considered inaugural in discussions of the "attitude of modernity."[63] "Enlightenment," writes Kant, "is the emergence of man from his self-imposed infancy" (*selbst verschuldeten Unmündigkeit*). Kant's *Unmündigkeit* is often translated as "infancy," derived from the Latin *infans* (unable to speak), and also as "minority," which is more correct in the legal sense, "tutelage," and "immaturity."[64] In Kant's time, *Unmündigkeit* had the more technical meaning of legal minority. Locke's translation of Kant's general argument to the African American metropolis is therefore unmistakable: "the Negro today . . . resents being spoken for as a social ward or minor"; "Having weaned the Negro, public opinion cannot continue to paternalize" (NN 11, 10). And from Locke's first unveiling of the New Negro in the issue of *The Survey Graphic* from March 1925 (the "nucleus" of *The New Negro*), "the Negro of the Northern centers has reached a stage where tutelage, even of the most interested and well-intentioned sort, must give place to new relationships, where positive self-direction must be reckoned with in ever increasing measure."[65] Furthermore, although the adjective *enlightened* was commonly used in Locke's time, it is not coincidental here that the Locke of *The Survey Graphic* refers to the black intelligentsia as an "enlightened minority" and to the "enlightened minorities" of both blacks and whites (630, 632);

and in the foreword to *The New Negro* he writes of needing to seek the "enlightenment of that self-portraiture which the present developments of Negro culture are offering" (NN xxv).

In spite of its brevity, Kant's newspaper article choreographs complexities that both determine Locke's representation of the New Negro and are displaced or reworked by it. We begin with *Unmündigkeit*, the condition of minority or infancy from which humanity in Kant's time seems to be freeing itself. The translation option of "infancy" is of interest because it captures a semantic shift in the German terms *Mündigkeit* and *Unmündigkeit* during the nineteenth century. *Münd* in these words derives from the old-high-German *Munt*, meaning "force," "power," "protection," especially of a patriarchal type. It is "related to the Latin *manus* (hand)."[66] *Mündigkeit* signifies a power of nondependency, becoming in Germany the legal term for majority.[67] A false etymology came to "contaminate" the *Münd* in these words with the German word for mouth, *Mund*, and thus to give the impression of an equivalence between *Mündigkeit* (accession to the age of responsibility, or majority) and *Mündlichkeit* (mouthyness, capacity to speak).[68] A play on words allowed *Unmündigkeit* to carry the shadow-sense of inability to speak, like the infant. Theodor Adorno also inhabits this mindset when he writes, of Kant's essay, "politically mature [*mündig*] is the person who speaks for himself, because he has thought for himself and is not merely repeating [*nachredet*] someone else; he stands free of any guardian."[69] Kant's essay already exploits the semantic mix-up and its uncontrollable, punning play of meaning. The Kantian pun shadows "hand" with "mouth," rhetorically allying independence and speech, but also force and speech, might and reason.

In *Anthropology from a Pragmatic Point of View* (1798), Kant makes a further play on this pun that reveals how profoundly it is connected with a historical gendering of the public sphere. In the section "On Mental Deficiencies in the Cognitive Faculty," he opens the question of a normally functioning understanding that is immature (*unreif*), as with a child, and therefore deferred in exercise until ripening (a temporal deferral), or one that always requires representation by proxy (*Stellvertretung*) in the civil sphere (a spatial displacement). The latter concerns woman, "immature in the civil sphere" regardless of age (*bürgerlich-unmündig*).[70] "It is true," writes Kant, "that when it comes to talking [*Sprechen*], woman by the nature of her sex has enough of a mouth [*Mundwerks genug hat*; has enough of a motormouth] to represent [*vertreten*] both herself and her husband, even in court (where it concerns mine and thine), and so could literally be declared to be *over-mature* [übermündig]" (103/522, emphasis Kant's with the shadowed pun sense of "overmouthy"). By having a big mouth, woman falls short and simultaneously exceeds the measure of *Mündigkeit* that marks a subject with legal status in civil society. We will see remote lines of this gendered fracture played out across the (post)colonial world in the chapters that follow.[71]

These questions also touch Locke's *New Negro*. Eight of the anthology's thirty-six contributors were women. The idea that the New Negro will be given a place to speak "so far as he is culturally articulate" (NN xxv) opens onto a historical narrative of epistemic and social fissuring that intersects discontinuously with the story of sexual difference and ultimately desta-bilizes Locke's schema of nationhood.[72] One sign of this dilemma can be seen in the retitling of Elise Johnson McDougald's contribution to the *Survey Graphic* issue, an essay reprinted in *The New Negro*. From the *Survey Graphic*'s "The Double Task: The Struggle of Negro Women for Sex and Race Emancipation," the essay becomes "The Task of Negro Womanhood." Although the essay's text remains identical, the retitling suggests a one-dimensional "task" for an unproblematic "Negro Womanhood," rather than the complexity of a double task across fractures between race and sex indicated in the *Survey Graphic*. Locke thereby both acknowledges and works to occlude these sites of potential incommensurability, and some-times occludes them in acknowledging them.

In the *Anthropology*, Kant immediately proceeds to link his remarks spe-cifically to the discussion in "Enlightenment" by invoking the "docility of the masses" (*Lenksamkeit des großen Haufens*). The people find it more "com-fortable" to make themselves *unmündig*, to the benefit of heads of state who thereby take on the patriarchal moniker of *Landesväter*, or "Fathers of the Country." These leaders actively promote dependency by representing (*vorzustellen*) "the use of one's own understanding without the guidance of another" as deadly. Thus "the people [*das Volk*] are condemned to perma-nent immaturity [*Unmündigkeit*] with regard to their own best interest [*seines eigenen besten Wegen*]" (103/523). Children, mouthy women, and folk masses: Kant both inhabits and critically oversteps a discourse that situ-ates these three (nonequivalent) protosubaltern, even primitivist, crowd-like figures as having to be represented and "mechanically handled" (*mech-

anische Handhabung) "under the reign of others" (*unter dem Regiment anderer*) in the interest of maintaining a legal order (104/523). We return to the question of how these asymmetrically positioned groups of unripe primitives can step out of *Unmündigkeit*—their lack of independent power, which is also the power of a speaking mouth.[73]

Although Enlightenment was for Kant certainly a matter of emerging from a feudal-patriarchal dependency on authority figures, freedom to speak reason was not its sole condition. As Kant was acutely aware, to speak and reason independently and publicly was not simply a matter of being freed to do so by being "given a voice." Something had to intervene, to prepare for the public use of (the voice of) reason, with no guarantee of success. Kant writes as follows: "Daß aber ein Publikum sich selbst aufkläre, ist eher möglich; ja es ist, wenn man ihm nur Freiheit läßt, beinahe unausbleiblich." "That, however, a public could enlighten itself is quite possible; yes, if it were only allowed freedom, it is almost inevitable." This complex, puzzling sentence, hedged with conditions and laced with adverbs and conjunctions, calls for an interminable analysis. I will examine the last phrase as a metonymy for the questions raised by the logic and structure of the entire sentence: *beinahe unausbleiblich*; almost, nearly, inevitable. How can something be *almost* inevitable? The components of *beinahe* each connote proximity, nearness, in space or time, but a proximity that is also a not-quite-thereness. And the unconventional oddity of this adverb modifying an adjective calls attention to rhetorical structure, semantic mutation. By inserting the logically peculiar "almost" here, Kant points to a fissure—between the acquisition of freedom and the ability to exercise it—that can expand into an abyss.[74] Having a freedom in no way means that freedom will be practiced so that it turns into self-enlightenment. Everything hangs on the "almost." What will occupy its position? What will be the articulating hinge, or power, of the almost? What sort of interface between the condition of unfreedom and a step into nondependency can "almost" represent?

It is precisely at this point that Fichte stepped in to revise the Kantian account, to try to close the fissures of gender and class that remain presupposed in Kant. In "What Is Enlightenment?" it is those able to speak "as scholars" (*als Gelehrter*, as "the educated") "through writing" (*durch Schriften*)—both phrases are repeatedly used—who will function as the vanguard of general enlightenment. The institutions and processes by which this generalization will happen are implicit, though not spelled out: "the obstacles to general enlightenment or to the exit out of this self-incurred immaturity become ever fewer."[75] Bernard Stiegler elaborates the generalization as the existence of "readers, as the receivers of reason's public exercise ... who are at least by right writers, have had access, by the fact of the circulation of letters—epistolary exchanges, gazettes, reviews, books—to the formation of a kind of attention that, *in Kant's epoch*, in the century of Enlightenment, addresses itself to *all* as 'the people.' Even if they are serfs or even slaves."[76] The problem hangs on the "at least by right [*au moins en droit*]." If serfs and slaves are addressed as part of a "people," or as Kant's "*Welt*," how does such "right" become legible to them? A right is no small thing, but Stiegler's book itself demonstrates that "access" as such to literacy (or information) in a narrow sense does not guarantee the "mature" capability of "reading, being read, and being capable of writing" in the expanded critical sense of knowing and exercising "the usage of the book." An educational supplement is needed.[77] Fichte perceived that that without a generalized (what he calls "national") education that brings in all children of whatever class or gender, this impulse of Enlightenment will falter. In his own terms, the stake of Fichte's radical, even avant-garde, *Erziehung* is precisely the transformation of the *Unmündige* to a condition of *Mündigkeit* (AG 117, 130, 135). "The majority of the citizens [*Mehrheit der Bürger*] must be educated to this patriotic sentiment [*vaterländischen Sinne*] and, so that we can be assured of the majority, this education must be attempted on all [*an der Allheit*]" (116/148); "If these wards [*Unmündige*] are not to become slaves, they must leave their tutelage [*Vormundschaft*], and to enable them to do so, they must first of all be educated to maturity [*Mündigkeit*]" (117/148); the new national education must be extended to "even those born into the lowest rank" (128/162); and "both sexes [*beiden Geschlechtern*] must receive this education in the same way" (136/173).[78]

Beside the fissure of sexual difference (an uncontrollable signification of *Geschlecht*), therefore, a social difference also enables the existence of modernized New Negroes and is veiled by their articulation of a "folk" they have left behind. The folk will return us to another locus of translation questions.

❖   ❖   ❖

Locke revisits these Kantian and Fichtean problematics, making double binds single by playing midwife to a spectacularly talented array of voices (Jean Toomer, Countee Cullen, Zora Neale Hurston, Langston Hughes, Eric Walrond, Claude McKay, Jessie Fauset, and many others). All already recipients, in one way or another, of excellent humanistic educations, these New Negroes appear in the collection as having already traversed the gulf of the "almost" to the space in which they are "spiritually free" and able to offer "an emancipating vision to America" (NN 53). While Locke rightly places them at the forefront of modernist experimental literary and artistic production, we must yet examine here how the paradox of the Kantian "almost" remains to determine his vanguard maieutic role, his pattern of argument, and his aesthetic of presentation.

Locke stakes *The New Negro*'s claim to "national and even international scope," and this scope remains defined by a point of maximum advancement defined as a black vanguard. Locke stands at the head of the collection (or at the end of its birth canal?), his foreword and prefaces to several of its sections demarcating the places of the pronged points of the collection's vanguard wedges. As Locke goes on to detail in the book's introductory essay, it is Harlem that is "center" of a "new spirit" of renewal in black American life (NN 14, 3), the site of "consciousness of acting as the advanceguard of the African peoples in their contact with Twentieth Century civilization" (14). This vanguard exists on a line that readers of modernity's topoi will immediately recognize as archetypal: a line "from countryside to city . . . from medieval America to modern" (6). History and geography here also encode a line of social change from peasant to proletarian that is the way the revolutionary vanguardism of Locke's times had revised an older story of country-to-city as modernity. Thus, on the one hand, the country-to-city story told by Locke patterns the black American experience within a conventional "transition narrative," while, on the other, his revision of the figure of modernity as a black visage and *Geschlecht* can perhaps accommodate David Nicholls's more general view that holds the history of slavery and emancipation to be at odds with a more conventional modes of production narrative.[79]

The New Negro assigns itself the task of creating a site at which literary artists can articulate what the inarticulate mass cannot. The mouthpiece is necessarily separated in space and time and class from the vast body it speaks (regional, national and transnational, masses and African peoples).

Locke lays claim to a vanguard position and simultaneously, perhaps necessarily, disavows its mouthpiece function: "it is a presumption to speak further for those who . . . speak so adequately for themselves" (53). In this intricate relay, Locke seeks to avoid being a mouthpiece of a mouthpiece, refusing to speak for those who can eloquently articulate what the inarticulate cannot. This is a description of the cultural activist's responsibility: to represent without attempting to be "representative"; to make a stage where American blacks can speak "*as* Negroes" rather than "*for* the Negro" (48). Rather than "people," the name Locke gives to the collectivity thereby claimed is "folk." It is a shared "peasant matrix" of the folk that permits the articulate to voice the inarticulate (15).

The relation between the terms *folk* and *people* is a complex one; I can only note the possible displacements and translations of the eighteenth and nineteenth century collective cognates (nationalist and/or revolutionary or republican) *das Volk* and *le peuple*.[80] As we saw earlier with Fichte and Kant, the German *Volk* is often translated without remark as "people," as if the terms were neatly synonymous. For neither thinker was this the case in his own idiom.[81] In a U.S. context where the name of the national collectivity appears in the political field under the heading "We the People," the posing of the term *folk* by Locke (and Du Bois before him) signifies an interested refusal of this translation in at least a dual register. *Folk* belongs (though not exclusively) to the lexicon of popular African American speech and shifts a symbolic political allegiance from "French" to "German." Following Du Bois, but adding a modernist and aesthetic interpretation, Locke deploys the term cognate with German rather than French to assign a national subject of cultural spirit as distinct from an abstract political (republican) subject.[82]

The name Locke gives to the collectivity claimed is "folk." He conceptualizes its ground as a shared "peasant matrix"—a residuum of the rural regions they have left. This also provides the material voiced by the articulate on behalf of the inarticulate (NN 15). Barbara Foley refers to this "folk" aspect of Locke's aesthetic as a "metonymic nationalism," an indigenizing figure of the "racy peasant undersoil of the race life" whose "signifying chain connects folk with soil with region with nation."[83] It is this folk-ness that will enter modernity in the cultural advance guard that speaks it. Beyond this nationalist signification, it is the folk that occupies the place of the Kantian *almost* in Locke's *New Negro* writings; here it plays the role of an imaginary suturing of the gap between enlightened articulate cultural avant-garde and inarticulate mass.

Locke territorializes the originary bond sharable in the "folk" form: a "humble, unacknowledged source" has informed the South's specific (subnational) regionality. The Negro is the "peasant matrix" of the American South ("that section of America which has most undervalued him") because "he" is a material and also a "spiritual" infrastructure of that region (NN 15). It is here, therefore, that Locke initially locates the black claim to a specifically American spiritual purchase that overspills the limits and segregations imposed by the racialization of blacks. Furthermore, the terms *matrix* and *undersoil* both suggest a philosophical schema of derivation in which the matrixial space approaches the condition of an a priori bond, and this bond is only representable in the derived form of the various modes of "folk"-ness delineated by Locke. Representable, therefore, in the assorted aesthetic and cultural practices he collects in the book.

The peasant matrix is not dissolved in movement to the metropolis, but aesthetically transfigured into a phenomenalized bond or alliance for the new and more general *Geschlecht*. The peasant matrix rises—as folk—into national representation ("a collaborator and participant in American civilization") on being articulated by a "conscious contributor" (15). Then it is legible/audible/visible in its various derived folk forms. Locke's phrase "peasant matrix" is unusual and calls attention to itself. He is here sufficiently philosophical to choose a term that denotes no particular territory but rather the possibility of territorialization as such. Yet in this context I must emphasize the powerful gendering of "matrix" as a feminine envelope or container, womb, repository in which type is set, the unrepresentable base of representation.[84] It is only in some sort of instituted articulation that the matrixial (peasant) infrastructure receives determinations such as a face and an audible mouth. Indeed, the adjectival "peasant" already gives the matrix an empirical content that a pure matrix could not have, the latter being the condition of any such content. In Locke's usage, the matrix falls into a heteronormative, reproductive understanding of nationality as the privilege of birth in or of this place (autochthony) that has a powerful and lengthy genealogy; the peasant's metonymic link to the soil is clearly a part of this.[85] Autochthony and genealogy tie us back to the threads of *Geschlecht*, wherein the vehicle of genealogy itself—the mother—is condemned to abjection or glorification, each equally unlivable. We must turn once again to the *Brown Madonna*.

It is only in articulation that the matrixial peasant infrastructure receives a face and an audible mouth. Can we hear it otherwise? As matrix it also offers the trace in Locke's discourse of a foreclosed opening onto the relation between voice, place, and sexual difference. Could it also therefore mark the site of a desire to engender an emancipatory speech other than that of a New Negress who would simply be the New Negro's female counterpart, his honorary brother?

❖   ❖   ❖

We have seen that Locke gives minimal empirical predicates to the matrix, naming it "peasant" and supplying a regional determination. While this may be a "mistake" in terms of strict philosophical protocols because the matrix can by definition have no such predication, Locke commits the error and thereby wrests a conditional and empirical place for the speaking subject from the unconditionality of the matrix. As we have seen, Locke similarly empiricized or phenomenalized Fichte in a botching way so as to define a place from which the African American could speak as national subject. Following in the spirit of Locke's own gestures, then, I ask the following question: Of what could his peasant matrix have consisted around 1925?

In Locke's account, the transformations involved in forming an urban cultural vanguard from the peasant matrix involve cultural valorization or intensification of figures of regional territorial concretion and connectedness, even as the historical story is one of urban-centric migration and disconnection from a land that was, even for postslavery southern blacks, never widely coded as property. The new modes of community and sociality developed by blacks in the rural South after Reconstruction are the implicit ingredients of Locke's sense of a peasant matrix.

In 1926, a year after publication of *The New Negro*, the Association for the Study of Negro Life and History undertook a "three year survey of the social and economic conditions of the Negroes of the United States since the Civil War."[86] It focused in particular on the conditions of rural blacks in the South, still the majority black population in the United States. In other words, the Association took as its object the "peasant matrix" insofar as it could be maximally empiricized through documentary social science, fieldwork, and statistics.[87] The book that emerged from this study, Carter G. Woodson's *The Rural Negro* (1930), has been described as "the only seminal work concerning this population," and it offers a stark demarcation of the peasant matrix's lines of class and subalternity.[88]

In the words of *The Rural Negro*, examination of the quotidian normality of our matrixial area discloses a "transitory, migratory class which has no permanent attachment to and no abiding interest in the communities in which they sojourn" (RN 46). This deterritorialized, homeless condition is arguably the situation, in the mid- and late 1920s, of the majority of tenants, croppers, and peons that will have constituted Locke's peasants: mobile groups, banded together for survival precisely in the *absence* of opportunity for "building a desirable rural civilization" (46).

As William P. Browne confirms, black peasants subsisted in the interstices of capitalist farming and were also marginalized by the State's efforts to bring agricultural "modernization and development" through "ever more applied scientific research" in the interests of "social progress not of social justice."[89] Sidelining a redistributive function (social justice), capital and State together pushed to improve yields and techniques through technoscientific innovation (social progress), a process that mattered only to "farmers who were newly committed to reorganizing to enter a market-driven economy" (134). The "most needy and subsistence type" of farmers remained "reluctant to be saved by science and service interventionists" (133). Although black land ownership was in fact at a historic high point during this period, the great majority of rural blacks were in various forms of tenanted holdings.[90] Beyond its statistics, *The Rural Negro* provides a qualitative mapping of landed and social relations and a devastating account of the subalternized conditions of "tenancy" and "peonage," neither of which was within the wage-labor system.

Tenancy, as Woodson defines it, is a ramified post-Reconstruction system of contract labor for landless itinerant workers whose payments are usually made in kind. Sharecropping is the most common example, and the system is characterized by almost complete dependency; "their will is subject almost altogether to that of the landlords to whom they are attached . . . law is the will of the particular planter" (RN 47–48). According to Woodson, the tenancy system is a mode of sustained mental and material underdevelopment for its subjects, the production of a "landless, homeless, illiterate class" understandably riven with "selfishness or short-sightedness," and unable to "reach any definite stage of mental development" (61, 63).

Peonage is engendered by tenancy "manifested in its most undesirable form" (RN 67). A mode of "force upheld by the law," an updated vagrancy law, peonage is the system by which the migrating tenants are tied to a particular territory and employer through debt bondage.[91] Woodson defines it as a de facto slavery, an "involuntary servitude" (69). The deterritorialized tenant peasants (a large, landless, disconnected group forced into cyclical labor migration) are reterritorialized by peonage (extraeconomic compulsion to stay in one place to work). The "worst form" is the chain gang, which produces unpaid bonded workers from people convicted of minor crimes (73). Indeed, a further ramification of the process is the prior production of "criminals" who are then compelled into "the working out of the debts thus incurred" (74). In other words, not only peonage itself, but also the institution of the chain gang are a logical outcome of, not an aberrant slide from, the actualized peasant matrix.

Locke's point is of course that in spite of all this, the peasant matrix aesthetically translated via folk spirit to new race spirit describes a practice of freedom that can form a new, irreducibly national bond. Locke imagines the representability of the folk within a framework in which something of the folk has been freed into the possibility of appearing on a cultural stage. "Countryside to city, . . . medieval America to modern" (NN 6): a culturalized reflection of a historical process that "frees" the peasant into being a wage laborer, economically independent and at liberty to sell labor-power in a marketplace (result of Marxian "so-called primitive accumulation").[92] Transposed as it is here to the cultural sphere, the migrant is a privileged emblem of this process, which becomes thereby a peculiar prefiguration of the properly postcolonial celebration of migrant cultural diversities.

Something can be added to Locke's reading of this situation if we juxtapose The New Negro and The Rural Negro. It may not even be far-fetched to suppose that the name of the latter was conceived in response to the former. In any case, Woodson's The Rural Negro reminds us that processes of subalternization keep churning in the background, falling away from the capital logic within which the educated migrant is freed to represent his or her cultural heritage in the metropolitan public sphere.[93] Locke is of course far from blind to these problems; but consider the following, not as an attempt to correct Locke's position, but rather as a monitory instance that will ever shadow Locke's vanguard icon of the "migrating peasant, . . . the man 'farthest down' who is most active in getting up" (NN 7):

> [In 1928] a peon of this class was taken by a Southern family to serve them for life in New Jersey. Public spirited citizens, having found out that there was a case of involuntary servitude in their midst, protested and interceded on behalf of the peon. The Negro girl was taken away from the white family and placed in another home where she would have the freedom formerly denied her. A few days thereafter the girl expressed herself as being tired of her independent life. She had been dependent on others so long that she doubted her ability to provide properly for all of her needs. She grieved to get back to her master.
>
> (RN 84)

In Woodson's account, the peon girl is returned to her employers. So used to an utterly dependent confinement is she that being taken out of it with no practical, intellectual, or indeed spiritual preparation for that change is counterproductive. Freedom—as being abruptly freed by others—is feared and refused. "They have lost their initiative or they have never had the chance to develop any" (84). The young woman, who remains unnamed by Woodson, might have been a fifteen year old called Anna Belle Wilder. There are several syndicated reports of Wilder's story from 1923, in which this peon girl rescued from servitude in New Jersey is named; and it is thus possible that a typographical error in *The Rural Negro* changed the date 1923 into 1928.[94] Typography here plays interference with the researcher's impulse to "rescue" the subaltern from the archive, perhaps, keeping the peon girl in history's shadows indefinitely. Following Woodson's argument, though, it is hardly likely that Anna Belle Wilder was the only such case of a trafficked indentured servant in the 1920s; and if Woodson's peon girl remains unverified and unconfirmed, this itself attests to the lot of the subaltern then and now—paradox of an ungeneralizable "type-case," uncanny prefiguration of today's trafficked border crossers.[95]

Woodson cites, without quotation marks, the testimony of Thelma Duncan, a rural schoolteacher who was his informant in 1928:

> She found families of Negroes [in rural North Carolina] bound to white landlords for debts which they were never permitted to pay. They remain there in this state, uneducated, unenlightened, not knowing what is going on in the world, and believing that they must remain forever in the slave relation which they sustain to the planters. [Here Woodson inserts a footnote reading, "Statement made to the author by Thelma Duncan."] There comes little light upon their pathway, and they would hardly know how to heed the call if they were told that the world is theirs if they would go forth and possess it.
>
> (RN 88)

How will Anna Belle Wilder—one possible figure of Woodson's lost peon—play in the cultural calculus of the upwardly mobile migrant who is the producer (the ideal subject) of modernism and its modernizing spirit? What if she is taken as an example of the *Geschlecht*? With this question, we reach the limit of an investigation into modernist literary and aesthetic practices. Something other than an "alternative modernism" will be found on the other side of that limit.

Coda: Apocalypse

Locke's effort is to *détourne* Enlightenment by giving it a new face, a new *Geschlecht* that will take up its place as spiritual subject of the world's leading nation. The New Negro is culturally and intellectually continuous with American democracy. This continuity is achieved through the paradoxical means of a counterdeclaration of independence that in effect says, "We the Folk." Yet Locke's framing of the violent, muting history of mind-closure also calls for a transformation of the very task he assigns himself: to midwife the birth of the new generation. That task cannot be achieved just by the creation of spaces where folkish voices can be spoken and heard. The work of staging those voices, as in *The New Negro*, accedes to the hyperreality of the cultural pageant, so that the modernized folk can appear in the metropolitan cultural public sphere. Locke's editorial work is far from being an act of cultural or political bad faith, and my argument has not been that he has an undeclared interest in constructing a cultural alibi for ongoing processes of subalternization in the zone of the peasant matrix. I am concerned, rather, to underline sometimes unintended effects of concerned, benevolent cultural vanguardism, even when it strikes against the depths of racial abjection. Locke himself closes the introduction to *The New Negro* with an invocation of work still to be done, and it is to a different sense of what is to be done that we shall now turn.

It is a mark of Locke's editorial acuity that he gave the last word of *The New Negro* to an essay that questions his own account and organization of the collection's particular mode of metrocentric vanguardism. Giving renewed life to the book's subtitle (*An Interpretation*), this final essay, "The Negro Mind Reaches Out" by W. E. B. Du Bois, adds another twist to our readings and hints at epistemic formations that may divert prevailing vanguard currents. Steve Pinkerton has, in my view correctly, described this concluding section as a parallel structure in *The New Negro*'s New Testament. We have already touched upon the manifesto-form as being a tributary of the apocalyptic and revelatory mode in general, a mode that can also encompass the theory, practice, and desire for *Aufklärung*—bringing into visibility.[96] Locke's midwife writings in the book occur in the play of an apocalyptic mode so defined, revealing visions of the end of the old and the coming of the previously unseen. As everyone knows, the Revelation (*Apokalypsis*) of John the Divine is located at the end of the New Testament. Thus, even with the revelatory tonality that imbues *The New Negro* from start to finish, the placing of Du Bois's essay may be read as giving it an extra (even meta-) apocalyptic charge. As Pinkerton suggests, this essay, with its eschatological and prophetic tone and its final evocation of the postcatastrophic Holy City (Monrovia), may be read as *The New Negro*'s Book of Revelation.[97]

I cannot analyze all the textual details regarding the inclusion of Du Bois's essay in *The New Negro* and its editing and expansion with extra material at Locke's hands. Schematically: Du Bois was by this time an elder figure, and as such contributed a kind of upper-generational seal of approval to the collection. Locke had solicited a contribution from Du Bois, and by Locke's later account Du Bois's "article in *The New Negro* I rewrote for him from two old articles of his that he contemptuously tossed over his desk top to me."[98] The entire framing of Du Bois's piece in *The New Negro* is remarkable. Apart from the inclusion of a significant new section, it is assembled from draft versions of an essay that had appeared as "Worlds of Color" in *Foreign Affairs* in April 1925. As Pinkerton suggests, the new section that is added between pages 409 and 413 of *The New Negro* is drawn from unpublished drafts for the *Foreign Affairs* essay and in part from another typescript, all now located at the University of Massachusetts, Amherst.[99] The revamped essay is retitled "The Negro Mind Reaches Out" for *The New Negro*, but it sits in its own section of the book that is called "Worlds of Color" (the essay's original title). More puzzling still, given Locke's later account of the active way he "rewrote" the essay, is a footnote to the title that reads, "Reprinted, with revisions by the author, from *Foreign Affairs*, an American Quarterly Review, New York, Vol. III, No. 3" (NN 385). Pinkerton's reading is that the manuscript edits and the new section intensify Du Bois's apocalyptic tone. This is certainly one of their effects; but I would also highlight the palpable, properly apocalyptic, and for now unverifiable struggle over the text, its title, the holder and envoy of its voice or voices, and the related attribution of the editorial changes. It is as if Locke tries to atone for the violence of his alterations to the other man's essay, first by paying tribute to its original title by making a standalone section in its name, and second by attributing his revisions to "the author."

On the one hand, what is "revealed" here is less the end (or the beyond of the end) than a scene of ongoing representational struggles between competing generations of male intellectuals on the Harlem turf. On the other hand, if, in spite of this local quarrel, "Negro Mind" ultimately does point beyond the Harlem vision delineated by Locke, then Locke's own editorializations, heightening Du Bois's tone of revelation, make the indication of that beyond more emphatic. The way in which "Negro Mind" gestures toward a beyond-the-limit entails a dismantling of the provincial Negro Renaissance project's scenography. Locke cannot or will not sign or attribute to himself this autodestruction of *The New Negro*, but rather enacts it in Du Bois's name: "revisions by the author."

The end of *The New Negro* sounds notes that caution against Locke's celebration of black metropolitan cultural vanguardism. "Negro Mind" casts a retrospective shadow upon the anthology of experiments in black cultural production that precedes it. Writing of class and race in a worldwide frame, shifting his gaze outside modernist Harlem, Du Bois advises his reader not to remain trapped within "the labor we see and feel and exercise around us," but to turn to "the periphery of the vast circle, where unseen and inarticulate, the determining factors are at work."[100] World-historical reality is larger than "our concern and good will," and so the reader must try to look—or think—farther than she or he can immediately see (385).

Capitalist imperialism, determining new formations of class, has also drawn new racial lines on a world scale. It is not about a matter of choice, of some spurious priority of race over class (or vice versa), that Du Bois speaks. Race and capital combine, "the race problem is the other side of the labor problem," he says; "modern imperialism and modern industrialism are one and the same system," "two sides of the same human tangle" (386, 408). Yet he asks if only "baffling" and "failure" may result if the invisible periphery of this system is not attended to. So it is to these colonial shadows that Du Bois turns as he suggests what might be of imperative interest for the mind of the New Negro:

> With nearly every great European empire to-day walks its dark colonial shadow, while all over Europe there stretches the yellow shadow of Asia that lies across the world. One might indeed read the riddle of Europe by making its present plight a matter of colonial shadows, speculating on what might happen if Europe became suddenly shadowless—if Asia and Africa and the islands were cut permanently away. At any rate here is a field of inquiry, of likening and contrasting each land and its far-off shadow.
>
> (386)

In asking what might become of Europe if its colonial shadows were cut away, Du Bois prefigures Frantz Fanon's extraordinary double-edged statement that "Europe is literally the creation of the Third World" (*L'Europe est littéralement la création du tiers monde*).[101] What kind of profile or identity can a figure without a shadow have? What would Europe be, or resemble, without its vast colonial shadows? What kind of visage would it have, if any? Du Bois proposes the "shadows" as an allegory for reading "Europe," rather than the other way around: "One might indeed read the riddle of Europe by making its present plight a matter of colonial shadows." The "crisis" of Europe, diagnosed in so many ways during the interwar years, is here constitutively linked to the question of its colonial shadows. Anticipating the

double meaning of Fanon's sentence, Du Bois asks to what extent such shadows *produce* the figure that seems to cast them, as much as they are projected by that figure. What else, besides some (negative or positive) figure
of the Europe they helped to shape, lies in the colonial shadows? How can
its enigma be read?

As he goes on to open up his field of inquiry, Du Bois creates a comparative taxonomy of the colonial "shadows" of imperialist European
nation-states in Africa and the Caribbean. Contemporary Africa is split
by various imperialisms, a collection of overlapping sets with zones of
difference and knots of complicity. In theory, writes Du Bois, French
colonial policy offers citizenship and the outlines of a democratic civil
society, whereas by contrast that of England offers "segregation, disen-
franchisement" (398). The French raise and educate the brightest Africans into the ranks of "the exploiters" so that most educated Africans
in the French colonies "are Europeans" (396), whereas by contrast the
English "feared and despised the educated West African" and are "interested in the primitive black" (399). On the one hand the semblance of
equality, and on the other the desire to keep the "primitive" a primitive.
In each case a kind of double bind for the colonized African, and yet the
complicity between the two colonial formations is that "white Frenchmen were exploiting black Africans in practically the same way as white
Englishmen" but without the same overlay of racial segregation (or
"caste lines" as Du Bois puts it) (395).

Du Bois's sketch of "a field of inquiry" in "Negro Mind" provides the outlines of a more broadly applicable comparative approach to interwar
modernist culture. First, he reflects on the localized scene of a modernist
cultural milieu, asking it to think outside its field of vision to the peripheries. Get out of your own cultural vanguardism, he seems to say to Harlem, and try to think and read what you cannot immediately see.

Second, Du Bois looks at a world both divided by imperialism and being
unified by the emergent economic links of a specifically capitalist modernity, a "world-embracing industrial machine" (385). He thus points to the
differences between colonial formations that produce different kinds of
subjects and new kinds of frontiers, even as strange and unexpected collectivities and units are engendered by these very divisions. The racism of
the white labor movement; capitalism against slavery: "Liberalism, anti-
slavery, and cocoa capitalism fighting Toryism, free Negro proprietors and

economic independence" (388). Or, "how curious are these bedfellows—English capital and African black labor against Dutch home-rulers and the trade unions," he writes of South Africa. "The combinations are as illogical as they are thought-producing" (403). These new divisions and unifications overwrite other combinations and conjunctures that are cast into an artificial realm of the premodern or the primitive. Such types of relations between hyperreal premodernities and hybrid vanguard positions concern the present study more generally.

Third, Du Bois raises the question of the "shadow of shadows" (408)—the question of what resistant alliances are emerging in the unequal development between metropole and colony, shot through with racism and class segmentation. He frames the new vanguard formations thrown up on the seething surfaces of the colonial world in terms of "intelligent organization" (408), an advanced fraction within the shadows that has the relevant epistemological and practical preparation to be able to work together across imperial, class, and race lines. Emphasizing the extent to which those lines are fraught, he writes that "the attitude of white labor toward colored folk" is shot through with racism (407). This is an essential part of the problem: How will *this* color line be crossed when "the myth of mass inferiority of most men" prevails (407)? Du Bois senses a coming world in which modernization and development represent a travestied fetish of progress as "efficient organization," measured solely by volume of commodities and size of profit and "held together by militarism" (410). He sees one colonial zone in which "the English fear black folk who have even tasted freedom," a cliché of "bad" imperialist policy (398). Yet there is another colonial zone where "these dark men"—those Africans made upwardly mobile in the French colonies—"were also exploiters. . . . They looked upon the mass of people as a means of wealth" (396). Between these two options, what is to choose?

In the large section purportedly spliced into "Negro Mind" by Locke, Du Bois brings up the question of a means to *détourne* the quandary of "Western civilization, . . . [which is] spiritually bankrupt and unhappy" in spite of its "labor-saving devices, its harnessing of vast radical forces, its conquest of time and space by goods-production, railway, telephone, telegraph and flying machine" (409). Raising the issue of the social cost of capitalist modernity's rapid technoscientific, industrial, and economic development, he suggests that "the efficient West and North can learn of the lazy South and sleepy East" (410).

What if "life, without a surplus or even a sufficiency of modern comfort may for a moment be held an end and ideal of existence"? asks Du Bois (410). It is a thought experiment made under the sign of the subjunctive rather than a prescription. The "what if" here saves Du Bois from falling immediately into naïveté or embarrassing primitivism as he makes positive claims for the values of "African leisure and Asiatic contemplation" (410). In spite of the potential "civilizationism"[102] of this section of "Negro Mind," I wish to establish that it tries to define a position that is one neither of artificially keeping the primitive a primitive (British imperialism) nor of the "colored worlds . . . subordinat[ing] themselves to its interests, becom[ing] part of its machine" (the French option) (410). In other words, one of the tasks Du Bois assigns is that of stepping outside the restricted domain of the prevailing opposition between backwardness and progress so as to be able to see what remains in those systems of thought and ways of life that are otherwise trivialized as merely idle, irrational, or primitive. His is a mere suggestion, unelaborated with methodological or empirical detail. Yet as a theoretical proposition, it is an important supplement to Locke's particular formulation of an American black cultural vanguard.

Most interpretations of Du Bois's thought of internationalism emphasize (as does Du Bois himself) the role of vanguard groups providing conscious leadership to the Afro-Asian masses.[103] "Negro Mind" itself does this, as it argues that it is the American Negro who provides the "intelligent, thoughtful leadership" and the "main seat of . . . leadership" for the millions of colonially subjected blacks around the world (411). This echoes Locke's own words from earlier in The New Negro. "Led by American Negroes, the Negroes of the world are reaching out hands toward each other" (412). The vanguard dream—placing the group speaking for itself at the representative head of the blacks of the colonial world. Continuing to echo Locke (no wonder Locke included these pages), he writes that "for the first time in America, the American Negro is to-day universally recognized as speaking for himself" (411). And this is entirely a salutary event in a context in which conferences and journals could, without seeming anomalous, discuss "the Negro problem" without contributions from any black intellectuals (412).

Yet the seemingly embarrassing invocation of laziness, reiterated in several places during this period, including, for example, the essay "What Is

Civilization? Africa's Answer" (1925), puts us onto the trail of what diverts or withdraws from the vanguard formations that Du Bois imagines remaking world civilization in the Spenglerian image of an upsurge of Afro-Asia or the "darker races."[104] Du Bois soon afterward gives a hyperreal and phantasmatic depiction of an elite-led cosmopolitan Pan-Asiatic/African vanguard movement in his novel *Dark Princess* (1927), picking up on some of the most ominous contemporary threads of interpretation that relate to *Geschlecht* as race, lineage, and reproduction.[105] Yet in "Negro Mind," risking the worst kind of (colonial) stereotypes, he honors a laziness that must be excessive to and not immediately useful for such real or imagined vanguard movements. Laziness would also be a kind of withdrawal from the busy cultural frenzy of Locke's youthful vanguard of creative New Negroes in "stepping alignment with contemporary artistic thought, mood and style" (50).

In commemorating laziness as something dysfunctional for imperialist efficiencies of exploitation and vanguard fixes alike, Du Bois cannot throw out the vanguard question. It is a question not of rejecting vanguardism, but of defining a "field of inquiry" that points to *what else* might remain in the colonial shadows of Europe, possibilities that might inflect the "shadow of shadows," modulate the "intelligent organization" of new collectivities emerging as "intelligent and thoughtful leadership."[106] Laziness is an epistemological category here, even if its current deployment likely cleaves too close to a troubling primitivism that too confidently empiricizes "a land of sleep and happiness, . . . [a life] for this earth, happiest and most natural."[107]

In spite of this questionable primitivism, two consequences flow from the inclusion of the emphatic passages on laziness. First, a merely cultural and metropolitan-centered vanguardism will not suffice (this is an implicit critique of Locke and of remaining bound by visions of Harlem made by the lucky few). Second, and more important, the "shadow of shadows" must go beyond an unquestioning embrace of technoscientific social productivity and development as an outcome of capitalism-as-imperialism. With "laziness," Du Bois minimally indicates other areas of subject formation that mere economic/industrial/technocratic development leaves to decay or to ossify. Thus, the emergent, prefigurative, vanguard-like formations (and Du Bois names several possibilities here—the "American Negroes," the Pan-African Congress, Liberia) might learn from the subject space that "laziness" stands for. The right to laziness would at least be the right to something other than the mind- and happiness-destroying work of capitalist development; and in his words, it "may for a moment be held to be an end and ideal of existence" (410). Such a momentary end would call into question the self-assurance of the vanguard march insofar as it is compatible with capitalist development, opening an indeterminate space in which thoughts and practices may be developed that do not leave it "enslaved by its own ingenuity, mechanized by its own machinery" (409).[108]

Sounding a final note that resounds between optimism and pessimism, Du Bois writes that Liberia "represents to me the world" and that its fate— its "partial failure"—metonymizes the failure of the world to "resist the power of modern capital" (414). "Can Liberia escape the power that rules the world?" asks Du Bois at the end (414). The astuteness, naïveté, or instrumentality of Du Bois's position on Liberia remains an open question.[109] His closing invocation of Liberia tightens a knot of paradoxes concerning a vanguard of black "intelligent and thoughtful leadership." Liberia is here a comparatively recently formed African nation in which the State is run by blacks and is not formally under the control of a colonial power. Its formal independence is symbolically crucial, yet Liberia's existence derives from a settler colony of ex-slaves returned to the continent. This is the essay's final figure for the development of Africa and—by Du Bois's own metonymy—the world "led by American Negroes" (412). The struggles in Liberia between the settlers (the majority of whom were emancipated slaves) and the greatly vaster indigenous population certainly give pause for thought as to how black American leadership might have been made translatable.[110] Du Bois himself had high hopes for it, entering at this very moment into a fateful (but brief) expression of solidary encouragement toward the Firestone Tire and Rubber Company as it established its Liberian rubber plantations.[111] Effectively advocating a softer imperialism prefiguring postwar and postcolonial global economic developments, Du Bois writes to Harvey Firestone and suggests following in Liberia the model of industrialization in "Australia:. . . invade it, reform it and uplift it by incorporating the native born into the imported industry and thus make the industry a part of the country."[112] Firestone should train both African and American blacks in industrial leadership and management, and not organize management on the basis of a color line. Capital, he imagines, can thereby be set to work in a controlled way for social development and as a wedge for black American leadership in Africa. In more than one public statement on the question, Du Bois suggests that the voting power of American blacks can control the excesses of capitalist development in Liberia, thereby acknowledging its condition of dependency (albeit in an original and strange configuration of the diasporic and the indigenous in the political sphere).[113] "Everything," he writes in "Liberia and Rubber," "really depends upon the attitude of white capital in America. If they want to do a fine and unusual job in imperialism they have the opportunity here in Liberia"; or Firestone "can repeat in Liberia all the hell that white imperialism has perpetrated heretofore in Africa and Asia" (329).

Du Bois's fears for the future were in any case realized as *The New Negro* was being readied for publication. In the terse words of George Padmore a few years later:

> In July, 1925, the Firestone Rubber Corporation, one of the biggest rubber trusts in the world, entered into negotiations with the Liberian Government for a lease on rubber producing lands. The company secured the concession of a million acres of land at the cost of six cents per acre.
>
> After the negotiations were completed the Firestone Company demanded that the Liberian Government accept a loan of $5,000,000 at the rate of 7 per cent interest, failing which they (Firestone) would not carry through the proposed development scheme. The Liberian people were reluctant to accept this heavy financial obligation, but finally succumbed to the coercion of the great colossus of the North.[114]

Du Bois would now also condemn Firestone in similar language in a detailed article for *Foreign Affairs* in 1933, and would even write of Firestone's "capitalistic exploitation and imperial domination of the Black race" in a letter to Bishop Francis F. McConnell of the Federal Council of Churches that same year.[115]

The New Negro's final revelatory move from "laziness" to "Liberia" discloses a scene that cannot be managed by the aesthetics of a metropolitan cultural vanguard. Nor does it entirely escape the latter's force field. As with the book's relation to Anna Belle Wilder, then, the apocalyptic gesture that concludes *The New Negro* brings us to the disciplinary and epistemological limits of an investigation into modernist literary and aesthetic practices.

7

NÉGRITUDE (SLIGHT RETURN)

The African Laboratory of Bicephalingualism

In April 1937 Léon-Gontran Damas, a graduate student and poet from French Guiana working in Paris, published a volume of poems titled *Pigments*. It appeared in a limited edition under the G. L. M. imprint of Guy Lévis Mano, a poet and book designer and a significant figure in the samizdat-like world of small-press surrealist and avant-garde art publishing.[1] *Pigments* had a preface by the surrealist poet Robert Desnos and a woodcut frontispiece by Frans Masereel, a Flemish graphic artist living in France. It is likely that the connection to Masereel was brokered by Mano, whose network of connections in the literary and artistic world was extensive. We know little, however, about the exact circumstances of the commissioning and production of the graphic. In any case, the frontispiece represents a kind of "reading" of the collection. It reads and metonymizes aspects of the emergent Négritude movement that are the concern of this and the following chapter.

Masereel's woodcut depicts a naked black male figure emerging from the empty neck hole of the wing-collar shirt and bow tie of an immense, formally dressed male torso. To the left of the image the background shows an urban metropolitan scene with high-rise buildings and smoking chimneystacks; in the right-hand background appears the top of a palm tree, with shapes that could depict long flames or—more likely—vegetation below it. Underneath the palm tree are human figures, one of which is

FIGURE 2.1 Frans Masereel, Boisgravé de Frans Masereel, pour l'edition (1st) de 1937 de Pigments, par L. G. Damas. Woodcut, 1937. Schomburg Center for Research in Black Culture, Photographs and Prints Division, New York Public Library.

raising its arms. The black figure emerging from the neck hole faces upward, right arm raised with open hand, while its left hand rests just below the neck. It is an ambivalent gesture evoking appeal and self-protection, workerist iconography and certain early modern depictions of Christian martyrs.[2] Two white slashes on the face depict an opened mouth, and two white slits stand for eyes either open or closed. The far background of the woodcut contains a starburst-like aureole that carries the energy of the emergent figure's vertical movement into the surrounding space. Shardlike black lines perpendicular to the figure's head, and seeming to emanate from it, might be graphic representations of sound coming from its mouth. An infant cry? For this is an image of birth, or of rebirth.

The sex of the mother-figure is represented only by the collar-hole from which the man emerges; and even this possible sign of the female-sexed body is displaced by the strong suggestion of autogenesis. The naked, new black man appears to be birthing himself from the apparel that formerly covered him; it is happening in the void where the head of a bourgeois metropolitan man would be: birth from the hollow body of that figure, the neck hole as the orifice from which, fully formed, the black man steps out. As if Négritude has gestated inside the shirt and frock coat of the headless European bourgeoisie—a body *and* a head where there was no head at all. Thus, a new hea*ding* for modernism. Born of metropolitan vestments, but seemingly leaving them behind, the figure occupies the space between tropical foliage and urban buildup, as if the exposed body itself must mediate the relation between colony and metropolis.[3]

Carrie Noland has observed that Masereel's image corresponds most closely to the thematics of the poem "Solde" in *Pigments*, which begins:

> J'ai l'impression d'être ridicule
> dans leurs souliers
> dans leur smoking
> dans leur plastron
> dans leur faux-col
> dans leur monocle
> dans leur melon
>
> [I have the impression of being ridiculous
> in their shoes
> in their tuxedo
> in their shirtfront
> in their collar
> in their monocle
> in their bowler.[4]]

The speaker of "Solde" is reborn to the extent of its self-lacerating, self-conscious sense of complicity, a reflexive self-distance and self-accusation generative of poetry. This is not the overall tonality of *Pigments*. Masereel's graphic catches something else about complicity, and about the situation from which the Négritude group emerged. For these poets were, precisely, also men of the metropolis wearing formal suits. Their figurations of the renaissance (or indeed the desolation) of the black man in body, soul, or spirit emerged from the hole of an excellent European education. Masereel's "reading" stages this without accusation or exculpation, though of course his woodcut also requires "reading" to get it. The woodcut presupposes the kind of general epistemological and aesthetic educative background that will make it and the poetry of *Pigments* legible. This is the double bind of the cultural vanguard. The double bind of a preparation—an education—for the possibility of such reading is precisely the problem addressed by Damas and his friends in the 1930s that I focus on here.

In the previous chapter we saw how the frontispiece of *The New Negro* visualized the infant representative of a new black generation: a child born, as both pictorial convention and editorial proprietorship demanded, of a virgin mother. Both abject and phallically monumentalized, the woman-vessel serves little further purpose than to symbolically transfer the new generation into the hands of the midwife: Alain Locke himself. *The New Negro* was to become "a touchstone text for Francophone intellectuals in the late 1920s and early 1930s."[5] How its epistemology, aesthetic, and actual examples of black cultural modernity translated (or not) into the Francophone field may itself perhaps only be read between the lines of the works that appeared in its wake.

❖ ❖ ❖

It has become a truism about Négritude to remark on the paradox that "you discover and affirm your difference in the very seat of the imperial power that, in your home countries, denies your originality in support of its own norms."[6] Correspondingly: Négritude "was hatched, born, and propagated in and from Paris."[7] This paradox, however, represents neither a collusion to be denounced nor a moment of mere pathos. This and the next chapter examine the productive and fragile critical complicity with metropolitan *enseignement*—teaching, education—for the formative gestures of Négritude's aesthetic-political vanguard in the 1930s. Négritude's entanglement in the knots of a French *enseignement* assuredly makes the former appear less politically "radical" than what came before, or even what currently surrounded it.[8] On the other hand, the idiosyncratic modernist investigations of the mind-, soul- and spirit-making functions of education by Aimé Césaire, Léopold Sédar Senghor, and Léon-Gontran Damas in particular are varieties of representations of how colonial subjects imagine (or fantasize) access to their own roots, or to the radicality of possible alternative epistemic and gnostic formations.[9] Even to the "preschool past" (*antiquité pre-scolaire*) that figures "the root of the root, before the root, . . . [an] ultra-radicality" that is only representable after the event of *enseignement* and acculturation that both roots and deracinates.[10] Thus origins, place of birth, roots, all the dangerous figures of reproduction, rediscovery, renaissance, and autochthony that appear when Négritude is discussed are instruments of its work but also do not evade questioning and unraveling as it proceeds. An elite colonial education appears in Négritude as *phar-*

makon, both poison and medicine: means of knowing the very ills it symptomatizes, to which it gives rise, and which it attempts to heal, without guaranteed success. If Négritude is thereby compromised in terms of a retrospectively wished-for *political* radicalism, its unique contribution may be in its reminder that *all* vanguard subjects, "radicals," are also formed by what they set out to critique and remain complicit with it in definite ways. It reminds us of the price and stakes of class-divided *enseignement*, of what and who gets left behind; but it also offers aesthetic and imaginative resources with which (perhaps) to heal those wounding divisions. Its most disorienting means of discovering this complicity is precisely its attempt to reach the hinterlands of assimilative metropolitan education by returning—to someplace, sometimes an *arche*-place—so as to project or discover a new/old language of spirit. Such returns can be largely fantasmatic, as in Senghor's famous "kingdom of childhood."[11] They can also involve other kinds of work: Senghor himself investigating and reporting on the conditions of the Senegalese "rural popular schools" of the colonial interior in 1937; Damas's nightmare ethnographic journey back to the prison colony/goldmine of Guiana in the summer of 1934.[12] These are returns that involve a reality check of sorts, such as that also staged poetically in Césaire's *Notebook of a Return to the Native Land* (1939).

In this light, Césaire, Senghor, and Damas describe trajectories that are different, singular investigations of the shared desire for a "preschool past," a root or preradicality that could be accessed and elaborated as ground for a new cultural politics. Such a critical primitivist quest involves negotiating folds of complicity in structures and processes of assimilation as *enseignement* from the ground up. The language and cultural accretions of "French" have been desired, willed, accepted, and internalized by these elite students prior to any intended decision, and are structural to any subsequent intended actions. The meanings of desiring, willing, acceptance, and internalization, however, no doubt open themselves to questioning in the course of the inquiry into the workings of assimilation and *enseignement*.

I emphasize the literality of the French *enseignement* as ensign, marking, sealing, stamping, or even inscription. In imperial France, one meaning of being educated was to be stamped by—and to emit the signs of—a mode of cultural belonging that would visibilize development or evolution and thereby fittingness for citizenship. This in fact goes for all subjects of the nation-state and not just those of empire, but not in exactly the same ways.[13] Outside the hexagon, the imaginary geometric outline that symbolizes matricial French territory, the exclusions—and thus also the conditions of admission—are marked with greater rigidity and reach. The metric of these markings of subjection and formation gauged something like the transition from *Unmündigkeit* to *Mündigkeit* (see chapter 1). We must of course account for the displacements or questions of translatability from a Germanic language of Enlightenment as maturity and nondependence to the French (*mineur, minorité, évolution, évolué*, and so forth). A search for preschool roots—or even the preradicality of the roots—thus necessitated for these vanguard intellectuals a thinking, imagining, and aesthetic representation, if not yet the risk of an elaborated practical interface, with the diverse *mineurs* and subalternized spaces of the French empire and beyond. The gestures of Négritude that concern us here lodge on a threshold between a concern for the politics of cultural difference in colonialism and an alertness to the predicaments of the subaltern, and they get there by an unavoidable passage *through* the school.

The modernist investigations of Césaire, Senghor, and Damas, carried out in polemical prose experiments, epic and lyric poetry, and ethnological exposé, were attempts to turn an elite French education back on itself so as to delineate its outside, to think—and represent—the blurry mass of those who cannot think "French." This early focus on *enseignement* revises the assumption that Négritude is from the start an assertion of an essential, shared blackness or Africanity that short-circuits other structural social differences. These investigations dramatically engage problems that would haunt both modernist experiments and the postcolonial realities that followed political independence—problems springing from fissures reproduced within education in terms of groups treated as culturally, evolutionarily, racially, or sexually capable or incapable, those who are treated as evolved, and those treated as constitutionally in need of help or development (or, alternatively, who are left to ossify or rot, or turned into "a robot or a rubber stamp").[14]

◆ ◆ ◆

French policy regarding education's role in—or as—colonial governance was both regionally differentiated and continually revised between the 1880s and the 1930s. In spite of all of its twists and turns, amply documented and critically discussed in excellent empirical scholarship on French colonial history, certain key presuppositions remained intact.[15] In a nutshell: a difference exists such that the superior, colonizing group must help the inferior one "evolve" by teaching it, by developing it through a teaching broadly understood. The groups may be characterized in the typical terms of interwar European cultural discourse as "races" or "societies," "cultures" or "civilizations." While the slippage between these terms cannot be underestimated, the presupposition of an originary cleft, projected onto a human reality bigger than the classroom or narrowly educational institution, remains. Thus, at the level of the politics of State, a Jules Ferry can say in 1884, in the context of Madagascar, that French policy is "the right of superior races vis-à-vis inferior races and [is] also the exercise of a duty. . . . There is, gentlemen, between these races and ourselves, a genuine process of education [*education*] that is the most effective, the most penetrating of all."[16] This as opposed to the overt violence of military intervention. And in 1929 Georges Hardy, State official, spokesman, director of education in French West Africa, could write of colonialism as a relation of "tutor-societies and pupil-societies" (*sociétés-tutrices et sociétés-pupilles*).[17] Policy-talk of the period is replete with such formulations. Thus the general *ideology* of modern French colonialism across this period was one of pedagogy across an abyss that seemed to have no far side. One might speak of a constitutively interminable *mission pédagogique* as much as of a *mission civilatrice*. "All native policy is a type of pedagogy," wrote Jules Carde, governor-general of AOF from 1923 to 1930, who was especially interested in education. Jules Brévié, his successor, reiterated the assertion.[18]

As such examples illustrate, the presupposition of a typological difference between races or societies survives the early-twentieth-century shift from a harder policy of (universalizing) assimilation to its softer, gradated, and benevolently paternalistic modality that is known as "colonial humanism."[19] Divorced from a critical philosophy of education, the presupposition becomes an epistemic and ideological instrument of inferiorization without end. It is given ideological shape as a narrative philosopheme of servitude-as-being-helped-to-evolve that cuts across and mixes up the lines of race and class and gender (and indeed, in other contexts, caste).

Any educative relation presupposes a species of inequality between teacher and student. This inequality is worked through not by the student becoming the identical *semblable* of the teacher, but in the process by which she or he will, in turn, become able to occupy an analogous educative position.[20] The logic of working by turns does not have to be exclusively defined by the generational sequentiality of human life, where the "turn" is that of graduating cohorts. Antonio Gramsci, who was writing notes for future work in a Roman jail as the Négritude group attended university in Paris, devised the bare outlines of a critical philosophy of education "by turns" that linked it to political structures of democracy and citizenship that were concerns of the policymakers and practitioners of the French empire. Gramsci's projection revises the formula of the tutor-pupil relation: "The relationship between the teacher and pupil is active and reciprocal so that every teacher is a pupil and every pupil a teacher."[21] This formulation of "taking turns" or swapping places does not mean that the uneducated pupils are the immediate *semblables* of the teachers; what need would there be for any educative process at all were that the case? It rather says that the teachers must continually learn from the pupils how to loop back into teaching them. Rather than emit content, the teacher must learn to become the "disciple" of a strange new "master," the "environment," critically overcoming his or her sense of superiority to it while not abandoning the responsibility of working to change it. Gramsci's figure of a new, activist philosopher emerges in the "active relationship that exists between him and the cultural environment he is proposing to modify. The environment reacts back on the philosopher and imposes on him a continual process of self-criticism. It is his 'teacher'" (SPN, 350).

In an epistemic field defined by racialized or anthropologized definitions of evolutionary differences between groups and societies, generalized into ideologemes such as "tutor-societies and pupil-societies," Gramsci, too, noticed an "educational relationship [that] exists *throughout society as a whole* and for every individual relative to other individuals. It exists between intellectual and non-intellectual sections of the population, between the rulers and the ruled, élites and their followers, leaders and led, the vanguard and the body of the army."[22] Gramsci's analysis is pertinent in this French context because debates about citizens and subjects, assimilation and association, were general discussions about not just how to live together, but about democratic citizenship. Thus he writes, "every relationship of 'hegemony' is necessarily an educational relationship" (PN 350). Hegemony: the production of desire for, consent to, or participation in a relation that can be called *citizenship* in the (imperial) nation-state.

The critical philosopher of education thus concurs with the general truth, if not the practical application, of the colonial construction of the modern educational relation as something that permeates and structures all manner of other social relations. Gramsci shows that his critical philosophical practice of teacher and pupil taking turns to be master and disciple is already necessarily generalizable to larger social scales in modernity because modernity's social landscape is a forcefully pedagogical one. Turn-taking is truncated in the cruelty, racism, and exploitation of actual colonial relations that severely limited even basic school education, let alone wider possibilities.

It may be remarked here that Louis Althusser, who sketchily yet productively structuralized and systematized Gramsci's suggestions, situates the "educational ideological apparatus" as the "dominant ideological State apparatus" in "mature capitalist social formations" (where it has displaced the role of the Church).[23] This development is concurrent, in France, with the expansion of its empire, hence the dual role of a Jules Ferry as both imperial pioneer and architect of the farthest-reaching modernizing (including "secularizing") school reforms of the nineteenth century. The educational apparatus is a key site of subject-production, *the* key site for Althusser. Its ideological representation "makes the School today … 'natural,' indispensable-useful and even beneficial" (IS 157). Something of the phantasmatic nature of this naturalness is made more visible in colonial space—a phenomenon we can also discern today in the fetishization of mere "literacy" in education for the children of the non-Western poor. Listen to the words of Robert Delavignette in 1935, as he effuses poetically about the West African "popular rural school":

It does not issue diplomas; it does not open the door to positions. It is turned toward the land [*pays*]. It will reside in the truth of a given land; here riverside school; savannah school; forest school. It will express the whole rural and artisanal truth of this land. It will put the entire village to school. The master will not wait until a dozen children can spell French before telling old women and men, as well the young, that it is a fly that carries sleeping sickness. He will intervene in everyday life in the indigenous language to circulate ideas on village hygiene. And he will also intervene to re-establish work. He is a clerk who will become one [*communiera*] with the village in labor, in the local works character-istic of the land. Instead of skimming over subjects best suited for bookish teaching and losing interest in the illiterate mass, instead of making graduates for positions, he will live with the land; he will act there as a ferment. Then, according to the predictions of Governor Gen-eral Brévié, we will build "The School of Africa" where the currents of ideas coming from the French countries of Europe and the French countries of A.O.F. will mix.[24]

Delavignette is a "good," liberal, experienced imperialist. His words are nevertheless a screen that clarifies the mode of "material existence" phan-tasmatically envisioned for the apparatus: its "material practices gov-erned by material rituals," which are the actual locus of ideology—the site at which subject positions are "assigned" ("Ideology" 167, 169, 176). As Althusser tells us, ideology represents the imaginary relation of indi-viduals to the real relations in which they live, and not the system of real relations itself (162–65). We must pay as much attention to the ideology-*form* as to the various "contents" that fill it out (some of which are not in principle necessarily "bad" practical suggestions, such as working in the languages of the peoples taught).[25] Expressing the truth of the land, advis-ing the ignorant, living as one, developing Africans through fermenting: these are the ideological markers of an "imaginary relation" to "real rela-tions" (165).

The fact that the educational apparatus is the dominant ideological apparatus in a regionalized, contradictory, and fissured field of ideologi-cal contestation gives it a special place as both "stake" and "site" of class struggle (147). The Négritude writers among others perceived this very early on because of the constitutive linkage between French colonial practices and educational ones. Both stake *and* site of struggle, the educa-tional apparatus is thus both instrument and object of struggles for hege-mony, struggles that, moreover, may not immediately (or ever) make themselves legible simply as *class* struggles. The demand *for* particular types of education, or reforms of education, is not necessarily to be under-stood as a demand that will guarantee the reproduction of "good" capi-talist or imperial subjects.[26]

Accordingly, Kojo Tovalou-Houéno, Paris-based African activist of the Ligue Universelle de Défense de la Race Noire and editor of the newspaper *Les Continents*, wrote a scathing denunciation of colonial education in Africa in 1924. "The colonial program is thus the following," he concluded: "no teaching [*instruction*], no civil, economic, or political liberty, the condemnation of the entire black race to forced labor; for justice, the law of the victor: the whip. Preservation of the customary to halt and freeze all evolution. The teaching of French considered a crime."[27] This criticism reflects the way French colonial policy had been obliged to "learn" from the aporia of a fantasmatic "Greater France," where the projected unification and integration of a vast empire-nation faltered on the exclusion and nonintegration of the great majority of its peoples. In 1932, Jules Brévié, governor-general of AOF from 1930 to 1936, gives a brutally concise summary of the articulation between a "Greater France" and paternalist management:

> Under the influence of the generous ideas of the Revolution, France, at the beginning of the last century, wished to practice total assimilation [*assimilation intégrale*] and admit all the indigenes to citizenship [*droit de cité*]. This doctrine did not hold out long against the shock of reality. . . . The indigene appeared to the colonialists in his true aspect: an incapable minor whose education needed to be undertaken without futile precipitation, allowing him to evolve within the framework of his customary institutions, gradually raising him by vigilant direction toward an ever-closer collaboration.[28]

In the name of preserving the meaning of citizenship, citizenship must be withheld from the vast majority of a republic-empire. Or as Laurent Dubreuil puts it, "assimilation must not succeed, precisely because its completion would coincide with the end of the colonies"; it is "threatened with cancellation by [its] very execution" because the entire empire would be filled with citizens, thereby annulling politically the metropolis/colony distinction.[29] The question of number, of majority (of citizens), would induce a crisis of democracy. Brévié continues that "the policy of assimilation was succeeded by the policy of association," the latter being, by the 1930s, a broad name for the ethnographically informed protective management of indigenous evolution and welfare. Yet these two logics were in fact discontinuously articulated as two faces of a colonial front. The ongoing crisis of the coconstitutive yet disjunctive relation between assimilation and association was managed not only through the spatial separation of colonial territory itself but by a temporal deferral: "education . . . without futile precipitation" (*Circulaires* 7). "Association" becomes the figure of a perpetually deferred assimilation; citizenship is indefinitely adjourned until we decide the minors have grown up, and even then. . . . Tovalou-Houéno's "preservation of the customary" (*maintien des coutumes*) alludes to the logic of this culturally relativistic approach of recognizing, supporting, and even "protecting" the social and cultural differences of indigenous societies so as to help their "long apprenticeship for liberty" (*long apprentissage de la liberté*).[30] Colonial policy had taken lessons from extensive ethnographic investigations of social structures in Africa that provided a rationale for "protecting" the integrity of African societies from the very fragmentation threatened by integration into an advanced, industrialized imperial nation-state.[31] In order to develop Africa, France had to postpone the development of its people by preserving an ideal of African indigenous integrity constructed from ethnographic scholarship.

❖   ❖   ❖

"How many are we?" was a live question for politically conscientized blacks from far-flung areas of the empire in interwar Paris.[32] According to census figures obtained by Philippe Dewitte, there were approximately twenty-three black African and Madagascan university students in Paris in 1926.[33] The number cannot have been very much higher in the early 1930s. As Dewitte acknowledges, French Caribbeans were classified as citizens and thus do not show up as a separate grouping in official statistics. There was a small but established and culturally active middle-class Antillean community in Paris.[34] The majority of the ten to fifteen thousand Antilleans, Africans, and Madagascans estimated by Dewitte to have lived in the Paris region were workers and domestic servants, and included significant numbers of demobilized Senegalese soldiers recruited to fight in the First World War. It is not surprising, therefore, that many of the interwar social movements that involved blacks were organized unevenly along shifting lines of race, class, and anti-imperialism. The vicissitudes of these turbulent groupings are gradually being documented.[35]

A marked investment in the aesthetics and politics of education (both narrowly and generally conceived) is one of the features that distinguished the formative Négritude alliance from the manifold and shifting other groups and currents of black cultural-political activism in the metropolis of French imperialism in the 1930s. It is not a coincidence that the Négritude group emerged from Parisian black student organizations and newspapers, or that two of its main figures, Césaire and Léopold Senghor, were working toward the *licence* (teacher's diploma) and *agrégation* (selective examination for the most elite *lycée* teaching jobs) in the period. The intense pipeline of study for the *hypokhâgne*, then the *khâgne* at Lycée Louis-le-Grand, leading, for the successful, to *agrégation* from the École Normale Supérieure, was the guarantee of a good teaching position. (There were other routes post-Lycée too, including the one taken by Senghor who studied for a diploma and then the *agrégation* at the Sorbonne.)[36] Damas had relinquished his legal studies in 1932 and begun studying at the Institute of Ethnology. The situational determination of this investment in education opened a space in which these young students could elaborate more intensively its structures of interpellation and complicity. This necessitated a reappraisal of the debates on assimilation and association.[37]

Work in and on education did not distinguish the students essentially but rather generationally from the affiliates of the other active groupings with which they were most directly connected and sometimes in competition. Both Paulette and Jane Nardal, vital contributors to the internationalizing Parisian cultural ferment, were older *licenciées*, and Jane worked as a classics teacher.[38] Of the major black communist figures in Paris, Tiemoko Garan Kouyaté had been a schoolteacher. An important exception is the militant Marxist Lamine Senghor. He was dead before Léopold Senghor, Césaire, and Damas arrived in France, but his spirit haunted the scene of metropolitan black anticolonialism through the 1930s. Raised illiterate in a peasant family, the recipient of "subhuman" treatment as a servant in Dakar, and having served as a soldier in Europe's theater of war and a mailman in France, Lamine Senghor would become "the most charismatic and eloquent black Marxist of the interwar era."[39] At the end of his short life as a political activist—and hence as a kind of parainstitutional educator—Senghor attempted what can only be described as an alternative radical textbook for use among the colonial underclass.[40]

In the interwar period examined here, *négritude* was not so much a movement as an occasionally used neologism. As Abiola Irele has observed, *négritude* became Négritude as a proper name for a more systematized movement in the wake of the publication of Jean-Paul Sartre's strident essay "Orphée noir," the introduction to a poetry collection published in 1948 edited by Léopold Senghor, the *Anthologie de la nouvelle poésie nègre et malgache*.[41] As his political career took off, Senghor gave Négritude a more elaborated framework between the 1950s and the 1970s. I underline the important fact that the more systemic Sartrean and Senghorian interpretations and explanations of Négritude were made during and immediately after the wave of independence movements and decolonization across Asia and Africa (including Senegal in 1960) starting in the mid-1950s.[42]

Like many avant-garde monikers, Négritude came retrospectively to represent a certain coherence, occluding unresolvable heterogeneities and dilemmas behind the apparent univocality of a name. In the 1920s and 1930s, students in Paris from Africa and the French West Indies formed interest groups that engaged with questions specific to student life (especially scholarships) and politics in general, and black student life and politics in particular. An issue of the student newsletter of the *Association des Étudiants Martiniquais en France* from 1934 lists three "sister organizations": the Association des Étudiants Guadeloupiens en France, the Association des Étudiants Guyanais, and the Association des Étudiants Ouest-Africains.[43] One mythologeme of Négritude that should be questioned is that Césaire was instrumental in symbolically uniting these groups when the Martinican Students' Association renamed their newsletter from *L'Étudiant Martiniquais* to *L'Étudiant Noir*.[44] Our point is rather to take seriously the fact that these were students with student concerns beginning to try to generalize them beyond immediate self-interest. They made the specificity of their training (educators being educated) into an instance that could aesthetically and intellectually both represent a struggle and become the site and stake of that struggle.

The spaces and practices of education became the topoi of an investigation of the epistemic, cultural, historical, and racial policies and practices of a modern imperial nation-state. Brought together as students from very different parts of the empire (and to an extent thereby finding common cause in the metropolitan student world), these young black intellectuals began to write critically on the subject of assimilation. They questioned both its sacrificial injunction and its asymptotic racial logic. Sacrificial injunction: What, in terms of culture, tradition, habit, ethics, must be given up in order to be assimilated? As we have seen, by

1935 "global" or "total" assimilation (*assimilation globale*) had been rejected as "outdated" in an official communiqué by Jules Brévié, governor-general of French West Africa. Nevertheless most Africans' accession to the *Cité française* (citizenship) remained in principle conditional upon a "total and definitive renunciation of the morality, the institutions, and the rules of customary status" (*une renonciation totale et définitive aux moeurs, aux institutions, aux règles du statut coutumier*).[45] "Customary status" here means everything that had been fixed by a humanistic contemporary French ethnography as the structures of indigenous social and cultural life in their Africanity, anthropologically defined civilizational differences that colonial policy aimed simultaneously to preserve and modernize. The developmental rationale of French colonialism in Africa had become at once explicitly pedagogical and indigenizing. It would secure production of "healthy emulation" under the "tutelage of an authority" sufficiently attuned to the specificities of the pupils' environment and culture to ensure that they progressed and rose at the same time as remaining rooted in their own civilization (*Circulaires* 9–10). Brévié regards the potential that indigenous elites might become "deracinated" as the greatest possible risk, and he sets out the parameters within which an indigenous vanguard among Africans will be prepared for a future emancipation while being kept in their place *by being helped* by a superior, dictatorial authority because they are incapable of helping themselves:

> To the extent the minor peoples rise toward the higher planes of the social order, institutions must necessarily follow this evolution and adapt themselves to each phase of rising movement. Attentive from the start to observe [*surveillir*] the first steps of infancy, to soothe growing pains, to quash the unruliness of adolescence, the tutor soon becomes preoccupied with engaging the pupil in business; he instructs him, develops his skills, then apprentices him until the day that release [*emancipation*] allows him to make the pupil a partner. Thus the indigenous societies, in contact with our civilization, are progressively transformed, organized, become conscious of their personality, and, in successive stages, put themselves on the road to free will [*le libre arbitre*]. But primitive peoples need a long apprenticeship in liberty. Strong authority is first necessary to establish the domination of the tutelary Power.
>
> (Communiqués, 29–30)

This leads inevitably to an asymptotic racial logic. In a displacement of its signs, assimilation is now both rejected and ideally reimagined—it remains an ideology—as a pedagogical process of helping to develop the colonized indigenes out of their infancy, their *minorité* or *Unmündigkeit*. Perfection of this development remains constitutively unachievable because there is always a difference (the stain of a cultural, customary, moral, or habitual atavism) that can be racialized in the form of a temporal backwardness. The closer blacks get to being assimilated, to emitting the signs of sacrifice, intellectual and moral advancement that will secure citizenship, the further they are from being so; and therefore, in spite of the exceptions that merely prove the rule, Africans and blacks in general will collectively always remain unassimilated, as well as second-class citizens if granted citizenship. Gary Wilder concludes that in this period, the figure of "political immaturity" displaced that of "biological inferiority," but in such a way that "natives were constituted as *perpetual* political minors."[46] This double bind of political inclusive exclusion forges a coconstitutive link between republican humanism and racism under the headings of pedagogy and immaturity.

The situation in the French West Indies was different in important respects (especially regarding the question of formal citizenship), and I discuss its specificity in more detail in the next chapter. The racialized educational and psychosocial practices of assimilation/adaptation between the Antilles and AOF were differentiated enough to determine legible positional fissures within Négritude, and yet similar enough to provide material for the provisional working out of a shared predicament in the metropolis. A key stake of Négritude was precisely whether there was enough usable *semblance* in a shared blackness (or Africanity) to ground solidary experiences of "global subjection to the political, social, and moral domination of the West" beyond the negativity of racism and in terms of "the black world in its historical being, . . . the total consciousness of belonging to the black race."[47] The question of race or blackness was general enough to be the means of forging links between young people from quite different colonial situations while they were embattled and impoverished students in the metropolis.

❖ ❖ ❖

In September 1937, Léopold Senghor gave two important presentations that engaged directly with the cultural politics of education. These linked speeches are his first significant public statements after the essays of *L'Étudiant Noir*, which was a student publication rather more limited in reach. The first, "Le problème culturel en A.O.F." (The cultural problem in French West Africa) was sponsored by the Franco-Senegalese Friendship Society and took place at the Chamber of Commerce in Dakar. It was delivered during Senghor's first visit to Senegal in almost a decade. His visit had been funded by the organizers of the International Congress on the Cultural Evolution of Colonial Peoples (Paris), at which he would give his second presentation later in September.[48] The overarching thematic of this latter conference on "evolution" was in fact education, and the support given to Senghor was for preliminary research into the topic in Senegal.

"Le problème culturel" was published serially in the newspaper *Paris-Dakar* between September 6 and September 11, 1937, immediately after the speech itself.[49] It is a public address—Senghor's first in Senegal—to a significant sector of the colonial administration and bourgeoisie, both African and French.[50] It is also, at least as represented in its published form, a rhetorically complex modernist artifact: a general statement of a critical philosophical and aesthetic primitivism as much as an angular, manifesto-like outline of principles for revising colonial policies of education in French West Africa. It is an argument for the role of indigenized modernist literary art in the formation of an African cultural base, taking avant-garde literature as both example and illustration of its problematic. "Le problème culturel" probes the limits of the sayable within the surveilled, censored, policed, and constricted "public sphere" of the colony.[51] With its supplementary Congress lecture, it also discloses once more the limits of the search for an epistemology of "alternative" modernisms.

Senghor posits the formation of an indigenous vanguard of the spirit through primary education.[52] An indigenized (Africanized) primary education in AOF would preserve the spiritual integrity of the child's cultural base—the child's "soul." It would allow children to consolidate and retain their indigenous spirit before entering into an alien world represented by "French"—which means narrowly the language itself, and more broadly a cultural and gnostic framework other than the African background. The specificity of the African spirit thus preserved and transmitted by education represents a vanguard of cultural insurgency within the *Cité*.

Senghor posits the prioritization of a cultural episteme (spirit and soul, *esprit* and *âme*) as the basis of future political transformation, though this is not the revolutionary overthrow of the State. Rather it is the wish to prevent loss of indigenous idiom by preserving it within a modernized Eurafrican world, and the projection of a mutual supplementation of "African" and "French" cultural forms. Also, therefore, it is a matter of survival within an inescapable and ever-more "Afro-French" environment (PD September 7).

Toward the end of the speech Senghor evokes the New Negro in a tacit acknowledgment that he is adapting his epistemology from Alain Locke's formula of an insurgent black spirit—located at the ground level of culture—that would transform "America" from within.[53] "It is precisely bilingualism," he writes, "that would allow for a total expression [*expression intégrale*] of the New Negro [*Nègre nouveau*]" (PD September 11). Bilingualism—in an African language such as "Mandingo, Hausa, Yoruba, Peul, Wolof," and French—is, as we shall see, the means for grasping, preserving, and indeed "restoring black values" (PD September 11).

Culture is an autochthonous phenomenon, Senghor tells us. But from the first words of the speech, Senghor places the relation between the modernist intellectual and his presupposition of cultural autochthony in question. "Would you admit it to me if I disappointed you? The press and the eminence of my listeners have made me recall that I reckoned on speaking as [*je comptais parler en*] a peasant of the Sine this evening" (PD September 6). Contrary to what other readers have understood, Senghor does not claim to speak as a peasant of the Sine.[54] His thought of doing so appears as a remembrance haunted by the possibility of a desire unfulfilled, or a disappointment, especially as the movement of his speech unfolds with the exquisite structuring of a kind that can be written only by a highly trained *lycéen*. Would it have been disappointing if Senghor *had* been able to speak "as a peasant of the Sine" when everybody was expecting a metropolitan professor? In any case, we must reckon with an internal determination by metropolitan scholarly norms even as Senghor plots their transformation. These norms are both what prevents him from being able to speak as a peasant of the Sine and the condition of his desire to do so. Immediately following the moment when, like a brilliant student, Senghor has plotted in advance the logical course of his lecture (definition, clarification, "deduction of general principle"), he makes the most violent and shocking outburst of the entire speech: "The time of seduction is past, it is high time to hang the seducers" (PD September 6).

Is the violence of a death penalty for seducers the only recourse for those who are unseduced or wish to undo their seduction? There is already an unresolvable epistemological tangle between those two positions, since to what extent is it possible to know oneself as seduced or seducer, or not? As led away from oneself? How long after the event does the truth of seduction become knowable, if ever? The security of rootedness in a knowable or sensible base will be a matter of Senghor's discussion of culture and assimilation. If seduction here means assimilation, then his alternative option for the bodies of seducer and seduced is no less dangerous. Assimilation will not be abandoned but redone as mutual devouring.

Senghor's rhetorical turn goes beyond the measure of the gracious *professeur agrégé*'s demeanor, as if he must break symbolically with it so as to say what he needs to say. Such a hanging would be suicide as well as murder for a Senghor; if seduction names any degree of assimilation, he cannot speak this way—as a *professeur agrégé*—without being both seducer and seduced. This staging of an impossible dilemma between murder and suicide designates the real ethico-political extremes of a colonial double bind that Senghor must negotiate. The structure of feeling that reflects a desire or frenzy for educational assimilation among the elite has its counterpart in this (self-)destructive movement of homi-suicidal vengeance. However, Senghor's eye is also fixed on the wound of the fissure between this elite and the rest of the people, coded in terms of a rural/urban division. His bid to heal the rift between classes is posed at the level of a culture assumed as shared across the abyss of epistemic difference.

It is immediately after the evocation of murder-suicide that Senghor ventriloquizes the first of his peasants, as if to reground the discourse in an unseduced and popular voice that doubts the very topic of the talk: "—A big word that, your culture, Samba Sène said to me" (PD September 6). Senghor can only "speak as" a peasant by ventriloquizing regional peasant voices within the dialogue interludes of his lecture. Samba Sène (who "cultivates his own field and feeds his family with it"), Demba N'Diaye, Silmang Faye ("my village neighbor"), and another unnamed interlocutor appear in direct speech as characterological archetypes of peasant wisdom and skepticism (PD September 6).[55] The skeptical cultivator transitions the lecture to its preliminary definition of culture.

Culture is by definition *raciale*, which in French permits a play between "racial" and "racinating" that remains less visible in English: culture is a "*raciale* reaction between Man and his milieu" (PD September 6). Thus, within an admissible semantic play, a reaction that both roots Man to his milieu and is definitive of the racial differences of humanity. "Imagination, active spirit, . . . creative dynamism": this Bergsonian conjunction additionally proposes culture, as well as race and environment (*milieu*), as historically changeable, in flux, on the move.[56] If a specific culture enracinates each human in its place, then each cultural dynamic may be progressively formalized such that a "civilization" is "the ensemble of concepts and techniques of a given people at a given moment in its history," the "accumulated experience of previous generations" (PD September 6). A further level of formalization makes that civilization *teachable*, such that education (*enseignement*) is the "instrument" of culture because it transmits this "accumulated experience" in the form of the study of successive civilizations. Education is the "study of the civilizations of a specific people" (PD September 6).

Education is the instrument of culture, the passing on of its "accumulated experience" through the study of civilizations. Thus, if education expands a particular milieu to take on board further-flung civilizations, this recursively alters the relation between humans and their milieu; it *changes* their cultural base. When, for example, educational programs in France devote more and more effort to "the study of foreign civilizations," this fact in itself has an effect on what the humanity of tomorrow will be: "our idea of Man is modified with the great developments of international relations, of economic and social sciences" (PD September 6). The cultural base itself shifts because its instrument, education, is mediating a more and more "international" milieu, and this leads Senghor to the question of what we will "make of the black man of tomorrow, more precisely of the West African of tomorrow" (PD September 6).

This question opens up another staged dialogue with Senegalese interlocutors in which the Senghor-voice asserts racial difference as difference without hierarchy. Each race is held to have its own capabilities different from others. Yet Senghor does not make of this an argument for racial purity or segregation. Rather, secreted in the dialogue-form of this section is one of Senghor's more politically complex and forceful points, hedged so as perhaps to mitigate its impact on a room full of powerful colonial functionaries. The fact of difference, he quotes himself as saying, might be honored by detaching French citizenship from the requirement of cultural identity. Given everything Senghor has made "culture" mean, this would imply a citizenship without *semblance*, isomorphism, or equality of birth in a place (*isogonía*).[57]

The violent recognition of racial difference manifests itself in the extreme of Hitler's Germany and the spectacle of the 1936 Olympics. Senghor's speech invokes the Nazis and ventures up to the line of racist ethnocentrism. The games were a site at which certain specifically black racial qualities were made visible, but they also serve as a foil for the points of general difference: "we are not an abstract race," meaning "we" are not constituted to perform abstract operations such as mathematics well (September 6). Senghor translates into French, and then quotes in Wolof, a Wolof proverb to support this sense of racial difference and of mutually defining limits: "To want to depart does not allow departure; it is the ability to depart [*pouvoir partir*] that allows departure" (PD September 6).[58] There is no point wanting to do something that you are essentially unable to do. In terms of the conduct of the text itself, it seems that translatability does not dissolve but reaffirms differences in which "race is a reality; I do not say racial purity" (Sept 6).

If race is a matter of being " 'different and together,' " then, asks Senghor, citing his own direct speech, "I shall propose to you: 'let us work to make of the West African, politically, a French citizen; but culturally?' "[59] This destabilizing formulation, which moves strangely from an imperative mode to something like a rhetorical question, is further hedged in quotation marks within the fictive polylogue about race that "Senghor" is having with other interlocutors. The utterance questions the terms by which the new philosophy of colonial education demanded adaptation as displaced assimilation—an order that made it impossible for the vast majority of colonial subjects to "grow up" to the point of qualifying as citizens. As I have shown, that qualification required the emission of signs of similarity, of homogeneity, of *semblance*, the symbolic sacrifice of (signs of) difference. Thus appears a horizon of recognition, the vanishing point of which is constituted by a formalism of sorts, a concern for form or isomorphism constructed between historically variable limits. Such imperatives are not new but are linked to a millennial history of democratic political citizenship structured in terms of "the bond between the political and autochthonous consanguinity" (PF 99), a baseline of equality as sameness that is founded on the figure (or the fantasy) of common birth in a native community, even as it has symbolic procedures for making-same by which the nonnative may be naturalized.[60] Racialization (racism) plays interference with equalization through visibilized phenomena of bodies marked as different, made to signify different hereditary capabilities, as well as formal phenomena of a shared culture in Senghor's sense (forms held to be specific to the racinated race of a place—languages, "customs," and so on).[61]

Senghor protects his challenge to the link between autochthony and citizenship by insisting that Africans are *culturally* autochthonous, too. Yet his equivocally demanded mutation in the structure of French citizenship—"I shall propose to you: 'let us work to make of the West African, politically, a French citizen; but culturally?'"—also questions the "genealogical schema" underlying an educational philosophy that demands the *semblance* of a maturity while systematically deferring it.[62]

"Le problème" thus returns to the "goal" of education. Rather than perform a narrowly instrumental function (oriented toward jobs and income, or toward a constrained pattern of sociocultural conformity such as "honor"), it should construct a *new Man* of the future. In a move typical for Senghor, he brings together West African and Greco-Latin conceptions of the ideal life: the Wolof *Samba-Linguer*, the Greek *kalos-kagathos*, the Roman *vir bonus*, and the seventeenth-century French *honnête homme* (PD September 6). These represent the goal of education. Symptomatically, such conceptions of the rounded or fully formed human being are aristocratic codings of virtue, cultivation, and character. They are given no more expansion or detail by Senghor here, precisely because they can be assumed as a part of the furniture of the well-educated "Afro-French" mind.[63] This is not to downplay their possible generalized value, but it is to raise a question that will resonate through what follows. What actually are these values, and how are they produced? Such conceptions of the good and virtuous life are at the very least powerfully marked by class assumptions about their desirability. Senghor himself notices that they do not permeate all class strata in advance.

Rejecting a means-ends justification for education, i.e., a "profession" or an income, Senghor remarks that if education were such a program, the "future engineer" would have no reason to study "Spanish literature" (PD

September 6). The tacit acknowledgment is that while a desire for a job and income might be quite reasonable for both rural and urban poor, this must be transformed with a "cultural" supplement. Correspondingly, when Senghor is criticizing the parallel instance of education for the limited cultural conformity of *honneur*, his example is a domestic servant who tried to kill himself because his feeling of honor was wounded when his employer falsely accused him of lying. "What do you think of a feeling that robs society of the best of us?" he asks his fictive rustic interlocutor (PD September 6). This argument cannot, however, account for how the desire to be a disinterested gentleman—or to learn to read literature—will be produced in the domestic servant or engineer.

In a world that is internationalizing in ways profounder than communications technology, the stake is continuing to *live* (*vivre*).[64] It is a matter of (cultural) life or death. Colonialism (though this word is not used by Senghor here) has willy-nilly made possible new international connections: "We are united [*solidaires*] with the other parts of the world by stronger links than the wires [*câbles*] that connect us to them—especially [*singulière-ment*] from France." The link to France is not exclusive: Senghor will speak of other kinds of solidarities of soul or spirit within a black world comprising Antilleans and black Americans as well as Africans, and such solidarities of négritude will remain suspended between a sense of a shared social predicament and a claim to unity of essence. Yet the apparent singularity of this French connection determines the way Senghor proposes a predominantly bilateral ("bicephalous" and "bilingual") relation between the units "Africa" and "France." This bilateralism extends to other colonial zones. Senghor speaks of the "Afro-French" and the "Antillo-French," leaving the ambiguity of these hyphenations and the units they conjoin intact. "If we wish to live," the inescapable international linkage necessitates adaptation and assimilation rather than a protective clinging to outmoded ideals. Culture is active racination in and to the *milieu*, and so a changing milieu demands self-change: "our environment [*milieu*] is no longer West African, it is also French, it is international; in sum, it is Afro-French" (PD September 7).

The paradox is that the self-change must not shake or threaten a fundamental cultural ipseity, identity, or selfsameness that carries the name of soul or spirit. "Thus for spirit and culture. The education of a people presupposes in the latter an ethnic personality, a civilization, however humble it may be" (PD September 7). This "personality," with its animating spirit, is the agent of a counterassimilation that will preserve the integrity and dynamics of the "Afro-" as it hyphenates with "-French." "Active personality" is the "necessary condition" of assimilation, or the capability, the power, of active assimilation. It is therefore no longer a question of an opposition between assimilation and nonassimilation. For "what does one understand by assimilation?" asks Senghor (PD September 7). "It is the action of being made similar but also of rendering as similar [*l'action d'être fait semblable, mais aussi de rendre semblable*]."[65]

Senghor's revision of assimilation theory denotes the desire for a return—*to* an indigenous African base so as to empower the return—*of* that base in a modernized mode. Who or what is the agent of rendering here? And what weight must we give to the change in verbs, where *faire* describes the being-made-same, whereas *rendre*, with its suggestion of return, repetition, or restoration, denotes the Senghorian supplement of the theory? If the "active" and "passive" sides of assimilation are not symmetrical, the active, like Echo, returns or reflects with a difference. How *semblable* does the *semblable* have to be rendered?

Questioning the *semblance*, Senghor values the making-same aspect of assimilation, but not its one-way movement in favor of the metropolis. To illustrate a counteractivated assimilation, he computes the cultural phenomenon as a biological one: "to assimilate a foodstuff is to transform it to the point of making it one's flesh and blood, to enhance oneself in absorbing foreign bodies. You do not become millet or beef; it is the millet, the beef that becomes our flesh and blood, . . . active, assimilating assimilation. The point is to assimilate not to be assimilated [*il s'agit d'assimiler, non d'être assimilé*]" (PD September 7).[66]

"If we want to live . . .": the future of humanity appears to be at stake in the "necessity" that cultures assimilate—eat—one another, and by so doing incorporate the benefits of the other's (spiritual) nutrients without loss of identity (PD September 7). Senghor mines a deep philosophical and indeed "spiritual" seam in these passages, where devouring the other's body in sublimated or metonymic form is a rich and general figure of cultural and political transformation.[67] It is not that you eat, for you cannot not eat; it is what and how you eat that matters. Thus, "foreign elements become nothing other than foodstuffs [*aliments*]. They enrich a civilization, they give it another quality not another direction, developing while remaining oneself, evolution not revolution" (PD September 7). "Le problème" allows for a certain degree of change (enrichment, another quality, evolution), but nothing that will subvert the essential identity of the assimilating agent. Assimilation mirrors the general form of the colonial model, which seemed to have little to say about self-enrichment by the foreign except in a material sense. Unshakeable in its sense of superiority, the metropolis devours and incorporates territory and material goods, though it is not this process that is named "assimilation" (a term reserved solely for the acculturative process of spiritual Frenchification, which, at least ideally and in principle, leaves no alien residue in the host culture). Senghor's alteration of this model posits "active" incorporation of chosen foreign (French/European) cultural elements—their being-made-African by Africans; and the *political* incorporation of this collective body into the French State as a citizenry that retains an essential *cultural* foreignness ("difference" in Senghor's terms).

This combination of schemas and formulae sets out the double bind of assimilation as imagined between cultural units. On the one hand, the *semblable*: rendering same, making identical; an ethnocentrism at the level of a cultural subject that necessarily produces centering effects, self-resembling effects so as to sustain agency and the power to calculate. On the other hand, consequently: an opening onto the incalculable, the risk of introjecting "foreign bodies," the cultural effect of which is not necessarily calculable in advance as "enriching." The foreign may always be an element that hijacks, diverts, or *détournes* the ethnocultural agent from its (sense of) itself. By assimilating the foreign, the "ethnic personality" opens itself to incalculable transformation whether Senghor wishes it or not; he touches on the possibility and risk of the incalculable and pushes it away ("not another direction . . . not revolution"), but this assertion has the character of a denegation. In order to remain itself, the cultural entity must destroy—even if only partially—its own defense mechanisms or protections so as to chew and swallow that which it desires to digest. "Civilizations, like races, perish from too great a purity"—the example of which is France itself, the "few materials with which it is vested [*matières dont elle est chargée*]" necessitating repeated renewals and "renaissances . . . under foreign influences" (PD September 7). Assimilation is therefore a supplementarity: it is only possible to assimilate something if the assimilating "I" is constitutively incomplete.

That question—who and what changes or remains "the same" (or identical, *semblable*) and how it does so—is a lacuna here. Senghor, because he is well educated, knows French culture up and down, knows himself to be in a position to know what is good and what is bad, what is good food and what is poison, and in which amounts the one becomes the other. To know a culture, in these terms, is to know what it is eating, excreting as inassimilable, vomiting as partly digested, to allow oneself to be eaten a bit. Such calculations must be made. That is the stuff of cultural *politics* itself. But he also suspects that in the movements (the flux) of cultural change, the specific benefit of eating the other—and being eaten a bit—is unknowable, at least in advance. Who or what is the subject of assimilation when it comes to a cultural form or current? Who will teach it?

Senghor's remarks do not take place in a vacuum. His manifesto addresses the colonial establishment in Dakar under conditions of surveillance and the pressure of (self-)censorship, and is thus unable to tackle in detail the colonial destruction or scrambling of indigenous cultural codes and practices. At the same time, he is pushing against the general colonial denegation of Africa, which, even if it no longer officially sanctioned the image of a barbaric dark continent, still ethnographically constructed the majority of Africans as backward child-subjects locked into a protective enclosure of their "customs" that guaranteed the interminability of their development. Yet even beyond the constraints of this situational limitation, Senghor's representation of the colonial relation would remain notably conciliatory and consistent with that of "Le problème culturel."[68] What but a highly educated, self-ethnicizing upper middle class can see itself as capable of making an active choice about what to assimilate from the metropole, meanwhile keeping its ethnocultural base intact? A hybrid wherein the hybridized elements secrete a self-identical spirit. We cannot question the justice of Senghor's demand that assimilation work both ways; his formulations anticipate the cultural politics of postcoloniality, for better and worse.[69] He delineates the active dilemmas and desiring-flows of a colonial elite schizophrenically inhabiting the post-tertiary-educated tier of the colonial machinery, an inevitable (perhaps necessary) ethnocentrism as bulwark against engulfment or abjection.

Fanon's phenomenology of violence had to be written later because of the failure to realize a Senghorian politics of culture in colonial conditions. In the absence of redress or even acknowledgment, citizenship without *semblance* remained an open wound; and the dynamics of anticolonial conflict were determined by the intractable knots of assimilation: in Algeria, "a war for independence waged in the very name of the political ideals extolled by the colonial power," i.e., republican democracy, because the "violent imposition of a culture and political language" ostensibly confirming to those ideals had "ended up producing exactly the opposite of democracy."[70] Algeria is not French West Africa, of course; but nevertheless we can see Senghor fighting a last-ditch effort within the colonial parameters so as to forestall the worst. The evocations of murder, suicide, sacrifice are enough to indicate his sense of how bad things may become if no effortful change emerges. If assimilation and imperial State there must be, then let there also be citizenship without *semblance*—or with the modified semblance that can teach and learn to live with the enabling violation of colonization such that the international lines (that will continue to spread whether we like it or not) can be humanized and diversified.

The theory of assimilation leads to the main axiom: how counterassimilation can work; how the African child can avoid being devoured by "French" and instead become a reasonable schizophrenic. "France" and "West Africa" name bipolar cultural units secure in their discrete civilizational identities. The energy of Senghor's program would be directed toward nurturing and protecting the African child's indigenous cultural base at the start, and then leading it from the security of this base toward "French" (language, culture). This leads to his proposition of a "bicephalism" in primary education, which becomes a bicephalism-bilingualism (bicephalingualism?) pair: "the study of West Africa and France should constitute the two poles of education [*enseignement*] in A.O.F., and this bicephalism will be found at all grades." Practically, the child begins learning in the mother tongue and graduates to French. Thus "bicephalism means [*veut*] bilingualism" (PD September 7).

Senghor proposes that this kind of program will train children to retain their indigenous spirit before venturing into French, thus enabling them to carry regionalized versions of a general African soul into the foreignness of an alien cultural realm: "To the extent one advances, the Africa pole will lose its magnetic force to the benefit of the French pole. The point is to set out from the environment [*milieu*] and Negro-African civilizations in which the infant bathes" (PD September 7). Baptized by its African milieu in language and cultural formation, the child will be able to internalize the foreign, absorb it, and make it its own. Without this primary spirit-soul training, "character" is corrupted by unprepared-for culture-contact. "Customs" (*moeurs*) develop faster than the spirit (or mind, *esprit*) that should be guiding them; and so our "evolved persons [*évolués*] . . . abandon the moral traditions [*traditions morales*] of our fathers" (PD September 7). With regard to pedagogical traditions, which have a moral resonance, the Catholic Senghor occludes the long history of Islamic education in Senegal in particular and West Africa more generally.

Here as elsewhere I would question Senghor's endorsement of an unexamined patriarchal inheritance. His position is paradoxically grounded in a close affiliation with the European ethnography of his times, and thus his own education places him in the field of some of the most torturous, difficult, and necessary questions about the politics of education more generally. It is those at the top, who, educated in a manner that gives them anthropological access to an ancestral culture, can idealize and formalize the "moral traditions of our fathers" in such a way. Moreover, it is by virtue of high-level and excellent education that cultural/civilizational units or traditions may be understood both aesthetico-formally and as objects of knowledge, and thereby also as kinds of reflexive *choices*, as choosable, or at least as legible in their premises, as options within a reimagined and modernized education. The projected ability to be able to select the "good" from the "bad" within each cultural formation is lacking without a prior training in a certain epistemological capability. In Senghor's own terms, "active assimilation" could not make any sense without the assumption of the ability to distinguish and evaluate what should and should not be assimilated.

This is not to say that the multiplicity of heterogeneous African cultural formations is static or unreflexive; nor is it necessarily to question the value of whatever kinds of African gnosis, ethics, or aesthetic-cultural traditions Senghor may have had in mind. It is rather to recognize: (a) that the same provisos would apply to them; and (b) that the ability to discuss and comprehend these things *in the kind of terms Senghor uses* is something that itself *has to be taught and learned*. Not taught and learned as cultural information or as moral code to be obeyed, but rather within the frame of epistemological exercise and imaginative capability. Recall, then, the way the sole example of a Senegalese subaltern appears in "Le problème culturel": as a domestic servant so deeply inserted into the cultural conformity of a pattern of morality and authority that his recourse when his honesty is unjustly challenged is to try to commit suicide. (And recall that Senghor contrasts this notion of honor with a highly aristocratic "ideal of Man in West Africa"—the Wolof *Samba-Linguer*).[71]

The difficulty therefore comes with identifying one's own already-fulfilled spiritual education with the interests of the universal. Put in a more prosaic way, it is the problem of assuming the general capacity of comprehending the semantic content of a teaching in advance. Senghor's philosophy of education and culture does not fall simply on either side of the problem. As we will see, his investigations of the "rural popular school" underline further the scope of the predicament. Thus, the significance of Senghor's philosophy is that it is worked over by these dilemmas as well as giving them discursive shape. If we now return to the catchphrase "the point is to assimilate not to be assimilated" (a formula that Senghor never abandoned), we see that it sums up in a nutshell the ethico-political stakes of his philosophy of education. Bicephalingualism could lead in the direction of the inner preparation of the non-*semblable* citizen. Alternatively, Senghor's philosophy could falter, as it often does, on the unquestioning ontologization of an indigenous, black, racialized soul assumed as cultural ground and thus as already-secured epistemological and spiritual apparatus for a workable counterassimilation.[72]

If the rudiments of primary education are given in the mother tongue, including "indigenous morality," then "at the age of six or eight, soul impregnated with our newly restored ideal, mind [*l'ésprit*] exercised and already equipped, well-furnished [*meublé*], the child would more fruitfully approach its primary studies" (PD September 7). These are the outlines of Senghor's thesis of an indigenous vanguard that will be capable of entering actively into the French "pole" of culture while retaining an essentially unthreatened indigenous ipseity.

Internal social and cultural differences within the West African zone will be recognized in terms of different kinds of gradations and adaptations of the schoolbooks and teaching practices to be employed. The great sociocultural rift is between rural and urban, and this split plays out in a double way. There is, first, a seemingly irreducible recourse to figures of the autochthonous originarity of culture as such. The great source of culture is extraurban, in the people closest to the earth and thereby the most rooted. "We want agriculture to lead to culture. . . . Will I speak of agricultural work, of the mystical sense of the Earth [*Terre*] which was that of our peasants? Shall I teach you that the healthiest, the strongest, are those in whom the sense [*sens*] of the Earth is strongest?" (PD September 7).

Culture as agri-culture, as farming and cultivation, has, in the Latinate tradition of Senghor's training, a nontrivial relationship with colonialism. The *colonus* was a cultivator, a settler, and this leads us to the sense of "a coloniality of culture, . . . the colonial structure of any culture" that, I would argue, is a presupposition for Senghor even if unacknowledged.[73] If etymology can too easily slide over the wounds and violence of specific histories of colonialism and imperialism, it is nevertheless perhaps this complicity between culture as such and colonization that allows Senghor to regard (French) colonization as carrying with it a chance as well as being an instrument of domination and exploitation. The all-too-visible extremities of modern colonialism disclose deviations from "normal" structural patterns common to the ongoing self-institution of culture as such. Thus, as Derrida suggests, we are "colonized" into "culture" in an underived way, making any actual cultural formation a double bind; "culture" is established by an originary usurpation that metaleptically grounds the possibility and desire for identity, propriety, belonging. "Alienation without alienation," underived or "inalienable" alienation energizes culture as its own auto-"*re*-appropriation" and as a movement of returns that seeks to grasp these inaccessible origins (*Monolingualism* 25, 27). If the subject of acculturating education is inextricably inserted into what Spivak calls the "enabling violation" of colonialism, then Senghor offers one possible philosophico-political response to it: rather than declare nativist opposition, *use* critically the cultural resources brought by colonialism, and supplement them with something of our own.[74]

Senghor imagines peasants as the guardians of ancestral African culture, most proximate to the soil. They metonymize the racial roots and therefore the primordial roots of culture. They are also by implication the least touched by European culture. While the category of the peasant (*paysan*) is central to both the rhetoric and the conceptuality of Senghor's presentation, it was a recent transposition of a formulaic French typology to the colonially scrambled structures of African rural society. A simulacral "black peasantry" delineated a template for benevolent modernization and development.[75] We must acknowledge that this morally weighted figuration of a slowly modernizing peasantry was posed against the rapacious practices of concessionary companies across AOF and the social chaos brought about by coercive labor recruitment and forced migration. On the other hand, it was an ideological bulwark against the formation of a West African working class.[76] In this context, Véronique Dimier has shown that Delavignette's novel *Paysans noirs*, taken as an inspiring representation of morally benevolent colonial behavior, played a significant role in the founding of postwar Europe's policies of "sustainable development."[77]

As Senghor had put it two years earlier in *L'Étudiant Noir*, the African communities most isolated from European colonization were the ones best able to preserve "their plastic beauty, their artistic and moral riches."[78] The only way the intellectual elite can now play the role of "example and intermediary" that history has assigned it is to avoid being "cut from the roots of its race" (*coupée des racines de sa race*) (PD September 11). The cut is also socially an epistemological or gnostic one, a cut in the social text. It is ignorance of the people—which fundamentally means ignorance of their indigenous languages, because those languages encompass "the grammar, the folklore, the civilization of the people in question" (PD September 11). That is, culture itself *as teachable.*

However—and this is the second direction of the rural/urban split—these human roots are also subject to a problematic class segregation in terms of education, both actually and in terms of the Senghorian schema. The rhetorical mode here recalls Senghor's opening gesture in which the question of speaking as a peasant appears as a desire that might not be fulfilled or fulfillable. Senghor's shift from an expressed desire that is literally impersonal ("one wants [*on veut*] agriculture to lead to culture") to the form of rhetorical questions ("shall I speak, . . . shall I teach you . . .?") calls for other readings.

Rather than give the obvious negative answer to rhetorical questions (of course I won't teach you about peasants), Senghor does presume to lecture his audience on the rural/urban division. It is as if a deliberate misconstrual of the function of the rhetorical question gives Senghor permission to transgress propriety if not to speak as a peasant. "I know what little success this work would have in the towns," he goes on (PD September 9). It becomes clear that Senghor's modernist manifesto addresses itself as much to the *évolué* and *assimilé* urban-dwelling members of the commune of Dakar (and perhaps some of those of the adjoining Gorée and

Rufisque and even more distant Saint-Louis) as much as to the white and black personnel of the colonial administration as such. The *originaires* of the urban Four Communes of Senegal had a different civil status than the inhabitants of any of the other territories in AOF, including enfranchisement and rights to citizenship, a difference proudly protected and cultivated.[79] The point here is that Senghor, not an *originaire* but from a provincial town dominated by the colonial cash-crop trade, maps his account of the rural/urban divide onto a further civic and social difference within the colony.[80] Even though the Four Communes were not, of course, the only urban centers in Senegal, he proposes a disconcerting alteration of the commune-dwellers' relation to the massive disenfranchised rural hinterlands, noting that the "hostility of the petit bourgeoisie" is unsurprising (PD September 9).[81]

An already-established differentiation between rural and urban schooling was reflected in AOF's "rural popular schools." These "adapted" schools were designed to train village children in applied manual work, agronomy, basic literacy, numeracy, hygiene, economic skills, and so forth. Hence, the production of pragmatically functional village subjects who were to remain broadly within the epistemic and cultural horizons of ethnographically framed African tribal society. The great ideological task of the rural schools was to protect customary and cultural specificity while according interminable development; practically, it was to keep agrarian inhabitants racinated, in place, tribalized, and peasantized, so as to avoid destabilizing flows of uprooted subproletarians to the cities. Senghor negotiates this situation by endorsing the practice of differentiated rural/urban educational institutions. "*Mamadou et Bineta* works marvels in the bush. But it is not made for pupils in Dakar," he writes, because its rural examples and illustrations are unfamiliar to urban children (PD September 9). *Mamadou et Bineta* was an Africanized primary textbook introduced in 1929, altering the prevailing educational practice of using metropolitan textbooks in the French colonies.[82] This innovation was aimed at the emerging rural schools to both suit the capabilities of working village children and revise the curriculum to reflect the kind of future envisaged for them. Even if teaching is tailored individually to the specific needs of each student, Senghor acknowledges that intellectual difference will remain at the level of instruction between rural and urban schools. The fantasmatic cure for that difference, the thing that will cover it over, is the cultural riches brought from the agriculturalists. Thus he declares that the "cultural level" of the rural students will make up for any intellectual difference they have with the urban. While this type of gesture could be salutary in terms of overcoming prejudices between rural and urban groups (see Gramsci's "Southern Question," note 22), it dangerously presumes that "culture" alone can bridge the gap of intellectual difference.

Senghor's manifesto holds out its highest hope for change in the agency of the literary humanities. The "indigenes of AOF, apart from the exceptions, are more gifted in Letters than in Sciences" (PD September 9). This literary predisposition is destroyed by the type of instrumentalized vocational education that produces a bored agronomist rather than "a zesty poet of the soil [*un savoreux poete du terroir*]" (PD September 9). Humanities (literature) will supplement a universality of reason that can be expressed in mathematics and the sciences.[83] Literature assumes that cultural specificity is only accessible through languages, and for Senghor languages are (more or less) continuous with civilizations. Thus, the cultural supplement of the universal will be autochthonous (because racinated) cultural creations manifested in various idiomatic forms of literary art.

This cements the principle of bilingualism: technoscientific knowledge is to be written and accessed in French, which thereby not only plays the role of lingua franca but also stands in for the universal. Correlatively, "we would employ the indigenous language in literary genres that express the genius of the race: poetry, theater, narrative [*conte*]" (PD September 9). Senghor thus posits an intellectual division of labor between languages, not in the traditional manner of linguistics (between "private" and "public" functions), but epistemically and disciplinarily. When he collected a revised version of this piece in *Liberté I* in 1963, Senghor noted that he had gone back on this judgment about the linguistic division of labor (*Liberté* 19).

Restored "black values," mediated by intellectuals in literary forms and indigenous languages, will awaken a people to otherwise inexpressible and intimate regions of its soul. "Tastes, . . . the play of spirit, . . . savor, . . . odor, . . . accent, . . . timbre." "Literature above all" will convey these intangible and sensual aspects of soul and spirit that can only be named in terms of transient sensory experiences (PD September 11). These things name the worldly, trace-y quality of that which the colonial lingua franca can neither translate nor catch; and it is literary art in African mother tongues that will awaken the "taste" (*gout*) of or for them. Senghor recognizes that the vanguardism of literature on its own cannot in fact achieve this as a general end. Education *for* such changes needs to happen, and thus the avant-garde can no longer hunker in its hermetic urban milieu. This is why he (and Césaire, Damas, and others) turned so quickly first to education and ultimately to the politics of State—to affect institutions that will enable such change.

At this point, however, Senghor's manifesto plays interference with itself. The principle of bilingualism, which is in many ways radical and admirable in its moment, is formulated as a bilateral arrangement between separated African languages and French taken as linguistic-civilizational units.[84] Each African language would individually be oriented toward the metropolitan pole: "For us Afro-French, this implies the teaching of French and one indigenous language which will be able to stand as a second living language. Each African language, "Mandingo, Hausa, Yoruba, Peul, Wolof," carries along with a grammar the "history, geography, folklore, civilization of the people in question" (PD September 11). And each of these civilizational language-constructs, implicitly not interwoven with its neighbors, looks only to France as its bipolar other.

The concept of bicephalingualism thereby reflects both a separation between African languages and an individualized bilateral relation between each of them and French, such that each African language/civilization relates itself only to that of the colonial center. The question of the relation *among themselves* of the African languages is left entirely unaddressed, with political implications that would play out in a baleful way in decolonization. The structure is many locals and a single universal, each African language's compass needle magnetized by the metropolitan pole, a divided Africa with the language-areas competing with one another for the attention of France.[85] Fewer than twenty years later, George Padmore would warn that "tribalism is, undoubtedly, the biggest obstacle in creating a modern democratic State and an integrated nation out of small regional units inhabited by backward people still under the influence of traditional authority."[86] Padmore's point is that modern capitalist imperialism happened only yesterday. Communism began the following morning. If you look to the *longue durée* of the past and the long-term prospects for the future, then "tribalism" is the more deeply seated problem than these more recent phenomena. What must be changed is much more sedimented in the social text, in its languages, practices, and idioms, in "culture" to put it in Senghor's terms. Fanon, too, would warn of tribalism and internal fracturing in similar terms in *The Wretched of the Earth*, though he sees the process as the playing out of class privilege in ethnocentric terms within postcoloniality. "We have switched from nationalism to ultranationalism, chauvinism, and racism," where the "ethnic group" sets itself up as party, giving rise to "ethnic" or "tribal" dictatorship, the "tribalization of power, . . . a regionalist spirit and separatism"; the nation "dislocates and dismembers itself."[87]

This early Senghorian position also prefigures the kinds of postcolonial problems later identified by C. L. R. James, among others. In the preface to the Vintage edition of *The Black Jacobins* published in 1962, James observes that "writers on the West Indies always relate them to their approximation to Britain, France, Spain, and America, that is to say, to Western civilization, never in relation to their own history."[88] Each former colony is considered only in terms of its relation to the old metropolitan center; intra-Caribbean historical, cultural, social, and political connections are occluded by silos of bilaterality.

While Senghor's particular way of formulating bilingualism may appear problematic today, it remains compelling because it also prefigures and frankly states what the vast majority of postcolonial studies or world literature scholars still actually do in practice. That is, they transcode the idiomatic specificities of a colonial or now supposedly postcolonial situation into the seemingly more universal format of the big, former colonial languages and their disciplinary and pedagogical frames. The relations *between* indigenous languages of Africa and Asia are barely imagined or practiced at this level. This is not a value judgment or a moral evaluation of a young man writing about these problems nearly a century ago; it is rather to state that his predicament is not merely of historical interest but remains general. We still share much of it with Senghor, this book included. The problems that furrowed his writing have not disappeared, and we can learn from them afresh in the altered frame of a globality that demands ever more uniformization and transcoding in the limited sphere of its operations.

"Le problème culturel" continues in this vein, underlining this systematizing, bilateralizing, and aestheticizing impulse that we still inhabit and that remains an urgent problem: "Today Malagasy is a literary language; yesterday it did not have a written grammar. A Paul Laurence

Dunbar, a Claude MacKay [*sic*], a Langston Hughes, a Sterling Brown have made a marvel of beauty, '*a thing of beauty*,' out of the impoverished blabbering of deracinated slaves" (PD September 11; italicized words in English in original). I remain troubled by the idea that a (literary) culture is built on the aesthetic transfiguration of subaltern voices or on the linguistic systematization of languages previously not subjected to the grammatization of academic experts. Yet these are in fact perfectly regular ways in which modern literary culture has been made; one might say that Senghor gives a summary (inadvertently pitiless, perhaps) of post-Romantic modernism's main acquisitive/reductive drive—to bring ever more margins into the sphere of representability, and ruthlessly to formalize them.

"Le problème culturel" ends with three summary gestures. First it offers a counterexample (though its purpose is to shore up the argument) that brings us to Aimé Césaire:

> I wish . . . to end; and, by way of a counterproof, to take an example you would think counted against me: the example of the old colonies, where diplomas abound, where the education [*enseignement*] is modeled exactly on that of the Metropole. I will question the Antillo-French of my generation: an Aliker, intern of the hospitals of Paris; a Césaire, student at the École Normale Supérieure; a Monnerot, essayist and critic; a Sauphanor, Professor *agrégé* of physics. What do they tell us? That in the French Antilles they have many diplomas and little culture in spite of their very lively intelligence; that they certainly have a literature, but that it is only the negative, the pale copy of the metropolitan; that at the assembly of peoples, "at the meeting place [*rendez-vous*] of giving and receiving," as Césaire puts it, they are forced to come empty-handed; that the fault lies in the education given them, since they have never been taught either the history or the civilizations of their African ancestors.
>
> (PD September 11)

Good education (successful professionals, many diplomas) can actually be bad education if it does not include the study of the history and civilizations of Africa. The peoples of the Antilles are generationally culturally "deracinated" by hundreds of years of plantation slavery. They are structurally denied meaningful dialogue—no give and take—with the metropole because its education condemns them to reflect a "pale copy" back to it (e.g., in literature). Antilleans cannot even know what they might have to bring to this give and take. Curricularized study of Africa would offer a context by which to find out if it would make a difference. As Senghor's argument so far has suggested, the very history of colonialism demonstrates that the European model of an enlightened republican civic polity cannot possibly exhaust the ethico-political and cultural (in Senghor's expanded sense) dimensions of civic virtue and practices of citizenship. Subsequent essays would attempt to delineate in more detail the intellectual, political, ethical—culture-civilizational—options that could be brought to the civic table if the black soul and spirit were attended to.

("Le problème culturel" emphasizes a discontinuity that Senghor would soon modify in positing a "single and unitary" *culture nègre* that has "not been extinguished" in spite of the diaspora.[89] We must, however, note the particular class fix of Senghor's argument. He is talking about elite, assimilated intellectuals and professionals, not hybrid cultural patterns from residual to emergent in the working class and underclass across the Caribbean. This is notable because Senghor was not unaware of the pioneering work of the Haitian intellectual Jean Price-Mars, who had published his eye-opening ethnographic experiment *Ainsi parla l'oncle* [Thus spoke the uncle] in 1928.[90] On the one hand, Price-Mars attempted to institute in the Caribbean the study of precolonial African social and cultural forms. On the other hand, a major impetus of this work was to document the hybridized transformation/survival of African cultural forms in Haitian popular thought and practice. Although informed by this at some level, Senghor sticks to modernist high-cultural aesthetics in "Le problème culturel.")

Second, Senghor summons a poet's voice to show that after all, in spite of bad education in the "old colonies," the trace of the Negro-African spirit persists and may be encountered in vanguard literary art. "Listen rather to Léon Damas," he says, "who sings, in an instinctively rediscovered tom-tom rhythm, his spiritual nudity [*nudité spirituelle*] after the flayings that followed exile" (PD September 11). Senghor quotes and presumably read aloud at his lecture Damas's poem "Ils sont venus ce soir" ("They came that evening," alternatively titled "Fragment") in its entirety. "Ils sont venus" was the first poem in Damas's first collection, *Pigments*, published in April 1937. Senghor in fact quotes an earlier version of the poem that, as Noland informs us, had been published as "Fragment" in a French syndicalist journal, *Soutes*, in 1936.[91]

Having indicated what is lacking in Antillean literary production due to bad education, "Le problème culturel" asks its auditors/readers to listen to a poet's song. It is worth proceeding carefully here to follow what Senghor does and does not claim for the poem. The poet "sings . . . his spiritual nudity." He does so in "an instinctively rediscovered tom-tom rhythm"; and the spiritual nudity has been rediscovered "after the flayings [dépouillements] that followed exile." This is all extremely equivocal to say the least. I translated dépouillements as "flayings" to catch the literal sense of removal of skin, which presumably relates to Senghor's figure of spiritual nudity, nudity beneath or beyond a physical skin that has been flayed. A nudity more nude than nude, because the condition of nudity (a skin to be bared) has itself been removed. A nudity—an exposure—of spirit, but at the same time a nudity that ultimately saves or redeems the physical suffering of being flayed because it results in a spiritual, cultural, or artistic benefit: the poem-song itself. Damas was a student from French Guiana studying in Paris. Is that distance—colony-metropole—the skin-stripping "exile" to which Senghor alludes, or is it supposed to be a synecdoche of the transatlantic slave trade? Or both? Again, neither Senghor's words nor the poem itself will answer the question definitively. Next we must address the "instinctively rediscovered tom-tom rhythm" in which the poet is said to sing. This is the condensation-point of the claim that literary art can short-circuit bad education. It follows this logic: the "tom-tom rhythm" is, again, a synecdoche for a rediscoverable Africa, or at least the spirit of a general Africanity (or "black soul") that remains after the severing of empirical or lived connection.[92] It is both "rediscovered" by the artist and instantiated in his poem. Instinct is precisely that part of the subject that remains pre- or noneducated, and therefore instinctive rediscovery means a short-circuiting of education as such. In spite of his bad (good) education, the artist has rediscovered a breath of spirit in himself that was not conditional upon education. The specialness of literary art is in its power to catch this spirit (and perhaps to teach it?): in the absence of education in "history or the civilizations of . . . African ancestors," art can get us some of the way there, and right to the essential—spirit. Modern art will show the exiled black spirit what it already is without knowing that is what it is, what it knows without yet knowing that it knows itself, because it is not yet educated in the "history or the civilizations of . . . African ancestors." Literary art thereby becomes a kind of spiritual supplement of curricular education, folded into the temporal crease between already and not-yet.

Senghor's caution here is salutary. The claim that literature, as instinctual rediscovery of the naked spirit, could short-circuit *all* education would defeat his entire argument and be a massive gesture of bad faith. Senghor, Damas, the Antillean intelligentsia: they were all the beneficiaries of some of the best education in the world. It is a moment of extreme ambivalence and ambiguity in Senghor's argument, yet a productive one.

Carrie Noland has admirably questioned Senghor's claim that the song of "spiritual nudity" instantiates, via its practice of rhythm, a short circuit to the "history or the civilizations of . . . African ancestors." She argues that both the poem's rhythmic infrastructure and its referential imagery could relate or refer to a plurality of rhythmic times and instances (musical, idiomatic, rhetorical).[93] These would include hybrid musical forms in metropolis and colony, a spectrum of socially and culturally accented speech, and the rhythms specific to politically inflected discourse, that is, various rhythmically mediated worldly equivalents that tail off as traces from the poem's signifying and metrical patterns. While resonant with Noland's reading, my emphasis is different. I remain with Senghor's activist deployment of Damas's poem as part of an argument about education and the role his manifesto assigns to the literary humanities. I will focus on way that "Ils sont venus" gives indications for reading that enrich Senghor's equivocal use of it.

Some commentators read the poem's typographically determined rhythmic patterns, its evocation of the "tom tom," and its images of frenzied body parts as figuring a scene of precolonial Africans dancing. The subject of the phrase "they came that night" is then taken to signify colonial invaders or perhaps slave traders.[94] This extends Senghor's more cautious reading to make the poem the kind of instructive historical narrative that is precisely what he says is missing in the old colonies.

"Ils sont venus" repeats the phrase *pieds de statues* (feet of statues). When he quotes, Senghor makes a singular "statue" of Damas's plural "statues." The second instance of "statue(s)" is the poem's last word, and is linked each time to a frenzy of feet: the "frenzy of [the] statue's feet" (*pieds de statue* in Senghor's usage). As with English *feet*, the word *pieds* in French denotes the standard metrical units of verse. *Statue(s)*, like every other word in the poem, is willy-nilly subject to metrical organization, the movement of the feet that measure out its syllables and lines even if in a nonstandard or typographically disrupted way. (The legibility of disruption depends on a prior metrical order). The "frenzy of feet" is preceded by "the frenzy of eyes / the frenzy of hands," evoking an animated act of reading or writing, the scanning and turning of pages. "Statues," on the other hand, most obviously evokes stasis, the articulated unity of finished works of art. In Senghor's terms, the "statue," the unity that is the work, is patterned by its inner rhythmicity (perhaps deranged somewhat in the frenzy of modernist rule-breaking). For the poem, this is the rhythm of word-sounds and spaces, its metrical feet as framework for the play of the work's respiratory system. The poem's tom-tom turns or rolls (*roulait*) on its own rhythms. In the encounter with the rhythms of the reader, the movement of his or her hands and eyes, the transaction of forms and meanings between work and reader instantiates the time, the rhythm, of reading.

Damas's poem stages, nontrivially, the "death of the author" in this situation of active transaction between reader and work: "how many of ME / . . . are dead."[95] It is an aesthetic experiment in training how to read, but this does not deprive it of the spiritual dynamic or interest that Senghor desires. The rhythmic play of writing-reading is the medium in which a "past" may be posited: "they *came* . . . the tom-tom *rolled* . . . *since* . . . the tom-tom *rolled*." Between the poem as internally differentiated or rhythmicized gestalt and the movement of a reading, the work of art allows and invites reflection on the positing of a "past" that may or may not have been lost: the past as trace rather than as meaning-full sign of a present past. It is the poem's moving feet, their rhythmicity, that permits positing a past, which is the very past ("that night") in which the rhythm rolled out. It makes itself up as the instantiation of the past rhythmicity that it describes. The temporal logic of the poem contains the glitch of a "performative contradiction"—"an event that seems to produce itself by speaking of itself, . . . [that] projects the advent of the self, of the 'speaking' or 'writing' of itself as other, that is to say, *in the manner of the trace* [à la trace]."[96] Thus, the lines invoking the uncountable "dead" MEs, the question of whose incalculable number divides the poem's halves, are more than a making-trace of the figure of the author. They guide us to imagine the billions of singular whoevers murderously excluded from grasping the stakes of these modernist poems and manifestoes. Here the poem declares another limit to its reach, evoking such others only as dead, uncountable, a question, a trace.

Rather than disclosing knowledge of origins or of a restorable past, "Ils sont venus" offers the reader the chance to reflect on the felt—or indeed structural—need for racination, for a transcendental ancestrality, to see that need or desire as a life-or-death struggle available for questioning—and perhaps healing—at the level of epistemological care. The remarkable ambivalence and economy of Senghor's framing of the poem can accommodate this detranscendentalizing possibility. If at one level art's frenzy deranges the epistemological project of education (pointing to a "past" missing from the curriculum and the killing consequences of that exclusion), it cannot by itself suture the knowledge-gap. Poetry's aesthetic staging of its own impossible origin makes legible *as* a desire the desire to secure that origin. All it can do is delineate the missing space of a more formalized epistemological labor of teaching and instruction rather than suture or short-circuit it with "art." Far from denying any past to Africa or Africanity, Damas's poem calls for the necessary supplement of epistemological labor that would construct a publicizable, sharable, teachable history, and take part in the inner preparation of the non*semblable* citizen.

Third, "Le problème culturel" gives its last word to two literary works: Damas's poem and then Claude McKay's novel *Banjo*, published 1929. Senghor concludes as follows: "You will meditate on these words by Claude MacKay [*sic*], Negro-American poet and novelist, native of Jamaica. He speaks to us through the mouth of Ray in *Banjo*: 'Plunging down to the roots of our race and building upon our own foundation is not returning to the state of savagery: it is culture itself'" (PD September 11). As Brent Edwards has observed, there is a discrepancy between the words quoted by Senghor and the French translation of McKay's novel. Senghor quotes McKay as "Plonger jusqu'aux racines de notre race et bâtir sur notre propre fond, ce n'est pas retourner à l'état sauvage: c'est la culture même" (PD September 11).[97] In the place of Senghor's *race*, the French translation of *Banjo* has *peuple*.[98] The original's English line reads as follows: "'Getting down to our native roots and building up from our own people,' said Ray, 'is not savagery. It is culture'" (*Banjo* 200).

Banjo's Ray is arguing with a Martinican student about divisions and prejudices among blacks (the student is particularly down on the Senegalese). His evocation of "our own people" carries a faint resonance of the political signifier "the people"—the name that symbolically unifies the social collectivity in the field of politics.[99] Whichever group or linked chain of groups or struggles declares its identity as "the people" makes its particular claim to emancipation the condition of universal emancipation. Its difference is the one that represents all the differences. This is alluded to in the *Banjo* scene, where the metaphoricity of "roots" gets mixed into a signifying chain including "the bone and sinew and salt of any race or nation," the "common people," and other kinds of emancipation struggles such as "the Irish cultural and social movement, . . . Russian peasants, . . . Ghandi and . . . the common hordes of India" (*Banjo* 200–201). Turning back to "Le problème culturel," we might well ascribe Senghor's substitution of "race" for "people" to the slips of quoting from memory. But the substitution of "race" for the term that names the ideal constituency of the republican polity or the felicitous citizenry is surely still of symptomatic interest in a presentation of the year 1937 that has spoken of Hitler and the 1936 Berlin Olympics. Of course Senghor has not been advocating an ethnostate in which citizenship is defined racially, but this final substitution might be read as an equivocal modulation of the formula for a *citizenship* of the non-*semblable*. The French yet again permits a clearer play with "roots," such that it could be said that there are roots of roots, "*racines de . . . race*," an anxious-seeming proliferation of representations of roots and rootedness that expresses the apprehension that these representations are in fact all racination amounts to: representations of roots engendering more representations of roots to root them, and yet more roots for those roots, and so on; an unending textual "racinating function" subverting "radical essence."[100]

We must, however, also observe the way that Senghor has framed this final word from *Banjo*. He offers it to his audience as a parting nourishment before they disperse for elsewheres unknown, a "*viatique*": one for the road (PD September 11).

❖ ❖ ❖

Back in Paris later in September 1937, Senghor made a related presentation to the International Congress on the Cultural Evolution of Colonial Peoples. The three-day Congress was part of "Colonial Month" during the 1937 Paris International Exposition. Under the general rubric of *arts et techniques dans la vie moderne*, the Expo was a vast spectacle of technoscientific progress, artistic and spiritual development, and political competition among militarizing transnational forces. In spite of the now iconic faceoff between the Soviet and German (Nazi) pavilions across the mouth of the Pont d'Iéna, global fissures and centrifugal energies could not be contained or balanced aesthetically in the framework of the Expo-form. Senghor had returned from the colonial capital to the heart of the imperium where signs of the colonies, too, were visibilized and displayed as part of this general force field.[101]

Within this general spectacle of power, conflict, and unexamined celebration of technoscientific advance, the program and records of the International Congress point to a cluster of problems necessarily occluded by a spectacle designed to visibilize success and results. At the Congress, the question of colonial development is closely tied to the practice of education. This is so especially in noneconomic dimensions that cannot "be translated exactly by statistics" and are "more difficult to express" because it is a question of producing a "summary of colonial action on young minds [esprits neufs]."[102] In terms of the congress-form itself, such difficulties are given a provisional (ideological) fix in terms of incompatible yet unilateral resolution statements.

Resolutions adopted by the Congress thus disclose double binds in the ideological field of colonial humanism. They could at the same time encompass the call to establish a service to promote and support "indigenous arts and trades" and the call to ensure that "evolved indigenes" not be submitted to "customs contrary to the principles of our civilization." Prefiguring issues central to postcolonial gender-and-development action, the latter cluster of resolutions focused on the prepubescent girl's right not to be exchanged or married with or without her consent, the postpubescent girl's right not to marry without consent, restrictions on "customary" authority of the parents over female children, and the establishment of a right of widows and other women not to be "inherited" by a man according to "customary succession"[103]—a now-familiar usage of the sociocultural conditions of women as indices of development according to the scale of the developers. It is highly unlikely that these resolutions had any practical effects, but they serve to remind us of the already-active double imperative of preservation/ modernization that could represent itself through the contrast of specific figures and sociocultural areas: gender and production. Thus a bifurcation of the imperatives of colonial intervention wherein indigenous arts and trades are to be supported while customary practices of matrimony and relations between the sexes are to be aligned to French norms. Denis Blanche, the Congress's rapporteur, identified in contemporary terms this ideological split that assigns each aspect of the double bind to an apparently autonomous empirical area: "two theses confront each other; one that advocates respect for indigenous culture; one that advocates, on the contrary, the progressive assimilation of blacks to the West" (*Congrès* 18).

Senghor addresses obliquely the effect "of colonial action on young minds," making his brief presentation before a highly distinguished group of delegates that included anthropologists such as Marcel Griaule, Michel Leiris, Marcel Mauss, and Melville Herskovits, as well as the colonial ethnographer-administrator of AOF Maurice Delavignette, and many other functionaries of the French, British, and Portuguese colonial systems. The psychoanalyst Marie Bonaparte is also listed as a delegate.

"*La résistance de la bourgeoisie sénégalaise à l'école rurale populaire*" (the resistance of the Senegalese bourgeoisie to the rural popular school) supplements Senghor's Dakar speech. It is a subtle but pointed analysis of the class separation that revealed itself as both condition and effect of an attempt to "Africanize" primary schooling in AOF.[104] According to Harry Gamble, the institution of the rural school aimed to produce functionally literate and numerate agriculturalists who could understand basic economics and hygiene and become effective as sufficiently modernized workers for an expanding cash crop economy. This is how it reinforces already-existing formal and informal separations on regional and class lines. At the ideological level, it sustained transposition of an idealized image of the French peasant onto the rural population of western continental Africa.[105] Despite Gamble's retrospectively just evaluation of the rural schools, Senghor presents them once more as flashing forth a chance, however slim, to develop the non*semblable* future citizen.

"The rural popular school would be an excellent institution, on condition that it did not leave the village," writes Senghor, ventriloquizing a Senegalese urban middle class that does not wish for "Africanized" education to be generalized to its own children (RB 41). Apart from a small minority of metropolitan-educated intellectuals, the bourgeoisie does not object to rural schools for rural areas so long as it is not affected by them. On the one hand, Senghor attempts to understand and explain this resistance, its cultural and sociopolitical conditions; on the other hand, he contends that the rural schools represent more than a mind-numbingly narrow focus on practical education at the expense of the development of epistemological capability. Revisiting the position of the Dakar speech, he writes that "our bourgeoisie does not understand the Franco-African cultural movement, of which the popular rural school is an expression" (42). The rural schools represent a chance for the kind of future bifocal (Franco-African) cultural formation envisioned in "Le problème culturel." The movement for such schools is "born of a completely *modern* conception of culture" (42, my emphasis): first, " 'cultivating one's difference' [*cultiver sa différence*] as André Gide wishes"; and second, repeating exactly the phrase from "Le problème culturel," "in a racial reaction of man on his milieu" that will offer him an "instrument of moral and intellectual perfection" (42).

The *évolués* do not grasp this "completely modern conception of culture." They have inherited historically a prerevolutionary "scholastic-rhetorical" notion of culture from the early days of the establishment of French education. This is itself a kind of colonial hybrid, as it grafts on to a deeper "ancestral repugnance for experimental and exact sciences" and the "influence of Islamic [*coranique*] teaching" (42). Yet if such a "formal rhetorical conception of culture" holds sway among the bourgeoisie, it is profoundly out of step with "what is concrete and practical, perhaps with what is African" (42). Given its cultural sedimentation and its embattled material and civil circumstances, it is quite understandable that the urban middle class prefers the "lawyer" to the "agronomic engineer." Its fear is that the object lessons of the new French education are instrumental means to " 'know the new,' to be 'deracinated.' "[106]

The "political causes of resistance" are more important and more proximate, and stem from a double imperative: a *political* and historically determined self-interest, and a *social* demand of responsible (quasi-)citizenship. If education is an "instrument of culture," it is also "a kind of livelihood [*gagne-pain*]: it is preparation for the professions" (RB 42). In order to qualify for positions in the colonial bureaucracy, applicants "must possess qualifications [*un diplôme*] identical to that received in the Metropole" (43). Assimilation must take place at least at the level of qualifications and knowledge (*connaissances*); and therefore "assimilation must be at the base, in primary school: it proscribes the rural popular school and the Africanization of education in general" (43). Desire for upward mobility conditions the desire for assimilation. The bourgeoisie fears losing its small place in the sun—its access to professional positions in the colonial machinery—if it is not inserted into an educational apparatus identical to that of the French metropolis.

Senghor limits the meaning of "political" here to designate the defensive, self-interested side of the imperative. The linked (*lié*) phenomenon of desire for an active role in the polity is "social." Consequently, not only do "they think of their livelihoods"; they also "think of taking an increasingly greater place in the administration of the Polity [*Cité*]" (43). This social stake is in the arena of an admittedly limited—but still real—ability to exercise a degree of responsible citizenship in running the State. What must have been assumed by Senghor and legible to most of his audience is that his "bourgeoisie" must refer almost exclusively to the Senegalese *originaires* of the four coastal urban communes. With very few exceptions, Senegalese from outside a small fraction of this group would have been excluded from the possibility of qualifying to enter the administration. Senghor himself, not an *originaire*, had to undergo French naturalization in 1933 in order to be eligible for his *agrégation* at the Sorbonne.[107] Senghor cites an anonymous article from *Périscope Africain* (February 16, 1935) that underlines the double bind of the bourgeois political resistance to the rural schools: "we are obliged . . . to demand that the State permit the colonized to form intellectuals who will become the elites called to participate in the Administration of the territories that belong to them" (RB 43). If all schools are generally Africanized along the current lines of the rural schools (that is, turned into training centers for peasant farmers), the necessary epistemological and "cultural" preparation for running the State will be lacking. The rural school can appear as a cynical attempt to regulate the production of indigenous intellectuals and to further diminish the quality of citizenship enjoyed by the urban middle class. Yet this is at the same time a minute fragment of the elite fighting to protect its fragile privileges and willy-nilly endorsing the strengthening of social and epistemic barriers between itself and the masses of the rural hinterland. A short quarter-century later, Fanon would excoriate this section of the colonial bourgeoisie for its lack of "organic links" to the masses and for its failure to "put itself in the school of the people" (*se mettre à l'école du peuple*) so as to share the intellectual and cultural gains of metropolitan education.[108]

An even smaller segment of this elite—perhaps only Senghor himself— supports the institution of the rural school. Along with the "General Government," it "has advocated the return to the land and to indigenous crafts [*arts*] in which the economic future of the country resides" (RB 43). Paradoxically, the "tiny minority" group "from the very heart of this bourgeoisie" prepared to "defend the rural popular school" comprises "the majority of teachers and indigenes graduating from metropolitan institutions

[*Facultés*]" (40). Their interest is not the mere self-interest of the "political," but is "cultural and social" because other-directed: "they also want their fellows [*congénères*] increasingly to participate in the administration of the Polity [*Cité*]" (44). Senghor dreams that the rural schools could become the site of preparation for citizenship and for the capacity in principle to run the State.

The reality of the rural schools seems to have been baleful. Gamble writes of problems ranging from the "gutting of the primary school curriculum to the imposition of long hours of heavy farm labor" upon children.[109] Marcel de Coppet, who was the governor general of AOF during the Popular Front period and who hosted Senghor at the time of his Dakar speech in 1937, went on a fact-finding tour in 1938. In Gamble's words, he "learned that, in many areas, local populations did their best to avoid rural schools, which they saw as new form of *corvée*" (794). Upon returning to Dakar, he bluntly reported to members of his administration that "rural schools have not achieved their goal, namely, a mass education adapted to the native milieu and capable of improving living conditions."[110]

If Senghor's endorsement of the rural popular schools in 1937 seems overly idealistic, if not naive, we must bear in mind that we are following here the dream-figures of the intelligentsia's literary-aesthetic vanguard. The point has been to uncover some of the limits of modernist ambition at the same time as finding in those limits problems and questions that remain inescapable today. A decade older and rather more politically experienced, Senghor would be bitterly critical of the rural schools, acknowledging his prior naïveté.[111] However, his disappointment was that the rural schools had not really been set up to do what he hoped and believed they could. As a deputy to the French National Assembly in the late 1940s, therefore, Senghor would not abandon the double demand of citizenship plus an Africa-oriented education, and therefore a citizenry of the non*semblable* once again. The quick fix of the rural schools turned into a much more tangled and complicated political and epistemological endeavor. No more short circuits, but the residual hope for a longer-term possibility of the bourgeoisie "putting itself in the school of the people," as Fanon later said, to work toward a time when the *congénères*, whoever they may be, and even if they are not born alike or born nearby, may become the active citizens who could change the *Cité* from the inside out.

3

NÉGRITUDE (SLIGHT RETURN) II

Aimé Césaire and the Uprooting Apparatus

La trace d'un retour.

—Derrida, *Le monolinguisme de l'autre*

There is a bizarre, even mystifying moment concluding Aimé Césaire's first known piece of published writing, at which he announces to "Black Youth" that "it is a hair that prevents you from acting: it is the Identical, and it is you who carry it."[1] The text then exhorts Black Youth to "shave yourselves" as the "first condition of action and creation." "Long hair, it's affliction," it ends. More strident in tone, more self-assertively vanguardist than Senghor's writings of the 1930s, Césaire's "Jeunesse noire et assimilation" (Black youth and assimilation), published in 1935, presents itself as a manifesto for "action and creation." As with other modernist avant-garde manifestoes (even the most overweeningly programmatic), the founding gesture that Césaire's advocates is removal, reduction, cutting off ("destroy . . . extirpate . . . cut" he writes), to make "action and creation" possible (1203).

Haircutting is an odd, almost comical metaphor for the primary purging that is the condition of (avant-garde) action and creation, evoking a kind of inverted Samson held in thrall by a single uncut hair that has the power to disempower. If hair cannot but make us think of roots in the context of the young black students' fervent discussions of racination and assimilation, then cutting "the Identical" back to its root perhaps makes some kind of sense. To read the complexity and double bind of this concluding gesture, however, we must look more carefully at the manifesto.

"Jeunesse noire et assimilation" was published in the first number of *L'Étudiant Noir* (March 1935). It appears under the column heading "Nègre-ries," which as Gary Wilder observes is a "neologism that condenses *nègres* and *reveries*."[2] It is likely that "Nègreries" was a regular feature, as the only other issue of *L'Étudiant Noir* we have also places Césaire's contribution under the same banner.[3] It suggests a seriality of black dreamworks reflected in prose, a modernist experiment in genre suspended between desiring-phantasm and analysis, ideal for the manifesto-form.

"Jeunesse noire" seems on the surface to polemicize against assimila-tion, to find in its structures and imperatives something to negate and strip away to the point of finding new material ground from which to (re) start. In a tone of apodictic declaration, it advocates recovery or preser-vation of a "self" (*soi*) that is lost in the impossible project of assimila-tion. To "live truly or authentically" (*vivre vraiment*), black youth must "remain itself" (*rester soi*) (JN 1293). But to "be itself [*être soi*] it must struggle against (its)self [*lutter contre soi*]"; the self, *soi*, is both site and stake of this struggle. The self is self-divided. It must return to itself to become itself; and not only that, it must violently excise something, raze it to the root, guillotine it to institute a level playing field of the self to give itself its own power and law of action and creativity. The hair—the Identical—in the final passage is the proper name of the force in the self that must be struggled against, that must be "cut . . . at its root" (1293).

At one level, "the Identical" appears to be an apposite name for that which black youth must cut out because it evokes the mistake of identifi-cation made by the "tribe of Old Men" (*tribu des Vieux*) whose watchword is assimilation (1293). The exemplar of the tribe is depicted as a grotesque, passive, sterile, subservient mimic man in bowler hat and tie, who has "renounced his father whose name is Bush Spirit" (1292). A tribe of old men, not real fathers, who have adopted identity-signs that the self should strip away (shirtfront, bowler). Venturing further with moves of modernist primitivism, Césaire writes that the assimilated man is not even mad, because the madman at least has faith in (him)self (*foi en soi*). By contrast, the *assimilé* is a "*Nègre* who has killed the *Nègre* in him," has no " 'faith in himself [*soi*]' and thereby saves himself from madness." Youth therefore perhaps risks the madness of " 'faith in self' " because such faith involves the torment of self's nonidentity, its struggle against itself, the Identical, as it seeks to find itself.

Is the task for black youth to repudiate the imitative and ultimately self-defeating project of assimilation, to get back to the roots, to recover the real "self" lost to assimilation? Such gestures could be typified as the manifesto of a modernist primitivism: strip away the disempowering layers of acculturation; go back to the Africanized/authentic/original self; start again by rediscovering the "Bush Spirit"—symbolically secured as the name of the Father—that has been renounced by the *assimilés*, the fake tribe of old-men-not-fathers, thereby guaranteeing their horrifying "imbecility" (1292). Such wishes are neither pathological nor criminal, but the conduct of "Jeunesse noire" will nevertheless point to their entanglement in a double bind.

It turns out that assimilation has already been repudiated by another—unacceptable—agency, and questioning it is a correspondingly more confusing and elliptical proposition. Black youth is already caught under the doubly binding injunction of its assimilability/unassimilability, and the positing of its unassimilable difference has already been appropriated by popular racism. The text asserts that "to wish to be assimilated is to forget that nothing can change animal life [*faune*, fauna]; that is to misrecognize the 'alterity' that is a law of Nature" (1292). Who or what is speaking here, where the text invokes this law of a natural racial or species difference? Even though these words are not represented in direct speech (that will come later), we are told that this is the voice of the People: "This is so true that the People, eldest son of Nature, informs us of it every day" (1292). The People itself is the agency that rejects assimilation. This "People" is textually woven with the People celebrated by Jules Michelet, whose *Le Peuple* (1846) supplies Césaire's epigraph. "Jeunesse noire" seems to draw on and make itself compatible with the rhetorical conduct of Michelet's text in certain ways; but the eruption of popular racism forces the black student's primitivist gestures to take a pattern different from Michelet's celebratory, class-coded national-populist primitivism of the "child" and the "simple."[4] Roland Barthes writes that Michelet's image of the People puts it "above History, it opens Nature and grants access to the supernatural goal of a paradisal, reconciled humanity."[5] Acknowledging this, Césaire's intervention delineates a People that is voice and agent of violently marked division and difference under an ideology of the natural.

What follows is a formulation of the aporetic injunctions, where one agency proclaims assimilation and the other proclaims absolute inassimilable (natural, species) difference. The first statement is the political ruling of the "decree" (*décret*)—thus the abstract operation of the republican State—which interpellates black youth as follows: " 'You are the likenesses [*semblables*] of the Whites, you are assimilated' " (1292). This is countered by a "natural Law" proclaimed by the People: "the People, eldest son of Nature, . . . the People, wiser than decrees because it follows Nature, yells at us 'Get out of here, you're different from us; you're nothing but wops [*métèques*] and *nègres*' " (1292). Popular racism now appears as absolute as Nature itself in its ever-renewed efflorescence in the face of official decrees. Assimilation as State policy paradoxically intensifies the passions of naturalized difference, multiplying opportunities to "mock," and revealing its covert affiliation with racism in the scientized modern sense.[6]

"Jeunesse noire" rejects assimilation on metropolitan-colonialist terms, but it cannot simply do so in a racist vein by joining with the Peoples' voice. Mere reversal would paradoxically assimilate the black student to the People and its racism. The Césaireian "reply" is obliged to displace this double, disjunctive interpellation from the metropole. Interpellation by decree (juridical rule) is countered by norm (natural rule): "You are the same/you are a different species." The symbolic field of assimilation appears saturated by this ever-reversible opposition that predetermines the field of the sayable and the intelligible. What can "black youth," especially the upwardly mobile black student in the metropolis, possibly say in the face of this impossible dilemma of an insistence on sameness and an assertion of absolute difference? Submitting to both laws simultaneously, Césaire's response dislocates the reader by following both contradictory contours of the black student's symbolic place in the metropolitan center. The writing black student displaces these markers by at once addressing and cleaving to their contradictory demands—thereby producing the event of a bizarre and destabilizing enunciation where there could otherwise be none. (None because either in your sameness your enunciation cannot register, being identical, assimilated, or your animal difference is banished from the scene of intelligibility.) Césaire's pronouncement, later in the text, that rather than be assimilated, black youth wishes to contribute to "universal life, to the humanization of humanity" seems to support this reading at the thematic level (1293).[7] Yet the justified but predictable thematic affirmation of humanist universality turns the double bind into a single bind, occluding the insight that racism itself has a "humanist, universalist component" ideologically linked to colonialism as a transnational, cosmopolitan, "civilizing" project for which assimilation would be exhibit number one.[8] It is thus in the conduct of the text—rather than in its unconvincing appeal to universalist humanism—that the imaginative outline of a subject unhinging the snares of assimilation resides. To become a "self" (*soi*) unmarked by the stigmata of (failed) simulation or radical animal difference, the black student must open another way of inhabiting and addressing the cultural script and the language.

"Jeunesse noire" expands upon universalist assimilation's intensification of racist passions by insisting that in practice the "copies" remain markedly imitative. Assimilation unexpectedly engenders an affective landscape of disgust, hatred, and contempt as humanity's "fear of the 'other'" finds a complement in its "disgust at the likeness [*semblable*]"—"the contempt one has for the monkey and the parrot" (1292). Moreover, the colonized *semblable* does not understand this contempt of its white prototype and starts to hate it back in the way that "certain students [*disciples*] hate the master because the master always wants to remain master when the student has stopped being the student" (1292). Thus, "assimilation, born of fear and timidity, always ends in contempt and hate" (1293). Uncannily echoing the neoclassical discourse on the enemy and civil war that Carl Schmitt was producing in Germany at the time, Césaire writes that assimilation "carries within itself the germs of struggle; struggle of same against same [*lutte du même contre le même*], which is to say the worst of struggles" (1293).[9] Césaire undoubtedly evokes the classical definition of *stasis* (internal discord "between those who share kinship ties or origins," civil war) from his education rich in classical writings that described it as the worst kind of conflict.[10]

Yet if white and black are subject to an absolute and unchangeable natural difference as the piece asserts, then assimilation can only ever stall, leading to hate and contempt; but it cannot entail the final "struggle of same against same" because the parties to the conflict are not and can never be the same. This apparent logical contradiction is not the sign of a conceptual failing; it alerts us to the working of another logic or pattern of pressures pushing against the sequence of assertive unilateral statements and imperatives. Césaire now moves into a denunciation of the "actor . . . [who] brings to life a multitude of men . . . but he does not himself live [*il ne se fait pas vivre*]" (1293). Yet this text, "Jeunesse noire," is itself obliged to ventriloquize, to act out the voices inhabiting and assailing it so as to assert a "self" for which it advocates but that remains strangely undefined and obscure. Such a patchwork confirms our sense that the "self" is delineated here in terms of a scenographics of interpellations and experiences of origins rather than a primordial rootedness or gathered ipseity that could only derive from the latter. *Nègreries* and manifesto: the bringing-to-manifestation or phenomenalization of the iterable singularities of *black* dreamworks.

As these staged scenes play out then, "the history of the Negro is a drama in three acts [*un drame en trois épisodes*]": servitude-assimilation-emancipation (1293). If emancipation is also part of the drama, then no self can escape fully the position of the actor who does not "live authentically or truly" (*ne vit pas vraiment*). We have thus entered into two further aporias: first, civil war of the assimilated defined as "same against same" as it is harnessed to affirmation of racial difference as a law of Nature; second, declaration of emancipation into "primacy of the self" as an act in a drama as it yokes black youth's antitheatrical desire "not to play any role" (1293). Such contortions of logic follow from the text's displacement of the two contradictory injunctions of assimilation and racial schism.

These and the following gestures take otherwise categorical pronouncements into the unstable zone of complicity. Who can denounce assimilation? From where? When the People have already spoken to pronounce the impossibility of assimilation? The text is frank about the fact that assimilated status is an object of desire, emblem of an upward class mobility and inclusion reasonably sought by the colonized as they move from empire's margins to the metropolis (or indeed as they remain in the colony, though this latter question will have to wait for the *Cahier* before it is touched upon). The motif of upward mobility is spelled out explicitly in the epigraph from Michelet's *The People*: "The difficulty is not in moving up, but in moving up while remaining oneself" (Le difficile n'est pas de monter, mais en montant de rester soi) (1292). The *soi* of "Jeunesse noire," then, is a transformative borrowing from Michelet, who opens—in terms of upward *class* mobility—varieties of Césaire's predicaments: "They who rise, almost always lose by it; because they become changed, they become hybrids [*mixtes*], bastards; they lose the originality of their own class, without gaining that of another."[11] For the dreamwork manifesto, assimilation becomes a loss of self and vitality in pathetic mimicry of the dominant. Yet in pointing at Michelet, "Jeunesse noire" underlines two things: the putting-together of bits of an enunciating self from cut-outs snipped from materials of the dominant; and the often occluded element of class in the racialized terrain of diaspora and assimilation.

The search for "self," then, turns on the class position of being able to attack assimilation in these terms; and the text's follow-through of the double bind shows that this attacking energy comes from a zone of complicity. Complicity is here to be neither celebrated (as hybridity) nor condemned (as moral culpability): it is the particular imaginative gift that the black student assumes through intimacy with the high culture of an aggressively devouring colonizing system. Hence the organization of Césaire's text tells us that it is the assimilated or partly assimilated figure that, subject to the law of assimilation, must constitute the vanguard against assimilation. Accordingly, black youth "must struggle against (its)self" (*lutter contre soi*). But even if the text wills some secure foundation of a "primacy of self" prior to any assimilatory contamination, it cannot fix the ground of that struggle there. The word *self* is the index of a peculiar unease. It points to what has been left behind (disavowal of the Name of the Father, loss of self) as much as to what is sought ahead. The apparent addressee is the "Black Student" him- or herself, the *étudiant noir* whose name heads the very periodical edited by Césaire in which these writings appear. "Journal of the Association of Martiniquan Students in France" reads the newsletter's subtitle.

The black student speaks from within the internal margin of a metropole that is also desired, and not from a radical externality that can be domesticated precisely by being exoticized. Césaire's French already inhabits an impeccable tradition of French prose and poetry, here borrowing critically all manner of resources from Michelet and others. The "contradictory" turns of logic and rhetoric in "Jeunesse noire" map contours of the center's own fault lines, so as to develop an idiom that reworks the terms of struggle to enter hegemony. As we shall see, Césaire's *Cahier d'un retour au pays natal* (1939) will attempt to figure what has been cut out of this picture of the tribulations of the upwardly mobile migrant facing metropolitan racism, what gets drowned out by the vociferous and eloquent complaints of the black student.

"Jeunesse noire" turns next to characterizing the pervasive ideological doxa of the logic of assimilation, taking its address deeper into the realm of a dramatized complicity. It is no longer "I," "them," "us," "black youth" and "the People," "the colonizer" and the Negro. The treatise slips into the impersonal pronoun *on*, to ventriloquize a doxa that confuses lines of speech, address, and power:

> The Negroes were first enslaved: "idiots and animals," one said. Then one turned toward them with a more indulgent regard; one said to oneself: "they are worth more than their reputation," and the attempt was made to form them; they were "assimilated": they were at the school of the masters. "Big children," one said, because only the child is perpetually at the school of the masters.

> [Les Nègres furent d'abord asservis: "des idiots et des brutes," disait-on. Puis on tourna vers eux un regard plus indulgent; on s'est dit: "ils valent mieux que leur réputation," et on a essayé de les former; on les a "assimilés": ils furent à l'école des maîtres. "De grands enfants," disait-on, car seul l'enfant est perpétuellement à l'école des maîtres.[12]]

If the voice of "Jeunesse noire" is taken as representing a stitched-together *soi* of an *étudiant noir*, it is willy-nilly *in* assimilation; it is attending "the school of the masters" (1293). This is perhaps how one loses oneself: becoming one with permanent tutelage, *minorité, Unmündigkeit*, a big child forever merged into the general *on* of assimilatory doxa with a symbolic loss of the ability to make *soi, moi,* or *je* meaningful. In a vivid grammatical staging of assimilation, *on* marks the spot of its subject.

It is now the moment to return to hair. As we already saw, the manifesto ends with a call to black youth to shave their heads of the hair, the Identical, that prevents them from acting. "Meredith tells us what must be cut above all," it says, before directly addressing "Black Youth" (1293). Once more, Césaire's text operates a complex merging of voices: "Meredith tells us: Black Youth, there is a hair that prevents you from acting" (1293). Does the black student now speak through Meredith? As with Michelet, the reader has to follow up the intertextual signal to see what is happening.

Césaire is borrowing a bit of what makes his text work in order to make his point. The very thing that makes the text work is being illustrated in another mode by the text. Beside Michelet, Meredith gives the lie to the antiassimilationist argument from species-difference because Césaire can make European cultural riches his own, the basis for his own figuration of what must happen for "action and creation" to occur.

This Meredith is none other than George Meredith, the English Victorian novelist and poet probably best known for *The Egoist* (1879) and "The Lark Ascending" (1881). Césaire's text points us to a relatively obscure Meredith work of 1856, *The Shaving of Shagpat*.[13] This early novel is a hybrid arabesque fable set in a mythic Persia and telling the story of a protagonist, Shibli Bagarag, whose task is to shave the head of a certain Shagpat. Shagpat's extensive head of hair contains a single power-hair that holds the people of the city and surrounding areas in thrall and illusion. Césaire picks up on this motif of a magical hair that detours people from knowing themselves, and generalizes it to the Black Youth, whom he makes Meredith address in the *Étudiant Noir* text. The metaphor of cutting the power-holding hair is forceful, having a biblical resonance (Samson) as well as a field of possible connotations involving castration. Yet this figure remains mostly illegible unless the reader unravels it with actual knowledge of Meredith's novel (Césaire does not explain the power of the hair but alludes to the Meredith work as if it is preunderstood). It is possible that Césaire was imagining a small and perhaps very specific constituency for this piece of writing, one that consisted of Paulette Nardal, for instance, who had not only studied English literature but may have supplied Césaire with this very reference to Meredith.[14] As with all avant-garde statements, its coding is restricted, quasi-private, at the same time as making gestures of address to a shapeless, phantasmatic larger public (black students and those who would seek to assimilate them, thus "France" or "Europe" in a larger sense). As a published writing and not a private communication, "Jeunesse noire" is also destined for those for whom "Meredith" is not immediately decipherable. The short screed, bursting with avant-garde imperatives as it ends, impels the reader into following the lines of its own incompletion toward the ragged edge of a seam joining other material that countervails its emphatic avant-garde stress on the cleared ground and the new beginning.

The avant-garde gesture is clearest with the imperatives "*tondez-vous au ras, . . . rasez-vous*," "crop yourselves close, . . . shave yourselves" (1293). The *ras* and *rasez* evoke the tabula rasa, the writing surface scraped clean for a new beginning that is one of the key motifs of literary modernity and its unending gallery of primitivisms.[15] Meredith's novel is both ground and illustrative example for the imperatives to struggle against, to cut out, the forces in the self that hold it in thrall of illusory promises (*nègreries* of assimilation *and* of absolute difference). But if we also take *nègreries* as manifesto/manifestation, then this first installment of the black dream-work has been a showing, a display—of its scenography of wounds. What remains of "black youth" after it has been torn up between identity and animal difference? It manifests here, with razor *and* seams, the cultural shreds with which it has patched something together. An embarrassing exposure of the lesions left by an institution that combines the imperative of assimilation (absolute translatability) with that of racist purism (absolute untranslatability). Perhaps this echoes the old artistic tradition of *ostentatio vulnerum* (the displaying of wounds), to which the black student obviously had no "right."[16] But this is a *nègrerie*, after all.

❖ ❖ ❖

Between "Jeunesse noire" and the *Cahier*, one more *nègrerie* survives: "Conscience raciale et revolution sociale" (Racial consciousness and social revolution), published in the only other edition of *L'Étudiant Noir* that has so far come to light.[17] Space does not permit a detailed account of this important link in a possible chain of black modernist dream-scenes. Let us just say, summarily, that this rich, allusive, and typically grandiose text attempts to deconstitute the desire of "black revolutionaries" for whom the agenda of revolution is overly entangled with the values of assimilation and the "mechanical identification of races" (1299). In the apodictic and imperative (manifesto) tone that characterized "Jeunesse noire," Césaire demands that before entering into a revolutionary process programmed from elsewhere by others, blacks work on the self (*soi*) as the precondition for revolutionary work. "We must not be revolutionaries accidentally negro [*nègres*], but properly revolutionary negroes, and the accent should be placed as much on the substantive as on the qualifier" (1299). The "invisible nets" of a white culturation, civilization, morality (the general field of an *enseignement* and education) will remain even if the realm of sensible, material oppressions is attacked. Epistemic change, a change of mind-sets, knowledge, and consciousness, must precede unexamined and precipitate entry into a revolutionary activity that is not yet adequately understood. Otherwise, blacks will remain self-infantilized *ass-milés*, playthings or pawns of a predicament they cannot comprehend, gnawed at by an "evil" or "sick" (*mal*) denial of self whose lame alibi is that "it has nothing to say" because it is already spoken by a culture to which it has assimilated (1298).

This *nègrerie* thus dreams of a displacement of revolutionary struggle—for blacks at least—onto the terrain of culture, which is itself a task of re-forming the "natural substance" of the self (1298). There is little that is specifically Marxist about Césaire's sense of "the Revolution" here, beyond an avant-garde celebration of revolt, a "destructive groundswell and not the shaking of surfaces" (1299). To ask for more would be to mis-recognize its (strange and invented) genre, the *nègrerie*, and its corre-spondingly apodictic mode of address.

"Conscience raciale" has been made significant because it seems to be the place where the word *négritude* first appeared in print. While this is clearly an important event, I suspect that claims that it drastically rewrites the story of the "birth" of Négritude or discloses its "Marxist . . . origins" are overstated.[18] Here, *négritude* names the quality of black specificity that should not be sacrificed for a "revolution" that merely instrumentalizes blacks and redoubles their racial subjection. The imperative is to "plant our négritude like a lovely tree so that it can bear its most authentic fruits," and the piece's obsessive return to the question of (re)discovering authen-ticity of the "self" (*soi*) brings it into proximity with the concerns of our previous *nègrerie* (1299). Césaire's extraordinarily complex relationship with Communism is already manifest here, and the *nègrerie*'s dream-articulation calls attention to lacunae in Marxist theory and practice of the time (cultural formation of the subject, race, and racism). It makes sense, then, within the cultural and especially *literary* avant-garde modal-ity of the *nègrerie*, that the primary instances and examples are themselves literary. There is no significant engagement with any actual communist or Marxist text or practical example. Césaire chooses to make a point about complicities between communist revolutionaries, racial assimilationism, and imperialism by allusion to "Le tzar noir" (Black tsar), a short work of political science fiction by Paul Morand in which, thanks to the revolu-tionary but *assmilé* Occide, "Haiti has its Soviets [and] Port-au-Prince becomes Octoberville" (1299).[19] Morand depicts an indigenous vanguard run wild: a bizarrely primitivized Soviet model of dictatorship displacing the American occupation of the island. For Césaire, the allegorically named dictator Occide is the model of the "sterilely imitative monkey" that blacks are condemned to be if they remain caught in "official white culture, the 'spiritual rigging' of conquering imperialism" of east or west (1300). The *nègrerie*'s literary illustrations come from Charles Dickens's Gradgrind and G. K. Chesterton, while the repeated phrase "nous autres" ("nous autres exploités noirs, . . . nous autres nègres," we others exploited blacks . . . we other *nègres*) evokes Valéry (1298–99).[20] We must acknowledge that for Senghor and Césaire, the quest for racial justice and a refigured "human universal" within a generally socialist discursive field was compelled often to draw its conceptual and figurative resources from thinkers far more readily associated with "conservative" or right-wing currents than from those of the left.[21] This is no doubt because the former addressed racial, cultural, regional, and "civilizational" difference rather more explicitly than contemporary writers in the Marxist/socialist camp, who generally tended to suppress such differences in the attempt to construct an abstract collectivity of class.

In a further displacement within the sign-systems of the *enseignement-*apparatus, the clamorous dream-scream of the student *nègrerie* gives way, toward the end of the 1930s, to a concern for what lies below the purview of the metropolitan diploma student's place in the machine. This in two senses: first, what underlies the formal screen of the educational apparatus of secondary and tertiary levels (the scenography of elementary instruction); and second, who and what is silenced or drowned out by the vociferous protest of the activist metropolitan student (in 1939 it is the island subaltern, and later a more worldwide group of oppressed figures).

◈   ◈   ◈

Césaire's *Cahier d'un retour au pays natal* (Notebook of a return to the native land, 1939–56) dramatizes and formalizes an untimely "return" to the colonial primary school and the child's face-to-face with its classroom materials. The persistent formal and rhetorical patterning of this return traverses the palimpsest of edits and augmentations that Césaire made to the poem between 1939 and 1956, continuing to inflect the significant aesthetic and ideological changes undergone by the *Cahier* after the World War ended, the great wave of decolonization broke, and the fractured binarism of the Cold War began to play out. Given the interwar focus of this book, however, I remain primarily with the version from 1939 as it was published in the avant-garde literary journal *Volontés*.[22]

General critical consensus holds that the *Cahier* stages the making and unmaking of a subject, thematically legible as "the struggle, symbolic death and spiritual birth of the hero of Négritude" as prophet, leader or messiah of his people, or rhetorically legible as "the violent alienation of the subject through language, the radical recuperation of that subject by an active transformation of that language."[23] At the thematic level, an oracular voice instantiates the universalizable collectivity of négritude. The poem's speaker must come to "accept . . . totally, without reservation" (*entièrement, sans réserve*) a shared birth with *this* island people, "my race," so that he can finally say "US" (*NOUS*) possibilizing from this base the formation of the dispersed generality of négritude's collectivity (45, 55). The rhetorical critical current observes the many ways in which Césaire's *Cahier* destabilizes this thematic articulation of the speaker's relation to his people or race.[24] The *Cahier* is clearly deeply invested in the figure of the prophetic (anticolonial) leader-figure, shot through with the biblical rhetoric that permeated Césaire's environment as a young person, the grandiose and liberating civilizationism of Frobenius and Spengler that he discovered as a student in Paris, and the terrifying shadows of the populist leaders that sprang up everywhere in Europe in the 1920s and 1930s.[25] These elements—and more besides—are also identifiable in other anticolonial currents of the period, and such connections have been documented for the *Cahier*.

Additionally, Césaire's *Cahier* offers an unsettling staging of the child's innocent encounter with—and investment of—the pedagogical elements of the French colonial classroom. In particular, an ingenuous cathexis of the French schoolbook, the *cahier*, its formal exercises, illustrative pictures, and thematic topics. This staging of the pre-text of the protesting metropolitan student introduces the irreducible complication, for a postcolonial politics, of complicity (being folded together-with) with what is subsequently opposed or resisted. Rather than neutralize any future politics of the postcolony, Césaire's literary traversal of the lines and creases of the fold would open a certain space for imagining (if not solving in practice) some of the tormenting predicaments of achieving a postcolonial reality. Césaire would elaborate this gesture aesthetically, with more concretion but rather less focus on *enseignement*, in his subsequent dramatic work (especially in the plays *The Tragedy of King Christophe* and *A Season in the Congo*).[26] Frantz Fanon, Césaire's student, picks up this relay throughout *The Wretched of the Earth* (1963). In the chapter on national consciousness—possibly the most significant of the book—Fanon writes of the "making human" (*rendre humain*) of a people ruined by colonial depradation, the traumas of violent struggle, and the burgeoning neglect of its "leaders."[27] In other words, Fanon here makes his most vivid effort to imagine possibilities for coming *post*colonial societies. "Being responsible in an underdeveloped country is knowing that everything rests definitively on the education of the masses, on the elevation of thinking, and on what is too quickly called civic instruction [*la politisation*]" (138/187). As he underlines the centrality of education, Fanon immediately evokes Césaire: "Now, civic instruction is opening the mind [*l'esprit*], awakening the mind [*l'esprit*], putting the mind in the world [*mettre au monde l'esprit*]. It is, as Césaire said, 'inventing souls.'"[28] This process of "politicization," which clearly exceeds the sense of instrumentalizing thought for a narrowly political end, rests on *educative* work on spirit and soul.

"We, at the conjuncture we are in, we are the *propagators of souls*, the multipliers of souls, and at the limit, *the inventors of souls*," says Césaire in the speech from 1959 to which Fanon alludes ("L'homme," 118, Césaire's emphases). Césaire acknowledges, without naming names, that the formulae here are displacements of Stalin: "some have been able to say that the writer is an engineer of souls."[29] In a more extended discussion, we would have to account for the displacement from engineering souls for a Socialist imperium to propagation, multiplication, and invention of souls for the other "universal humanism" envisioned as the future of the other "colonized peoples" (122).

The speech is possibly Césaire's most powerful thematic avowal of cultural vanguardism, assigning to cultural producers the task of being the collective short circuit of breakout from and rupture with colonialism into freedom. On the one hand, *"decolonization is not automatic"* but is the "result of a struggle, . . . of a pressure"; on the other, decolonization is necessarily transitionless destruction, extirpation, "ripping out of the roots" (*arracher les racines*) of the entire colonial apparatus (119–20). A double imperative: decolonization must be worked for from within the colonial situation and it must be an immediate liberation achieved without transition. Colonialism negates the very resources that would be able to undo it: "slavery cannot be a school of liberty, colonialism cannot be a school of independence" (116, 120, Césaire's emphasis). The notion of an "apprenticeship in independence," leading the oppressed through *"necessary stages"* is a colonial alibi for transition without end, ultimately leaving the *"master and servant, . . . creator and consumer"* hierarchy in place (119, 118, Césaire's emphases). It is artistic creation that conducts the short circuit of this double bind, enacting the transition without transition that will open a future world. Thus, no *collective* transition, preparation, or "apprenticeship" in liberty for the colonized except for the vanguard work of the "man of culture" already toiling *within* colonial space, who "must make his people *do without the apprenticeship in liberty . . .* because in the colonial situation itself, creative cultural activity, going in advance of collective concrete experience, is already that *apprenticeship*" (120, Césaire's emphases). Awesome responsibility of an aesthetic education, as well as a kind of disavowal of that responsibility into faith in the power of art alone to develop and formalize the preexisting but amorphous and "immediate" "national sentiment" of the people into a "consciousness" (117). If the impoverished popular "sentiment . . . contains in advance the entire cultural rebirth [*renaissance*]," the task of art is to "find it, magnify it," make of "sentiment" a contour-defining and phenomenalizing "radiant sun" of consciousness (117). In a pedagogy without pedagogy, the people's sentiment must be made into what it already essentially is by the "creative" agency of the vanguard man of culture.

Fanon will subtly question this vanguardism over the length of *The Wretched of the Earth*, contextually altering and cumulatively qualifying the meaning of the phrase *sans transition* (without transition). His phenomenology of decolonization unravels the phantasmatic apparition of the rupture of decolonization. At first: "It is a total, complete, absolute substitution, without transition" (WTE 1/39). This apparently immediate reversing rupture is the great point of the first paragraph that presents violence as the "phenomenon" of "national liberation" (1/39). Yet each time the phrase *sans transition* is repeated in the book, it is more qualified, more legible as sustaining phantasm, until

> this spectacular voluntarism that understood itself leading the colonized people to absolute sovereignty in one fell swoop turns out in experience

to be a very great weakness. As long as he imagined being able to pass *without transition* from a colonized state to the state of sovereign citizen of an independent nation; as long as he assumed the mirage of the immediacy of his muscles, the colonized did not realize real progress on the path of knowledge.[30]

Césaire negotiates a simultaneous denial of and need for transition by filling the rupture with the work of a cultural vanguard that will achieve—aesthetically—the transition in advance and prepare the ground for the collective rupture of liberation that annuls the necessity of transition. He thereby does not quite fall prey to Fanon's "mirage of . . . immediacy," because the cultural vanguard remains as placeholder for the work—the transition-in-advance—of preparing a future world. Fanon's revision of the Césairian position is rather to agree that decolonization is not automatic but to doubt that the transitionless transition and the invention of souls can be accomplished by means of cultural vanguardism and a newly "*sacred art*" alone ("L'homme," 121, Césaire's emphasis). Césaire's *Cahier*, too, brushes against the grain of the poet-politician's more programmatic statement. Returning to the classroom, it formalizes the multiplication, propagation, invention of souls, the formation of the ordinary as well as the cultural vanguard within the colonial apparatus, and the intimation that "to utilize . . . the colonial structures" *in some way* may itself be an unavoidable condition of the desired "rupture" that would "smash the colonial structures in a definitive way."[31]

❖   ❖   ❖

Regarding one way of discerning formalization and the work of the vanguard, Renée Larrier has proposed that "literacy, often considered an individual achievement, brings with it, according to Césaire, a reciprocal responsibility, that is, its beneficiaries should function as '*la bouche des malheurs qui n'ont point de bouche*'" (the mouth of calamities that have no mouth).[32] This reading, apparently compatible with the expressive and formative task of the "Man of Culture," combines the staging of the production of a leader-subject with the question of *enseignement*. The quotation supporting Larrier's claim is drawn from Césaire's *Cahier*, and its deployment is symptomatic of readings of the poem that extract sympathetic but unmediated political or thematic points from it with insufficient attention to their staging. In this case, the sentence "My mouth shall be the mouth of calamities" (17) appears as a fragment of direct speech in the *Cahier*, under the sign of the conditional. The speaker announces, of his supposed "return," that "I would arrive [*je viendrais*]. . . . I would say [*dirais*] to this land of mine. . . . I would say [*dirais*]: / 'My mouth shall be the mouth of those calamities that have no mouth'" (17). In other words, this and related statements (again in direct speech), such as "if all I can do is speak, it is for you I shall speak" (17), are presented as something that *would* be done and said, articulating a specific kind of desire. The poem does not necessarily question the force and validity of this desire, but its conditional staging still must be taken into account. Rather, the scenography of this section, governed by a *"partir"* (to leave, 17), dramatizes a self caught in its own righteous yet unexamined benevolence toward its fellows. The conditional verbal mode tells us that the statements signify a grandiose wish to be a spokesman rather than a clear imperative to representative responsibility by the literate and educated. Indeed, the desire to speak-for could just as easily accommodate the structural denial of articulacy or literacy in those for whom one speaks. Yet it cannot be argued that it is lack of literacy that makes the *Cahier*'s Antillean crowd so "chattering and mute [*bavarde et muette*]" (5); nothing in the poem sanctions a reading that would allow us to say that it is about literacy as such. This would be epistemologically almost meaningless, and indeed one could as easily argue that the *Cahier* questions the value of merely functional literacy: bad education.[33] These first sections of the *Cahier* stage extreme affects of horror and justified anger as an educated subject, full of benevolent will-to-lead "returns" to a milieu of fellows whom he can barely recognize as *semblable*. The exact status of the "return" is ambiguous. Something very much at stake for any reading of Césaire's *Cahier*, therefore, is deciding what its speaker's relation is to the desire to speak-for; but this decision cannot be approached without closer consideration of the poem as a formal construction beyond its existence as a collection of thematic statements or phenomenological descriptions.

While Larrier's account does not establish a convincing link between Césaire's *Cahier* and French colonial education, the possibility of this connection remains worth exploring. In "Orphée noir," his famous introduction to Senghor's anthology of new black and Malagasy poetry in French, Sartre argued for a paradox: the French language was not foreign to the

Négritude poets, nor was it a proper vehicle by which they could express themselves.[34] "The herald of the black soul," writes Sartre, "has gone through white schools" (ON xv/20). Thus, the white school plays a part in forming the black vanguard—its "heralds," "evangelists," "prophets," and "partisans"—precisely by splitting them from the mass of blacks that they will represent and for whom they are enjoined to speak (xv/20). Entering into a certain continuity with metropolitan culture, the partisans experience a racist repudiation by it. The dialectical movement engendered by this double "shock of white culture" forces the poet to pass from "immediate existence to the reflected state . . . split [dédoublé]" into non-self-coincidence (xv/20). This split makes Négritude representable, but only in the mode of an inadequation of the language available to speak it. The ultimate trajectory will be to "return" to "his existential unity as a negro, . . . the original purity of his project, . . . to origins, . . . [to] coincidence with himself in négritude" (xxiii/29). We have already seen the extent to which Césaire's, Damas's, and Senghor's earliest writings exceed this kind of summary. Sartre portrays Négritude as a poetic/political project to overcome "the alienation that a foreign thinking [pensée étrangère] imposes upon [the black man] in the name of assimilation" (xxiii/29). One or other variety of primitivism is unavoidable here: either the poet must enact an Africanist culturalism ("allowing himself to be fascinated by primitive rhythms, letting his thoughts run in traditional forms of black poetry") so that these African "echoes" will "come to awaken timeless instincts sleeping within him," or else he takes the "subjective" option of an excavation of the primordial self so as to "descend below words and meanings" and touch a precultural "Nature" (xxiv/29; xxv/30). The first option obliges the black poet to simulate the cultural surface of an essentialized Africa, assuming the real thing will return from within the subject's crypt; the second obliges him to identify himself with Nature.

The black poet "must have recourse to the words of the oppressor" so that

> when the negro declares in French that he rejects French culture, he accepts with one hand what he rejects with the other; he installs in himself the enemy's thinking-machine [appareil-à-penser], like a grinder. This would not matter: but at the same time, this syntax and vocabulary,

forged in another time and in far off places to answer other needs and to designate other objects, are unsuitable [*impropres*] to furnish him with the means to speak of himself.

(xviii/23)

Sartre continues: "It is not true, however, that the black man expresses himself in a 'foreign' language, since he is taught French from a young age and since he is perfectly at ease there when he thinks as a technician, scholar, or politician. It would rather be necessary to speak of a faint [*léger*] and constant discrepancy [*décalage*] that separates what he says from what he would like to say, whenever he speaks of himself" (xix/24).

The language of expression is not foreign, yet it introduces a particular discrepancy between signification and what the speaker or writer wants to say, such that "if he abruptly pulls himself together, gathers himself and steps back, there are the words [*vocables*] lying *in front of him*, strange, half signs and semi things [*à moitié signes et choses à demi*]" (xix/24, Sartre's emphasis). Here the argument intersects with a more general modernist argument about poetic language, wherein the nontransparency, and consequent failure, of language-as-prose engenders the poetic experience as such; the language-system appears as a stuttering mechanism of aborted indexicality ("*pour indiquer dans la vide*"), and the poet insists on "making words mad" (*rendant les mots fous*) so as to utter the unutterable (Sartre calls this mode of speech "silence") in the ab-use of language.[35] Making language demented to the point of "autodestruction" is a "goal" of modern French poetry, and thus the specific problematic of Négritude coemerges with other modern poetry (xx/25). The language of Négritude is based on a hierarchized binary opposition (its type case being the opposition between black and white) that is communicated through the education system. The action Sartre singles out as the definitive poetic act is "reversing the hierarchy" (*renverser l'hiérarchie*) all the while working from within the French language (xxii/26).[36]

Without saying it in so many words, Sartre argued for the uncanniness (*Unheimlichkeit*) of French. It is alien *as* nonalien. In Sartre's schema this discrepancy of the language with itself, installed in the subject by the experience of French schooling, opened up the necessity of violently attacking and de-forming it, making it aphasic precisely so it could speak. Sartre concludes by quoting two lines from Césaire's "Les armes miraculeuses" (collected in the anthology), evoking a "great negro shout" (*grand cri nègre*) that will shake the world's foundations (xliv/52). He depicts the unmediated black voice—prefigured in poetic expression—as the force of negation that will destroy the values sustaining a hierarchical opposition between whites and blacks in the world.

While an influential strand of Césaire interpretation has (undialectically) followed one side of Sartre by reading the *Cahier* as dramatizing the assumption of a stable and powerful voice of black identity, a more convincing group of readings has underlined complexities and ambivalences in the poem's framing of problems of identification, messianic or prophetic utterance, speaking-for, testimony, history, and memory. It is not that the poem has some discernible aim of disabling political action, but it nevertheless deconstitutes and questions the fantasy of a transformative collective "*cri*," a shout of protest and negation that would simultaneously be an attestation of a new identity. Showing that the *Cahier* dramatizes the vicissitudes and difficulties of a desire for voice, such readings still often conclude on a redemptive note, ultimately endorsing the Sartrean interpretation of the speaker's dialectical passage through negation toward a "total identification with his people" that is formally accomplished through a tripartite sectional division in the poem.[37] The *Cahier* is taken to be a peculiarly expressed type of bildungsroman, a story of the dialectical growth of the consciousness of a colonized subject as he moves toward the possibility of collective emancipation in the name of humanity itself. Readings such as that of James Clifford, who further develops the "ambivalence" position, move outside the simplified one-two-three dialectical framework. Commenting on the poem's final neologism *verrition*, Clifford writes that "the poem 'stops' on a coinage. Césaire's great lyric about finding a voice, about returning to native ground, strands us, finally, with a made-up, Latinate, abstract-sounding question mark of a word."[38] Clifford's reading poses the problem especially clearly by suggesting that the *Cahier* "strands" its reader in a paradox of identity and disidentity.[39] Similarly, Brent Hayes Edwards reads the aporia of the final phrase ("*immobile verrition*") as an "insistence on founding collectivity on paradox, on antithesis without sublation."[40] He relates this to a consideration of the *Cahier*'s formal organization (especially anaphora) and concludes that "it may be that a Césairean poetics of anaphora, in delivering the possibility of infinite requalification and extension inherent in serial form, thereby forecloses the possibility of *any* ultimate term, any dialectical synthesis" (15).

Anaphora—the repetition of a word or phrase at the beginning of successive clauses—defines an insistent series of refrainlike terms that *textually* instantiate points of "return" suggested in the title of the poem (*retour*). Each strophe, however, is completed differently. Edwards rightly suggests that anaphoras seem repeatedly to restart the poem even as the intervals between them shorten in an intensified rhythmic movement toward the end.[41] This constantly figured restarting works against the sense of a sequential or dialectical progression, and structurally the poem appears as much an accretion of obsessive returns to an originary scene of writing as it appears the staging of a self-transformative spiritual quest. Anaphora carries back, returns, repeats. It is repetition of "the same" thing; but each time it inaugurates a different clausal extension, some different way of completing, extending, or qualifying the anaphoric phrase. Thus the phrase *au bout du petit matin* (At the end of daybreak) repetitively instantiates the first strophes of the *Cahier* and repeats like a signature or tattoo across the space-time of the poem.[42]

As the *au bout*s fade out toward the middle of the poem, other words and phrases come to function anaphorically. If one of the poem's developments is that the speaker can come, momentarily, to say "US," displacements occur between the anaphoras. The *Cahier* begins with many repeated *au bout*s, signifying the edge, end, or outer limit of "first light [*petit matin*]," and this is associated with a serial imagery of flatness and inertia. By the *Cahier*'s penultimate strophe, *au bout* has become *debout*, upright or standing, in thirteen anaphoric repetitions (52–55). The imagery— of a mobile, active, upright "nigger scum" (*négraille*) on board a ship—is woven into a cumulative strand of figures of erection and verticality. It is almost as if the poem tracks the slow motion rising of a phallus—and thus that achieved erection would be its implicit emblem of transformation. But what is also crucial here is that, for the poem, "change" is figured through a displacement in a sign-chain of prepositions: from *au* to *de*, each inclined differently to a *bout*. The attachment of preposition and noun between *au bout* and *debout*, the closure of the space between them, accelerates the poem's climaxing rhythmic pulse. At the same time, the ability to discern the preposition's separation from (or attachment to) the noun was exemplary of the kind of orthographic exercise central to modernized French education. The figuration of "change," therefore, is also the poeticized iteration of an elementary grammar exercise. Its site of practice for the child was a *cahier*.

❖ ❖ ❖

The poem's title asks us to understand that it represents its scene of writing as a *cahier*. It designates the pages you turn as (the representation of) some sort of notebook, written and being read; it would be even plausible to take this literally: the semantic field of *cahier* is broad enough to accommodate the sense that each copy of the poem book *is* itself a *cahier*, which is not an entirely unfamiliar type of poetic conceit or device. This impels the reader to a question: Is the *Cahier* the record of a return (representation of an antecedent event or returning), or is the writing (and ever-renewed present reading) of it the return itself, back to a scene of meaning-making? Or both? In this dilemma, true for all texts perhaps, but exemplarily posed by our *Cahier*, reading "returns" to something that does not preexist it. The text is a wager on (or dream of) the institution or production of a reader capable of making its "return" each time anew—institution as *teaching* or *training* that reader, without guarantee of success. Dream of a new *enseignement* for which, as with every new curriculum, a *cahier* will be necessary.

❖ ❖ ❖

It is surprising that in the many interpretations of the *Cahier d'un retour au pays natal*, little attention has been paid to the *Cahier* of its title. What is the general meaning of the word *cahier*? Its etymology is Latinate, *quaterni* (by fours or in fours) generally denoting a four-piece unit or set. The *quaer, quoyer, queer,* or *cayer* of Old French meant a small book produced by folding four sheets of parchment in two so as to make eight leaves.[43] This etymological sense is cognate with the English noun *quire*, which denotes a similar gathering of sheets. The word thus indicates paper, gathered and folded in a particular way, so as to form a surface for writing or printing, something with a higher level of organization and institutionality than scraps or loose sheets. Hence, in French, the now much more generalized usage of the term *cahier* for notebook, composition book, or exercise book. Anyone who has been in a French schoolroom in the last hundred years or so will know that the commonest referent for the noun *cahier* is the bound exercise books used by students. The *cahier* is the gathered surfaces upon which the student writes out answers and compositions, and performs exercises in orthography, grammar, arithmetic, drawing, and so on. It is the companion of the *manuel scolaire* (textbook). There is also the teacher's *cahier du maître* that contains lesson plans and exercises. While the word *cahier* is not limited to these significations, they are the most general and—as I will show—the most apropos for Césaire's poem. A *cahier* can of course signify the book in which one writes a diary or a travel journal, and existing translations and critical accounts of the poem's title appear to treat it as such: the dramatized or poeticized record of a personal journey. Maryse Condé's interesting appraisal of the *Cahier* suggests that it traces the "itinerary" of a young intellectual's return to the Antilles and his discovery there of an antiparadise. This provokes an act of rememoration, a staging of memory in which he recalls "all of his childhood and youth," and ultimately comes to a "total identification with his people and his race" attained by acceptance of their condition as "the starting point of revolt."[44] The *cahier* is here implicitly understood as the (journal-like) place in which this itinerary is registered: the "return to the native land" is recorded in a *cahier*, and this in turn becomes preparation for an extratextual act of revolt. Condé reads the poem within the generic strictures of the bildungsroman, although her overall analysis shows how it transgresses those strictures.

On a contiguous track, both Eshleman and Smith and Rosello and Pritchard translate *cahier* as "Notebook." The first English translation, by Lionel Abel and Yvan Goll, renders the title somewhat freely as "Memorandum on My Martinique." In a commentary on the poem, Gregson Davis proposes "Journal of a Homecoming," giving the title a chronicle-like sense. John Berger and Anna Bostock violently excise the word *cahier* from the title altogether ("Return to My Native Land").[45] Yet the heading under which the work is written casts its shadow over the poem's text and invites—or even demands—a reading or a response that accounts for it. Eshleman and Smith tentatively acknowledge that "the poet called this poem a 'notebook,' suggesting that it was notes of some sort as preparation for another finished work. . . . The poem . . . feels notational."[46] This indication of the poem's open-endedness, provisionality, or incompleteness is useful as a general caution against monolithic readings. However, the authors do not examine how the *Cahier*'s "nonnarrative" and "nongrammatical" elements do any more than give this sense of the notational. Likewise, Gregson Davis writes that "*Cahier* (literally 'exercise book, notebook') suggests a project that is incomplete, if not sketchy, and furnishes a clue to its experimental character, which is congruent with the history of its successive alterations."[47] Summarizing several of these themes, Wilder writes that the title "connotes both a documentary ambition and an improvisational attitude, . . . the notebooks carried by journalists, investigators, and ethnographers who bore witness, recorded field notes, and produced firsthand accounts of colonial realities through rational discourse" (*French Imperial Nation-State* 279, 282). While Wilder rightly finds that the *Cahier* is both "deploying and parodying the notebook-form" (282), in the remainder of his reading he does not explore why this might be significant, and what role the "notebook-form," as *form*, might play for the poem.[48]

If, as I propose, the *Cahier* returns (us) in some way to the scene of the Antillean classroom, what is the general order of that classroom? The discernible tensions animating representations and discussions of school in the Antilles are undoubtedly determined by the form, power, and significance of the French education system in Caribbean society. This apparatus contrasts with the contemporary setup in French West Africa. In principle, "the systems of education are . . . generally identical for DOMs, TOMs, and the *métropole*." Education has "provided the *entrée* to cultural and political life, and the school was the primary institution for the *francisation* of colonized peoples."[49] As we have seen in the discussion of Senghor, the educational systems of the continental African colonies and those of the *vieilles colonies* were roughly bifurcated along the lines of an attempt to "adapt" or Africanize education and an attempt to replicate the metropolitan system. In practice, even in the metropolis, the modern French education system did not fulfill its own principles. Yet there was a more marked discrepancy between metropole and old colony.

❖ ❖ ❖

Eugen Weber writes of the post-Ferry-reform era in France that "The school, notably the village school, compulsory and free, [may be] credited with the ultimate acculturation process that made the French people French—finally civilized them. . . . The schoolteachers in their worn, dark suits, appear as the militia of the new age, harbingers of enlightenment and of the Republican message that reconciled the benighted masses with a new world, superior in wellbeing and democracy."[50] It is a simplified picture, no doubt, but this cliché of the *hussards noirs de la République* does capture the way in which teachers and schools represented a vanguard of French modernization. There is a joke in the metaphor condensing the apparent opposites of the down-at-heel rural schoolmaster and the Hussar (the very type of the early-modern dashing and daredevil military man). Like all jokes, this one makes a serious point: its imagery creates an analogy with the military avant-garde. The Hussars were, after all, a vanguard military cavalry unit renowned for their speed and ability to make advance lightning strikes on enemy lines. You didn't live long if you were a Hussar in active service. By contrast, the modernizing *instituteur* fighting on the rural front in provincial France was a salaried (albeit poorly paid) employee of the State.[51]

In the metaphor comparing the flamboyant Hussar with the gray schoolmaster resides a displacement that recalls Michel Foucault's move from the spectacular theater of public execution to the technical workings of the panopticon in *Discipline and Punish*.[52] Harbored within the surface banality of a modernization process that is not outwardly spectacular lies a sublimated violence of the military strike, says the metaphor. It is surprising that Foucault never dedicated a volume or a lecture course to the school as a disciplinary institution.[53] Far more effective and diffused within the social fabric than the prison, the school was modernity's determining instrument of epistemic, bodily, and spatial reorganization. In an analysis relevant to the emergent construction of modern France, Louis Althusser would characterize the "educational apparatus" as the "dominant ideological State apparatus."[54] A system both obligatory and free, the system has "audience of the totality of children in the capitalist social formation, eight hours a day" (156).

Such a temporality articulates with what Althusser terms an "apprenticeship in a variety of know-how [*savoir-faire*]" that appears and is thought to be disinterested (and is indeed virtually indispensable) (156). For an example of the indispensable we need only recall that nineteenth-century French society confronted the vast and complex task of teaching all young people to read and write a difficult orthography, and largely succeeded in eradicating so-called functional illiteracy.[55] General—if not universal—functional literacy appears to be both condition and effect of an operative and modernized nation-state, and it would be hard to argue against literacy as a laudable pedagogical objective. However, this opens onto the question of what else "literacy" is supposed to be in practice; and this is why the question of literacy as such is inadequate for an analysis of Césaire's poetic politics and indeed Négritude in general. Literacy is an impoverished category in every sense, though as the imposition of French as a State language it is an important aspect of the construction of modern France. In 1863 around a quarter of the population did not speak French, and for a much larger number it was still an effortfully acquired second language.[56] Weber writes that 1863 was the *last* time a national survey was undertaken into the use of "patois" and "idiom." It was after the Revolution that linguistic nationalization became a significant State project, though its development goes back into the sixteenth century.[57] "Resistance to the Revolution was often interpreted by the revolutionaries as the result of linguistic force and form."[58] Brittany was a main center of resistance. In 1784 Jullien wrote to Robespierre that "the Bretons, bent under the yoke of feudalism for so long, are still too brutalized to perceive the benefits of the Revolution. . . . You could say they're a hundred years behind the Revolution."[59] As Daniel Guérin points out, a limit to linguistic and secularizing modernization was soon reached because it moved too fast: the undoing of centuries of oppression under a "yoke of feudalism" cannot be achieved only by closing the churches, hounding out the priests, and interdicting patois. One must ask: What happened instead of Jullien's hundred years of work to change "presuppositions, . . . habits, . . . crass ignorance" by this most enlightened of modern state-formations?[60] Nineteenth-century linguistic standardization was modernization on the run, quick fixes applied one after another as the emerging national school system raced to eradicate the regional patois with a functionalized single tongue.

André Chervel has shown that the specific innovative and modernized techniques by which literacy was installed in France appear as a coherent grammatical theory when they were installed as an ad hoc solution to a social problem.[61] Recodified French grammar was a social patch applied in order to make functional as many "illiterate" French children as possible in the shortest possible time. Chervel thus finds the ideological locus in the formation of a subject functionalized with a dysfunctionally "logical" grammar rather than in explicit moral didactics at the thematic level.

Chervel's argument augments that of Theodore Zeldin, who contends that the "heart of the new primary education developed by the Third

Republic was moral and civic training" aimed at civilizing the "dangerous classes."[62] While Zeldin is focused on the *content* of the moral lessons ("Alcohol is the Enemy" and so forth), he also shows that the early sermonlike transmission of such lessons was practically ineffective. This is not the level at which Althusser and Chervel suggest subject-formation takes place. Again, focus on superficial moral didacticism does not touch the key problems. Elaborating the Althusserian perspective in more historical detail, Chervel has argued that the epistemic intervention goes beyond the overt moral didacticism incorporated into classroom lessons: "The smallest dictation exercise, the smallest reading text, even the grammar examples, all entered into a huge program artfully combining 'formation' with indoctrination."[63] How this is so in practice remains to be seen. Though it is neither a smooth-running nor a mechanically deterministic apparatus, the system of formation-as-"reproduction" is broadly effective in arranging a socially functional organization of the heterogeneous epistemo-practical habits that Gramsci called "common sense."[64]

Faced with a classroom of "illiterate" children, teachers charged with teaching them orthographics developed a series of pedagogical techniques that displaced "grammar" as it was formerly understood. What Chervel terms "student grammar" or "school grammar" (*grammaire scolaire*) does not have a basis in the history of linguistic science, but emerged from the need to construct an easily teachable method, impersonally constructed through the aggregation of various teaching tricks (28). Developing a "functional" practice of language, the implicit argument of "student grammar" was that "the problems of orthography could be resolved upon a purely grammatical terrain, in terms of parts of speech and syntactic functions" (205). The agreement of the past participle with the auxiliary verb *avoir* (which had been a contingent convention of eighteenth-century prose) was raised to a syntactic principle, giving rise to a new grammatical logic that was constructed from unrepresentative examples. This arbitrarily selected rule of agreement in turn enabled a series of other rules turning on the grammatical status of the "adverbial" (*complément circonstantiel*), which opened grammatical terminology to a classification of the *functions* of words and propositions (171–81). While this may seem like an arcane point, Chervel elsewhere clarifies its epistemological significance in terms of the way modernized pedagogy institutionalizes an understanding (and practice) of language that makes it seem as if the experience of the sensory being is grammatized in the same way as language has been grammatized and systematized. "To seek the circumstantial is to seek the elements of experience within the enunciation [*énoncé*], and to attribute to them a grammatical characterization. . . . With the new academic grammar, it is the whole nature of the relationship between language and the real that changes."[65] It is as if language is split broadly into two categories: one that stands in for chunks of extralinguistic "experience" and another that designates the connections between them. It is hard to say whether common education is acting as poison or medicine here.

Chervel concludes that pedagogy was thereby transformed into the teaching of a functionalized notion of language according to syntactical principles that prepared the student to reproduce rules of agreement above all (and to separate out spelled words according to these functional principles). It was, he writes, the "reduction of orthographic problems to a type of algebra with two variables: parts of speech and functions in the statement. To spell well it is enough to recognize correctly the two elements and then apply the rules of orthographic construction" (153). This paradoxically resulted in an apparently more stimulating and liberal environment of language teaching. The child was encouraged to write its own texts (the composition exercise) as a development of ideas dictated in the classroom (166).[66] Yet an effect of this modernization was "the hijacking of grammar for utilitarian ends (10), resulting in, as Pierre Achard has put it, "phony exercises of schoolwork."[67]

The kind of language that emerges from this process is, according to Chervel, one that is akin to the learning of "weights and measures, arithmetic, and the rudiments of modern culture" (167). "Virtually indispensable" to life in a modern nation-state, as Althusser wrote; but also ideological inasmuch as it is placeholder for the "French language" as such, for the "objective realities of the language" (27). The self-representation of the French language is as a language of logic and reason, but practical pedagogy, oriented to maximize efficiency and speed of learning, produced a simulation of logic and reason that acted rather as damage-control against other kinds of "nonstandard" language use. In interrogating what correct "French" was constructed as, Chervel asks a question relevant to the problems of regional French languages (such as Breton) and also to the situation of Creole in the Antilles. How, he asks, do we "assess . . . the disappearance of regional languages and cultures that must be ascribed to passive effects of generalized French education?" (24). There is no easy answer.

The question is the matter of a substantial debate in the Antilles and beyond. In 1952, Fanon wrote of the displaced repetition of intrametropolitan center/periphery asymmetries as they appear in the difference between metropolis and colony: "in the Antilles, as in Brittany, there is a dialect and there is the French language."⁶⁸ Yet this analogy slides into asymmetry precisely to the extent that "the Bretons do not consider themselves inferior to the French. The Bretons were never civilized by the whites [le Blanc]" (12). It is for Fanon racialized colonial civilization that upsets the analogy and induces a kind of fetishization of "speaking French well"—which itself is a synecdoche for a tangle of colonial double binds (10). Fanon is doubtful about the likely future of Creole in the Antilles, endorsing Michel Leiris's judgment that as a class-specific idiom Creole will persist yet "become a relic of the past" (11).⁶⁹ In an important intervention into postcolonial studies, Derrida makes a point similar to Fanon's about "the language of the Metropole" as "the substitute for a mother tongue, . . . as language of the other."⁷⁰ "For the child from Provence or Brittany," writes Derrida, "there is surely an analogous phenomenon. Paris can always fill [assurer] the role of a metropolis and occupy that place for a provincial. . . . But the other, in this case, no longer has the same transcendence of the overthere [là-bas], the distancing of being-elsewhere [être-ailleurs], the inaccessible authority of a master who lives overseas [outre-mer]. There is a sea missing" (42–43/74). It is the overthereness that makes a difference here, seeming to engender an uncanny spectrality in its distanced intimacy: "The metropole, the Capital-City-Mother-Fatherland, the city of the mother tongue, there's a place that figured, without being a faraway land, near but far, not alien [étranger], that would be too simple, but strange [étrange], fantastic and fantasmal. At bottom I wonder if one of my first and most imposing figures of spectrality, spectrality itself, was not France" (42/73). Derrida immediately qualifies this spectrality to make it apply even to those who do consider themselves the most proximate subjects of a nation, suggesting that for the "most unsuspecting" of patriots too, the country or land (pays) is a "dreamland" (pays de rêve) (42/73).

That the colony represents a difference of degree and not kind will be an important matter for the Cahier of Césaire, which poses questions that prefigure Derrida's understanding of the intimate distance of the metropolitan *pays*. We find in Césaire, too, a spectralization, a rendering uncanny of the *pays natal* in the colonial classroom. The land of *birth* becomes available as a figure only in a certain separation from it. (Thus it can only ever be returned to; the return is originary.) It is this figuration that the *Cahier* dramatizes through its reenactment of elements of the colonial schoolroom, which becomes a universalizable figure of the schoolroom as such.

I have centered my discussion on questions of the transformation of French-language instruction in the nineteenth and twentieth centuries for two reasons. First because its grammar, in a broadly understood sense of a technique for speaking and writing French correctly, was a centerpiece of reform. Chervel has shown us that everything fell into place around a new theory of syntax and that "school grammar [*grammaire scolaire*]" represents "the set of grammatical 'knowledges' [*connaissances*] that school delivers to its public in its program of French language study."[71] The second reason, consequential upon the first, is that Césaire's syntactic and semantic play both engages and subverts the instrumentalized and utilitarian modality of the period's language instruction. Chervel shows us that the key methods of the new language instruction were formalized in exercises such as copying, dictation, spelling, error-correction, memorization of sequences with exceptions, definition, conjugation, synonyms and antonyms, and other pattern-drill-type rehearsals of variations (25 and passim). Moreover, a key aspect of the new pedagogy was its solicitation of the child's expressivity in compositional writings that supplemented mechanical exercises. Césaire draws upon this double repertoire as an inventory of elements so as to figure a repair of their instrumentality as tools for the construction of a constitutively limited epistemological range.

◆ ◆ ◆

The Republicans who held political power in Guadeloupe and Martinique from the beginning of the Third Republic dreamed of founding democracy in the islands. Their formula was the assimilation of the colonies to the Motherland, France. Under the ancien régime and prior to the abolition of slavery in 1848, the Antillean ruling class—the plantation owners and the *békés* (Caribbean-born white Creoles)—had sought autonomy from France. With the entry of *métis* and blacks into the structures of municipal government when universal male suffrage was declared, the texture of Antillean political society changed, and the Republican-allied groups "wanted France to put into practice the *assimilation* which it preached."[72] André Lucrèce argues that the fundamental objective for the emerging Martinican petit-bourgeoisie was "assimilation, political integration of Martinique as a French Overseas Department in the heart of the metropolis." School was a "means of civilizing a population that would deserve this integration," since religious instruction proved to be a much more limited means for inculcating French civilization.[73] The dream of political and economic freedom figured itself in terms of a full integration into the French State, and its means of assimilation for the actual subjects of the envisioned State was school.

Antillean schooling was consequently projected as that promoted by the Jules Ferry Laws, which, in France, instituted public, secular, free, compulsory primary education. Its ideological self-representation was as the school of the people, the school for all, the school of the Republic.[74] It contrasted with a secondary education reserved for the elites, up until the unification of these two school systems. As Sylvère Farraudière points out, there was a colonial discrepancy in the way in which the education system was actually put into practice in Martinique. Both Farraudière's *L'école aux Antilles françaises* and Joseph Jos's *La terre des gens sans terre* give historical documentation of the vicissitudes of establishing working educational institutions on the island.[75] Within the terms of Republicanism itself, of the three essential principles of the Jules Ferry laws it was only secularism that was fiercely defended. In the Antillean colonies before 1947, primary instruction was not compulsory except where the means existed (that is to say, in the urban milieu and in the occasional hamlet). Until then, school had been neither public, nor free, nor compulsory for the majority of the rural and hill population, which also constitutes the majority of the entire population. "Universal" schooling did not start in practice in the Antilles until the 1980s, a century after the Ferry Laws. Farraudière regards this colonial *décalage* as a betrayal of universalist Republican ideals in practice. However, the logic of this colonial discrepancy was something other than a betrayal of the highest ideals of the Republic. It stemmed also from the racial and cultural coding of a difference internal to the Republic that positioned the Antilles, like French West Africa, in terms of the "not-yet" grown up, of *minorité* or *Unmündigkeit*.

❖ ❖ ❖

I now extract the opening phrases of the *Cahier*'s first strophes in sequence. The ellipses represent the further elaboration of the strophes that in each case has been cut out here so as to illustrate the anaphoric pattern of repetition with variation.

Au bout du petit matin bourgeonnant d'anses frêles les Antilles qui ont faim
. . .
Au bout du petit matin, l'extrême, trompeuse desolée eschare
. . .
l'affreuse inanité de notre raison d'être
. . .
Au bout du petit matin, sur cette plus fragile épaisseur de terre
. . .
Au bout du petit matin, cette ville plate-étaleé trebuchée de bon sens,
. . .
Au bout du petit matin, cette ville plate-étalée . . .
. . .
Et dans cette ville inerte, cette foule criarde
. . .
Dans cette ville inerte, cette étrange foule
. . .
Dans cette ville inerte, cette foule désolée
. . .
Au bout du petit matin, cette ville inerte
. . .
Au bout du petit matin, le morne oublié,
. . .
Au bout du petit matin, le morne au sabot inquiet et docile—
. . .
Au bout du petit matin, l'incendie contenu du morne,
. . .
Au bout du petit matin, le morne accroupi devant la boulimi
. . .
Au bout du petit matin, le morne famélique[76]

The repetition of the phrase at the beginning of each strophe resembles a dystactically spaced series of repeated practice exercises in orthography, or an effortful composition exercise being started again and again at the speed of a learner.

The lone third strophe ("the dreadful inanity of our raison d'être"), quoted earlier in its entirety, may be read as reflecting on the horrifying compulsion to repeat such pattern drills—not because learning through repetition is bad in itself, but because in this case the completion of the drill is each time the writing of a deathscape. Repetition, variation, same-but-different panorama of abjection becoming visibilized each time with illumination of a rising sun—*au bout du petit matin*, "at the end of first light" (the translation here perhaps overemphasizes the

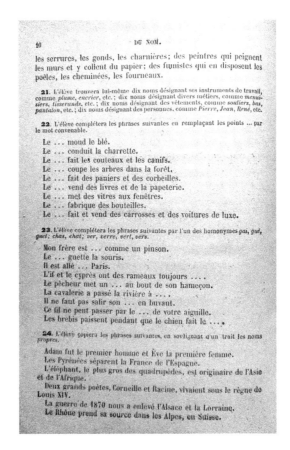

FIGURE 3.1 From Brachet and Dussouchet, *Grammaire française: Cours élémentaire* (Paris: Hachette, 1921).

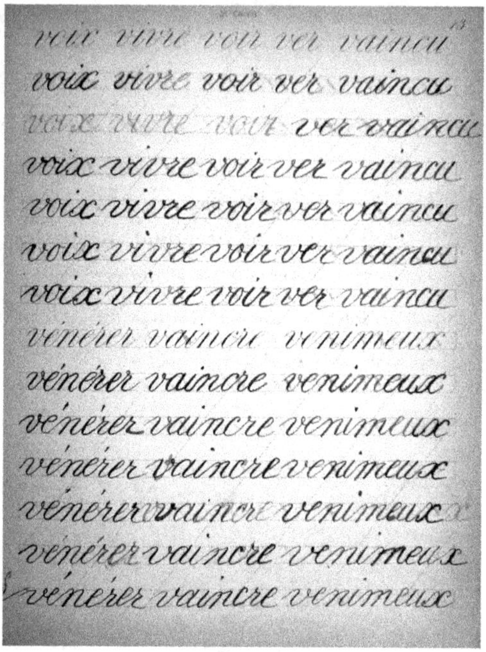

FIGURE 3.2 Page from primary schoolchild's *cahier*. Anonymous, French, c. 1920.

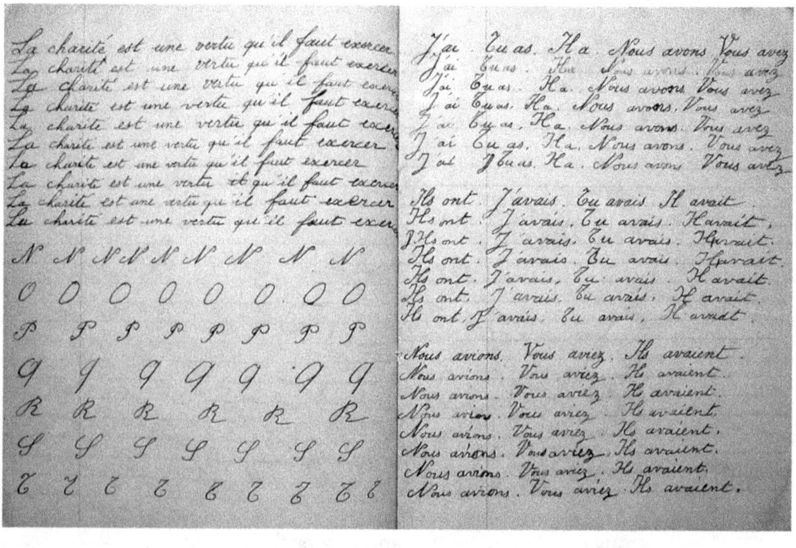

FIGURE 3.3 Page from primary schoolchild's *cahier*. Anonymous, French, c. 1920.

luminous coming of phenomenal day). Strophe 3 breaks the repetition/ variation pattern with a sort of aside. The "our" folds back upon the strophes themselves just as much as it names any "we" of the island; or rather, it underlines the tormented and tormenting relation between the performance of the drill and the possibility of an alliance that can say "our." How many are we?

The next significant break in the repetition/variation pattern— coming after the strophe that begins "Au bout du petit matin, le morne famélique"—gives a clear signal as to the poem's strategy: "And neither the teacher in his classroom, nor the priest at catechism will be able to get a word out of this sleepy little picaninny [négrillon]" (7). Recall that Althusser tells us that the education system is the apparatus that, within a certain European enclosure, displaces the church as modernity's predominant Ideological State Apparatus.[77] Teacher and priest, drummers-in of memory-exercises, fail to elicit a response from a child so hungry his brain does not work. Mind and body. The expression of the cognitive incapacity of the child, figured through an empty voice, echoes the short third strophe's reflection on the "inanity" of "our raison d'être": "c'est dans les marais de la faim que s'est enlisée sa voix d'inanition": it is in the swamps of hunger that his voice gets stuck from emptiness (or, because of the double genitive, "his voice of emptiness gets stuck").[78]

❖ ❖ ❖

Following each repetition/variation phrase, each strophe elaborates a descriptive imagery full of referential detail, thematizing a pathologized colonial island landscape:

> At the end of first light, the famished morne and no one knows better than this bastard morne why the suicide choked with a little help from his hypoglossal jamming his tongue backward to swallow it; why a woman seems to float belly up on the Capot River (her chiaroscuro body submissively organized at the command of her navel) but she is only a bundle of sonorous water.

> [Au bout du petit matin, le morne famélique et nul ne sait mieux que ce morne bâtard pourquoi le suicidé s'est étouffé avec complicité de son

hypoglosse en retournant sa langue pour l'avaler; pourquoi une femme semble faire la planche à la rivière Capot (son corps lumineusement obscur s'organise docilement au commandement de nombril) mais elle n'est qu'un paquet d'eau sonore.[79]]

With each of these strophes, the *Cahier* rehearses the student grammar sequence, proceeding from mechanically repetitive fill-in-the-gaps exercises to elaborated imaginative compositions. While this strophe does not contain the powerful motifs of disease and decay that prevail over this part of the poem, it condenses a number of other key themes of privation (the landscape itself as a metonymic body, starving), death, and muting. By choking himself with his own tongue the suicide has used the very instrument and metaphor of speech and language to kill himself, and this image relays a chain of motifs of silencing that includes an "aged silence bursting with tepid pustules" (3); "this town sprawled—flat, . . . mute" (3); "this squalling throng so astonishingly detoured from its cry, . . . detoured from its cry of hunger, of poverty, of revolt, of hatred, this throng so strangely chattering and mute" (3–5). The chain continues into the next strophe already discussed, which picks up the thematic of the schoolroom and the silent child. The suicide's turned-back tongue also brings us to the turns of "return" and a turning back on itself of language ("retournant sa langue")—figuring the swallowing, internalization, of a *langue* as a kind of suicide. Attempted assimilation as suicide. With bitter irony, the poem's speaker then states that the drowned woman, swollen and belly-up ("organized at the command of her navel") in a grotesque mimicry of pregnancy, is a "bundle of sonorous water" (4). Nonsensical sonority where the sign of natality should be emblematizes the speaker's relationship to the island's everyday wretchednesses.

In a pattern that recurs throughout the *Cahier*, the signifying chain from strophe to strophe is both linked and cut by the refrainlike mechanism of anaphoric repetition/variation. The "same" opening prepositional phrase, acting adverbially or adjectivally, is differed as it repeats in relation to the contents it modifies. As schoolbook exercises, all of the strophes would of course be wrong answers, mistakes. Finite verbs are missing, syntax is wild. But of course this is poetry. It is not meaningless word strings, nor is it referring verifiably or systematically to the schoolbook exercises to which I am trying to relate it. The grammatical incompletion of each anaphoric phrase promises meaning. "At the end of first light," "and," "Eia for," "my race," "upright," and so forth promise and solicit each time a meaningful completion that is fulfilled, but in a subverted way, by whatever composition follows them. Fulfillment in terms of thematic (political) content is the general material of Césaire interpretation for literary critics. Nesbitt's compelling political reading makes the *Cahier* a sort of literalization of the experience and overcoming of a colonial shame "primordial" to it through the power of an imaging of shameful experience. In reading the poem the reader must pass through the stages of consciousness described there because its words and images effect the same states in that reader.[80] "The production of (poetic) objects becomes productive in turn of consciousness" (129), and the "scene" of shame will "interpellate *every* reader" engendering a "poetic subject" that has "pass[ed] through the most desperate sense of shame" that emerges with the freedom to accept it (130).[81]

My question would be: Does a phenomenology of consciousness, no matter how poetically powerful, guarantee the interpellation of the reader such that she or he will pass through the process as represented? I would argue not, and suggest rather that the *Cahier* desediments originary scenes of interpellation in education—actually impossible to access as such—in terms of a poetic staging of returns to their scenographies. The poetic/literary work in general certainly solicits or tries to instruct its reader, and this process resembles what we understand as interpellation: each demands a countersignature given prior to some conscious act of consent by an intending subject. Recall that in interpellation, consent (" 'Yes; *it really is me!*' ... *recognition*") "happens" such that the becoming of an intending subject conscious of its "self" or "identity" derives from this underived but structural solicitation ("Ideology" 178). "Ideology has no history" (159–60). "I have had to present things in the form of a sequence," writes Althusser, "with a before and an after, and thus in terms of a temporal succession" (174). But this "theoretical theater" is a matter of exposition only; ideology has "always already interpellated individuals as subjects," "assigned" them as such in an impersonal classificatory system that makes possible subjective self-recognition (175, 177). The living "concrete individual" as trace becomes the subject as sign, meaningful as such to self and other. The entire phenomenological description of "hailing" is a means of (re)presenting this paradox of an always-already that is inscribed and practiced in unendingly repeated material "rituals of ideological recognition, which guarantee for us that we are indeed concrete, individual, distinguishable and (naturally) irreplaceable subjects" (172–73).

Interpellation does not happen just once and for all; it is an event constantly "reproduced" below the level of the intending subject and in ever-renewed ways (152). The fact that this happens in a material-ideological field fissured by struggle makes it possible for the artist, among others, to purloin its resources and represent (with) them. It is possible that exemplary or exceptional kinds of representation or statement stall the autodenegatory aspect of the ideological process as it is described by Althusser, to the extent that it becomes legible in ways analogous to his "theoretical theater."[82] Through competence or incompetence or the invention of new competences (these terms are clearly inadequate, but what to do?), the literary work dredges up and sets out the elements, signs, materials of an ideological process. There is an analogue here with what Sartre described as the writer discovering "words [vocables] lying in front of him, strange, half signs and semi things" (ON xix/24). The chance of literature; its space of enseignement, for better and worse.

The point of the new "student grammar" was instruction in the use of language as a sign-system (almost an algebra, according to Chervel's critique) for making meaning. The pedagogy's operative presupposition is that language is a system that makes it possible to create a demonstrable extralinguistic conceptual meaning using written signs according to a particular grammatical code. In returning to that scene, Césaire brings the trace to bear as a displacement of the operation. The Cahier would thereby figure (this is all it can do) a limit to the universalizability of this teaching system as it is a synecdoche for the mindfuck (epistemic violence) of French colonialism. This is the educative system there is; the Cahier institutes supplemental traces on the framework of an education and interpellation that it cannot do without—even this bad-good French education harbors the chance for something else (a Cahier inscribing itself upon a cahier—enriching it with new references to themes and histories, fleshed out in the thickness of imagery and allusion). But it also demands that the reader learn that the investment of the cahier and its exercises by the child is not identical everywhere. Martinique is not France, and the birth (interpellation) of the subject there will be otherwise than both metropolis and French West Africa, within the "same" language that differs from itself.[83] A striking expression of this possibility occurs right at the end of the poem, before the much-remarked neologism *verrition*. After a list of three *montes* apostrophized to a dove, the poem reads, "I follow you, imprinted on my ancestral white cornea" (je te suis, imprimée en mon ancestrale cornée blanche) (84/51). The writer writes as he is written (I follow you, imprinted); the organ of vision, of reading, though white like a blank page, is imprinted with the apostrophized entity or the "I," determined by an anterior textuality that stands guard over any present signification. The following clauses rush toward the final word, *verrition*, leaving us hanging in this Joycean way on the hook of a resonant trace-word, promising but not delivering "meaning," or wagering whether and how far the reader will go to reason it into a sign.[84]

Desedimentation of interpellation is a wishful, imaginative-poetic endeavor. A *nègrerie* of sorts, Césaire's intimate habitation of the landscape and repertoire of French poetry and classical literature furnishes resources with which further to formalize this wish. Césaire is clearly not the first Francophone poet systematically to deploy anaphora, for example; but his way of doing it accommodates the unusual moves that I have been describing.[85] Césaire's *Cahier* returns to the remnants of machineries of interpellation and elements left in reserve from childhood; an inventory of pattern drills, lists, and fill-in-the-blanks-type exercises comprising formal fragments from the repertoire of the child's composition book. Its *cahier* is one of the key institutional instruments in which the child learns to rehearse the grammatization and systematization of trace into sign. Disposed under the title of *Cahier*, a poem figures the form of the schoolroom training exercises as fill-in-the-blanks or repeat/vary drill that are, if not meaningless in themselves, then representative of a rehearsal for elaborated meaning-making in the *rédaction* exercise ("composition").

The *Cahier* does not reproduce content directly from any schoolbook (an exception is the syntagm "(retour au) pays natal," which I address later). The structural analogy between the *Cahier*'s anaphoric adverbial/adjectival phrases and actual schoolbook exercises exemplifies a different kind of signification, unverifiably referential but permitting the pre-text to be read between the lines. Between *Cahier* as common-noun-become-title and pattern drill in an exercise book, the reader may discern a possible pre-text, a traced "before," the secure presence of which is not verifiable as such *from within* the *Cahier*. There is not, nor can there be, a perfect isomorphism between Césaire's poetic *Cahier* and any empirical *cahier* belonging to a student. Indeed, as I have already indicated, the entire movement of

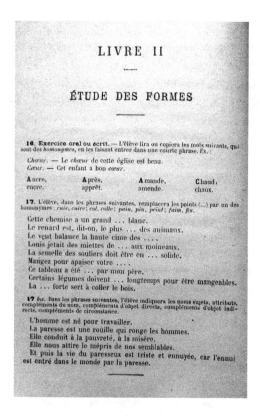

FIGURE 3.4 Brachet and Dussouchet, *Grammaire française: Cours élémentaire* (Paris: Hachette, 1921).

my argument takes place in the space and slippage between the *Cahier* and any actual *cahier*. Clearly there are actual French textbooks and student *cahiers* one can compare, and I have illustrated some here. But the pretext as trace "does not depend on any sensible plenitude, audible or visible, phonic or graphic. It is, on the contrary, the condition of that plenitude. . . . Its possibility is by rights anterior to all that one calls sign (signified/signifier, content/expression, etc.)."[86] This is a difficult point to grasp to the extent that there is no guaranteed documentary, anecdotal, or biographical "proof" that this pretext left *these* particular marks. This is why the pre-text is better called "trace." Schoolbook drills may have left their footprint in the sand of the *Cahier*, but are those footprints? That is ultimately something fragile that the reader must allow the poem to teach him or her to follow; and therein lies the difference from interpellation.

FIGURE 3.5 *Pour les petits: Année préparatoire* (Paris: H. Didier, 1921).

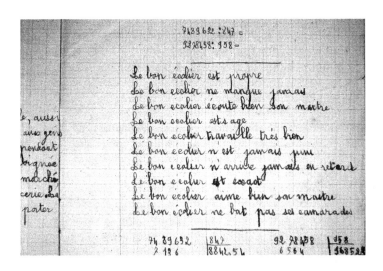

FIGURE 3.6 Page from primary schoolchild's *cahier*. Anonymous, French, c. 1920.

Interpellation turns the trace of the inchoate "concrete individual" into the sign of the subject that will "bear its Father's Name, and will therefore have an identity and be irreplaceable," be "called by his name," assigned a "personal identity" ("Ideology" 176–78).

The fragility of the trace discloses both the fragility and the power of the instituted structures of interpellation.

The *Cahier* tells that there may have been some *cahier* before the *Cahier*. This is its game with the title as proper name that points us to the way it participates in the commonality of the common noun and the unending traciness of all the *cahiers* that have been used to practice the moves of making meaning before it (and, indeed, ahead of it—the future trace/trace of a future). We have also displaced the primitivism of the tabula rasa, or blank sheet, since the *Cahier* appears in terms of the anteriority of a pre-traced space, an antecedent whose figure in the text is the (self-undoing) exercise book's babyish repetition-pattern.

A network of traces can appear to saturate in advance the ground of possibilities available to the poet; but in fact the degree or extent of this saturation is impossible to determine. The roots of the text never hit the dirt as such; and perhaps this is at stake in the poem's appellation as a *cahier* of a return to the native land, land of birth, *pays natal*. There is nothing wrong as such with the desire for locatedness, roots, for a sense of birthplace, origin, or home somewhere. As Derrida puts it, "the theme of birth is not in and of itself worrisome or something to be suspicious of";[87] or as Spivak says, writing of the subaltern below access to abstract nation-thinking: the need for a "rock-bottom comfort in one's language and one's home."[88] Placey-ness accommodates an extraordinarily complex range of affects, not all of them pathological in spite of the short circuit that conducts to nationalism, ethnicization, and racialization as soon as these thematics are raised to the level of the political. Homely or originary placey-ness when it is specifically attached to birth or gendered figures of reproduction often seems even more forbidding as well as powerful. As we have already seen in detail, these links were highly politicized for Césaire and his milieu, precisely around the question of citizenship by birth, place, blood, and the figure of the citizen (of empire) as *semblable* or not, marking differences of birth (race or place) and thus implicating the test of an ability to assimilate and make of oneself a legible or visible *figure* of the equality one already is (as human, "man," brother).

The unverifiable anteriority of the *Cahier*'s *cahiers* cannot be disentangled from the question of the *pays natal* itself, the designated object of "return." (As a student of Latin, soon to be teaching it in his old *lycée*, Césaire would have been aware that *pays* derives from *pagus*, the root of which also gives us *page*.[89] The connection is augmented by the shared sense of fixing or fastening-upon. Return to the native page? Perhaps. In any case, it serves to remind us that natality for the poem is not necessarily exclusively physical birth from the mother's body, that interpellation and education are other times and means of being born.)

Figured return of (or to) my "land of birth" is almost a formula for the uncanny, Freud's *Unheimliche* thing that in its doubled mode of apparition is homely as it is unhomely.[90] In the *Cahier*, even before the appearance of the speaker's mother and father, the landscape of the *pays natal* is endowed with the sexual characteristics of a female body: the "fat tits of the mornes [hills], . . . the hysterical grandsuck of the sea" (11). Uncanniness in Freud's account finds its most characteristic (most general or typical) instance in a returning fantasmatic *Örtlichkeit*, a dislocating placeyness, spaceyness, or affect of a spatiality that "I have been to before," rather than a specifically determinable location.[91] It is trace as symptom. If the uncanny as a symptomatic trace-effect of "return" is tracked back, it is found to be typified by the mother's womb/body (*Leib*), or her genitals as the "entrance" to that place. This place is most characteristic, for Freud, because most generalizably human: all human beings have lived inside the womb; they share the disquieted desire to return "home," in all their different idioms.[92] (Though it literally refers to a place of birth, *pays natal* is one way of saying "home," *Heimat*, *desh*, in French). Therefore to tie into the human being as such, the tracker of these traces would have to get to the places where all those human others practice the languaged expressions of these affects relating to this intimate thing. To follow this through would accommodate Senghor's sense that the "infant bathes" in an African mother tongue; that the mother tongue could be nurtured in and for education and advanced cultural production; and this nurture could ultimately limit or change the controlling ambitions of imperial sovereignty's way of infantilizing its subjects.[93]

The writings of Melanie Klein enrich the Freudian account of the uncanny by connecting its psychic relay to the schoolroom. In two essays from the 1920s, Klein analyzes elements of the school in terms of their fantasmatic dimension for the child.[94] Her interest is in the cathexis (libidinal investment) of elements of the schoolroom that can include pens, ink, individual letters and numbers, books and writing slates, formal exercises, desks, the schoolroom space itself, and the teacher.

In primary school, the child is newly focused upon acquiring the skills of shared (common or public) cognition, orientation, and meaning-making: how to read, write, count in the instituted ways. The psyche also fastens upon the material and structural elements used to accomplish this training. Between the lines of these operations, therefore, Klein discovers clusters of traces, investments of desire (libidinal energy) that pre-scribe—for each child in its own way—the pathway of accession to the common, shared systems of meaning-making. "For Fritz, when he was *writing*, the lines meant roads and the letters rode on motor-bicycles—on the pen—upon them. . . . 'i' and 'e' ride together on a motor-bicycle . . . [and] are the same, only in the middle the 'i' has a little stroke and the 'e' has a little hole. . . . Nine-year-old Grete associated with the curve of the letter 'u' the curve in which she saw little boys urinate. . . . For the libidinal significance of *grammar* . . . Grete spoke of an actual dismembering and dissection of a roast rabbit" ("School" 64–71, Klein's emphases). As the children are inserted into a common system of writing and sign-making, the analyst discerns instances of an unverifiable anteriority attested by each child, an originary writing (traces: worldly and bodily things and affective equivalents organized in another way) disclosed in the children's investments of the new and shared systems for constructing meaning.[95] The school is not the only site of such processes, of course; but like Althusser, Klein notes the "new reality" of the school for the child, its "extremely important [*überaus bedeutsame*] rôle" in the restructuring of the child's life around "new objects and realities" ("School" 59).

Klein's most explicit connection to Freud's essay on the uncanny comes at the moment she examines what she finds to be the most universal ("typical") of the "symbolizations" touching instruments of the school: "The maternal significance [*Mutterbedeutung*] of dais and also of desk and slate and everything that can be written upon, as well as the penis-meaning of penholder, slate-pencil and chalk, and of everything with which one can write," writes Klein, "became so evident for me in this and other analyses and was so constantly confirmed that I consider it to be *typical*."[96] The analysis of Fritz here and more extensively in "Early

Analysis" links the child's anxious relationship to the spatiality of the schoolroom (and indeed his entire ability to grasp spatial orientation) to the (typically uncanny) prescript of "the mental image of the inside of his mother's body … as a town, often as a country, and later on as the world."[97] We must of course be careful not to turn this into a master-code to unlock the system of Césaire's poem. Trying to access traced anteriority, in literary art as in life, does not guarantee a reliable translation from infantile cathexis to signified meaning. "These investments not only retain an opacity in the ideality of the object, but permit the liberation of that ideality. They give the force without which an objectivity in general would not be possible."[98]

❖ ❖ ❖

The syntagm "retour au pays natal" was and remains a French colloquialism, a cliché of the type "there's no place like home." It can accommodate a semantic and affective range from hominess and everyday belonging to nostalgically invested archaism or a defensive protonationalist investment

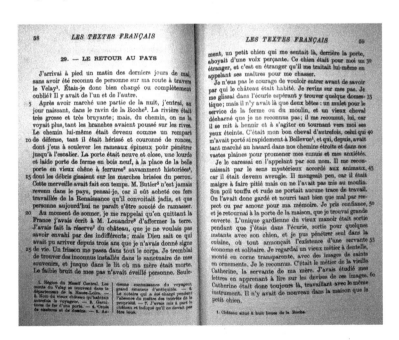

FIGURE 3.7 Extract from George Sand, "Le retour au pays." J.-R. Chevaillier and Pierre Audiat, *Les texts français*, sixième classe (Paris: Hachette, 1920).

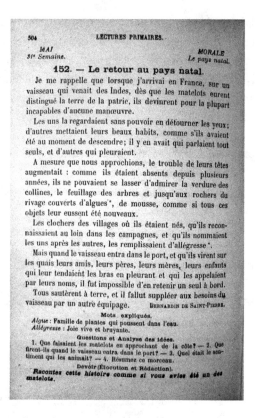

FIGURE 3.8 "Le retour au pays natal." Texts by St-Pierre and Lamartine in Emile Toutey, *Lectures primaires*, cours moyen (Paris: Hachette, 1920).

in native soil. In a public cultural context, it is associated most closely with regionalist sentiment in France (a structure of feeling that also responds to the prerevolutionary centralization of a nation-*state* in which the difference between citizen and national is possible).[99] It was a popular theme in primary and high school textbooks of the era.

Another popular and widely used French school textbook of the early twentieth century was Émile Toutey's *Lectures primaires*. The *cours moyen* edition, in print throughout the 1920s, contains two reading extracts entitled "Le retour au pays natal." One is by Bernardin de Saint-Pierre and the other is from Lamartine's *Harmonies poétiques* (1830).

Saint-Pierre's narrative describes a sailing vessel returning to France from "the Indies" that is abandoned by a crew overcome with nostalgic feelings for their coastal homes. Lamartine's poem concerns the pathos of remembering, through familiar sounds, the native country and paternal home. The exercises associated with these reading passages ask students to write compositions "as if you were one of the sailors," and to render the poem in prose. I therefore observe that one of the most widely used books of elementary readings within this system when Césaire was in school called upon students to imagine and rewrite, in their *cahiers*, a "retour au pays natal."

Each point on the spectrum of affects—as well as the logical possibility of the phrase as meaningful utterance—is conditional upon a separation from said "native land." As Saint-Pierre's narrative perfectly illustrates, a native land, a "home," cannot be returned to unless it has been lost or left in some way. Its evocation can only be predicated upon a loss, or at least a distance that symbolizes loss. Once we rise to the level of nation-thinking and its affective structures, "all national rootedness [*enracinement*], for example, is rooted [*s'enracine*] first of all in the memory or the anxiety of a displaced—or displaceable—population. It is not only time that is 'out of joint,' but space in time, spacing."[100] Both the temporality and spatiality of departure/return are unhinged and need not be predicated on the empirical story of going from A to B and back. Not only is "home" already made uncanny because you are "returned" to it in advance through the (colonial) schoolroom, but the poem's native land can also appear as the *cahier*, haunting it as a trace. A *cahier* that, as invested with desire by the child, is also an instrument of the very deracination I just outlined. Césaire's poem *Cahier*, with its staging of an island (hi)story of colonial suffering, sets forth the elements of an intimate but collective lexicon and grammar through which the Martiniquan child's desiring-investment of the classroom-*cahier* might begin to be deciphered.

❖ ❖ ❖

Do the following lines perhaps harbor the (trace of an) empirical scene of a child thumbing through a grubby hand-me-down school geography textbook in a tropical classroom?

And I say to myself Bordeaux and Nantes and Liverpool
and New-York and San-Francisco

not an inch of this world devoid of my fingerprint and my calcaneus on the spines of skyscrapers and my filth in the glitter of gems!

[Et je me dis Bordeaux et Nantes et Liverpool
et New-York et San-Francisco
pas un bout de ce monde qui ne porte mon empreinte digitale et mon
calcanéum sur le dos des gratte-ciel et ma crasse dans le scintillement des
gemmes!]

(*Cahier* 20–21)

It was uncanny, to say the least, to discover that on contiguous pages of several standard editions and variants of primary textbooks from Césaire's schooldays there were printed maps showing North America with the port cities of New York and San Francisco, maps of France that included the great ports of Nantes and Bordeaux, and maps of northern Europe on which the port of Liverpool was prominently marked in Great Britain. Nantes and Bordeaux were the two most important French ports for the

FIGURE 3.9 Map of North America and picture of skyscraper (*gratte-ciel*). H. Le Léap and J. Baudrillard, *La France: Métropole et colonies* (Paris: Delagrave, 1921).

FIGURE 3.10 Map of France. H. Le Léap and J. Baudrillard, *La France: Métropole et colonies* (Paris: Delagrave, 1921).

Atlantic slave trade and the associated shipping of commodities from the West Indies. Liverpool played the same role in England. A little constellation of the major ports of the European slave trade with their North American east and west coast counterparts known for gold rush shipping and mass immigration in the vanguard of capitalist development (the skyscraper being its emblem), and perhaps a link to other histories of the Americas where slaves were set to work in Brazilian diamond mines. But the reader of the *Cahier* must put these things together; the poem is not "history" as such but tells a telling of history by playing metonymically with the long-vanished pages of the textbook and the poetry of unintended juxtapositions found there. The speaker—figure of the poet in the text—lays claim to these geographies and their histories: "not a bit [*bout*] of this world that does not carry my fingerprint." But is "this world" (*ce monde*) the world depicted *in* the schoolbook, or *of* the schoolbook as thing; the world as figure of the universal; the world of the historic connections Bordeaux-Nantes-Liverpool-New-York-San-Francisco-skyscraper (slavery displacing into contemporary capitalism)? If each one of these options can be made as singular or as ordinarily "mine" as the uniqueness of my fingerprint, then each implies a different cut of identity from macro to micro (continents to fingers on the pages of a book).

You can cathect identity-parts in big bits (*bouts*), in terms of heavy proper names (France, Europe); or the bits can be as small as a *cahier*, letter, mathematical operation. The yearning for a beloved *pays natal*. Césaire stuffs his *Cahier* full of representations of extreme traumatic affects, banal wretchedness, history-stories, lists of cruelties—impossible contents for an everyday schoolroom *cahier*, contents rather bigger than the container.

—This is what I fill the *cahier* with, Césaire may be imagined as saying, this is the sketched figure of the ways I invest its already-existing contents with desire, making it into a new proper name, *Cahier*. "Europe" as trace rather than as the dispenser of all signs. Subtext for other scenes of meaning-making.

Not an anthropological exhibit of the inner workings of a "colonial subject" peddling cultural identity as a commodity, but an invitation to the reader to follow the stop-start do-it-again rehearsal of finding or making meaning on an unexceptional pre-figured ground. The *Cahier* can finally seem to rescue the population of the island *in poetry*, by ending with its *négraille* ("nigger scum") "arisen" ("standing," *debout*), just as it began with them as a "desolate throng" *beneath* the vertical statue of "Josephine, Empress of the French, . . . way up there above the nigger scum [*négraille*]" (4/5, 52/53). But bear in mind also the blanks, the stop-starts, the pattern drills that remind of errors, wrong answers, incompleted exercises. The *Cahier* folds into itself very many figures of those for whom neither the *Cahier* nor a school *cahier* would mean anything much at all. Each new one will have to cathect a *cahier* differently, but also collectively; and the poem knows enough to keep watch over blank spaces where the responses of unknown others, modern and contemporary but outside the fold of what is legible as "modernist poetry," will perhaps be written.

4

EDUCATING MEXICO

D. H. Lawrence and *Indigenismo* Between
Postcolonial Horror and Postcolonial Hope

D. H. Lawrence was born on the cusp of rural and industrial worlds in England's Nottinghamshire in the late nineteenth century. His father was a coalminer, a skilled and senior practitioner of that curious interstitial occupation neither agrarian nor then fully industrialized, representing a practical knowledge and exploitation of the body of the Earth. His mother was a former schoolteacher and sometime small shopkeeper. The tensions between the class feelings and aspirations of Lawrence's family have been recorded in his early fictions and well documented in the biographical accounts of his life. Lawrence was born into an upper stratum of a disenfranchised group, and the experiences and paradoxes of class mobility are writ large across his body of work.

Education figures as the central, paradoxical *pharmakon* of social mobility in Lawrence. Both poison and medicine, it appears at various times and places as that which both liberates from the restrictions of socially determined roles, and yet destroys "the intuitive and instinctive" subjectivity born of collective class experiences: "In my father's generation, with the old wild England behind them, and the lack of education, the man was not beaten down. But in my generation, the boys I went to school with, colliers now, have all been beaten down, what with the din-dinning of Board Schools, books, cinemas, clergymen, the whole national and human consciousness hammering on the fact of material prosperity above all things."[1]

The modern public sphere, "the whole national and human consciousness," appears as a great didactic scene (a national education) coercively imposing a single lesson. Here, movement out of the social limitations of the working class is barely even bought at the cost of a self-interest that is simultaneously inflated and restricted by being fixed on "material prosperity above all things." The demoralizing, scabbed ruination of the industrial landscape of modernity—"ugliness, ugliness, ugliness: meanness and formless and ugly surroundings, ugly ideals, ugly religion, ugly hope, ugly love, ugly clothes, ugly furniture, ugly houses, ugly relationship between workers and employers"—gives the lie to the democratizing promise of the State's new, modern educational institutions ("Mining" 138), or, for Lawrence, perhaps discloses its essence: equality of ugliness is the truth of "democracy." The class-divided scene of education, as with everything in Lawrence, is further crosshatched by sexual difference. If "the men are beaten down," it is via the instrument of "the nagging materialism of the woman" (137, 136). "She was taught to do it," says Lawrence, modifying his gender rage by acknowledging that women are as much subject to the pedagogical system as they are its unwitting agents (137).

Education proves to be a persistent motif in Lawrence's lifelong project of depicting an external position from which to critically focalize modernity, a position from which to give voice to what remains outside modernity so that this beyond might be made present and actual. As we shall see later in this chapter, the literary staging of this desire is most vividly realized in Lawrence's *The Plumed Serpent* (1926). In that novel, a non-European scene of revolutionary vanguardism is depicted as tapping into the unmediated voice of the colonial subaltern so as to unleash the precolonial secrets it is imagined to have guarded. Yet the vanguard must deploy the most modern, didactic modes of intervention in order to produce this newly naked voice. *The Plumed Serpent* dramatizes the permutations of this double bind in the context of an "ugly" modernity now thought in terms of the great transnational political and social developments of the interwar years, and also in terms of a parallel project of didactically converting Lawrence's favorite negative sign of the modern subject—the emancipated European woman—into a signifier within a new collective pattern.

Raymond Williams wrote of Lawrence that "he was one of the first English writers to have direct experience of ordinary teaching."[2] Lawrence had the experience of upward class mobility as a scholarship boy, followed by three years teaching in a large slum school in the London suburb of Croydon between 1908 and 1911. This would not be particularly interesting were it not for the fact that in his writing Lawrence returns to the scene of teaching—the place and the practice of education in a broad sense— again and again. For Lawrence, moreover, the fact of sexual difference represents perhaps the most fundamental fissure coded into the social, political, and cultural fields. In his writing, the asymmetry of that difference eventually finds its most prevalent coding metonymically extended into the relations master/servant, leader/led, teacher/student. The double bind of sexual difference is the bind of a difference or asymmetry that seems invariably to be coded into a hierarchy.[3] Lawrence's writings go through all the permutations of difference-hierarchy, repeatedly running up against a seemingly impassable paradox: the recognition of the difference and "individuality" of the sexes versus the desire to make that difference and individuality conform to the most traditional hierarchical codings of masculinity and femininity.[4] Lawrence's writings in their multiple genres depict, as it were, a vast landscape of codings of sexual difference. As sexual difference crosshatches the dilemmas of vanguardism-as-pedagogy in Lawrence's writing during the 1920s, the rhetoric of the writing attempts to align the polarities male/female with those of leader/led and teacher/student. Following the topographic lines of these strata, we can trace how Lawrence's texts register the effort to make this alignment work, as well as a struggle that resists the neat bipolarities of such an alignment.

This persistent complication in the scenography of teaching and learning occurs from the start, in Lawrence's first great novel, *Sons and Lovers* (1913). In *Sons and Lovers*, the didactic scene is one written also by eros and overdetermined by sexual difference. Paul Morel's relationship with Miriam Leivers is nothing if not didactic. Three intertwined interests are at play. Miriam has an innocent interest in learning so as to move out of the gender-fixed position of ignorant household drudge: "It's not fair, because I'm a woman. . . . I want to learn. Why *should* it be that I know nothing."[5] This desire for knowledge is overwritten by Paul and Miriam's mutual love. In her powerful reading of Lawrence in *Sexual Politics*, Kate Millett has described these scenes as "remarkable instances of sexual sadism disguised as masculine pedagogy."[6] "The algebra lesson," she writes, "is something of a symbol for the couple's entire relationship" (SP 253). The didactic pointer of Paul's pencil becomes, as Millett observes, figuratively linked to a penis (or to a phallus in the symbolic function). The erotic tension of the two main teaching scenes in *Sons and Lovers*, the algebra lesson and the subsequent French lesson, overpowers the two protagonists' capacities to teach or learn the ostensible topics, and the improvised classrooms become sites of erotic struggle.

If desire is here written into the scene of teaching, it is a desire that violently reduces its subjects to caricatures of a copulating heterosexual pair in Paul's erect, heated arousal and Miriam's dilated tremulousness. The chapter depicting the eventual consummation of their copulation is appropriately titled "The Test on Miriam." As Millett writes, Miriam "cannot pass [Paul's] demanding examination" (SP 254). While I am in substantial agreement with Millett's reading of these passages as the depiction of a dominating phallic interest, it can be enriched if we notice the gesture of innocence or disinterest in Miriam's learning. Outside of the surcharged exchanges with Paul, Miriam manages to turn the lessons to other ends, channeling the "interest" in Paul into the disinterest of language learning. Her French compositions—in the form of a diary—are "mostly a love-letter" to Paul (SL, 204, 245). Yet the fragment of Miriam's diary represented in French in the novel is written in a passable high school French, implying serious study snatched in the interstices of the working day. The time of this study is outside the novel's frame, but its trace is indexed by Miriam's diary fragment that narrates the writer's imagining of an absent person witnessing the same dawn as she does. Moreover, the thematic content of the diary fragment figures an activated imagination (making the absent present in language), and this imagination is activated and instantiated through the work of language study as much as through amorous yearning. In spite of the text's desire to code the scene of teaching as an erotic heterosexual *agon*, the arduous work of learning a language appears as a sign of the disinterested, as a wish for something the young woman might be able to do on her own beyond a call for recognition from the young man.[7]

Aside from a few brief remarks in his correspondence, Lawrence did not write directly about his own experiences of teaching in Croydon. Yet the unforgettable depictions of Ursula Brangwen's teaching days at Ilkeston in *The Rainbow* (1915) are surely a monument to the difficult experience of teaching resistant children from below his own social stratum in a very impoverished working-class board school.[8] These episodes, which compose a key sequence of the novel's movement, begin to focus the linked questions of the social vanguard and the *pharmakontic* pattern of education. School education here is a narrow figure for a more general exploration of the relationship between social leadership, the changing of minds, and popular enlightenment. Ursula is the troubled emblem of the "progressive" New Woman of the first decades of the twentieth century, whose own development is marked by the passage through higher educational institutions. Both processes—the upward mobility of the New Woman and the education of the slum children by her—are dealt with in a deeply ambivalent way in *The Rainbow*.

The passages in *The Rainbow* that map out the months between Ursula Brangwen's departure from high school and her arrival at college already engage the paradox of education as negotiating coercion and violence. (In Ursula's own class formation the scene of education is less starkly drawn, as she is the beneficiary of a fee-paying grammar school: class difference.) The homeopathic violence of the classroom is at odds with Ursula's naively benign desire to be adored by her students. "She dreamed how she would make the little, ugly children love her. She would be so *personal*. . . . She would give, give, give all her great stores of wealth to her children, she would make them *so* happy, and they would prefer her to any teacher on the face of the earth" (R 341). The entire school sequence is staged so as to complicate further the novel's established opposition between the phantasmatic spontaneity of the "personal and vivid" (R 341) and the "mechanical." Ursula's own agonizingly painful lesson is that it is impossible to humanize the school through the application of mere "personal" goodwill. "Ursula thought she was going to become the first wise teacher, by making the whole business personal and using no compulsion. She believed entirely in her own personality" (R 356). As the narration makes clear, this desire is ironized from the start ("Ursula thought"), and the irreducible compulsion in the scene of teaching/learning will apply as much to Ursula as it does to her pupils. Ursula must learn benign violence, must learn to be an *impersonal* instrument. She must also, however, learn disinterest. The narrator detaches itself from telling the diegetic sequence in order to state the lesson clearly: the teacher can function only through an "abnegation of his personal self" (R 356). Ursula's powerful resistance to this privation produces an outburst all the more extreme for its being resisted. Her assumption of violence is staged with brutal clarity and sacrificial logic. Unable to control the class with her personal goodwill, she beats a disruptive and insolent boy with a cane until he becomes a "writhing, howling . . . thing" (R 370).

While the extremity of this sacrifice is staged as inevitable and necessary, the novel withholds judgment on the lesson learned thereby. The prisonlike school environment is Ursula's teacher; the narrator describes her as "like a young filly that has been broken into the shafts"; the educator is unwillingly educated (R 377). Ursula becomes a merely competent instructor, resistant to the end to the scenes of violence with which she must be complicit, and produces a class of poor exam results (R 381). The fate of the students falls outside the frame of the novel. The novel also withholds any description of the content of the slum school teaching beside basic grammar, spelling, arithmetic, and a mention of history books; only its "mechanical" pedagogy is depicted, focalized by Ursula: "She was tortured by the voice of Mr Brunt. On it went, jarring, harsh, full of hate, but so monotonous, it nearly drove her mad. . . . The man was become a mechanism working on and on and on" (R 356). This is not necessarily the novel's verdict on Mr. Brunt, in spite of his allegorical name. This figure, and the entire scenario of the school, must be read against the grain of the powerful focalization by Ursula. To read this sequence against its prevailing focalization is to keep in play what the novel sets up as a double bind: working for the overcoming of class-divided educational asymmetry through a violence and sacrifice, a thingification, that appears to consolidate it. Otherwise, the negotiable double bind is reduced to a single bind, a one-way street: it becomes an opposition of values between the humane (the "individual soul" or "happy self" with its love of the bucolic) and the mechanical. In this contest, the humane can win only a symbolic victory, the price of which is bad education for the lowest classes (R 378, 380).

The scene of teaching displaces this opposition between the mechanical and the living. Though Ursula is "as if violated to death" by sacrificing the boy Williams, the classroom remains harsh but not just a sign of death. The sacrifice of self-interest turns out not to be a death: "When the work had become like habit to her, and her individual soul was left out . . . Then she could be almost happy" (R 378). The Rainbow is often supposed to valorize figures of an organically articulated architectonic totality, such as the "wondrous, cloistral origins of education" (R 399) or motifs of architecture-as-womb, which play on a metaphorics of bodily integrity and organic, heteronormative reproduction.[9] Here, the novel gestures toward a disinterested, "almost happy" mechanicity of habit, and thus a new axis of normality. It is an ordinary mechanicity that disarticulates, forces the body into the uncomfortable postures of study, displaces the "happy self" through newly learned reflexes. The "almost happy" condition that results names the ethics of teaching as an uncomfortable space, tormented by the double bind between the "happy . . . individual soul" and the *pharmakontic* violence of a sacrifice employed to displace a greater, invisible, and thoroughly normalized violence of class difference in the exercise of intellectual faculties. The fate of the children, with their failing teacher and compromised education, escapes the novel's frame.

❖   ❖   ❖

As is already evident, the scene of teaching haunts Lawrence's writing, cutting across its many genres to both enable and interrupt the articulation of desires for cultural and personal change, social leadership, or a just form of community. Lawrence bears witness to the emergence of a public sphere given over to the relentless endorsement of self-interest and "material prosperity above all things" ("Mining" 137). It is a public sphere with which the State education system appears, in his writings, to be complicit. During the War of 1914–18, Lawrence became noticeably more interested in depicting the problems of vanguardism and social leadership, and indeed a certain postwar stage of his literary career is often referred to as the "leadership phase."[10] As with Lawrence's modernist contemporaries (for example, Eliot, Pound, Wyndham Lewis, Woolf, and Joyce), an interest in vanguardism during the postwar years reflected a profound anxiety about the function and possibility of literary art itself. What could art's role possibly be as the end of the war ushered in an apparently new era of vast transnational political forces, material interests, and mass cultural forms? The quasi-feudal structures of patronage and reception within which art had once appeared to have a secure place seemed finally to be broken.[11] Fredric Jameson sees this moment as that of the destruction, in Europe, of the possibility of "national allegory" by the breakdown of the nation-state political system in the war. According to Jameson, what replaces that older system is "the dramatic appearance of the great post-national ideologies of Communism and Fascism."[12] If this new dispensation is supposed to have made possible a new narrative mode ("libidinal apparatus") as Jameson argues, then it also threw into crisis the old ones. And yet, while the principle of libidinal apparatus is an attempt to figure "unbound, transindividual forces," personae of vanguards, leaders, and didacts appear at every turn to manage, organize, and contain, to recode what has been unbound and to reterritorialize what has been deterritorialized. It is thus as if capitalism and communism, having apparently uprooted the last vestiges of feudal modes of production, opened the way for the return of *feudality* in the guise of vanguardism. A "feudality without feudalism" that rushes to fill the voids created where the states and revolutions of capitalism, communism, and postcolonial independence fail or stall.[13] As I presently show, Lawrence's The Plumed Serpent (1926) is his most powerful literary anticipation of this possibility.

The figures and scenes of leadership and education that permeate all of Lawrence's work receive an extra articulation when tested or tried out against the experience of travel outside Europe. It is not a coincidence that Lawrence's "leadership phase" largely coincided with his travels outside Europe, as well as with the emergence of the Soviet Union and the rise of Fascism. Not only did he observe firsthand the "unbound" forces of a mass-cultural capitalism in Australia and the United States, but he also witnessed the living struggles of Communist and Fascist forces in the underdeveloped Italian South and Mexico, and spent time in the colonized zones of Ceylon and Tahiti. In Lawrence's writings, a residual "spirit of place" possessed by precolonial, precapitalist societies comes to represent a counterpoint to the post-Enlightenment figures of norm, equality, exchange, proportion, and their apparent destiny in a collective fixation on "material prosperity above all things" ("Mining" 136). It is these residual elements that Lawrence depicts as becoming emergent, to put it in Raymond Williams's terms. And in a further step in The Plumed Serpent, he dramatizes a vanguard spirit that will take up the residual-emergent and reterritorialize what enlightened society has deterritorialized and abstracted. The desire to make the unenlightened, savage outside short-circuit into the vanguard of the inside—so as to save that inside from itself—becomes especially visible in Lawrence's writings of this "leadership phase."

Lawrence was not exceptional in that, like almost all the cultured Europeans of his generation, he accepted the axiom that Europe was the center of world civilization and human culture. "The whole tree of man has one supreme traveling apex, one culminating growing tip . . . Europe has been the growing tip on the tree of mankind."[14] He also accepted the commonly held axiom that Europe in the interwar years had entered into a possibly irrevocable condition of decline and crisis precipitated by its own civilizational mechanisms, when "the war came, and blew away forever our leading tip" (MEH 257).

In order to recapture what had been lost *to* civilization as well as *by* it, Lawrence made an errant journey to the "outside." Lawrence's quest involved experiments with literary form, seeking to render in language an external position that would focalize modernity's failures and project an alternative. Focalization describes the special relationship between "seeing" and "telling" in the literary text. The text may "voice" (or indeed veil) another's seeing beyond the simplified analytics of so-called narrative perspective, so that its narrator can project (or withhold) a view from "outside" without being located there.

It is impossible to mark an absolute beginning for Lawrence's journey in search of a focal position with which to voice the outside of modernity, but here let us agree with Neil Roberts and give a provisional starting point in the liminality of the Mediterranean, between Europe and Africa. Let us say that Lawrence's journey "outside the circuit of civilization" begins in Sardinia.[15] Or rather that it begins with his writings about Sardinia.

❖　❖　❖

Sea and Sardinia (1921) is a book of travel writing composed after the Lawrences' short visit to Sardinia in 1921. It is heavily marked by the conventions of the travelogue genre, episodically narrating in the first person a circuit of departure, journey, and return, and mixing vivid and comical descriptions of encounters with the locals and difficulties en route with more general observations about the history and culture of the natives. The book ambivalently marks and theatricalizes its own tourist vision by often framing its views of Sardinia through the windows of a railway car or a bus and by focusing descriptions on fellow travelers, innkeepers, and servants. The thematic terrain of a self-conscious, slightly impoverished, almost-bohemian travel experience is familiar to any reader of modernist literature. The heavy grandiosity of the ambition to find something "outside the circuit of civilization" is apparently undercut by the self-deflatingly trivial vignettes of the annoying/amusing everyday experiences undergone by the two travelers. While *Sea and Sardinia* has thus often been thoroughly aestheticized as a "delightful" and "charming" text, or, more seriously, as a text whose "ideological project is interrupted or complicated by vivid observation," what is important is that the generic constraints of travelogue mean that the "delight" or even the "vivid observation" are in fact inseparable from the book's "ideological project."[16] I do not contest these assessments of its charm—it *is* a wonderful book, and its aesthetic qualities may win assent to positions readers may otherwise not endorse. In it, the genuinely charming innocence of the everyday is recoded by the generic frame: the genealogy of "vivid observation" in—or, rather, *as*—the travel narrative constitutes precisely its self-exculpatory dimension, earlier formalized in eighteenth-century natural history and generalized into the travelogue as a genre.[17]

Thus, rather than interrupting the "ideological project" of the travelogue, "vivid observation" stands as the very alibi of that project. The mode of writing in *Sea and Sardinia* is episodic and fragmentary, composed in a free direct discourse that mimes an acute observer's autocommentary on the passage through time and space. The seductive, "delightful," and beautifully written constative descriptions of "how it is" in Sardinia are the material of an argument about Sardinia's place in the world. An episodic metonymy of "vivid observation" coheres retroactively into a pedagogical image of "Sardinia" as a colorful island of the archaic in modernity. The final sections of *Sea and Sardinia* stage a kind of demystification of its own representation of Sardinia in the scene of the marionette theater in Palermo. Lawrence writes of a captivating and colorful puppet figuration whose scene of writing is elsewhere: "A lad is grinding a broken street-piano under the stage" (SS 188). The allegory suggests that the book's dance of figures is the product of a bleak, unseen, mechanical scene of writing, hidden from view and performed with a broken apparatus. Yet the vivid observer switches immediately to the speech of the puppets as an unmediated "male voice that acts direct on the blood, not on the mind" (SS 189–90). The scenes of writing and reading can be forgotten, or at least displaced into another scene whose description elides representation and the pedagogical intermediary: "What does one care for precept and mental dictation?. . . The splendid recklessness and passion that knows no precept and no school-teacher, whose very molten spontaneity is its own guide" (SS 190). The desire for this naked voice, set against a certain pedagogy, will be a major aspect of the later *Plumed Serpent*.

Africa is an object of denegation in *Sea and Sardinia*: Should one go to "Tunis? Africa? Not yet. Not yet. Not the Arabs, not yet" (SS 9). While Africa figures as frightening, however, it is rejected also because the Africa of the Arabs is an example of one of the civilizations—one of the great premodern empires—that Sardinia has managed to remain without: "They say neither the Romans, nor Phoenicians, Greeks nor Arabs ever subdued Sardinia" (SS 9). Sardinia is especially magnetic because of its externality to the orbit of Greece and therefore, by a gigantic historical metonymy, because of its externality to Europe. An impressionistic and paratactic buildup of clauses held together by the quasi-logical formalism of colons gathers up the most important skein of *Sea and Sardinia*'s depictions of the Sardinians as inhabiting this outside. The place to focalize modernity otherwise might be found in this exteriority, and the text thus returns repeatedly to the eyes of the Sardinians. The eyes of the Sardinians "strike a stranger, older note: before the soul became self conscious: before the mentality of Greece appeared in the world . . . as if the intelligence lay deep within the cave" (SS 67). These clauses do not add up to a sentence, as if the logic of grammar must give way when trying to capture the sense of what was before the emergence from the cave into the light. The blackness and glittering impenetrability of the native eye is a motif systematically returned to in Lawrence's writing of the traveling phase: the savage's "dark eye . . . not wide open to study, to *learn* . . . What we call vision, that he has not."[18]

While its signification is not fixed, it is clear that the blackness and nonreflexive mirroring of the eye marks nonenlightenment, and externality to educated consciousness. Although Lawrence is not focalizing with the "dark eye," it marks the desired place of an alternative focalization, of a mordant yet unconscious judgment on how modernity appears from or beyond its ruined margins. The ruse of focalization is that the narrator can give voice to this blank spot, dubbing the preeducated "voice" into the place of the civilized one in a short circuit that makes it appear as if the former holds the agency of the focalizer. The very invocation of this eye begins the process.

The native is "as if" not devoid of intelligence, "as if" in possession of an uneducated intelligence (SS 67). Scenes of education and pedagogy (or of the lack of education) reappear in Lawrence's writings whenever it is a question of depicting a state of subalternity. In *Sea and Sardinia*, the allusion to the "cave" section of Plato's *Republic* and Socrates's opening remarks on the relation between *padeia* and *apaideusias*, education or culturation and noneducation or nonculturation, is an obvious literary marker.[19] Yet beyond this classic allusion, *Sea and Sardinia* introduces a peculiar topological figuration of the native or indigene's place that receives a number of permutations throughout Lawrence's travel writings.

Lawrence attempts a preliminary description of this topology as a "net" early in *Sea and Sardinia*. "There is an uncaptured Sardinia still. It lies within the net of this European civilization, but it isn't landed yet" (SS 9). Fishy, slippery, inside yet outside; inside a net that is by definition permeable, yet still outside the European civilization that the net metaphorizes: Lawrence will forever struggle with this puzzling topographic logic in his representations of indigenous difference, intelligence, potential, and accessibility. The net may signify civilization, but civilization here does not only mean empires. It is also the process of becoming-civilized, the educative transition to which Lawrence returned obsessively as soon as he arrived back in Sicily to work on *Fantasia of the Unconscious* (1922). To enter the "net" is to become educated, but Lawrence describes an education in "ideas" that is a process of deracination because it mechanically produces the abstraction of self-consciousness. So it is better that the outside remain rooted in its exteriority rather than being perverted into the aimless, deterritorialized itinerancy of modernity: "Our nation of errant Quixotes jumps on and off tramcars, trains, bicycles, motor-cars, buses, in one mad chase of the divine Dulcinea. . . . Ideas are the most dangerous germs mankind has ever been injected with . . . in schools and by way of newspapers" (FU 82). For Lawrence, the "idea" is the abstract representative as such. The mechanical, abstract rote of the "idea" produces a terrifying, dysfunctional (non) collectivity, a "people . . . of idiots, imbeciles and epileptics" (FU 83). This portrayal of the "idea" reaches a modernist manifesto-like extreme in *Fantasia*: "There should be no effort made to teach children to think, to have ideas. Only to lift them into dynamic activity. . . . Let us substitute action, all kinds of action, for the mass of people, in place of mental activity. . . . *The great mass of humanity should never learn to read and write—never*" (FU 78,

87, original emphasis). The tenor of Lawrence's hyperbolic attack on the despoiled culture of modern pedagogy must be grasped here. He is desperately diagnosing a problem but, with his limited experience of the classroom and no engaged activist responsibility in political work, he grasps at wildly idealistic, neofeudal "solutions": "Leaders—this is what mankind is craving for" (FU 88). Lawrence can afford such extremity precisely because he is no longer responsible in the arena of practical education. We will see this imaginative extremity taken to its own self-resisting limit in *The Plumed Serpent.*

As the representative of the uneducated man in the depths of the cave, the Sardinian native is imagined by Lawrence as "within" the tradition of Greek enlightenment and *politeia*, yet outside it. Inside it as a figure of its outside, the uneducated native is *not* to be coercively enlightened as in the *Republic*, but remains as the blank spot of a difference resisting and breaking through the "proletarian homogeneity and khaki all-alikeness" of the modern, enlightened world (SS 89). The subalternity of the Sardinian is raised to an antipolitical political principle. The men of Sardinia should remain subaltern, remain in "animal-bright stupidity," precisely so as to represent a difference from a homogenized enlightened society and the self-interested *ressentiment* of a badly educated working class that has rote-learned its way into a desire for "material prosperity above all things."[20]

In one of the key sections of *Sea and Sardinia*, Lawrence generalizes about the significance of the Sardinians in this direction. The section condenses the logic and the larger stakes of Lawrence's investment in the figure of the native. It concerns the outside of a certain Enlightenment, a certain internationalism, a certain socialism. Enlightenment comes first: "Coarse, vigorous, determined, they will stick to their own coarse dark stupidity and let the big world find its own way to its own enlightened hell. Their hell is their own hell, they prefer it unenlightened. . . . Will the last waves of enlightenment and world-unity break over them and wash away the stocking-caps? Or is the tide of enlightenment and world-unity already receding fast enough?" (SS 88). Enlightenment breaks up in the passage into the various figures of universalism, cosmopolitanism, "world-assimilation," and internationalism. The men of Sardinia, as remnants of humanity's past, come to represent an imminently arriving future of "vivid clan or nation-distinctions," emerging as the tide of Enlightenment and all its figures recedes (SS 89).

Lawrence's musings here compose an allegorical reading of the recent history of Europe's fall into ultranationalist conflict in the War of 1914–18. The allegory anticipates a repetition and intensification of identitarian nationalist conflicts, produced reactively by the attempt to reconfigure internationalism. According to Lawrence, as internationalism reemerges, so it provokes a repetition of the ferocious and purgative violence of "separation and sharp distinction" (SS 89). The more "universality . . . cosmopolitanisms and internationalism" assert themselves, the more "savage distinction" and "multifariousness" return to tear them apart (SS 89).

The communist Second International had collapsed precisely because the imminent war engendered a crisis in its internationalism when major European socialist parties voted in 1914 for war credits for their *national* governments. From that point it was arguably no longer possible to think unity outside of national outlines, and this moment marks the beginning of the assimilation of socialist parties as national parties in Western Europe.[21] The question of internationalism had been taken up once more as an organizational issue after 1917 by the Third International, which approached the problem of nationalism through the lens of colonialism. Lawrence diagnoses the "reaction": "A reaction is setting in, away from the old universality, back, away from cosmopolitanism and internationalism. Russia, with her Third International, is at the same time reacting most violently away from all other contact, back, recoiling on herself, into a fierce, unapproachable Russianism. Which motion will conquer? The workman's International, or the centripetal movement into national isolation?" (SS 88–89). Lawrence's answer is "probably both," because the International will itself generate the reaction against "grey proletarian homogeneity" (SS 89). Why for Lawrence does the very logic of internationalism produce this reactive nationalistic assault? By an almost mechanical logic, the abstraction of deterritorialization automatically produces a reterritorialization. In his works of the "leadership" or traveling phase Lawrence visits this dilemma again and again, worrying at its permutations of terms and holding on to their self-perpetuating oscillation as the engine of narrative.

Lawrence's figures of Enlightenment are emblems of a terrifying abstraction and deracination with which he remains fascinated and to which he remains bound. Of all the British modernists of his generation, it is Lawrence who takes this negative depiction of Enlightenment tropes furthest, and he who seeks to image how their negation might be represented. It is in a subaltern "otherness" that Lawrence will try to find the figure of a counter vanguard that can control the monstrously unbound signifying forces of modernity. "Modern democracy—socialism, conservatism, bolshevism, liberalism, republicanism, communism: all alike" in their endless and transverse unfolding: in precapitalist, precolonial social formations in the Americas these unboundedly proliferating signifiers of a whole chain of post-Enlightenment institutions and movements might be didactically recoded into an order.[22] To this list may be added feminism and fascism, internationalism and cosmopolitanism, and indeed "all the *isms*" that now call out for an ordering from the top (D 717). Lawrence's writings limn the desire for a short circuit between the social vanguard and the subaltern, and they register the complication of that desire at every turn. It is to Lawrence's most elaborated fictional braiding of the didactic, vanguardism, and sexual difference that we now turn.

◈ ◈ ◈

In 1926 Lawrence published *The Plumed Serpent* with Martin Secker in England and with Knopf in the United States.[23] The novel had been composed over three peripatetic, post-Sardinia years, and with many revisions, on the base of the "Quetzalcoatl" manuscript Lawrence wrote in approximately two months in Chapala, Mexico, in 1923.[24] The main rewrite was carried out between November 1924 and February 1925 in Oaxaca.

The Plumed Serpent is among the earliest works of British modernist fiction to engage extensively with a non-European (post)colonial scene and the wave of revolutionary vanguardism in the early twentieth century. The Mexican Revolution was the only such upheaval Lawrence had direct experience of, and he uses this experience to articulate a series of questions about the cultural script of revolution, what comes after colonialism, and the use to which the memory of precolonial cultural systems may be put in modernity. I read the book as an attempt to track processes of epistemic transformation, that is, of (re)learning and mind-changing, within and against the revolutionary scene, as an attempt to find a language with which to narrate epistemic transformations at individual and collective levels. The parallels and disjunctions between these levels are a major aspect of the work.

Lawrence draws on the centrality of education in the Mexican revolutionary state in order to construct his narrative of epistemic change. The Mexican Revolution was one of the most didactically organized revolutions of the twentieth century, and Lawrence mines this empirical contingency in order to imagine processes of change in individual and collective subjects.[25] Thus *The Plumed Serpent* stages all manner of scenes of education, reading, and training, and attempts to imagine their transformative effects: What are the processes by which a change from reader/student to writer/actor occurs for individual and collective subjects? What is the vanguard agent that draws out such change?

Bildungsroman and romance are the obvious literary genres in which *The Plumed Serpent* represents individual change. Lawrence troubles both genres by tracing, in extended psychonarration, something like a displacement into paranoiac collapse for the protagonist, a "negative" *Bildung* that precisely does *not* parallel a successful pedagogical revolutionary state- and nation-building process. At the collective level, Lawrence's novel tracks change in the "world" surrounding the protagonist: a neofeudal ordering of the rustic subalterns who join the Quetzalcoatl movement. The precolonial is depicted as a lost object, a signifier that may be reanimated in a vanguard movement in order to rectify the depredations of the postrevolutionary present. The narrative of loss and restoration is staged there as the basis of agency in the ruined present, as the search for a way to confront and gain a critical perspective on "modernity" without being obliged to insert oneself into its discursive mold.

While Lawrence's imagining of an utterly phantasmatic "restoration" of the defeated indigenous Mesoamerican culture must necessarily fail to project the complexity of the Mesoamerican past, the questions it raises and the way it does so bring out several interwoven issues that remain compelling. First, the vanguard imagined as agent of epistemic change and as didactic restorer of voice-agency to the subaltern; second, the related question of signifying (international) collectivity in a postrevolutionary situation of breakdown of the older signs of collectivity; third, the cross-hatching of these matters by the factor of sexual difference. Lawrence both captures the pathos of mourning the precolonial by restoring it, and stages that apparent restitution as caught in the abstractions of modernity that it would contest.

The Plumed Serpent situates the agency of violent and curative restoration of the precolonial in the hands of an extrastate vanguard group. The spiritual redemption of the white European is also at stake in this scenario, and the narrative intertwines interracial erotic romance with a story of how the vanguard group builds its mass movement and eventually takes over the Mexican State. Lawrence thereby sets up an explicitly counterfactual response to the Mexican Revolution. That is, he exploits fiction so as to imagine a history of revolution other than the one recorded historically or experienced by him during his Mexican travels. This counterfactuality is clearly registered in the disjunction between the tenses of narrator and character-focalizer in the novel. The entire sequence of the novel's events is narrated in past tenses that are interrupted at irregular but frequent intervals by an indeterminate, explanatory, or diagnostic narrator's voice in the present tense detached from the protagonist's focalization:

> *Clap! Clap! Clap! Clap!*—Why, I thought Concha was at school!—said Kate to herself. No!— there, in the darkness of the window-hole was Concha's swarthy face and mane, peering out like some animal from a cave, as she made the tortillas. Tortillas are flat pancakes of maize dough, baked dry on a flat earthenware plate over the fire. And the making consists of clapping a bit of new dough from the palm of one hand to the other, till the tortilla is of the requisite thinness, roundness, and so-called lightness.
>
> (PS 143)

Opening a register larger than Kate's focalization, and reflecting the presence of a reader to whom such items must be explained, the narrator here steps in—in the present tense—to clarify what a tortilla is. The relay is rhetorically switched by the word(s) "tortillas. Tortillas." This seemingly innocuous disjunction opens onto an entire, dystactically arranged sequence of statements in the present tense that wrenches us into the narrator's present each time it breaks with character-focalizers. That present is explicitly "outside" the story of the rise of the Quetzalcoatl movement, and is signaled grammatically by abrupt shifts into the present tense: "Stone buildings in Mexico have a peculiar hard, dry dreariness" (PS 8); "this is Mexico . . . smashed or raw and unfinished, with rusty bones of iron girders sticking out" (PS 96). These three examples of the novel's many swerves into a narratorial present tense enact a splitting of focal positions. The text directs us to notice that the grammatical expression of the most present predication ("is," not "was") is also the marker that the narrative present is *other than* the time of (past) narrated events, other than the time frame of Kate Leslie's Mexican adventure and the rise of the Quetzalcoatl movement. The narrator's tone is often anxious and hectoring, or diagnostic of a still-fragmentary present: "*now*, the race of the conquerors in Mexico *is* soft and boneless" (PS 79, my emphases). This is to say that the narrator speaks in a "present" in which the Quetzalcoatl movement has *not* taken place, has *not* transformed Mexico as it does in the story. The narration, logically coming "after" the events told in the book, takes place in the very "raw and unfinished" present that the Quetzalcoatl movement is portrayed as overcoming, and not in the timeless present of "the Now" purportedly instituted by that movement (PS 175–78).

In this temporal paradox, the tense shifts are the rhetorical signals that the time of the political movements and epistemic transformations staged in *The Plumed Serpent* is a rhetorical space, a space for a counterfactual narrative experiment figured forth from the presently predicated signs of a "Mexico . . . smashed or raw and unfinished" (PS 96), or a fantasy constructed from the empirical signs of revolutionary Mexico's disjointed and open-ended present. Taking that "present" as a kind of lexicon of sign fragments from which to extrapolate a possible history-to-come, Lawrence stages an imagined future-past story written in the residual signs of postrevolutionary Mexico. The text's temporal paradoxes signal that Lawrence is putting forward an alternative imagining of events, however unattractive, and not a program that should be mined for literal truths about Mexico, precolonial mythology, or Lawrence's own politics. We can produce the "politics" of this text only by seeing *how* the political is staged in it, not by inferring a politics selected from the actions or statements of the characters.

Lawrence's novel thereby both represents a desire for a particular heading for social change in modernity and enacts a number of paradoxes underlying the self-resistant articulation of this desire. The temptations of the educational vanguard are a *pharmakon*, both poison and medicine, and *The Plumed Serpent* dramatizes some parameters of this double bind.

❖ ❖ ❖

The story of *The Plumed Serpent* is that of Kate Leslie, an upper-middle-class, white European visitor to Mexico who becomes erotically embroiled in a feudalistic (counter)revolutionary vanguard movement. The movement presents itself as a countercolonial "return" of precolonial cultural systems ("the old gods") to Mexico (PS passim). The Quetzalcoatl movement is the novel's main emblem of a politicized and "positive" primitivism, a primitivism that seeks to ground social agency in the present by mobilizing the ghosts of the precolonial past. Refiguring aspects of Mexico's revolutionary millenarianism, Lawrence portrays religion as the code of the movement's bid for agency, and dramatizes its spread throughout the country in terms of didactic texts and performances.[26]

Kate Millett has written that "*The Plumed Serpent* is the story of a religious conversion," and this remains an instructive, albeit characterologically focused, way of reading the novel.[27] *The Plumed Serpent* tracks the signs of "conversion" in the protagonist's subjectivity, but also graphs the success or failure of broader processes of transformation discontinuous with her consciousness. The narrative's desire is to show how Kate the writer-actor is made by entering an alien collectivity, as Kate the individualist reader-tourist is unmade; but the representation of this event is persistently blocked. The novel thereby proves itself as much invested in depicting a failure of articulation as it is in imagining its success. Thus, rather than effecting an expansion of the protagonist's restricted vision as she enters a new world, purportedly to become a writer-actor within it rather than a reader of it, *The Plumed Serpent* hyperbolizes its initial impasses so as to question the value of the very "change" or revolution it depicts. In its ironic staging of an *arrivante* protagonist persistently misrecognizing or misreading the revolutionary signs around her, *The Plumed Serpent* places itself in a literary genealogy that includes forebears such as Flaubert's *Sentimental Education* (1869). As in Flaubert's novel, the depiction of sentimental education (or conversion) stalls on its own self-resistance.[28] And, as in Flaubert, the turning "world" surrounding the self-obsessed protagonist must be read beyond the limited frame of that protagonist's focalization. That "world" is also subject to transformations as complex as those depicted within the mental theater of the character. The interest of the work lies in the disjunctions and articulations between these two intermittently intersecting spaces of narration established by it, and its contrasting treatments of collective and individual transformation.

The scene of *The Plumed Serpent* is the scene of revolution and, to distort Régis Debray's formula, the "counterrevolution in the revolution."[29] The novel was written in the wake of the Bolshevik Revolution in Russia and the failed Easter Rising in Ireland in 1916, both of which are marked as signifiers behind *The Plumed Serpent*'s narrative present of the Mexican Revolution. The setting is Mexico in the early 1920s, and the country is still in the throes of militant upheaval following the Revolution of 1910 and its radicalization in 1917 after the events in Russia.[30] The revolution in the revolution depicted by *The Plumed Serpent* is also *against* the revolution. If the socialist revolution has upset the signs of order and the ordering of signs, the task of the novel's counterrevolutionary Quetzalcoatl movement is to reinstall a felicitous relation between signifier and signified, between voice and place, between vanguard and mass, and between man and woman. *The Plumed Serpent* fantasizes a deployment of the precolonial signifier to recontain the "anarchy" of postcolonial revolution (PS 52), portraying an archaized "neoterritoriality" on the ground of postrevolutionary Mexico, an ambiguous reterritorialization of revolutionary sign-meltdown.[31]

How can a white European woman be inscribed (and territorialized) as joining the rightful inheritors of another, dead culture? the novel asks. How can lost precolonial collective forms be reanimated? How can the signs be changed so that the European woman may enter this collectivity as an actor? As the narrative traces the tortuous path of Kate Leslie's stalled entry into the phantasmatic, exaggeratedly phallic system of the Quetzalcoatl movement, it makes of her and the Mexican subaltern the vehicles and stakes of its attempt to imagine the exorcism of colonial and revolutionary history.

❖ ❖ ❖

The Plumed Serpent deals with the Mexican revolution as the crisis of a "functional change in a sign system."[32] It represents revolution and counterrevolution in terms of warring sign-regimes. While socialism inverts the signs of the natural order, the Quetzalcoatl movement will, at least in appearance, pose a reterritorialized semiosis, a phantasmatic restoration of a precolonial sign-system stabilized by a primordial connection to earth and blood. It is thereby related by the narrative to the central topoi of nationalism. Ramón Carrasco, the leader of the Quetzalcoatl movement, wishes Mexicans to "speak with the tongues of their own blood" (PS 248), and matters of voice, text, and representation are central to the novel's depictions of reterritorialization.

The novel's Mexican revolution appears as proletarian, a socialist revolution that has engendered a "mob authority": "They were the People, and the revolutions had been their revolutions, and they had won them all" (PS 11). Appearing in terms that recall the "fear of the masses" of the early modern period, images of the apotheosis of the "mob" punctuate the opening chapters.[33] In chapter 1, the Mexico City bullfight stadium emblematizes the space of political spectacle in postrevolutionary Mexico, where the signs of hierarchy have been reversed: "In the seats of the Authorities were very few people.... A few commonplace people in an expanse of concrete were the elect" (PS 14). There is an element of comedy or satire in the way *The Plumed Serpent* frames the relation between the frightened white tourists and the ultimately harmless Mexican crowd. Yet bathos turns to horror as the expected "gallant toreadors" and "great Mithraic beast" (PS 14, 17) are dislocated by a scene of sexualized violence wherein bull and gored horse figure a tableau of murderous anal penetration: "the horse was up-ended absurdly, one of the bull's horns between his hind legs and deep in his inside, ... his rear was still heaved up, with the bull's horn working vigorously up and down inside him.... And a huge heap of bowels coming out. And a nauseous stench" (PS 18). An image of anal copulation, displaced onto an animal scene, is presented here as a horrific travesty of mythic figures.

The turn from an idealized mythical antiquity to its lurid, primitivized flipside is a common enough move in avant-garde arts by the 1920s, but it is newly set to work by Lawrence to signify an abject symptom of the failure of revolution.[34] The crowd's naive pleasure in the spectacle of the bullfight is focalized through Kate as an epitome of evil that is generalized to a Mexico always lacking in comparison to Europe: "Mexico had an underlying ugliness, a sort of squalid evil, which made Naples seem debonnaire in comparison" (21). Such ambiguously focalized statements (made in free indirect discourse) multiply throughout the novel, knotting together an extended sequence of primitivist descriptions of the darkness, evil, and primordiality of postrevolutionary Mexico.

In the second chapter's "tea-party" scene Ramón remarks to Kate, "'Whenever a Mexican cries *Viva!* he ends up with *Muera!* When he says *Viva!* he really means *Death for Somebody or Other!* I think of all the Mexican revolutions, and I see a skeleton walking ahead of a great number of people, waving a black banner with *Viva la Muerte!* written in large white letters'" (PS 40). In this mad semiosis, "life" comes to signify "death," and the chain of revolutions in Mexico appears as an inscription of a death-emblem. In spite of the fact that the tea party scene is, again, a satirical staging of metropolitan, middle-class cynicism toward revolutionary projects, the novel endorses the view expressed by Ramón. Revolution is another twist in the cycle of colonial and postcolonial deaths—modern deaths—that invert all the signs of real life.

While *The Plumed Serpent* clearly associates the sign, revolution, and death, this connection is larger than the novel and should be seen in the context of Lawrence's broader diagnosis of the substitutive representational sign as both condition and effect of the corrosive leveling and massification of modernity. The sign in its present representational modality is a figure of death itself: in the place of living contact it substitutes a dead, mediating representative. For Lawrence this type of sign-making is itself a mordant condition and effect of modernization, and is specifically associated by him with the democratic/socialistic tendency of rendering equal or commensurable. In the contemporaneous article "Democracy" Lawrence clarifies this structure in more detail. Exploring the unity that constitutes democracy according to a reading of Walt Whitman, Lawrence writes that "This Supreme Being, this Anima Mundi, this Logos . . . is surely the magnified Average, abstracted from men, and then clapped on to them again, like identity medals on wretched khaki soldiers."[35] He traces the perverse effects of this averaging system, which does a violence to the indefinable, indivisible individuality of the "spontaneous self," subjecting it to a *ratio* of calculability (D 710, 711). This is one of Lawrence's clearest statements of the sociopolitical implications of the sign as substitute: the average is abstracted from the different individuals and then reapplied to them all as a representative of identity, substituting the supposedly inert materiality of a signifier for what the individuals actually are. The representative (here, what represents the possibility of commensurability) is elevated to being a principle and end in itself. The result is that the metonymic part by which the subject is made a part of the whole—the possibility of equalization—is turned into the very principle and end of the entire system: "the reduction of the human being to a mathematical unit . . . we have mistaken the means for the end" (D 699, 702). Not only a peculiar kind of criticism of socialism, Lawrence's argument here is a criticism of any and all of modernity's sociopolitical systems: "modern democracy—socialism, conservatism, bolshevism, liberalism, republicanism, communism: all alike" (D 717). Lawrence participates in a routine and systematic reduction of the principle of abstract equalization of the constitutional subject to the making of everything and everyone essentially "the same."

The Plumed Serpent makes revolution the figure of this mordant leveling, and within the novel's Mexican deathscape are the shadowy figures of yet other collective events. The Mexican Revolution metonymizes the terrifying chain of modernity's revolutionary upheavals. The revolutions in Russia and Ireland were preceded by the Mexican Revolution of 1910, yet they enter the narrative, which takes place in the 1920s, as sinister precursors of the ruined present.[36] The narrator/focalizer holds a special contempt for Bolsheviks, exemplified by the "unhealthy and unclean-looking" Pole (PS 28). The paranoid structure of feeling reflected here (contagion, dirt, foreign agents) is a metonym of the imperial anxiety of the "Great Game," the sometimes covert, sometimes open war waged between imperial powers in Central and South Asia throughout the nineteenth century and replayed elsewhere ever since.[37] The exemplary literary expression of the Great Game is Rudyard Kipling's Kim (1901), and certain aspects of Kim's racial and political masquerade appear in Lawrence's Mexican vanguard figures. In The Plumed Serpent, the Great Game is displaced onto Mexican ground, even as Mexico was actually a remote player in a new Great Game, no longer confined to Central Asia.

In Lawrence's own day M. N. Roy, a Bengali intellectual and activist who was one of the founders of the Mexican Communist Party in 1919, had come to Mexico from the United States, where he had been consolidating contacts with Germany for the anti-imperialist movement in India.[38] Roy would become a key interlocutor of Lenin's at the Second Congress of the Socialist International in 1920, and then return to the older scene of the Great Game as a key member of the Comintern's Central Asiatic Bureau. From there he moved, via China, to become one of the founders of the Communist Party of India. These webs of international intrigue were not confined simply to figures such as Roy. The Marxist who drew Roy toward a more vigorous communist position was Mikhail Borodin, "a Comintern agent who visited Mexico in late 1919, [and] was only the first of a number of Comintern and communist figures who left their mark on the development of Mexican communism."[39] Who knows who the model for Lawrence's "polish bolshevist fellow" was, if there was one (PS 12).[40] No matter how small or actually influential the internationalist communist networks were in Latin America in the early 1920s, the image of communist internationalism as a "red tide of Bolshevism" attended the decade after 1917 and profoundly modified Lawrence's literary imagination.[41] And it must be emphasized that the Mexican revolution, as it entered its more radical phase after 1917, proceeded in the name of socialism. The paranoid structure of feeling articulated in Lawrence's novel owes much to the sense of a terrifying and engulfing, yet invisible, development of an international (deterritorialized) communist network. The Bolshevik Pole's voice, "that dingy voice, that spoke so many languages dingily" (PS 28) is yet another index of a fear of the degradation of signs—and yet their simultaneous international permeation—in this new situation.

The association of revolutionary significations with death is further underlined in the figure of Kate's dead husband, a "famous Irish leader" in the Irish nationalist movement (PS 70). Although not killed during the Easter Rising of 1916, he fatally "ruined his health" fighting for the cause (PS 71). The novel subtly commemorates this link between the Irish and Mexican revolutions by opening its first page with the line "It was the Sunday after Easter" (PS 7). The phrase "after Easter" may be read figuratively as "after the Easter rising," after failed revolution and death in Ireland.[42] This is linked to the next anniversary mentioned in the novel, Kate's fortieth birthday, which is yet another figure of death:

> She was forty: the first half of her life was over. The bright page with its flowers and its love and its stations of the Cross ended with a grave. Now she must turn over, and the page was black, black and empty. The first half of her life had been written on the bright, smooth vellum of hope, with initial letters all gorgeous upon a field of gold. But the glamour had gone from station to station of the Cross, and the last illumination was the tomb. Now the bright page was turned, and the dark page lay before her. How could one write on a page so profoundly black?
>
> (PS 50–51)

The place of writing a life has itself been reversed so as to make it both unreadable and unwritable, except perhaps as a reiteration of Ramón's "black banner with *Viva la Muerte!* written in large white letters" (PS 40). The novel thereby expresses a profound disillusion with revolutions, and its figuration of a new "writing"—reterritorialization as the possibility of action—emerges as the protagonist journeys through death to be remade as an actor in a different collective scene.

As Kate journeys into more remote parts of the country, instances of the deathly reversal of signs proliferate: the "broken hacienda" on the train ride to Orilla (PS 85); the "smashed or raw and unfinished . . . barbarism and broken brick work" of the rustic holiday resort at Orilla (PS 96); the public space of the plaza at Sayula village which "now belonged to the peons" rather than the "*elegancia*" (PS 113); or the feudal villas on the road to the remote hacienda of Jamiltepec, "smashed, with broken walls and smashed windows" (PS 159). As Kate is being rowed across the lake to her new accommodations, "In the great seething light of the lake, with the terrible blue-ribbed mountains of Mexico beyond, she seemed swallowed by some grisly skeleton, in the cage of his death-anatomy. She was afraid, mystically, of the man crouching there in the bows with his smooth thighs and supple loins like a snake, and his black eyes watching. A half-being, with a will to disintegration and death" (PS 106). It is in mapping Kate's subjectivity that *The Plumed Serpent* elaborates most extensively the affects of anxiety, fear, and paranoia that Mexico and its inhabitants call forth. This is also the site of the novel's most sustained attempt to graph the movements of epistemic change—of relearning—within the individual subject. Borrowing moves from Joseph Conrad's *Heart of Darkness*, Lawrence effortlessly tries to graph this shift in terms of a turn from signs of horror to signs of hope. If we contrast the elaborate charting of this (un)learning process with the novel's rather different treatment of subaltern learning, then it is possible to read *The Plumed Serpent* as dramatizing this very fissure between (elite, feudal) vanguard and subaltern. The difficult and painfully interminable "internal" epistemic change for Kate Leslie is contrasted with the automatized performance of a prescribed new role by the rustic subaltern. While the novel offers detailed representations of Kate's endless preparation for vanguard responsibility, for two-way dialogue in the movement, it depicts the subaltern (already taken as an anonymous collective entity) receiving a rote-training in how to react.

❖ ❖ ❖

Kate is an upper-class, independent Irishwoman who carries the ethnocentrism and sense of superiority typical of her day and class. The novel focalizes the aftereffects of revolution in the protagonist's paranoiac affect as a horrific, swarming invasion of the soul by modernized masses:

> It was her soul more than her body that knew fear. . . . Half-made, like insects that can run fast and be so busy and suddenly grow wings, but which are only winged grubs after all. A world full of half-made creatures on two legs, eating food and degrading the one mystery left to them: sex. Spinning a great lot of words, burying themselves inside the cocoons of words and ideas that they spin round themselves, and inside the cocoons, mostly perishing inert and overwhelmed. Half-made creatures, rarely more than half-responsible and half-accountable, acting in terrible swarms, like locusts. Awful thought! And with a collective insect-like will, to avoid the responsibility of achieving any more perfected being or identity. The queer, rabid hate of being urged on into purer self. The morbid fanaticism of the non-integrate.
>
> (PS 105–6)

It is the modern subject in general that is the object of Kate's and the narrator's horror here, a subject that will graft onto the "part-thing" Mexican masses if the process of revolution is left to run its current course (PS 106). The imagery of Kate's affect and thoughts here once more bears a striking resemblance to contemporary protofascist images of the communist and the crowd in Weimar Germany analyzed by Klaus Theweleit.[43] *The Plumed Serpent* engages protofascist discourses as a possible option for representing the symptoms of modernity, as if the "half-made" Mexican condensed the generality of "men today" (PS 105).

Using the language of terror and paranoia—the language of madness—Lawrence thus maps the horror of the socialist insect-flood onto parallel anxieties about the decoded flows unbound by capital and about the incorporating masses of the "dark races": "let the white man once have a misgiving about his own leadership, and the dark races will at once attack him, to pull him down into the old gulfs. To engulf him again" (PS 148). The fragile autonomy of the self is assaulted even by subaltern everydayness at the lakeside house Kate rents at Sayula. The house, a clear figure for the space of the self, is subject to all manner of external invasions, from bandits and terrifying storms to benign locals:

> No, it was no sinecure, being a Niña. At dawn began the scrape-scrape of the twig broom outside. Kate stayed on in bed, doors fastened but shutters open. Flutter outside! Somebody wanted to sell two eggs. Where is the Niña? She is sleeping! The visitor does not go. Continual flutter outside. . . . An ancient crone appeared at the window with a plate of chopped-up young cactus leaves, for three centavos. Kate didn't like cactus vegetable, but she bought it. An old man was thrusting a young cockerel through the window-bars.
>
> (PS 141, 238)

The delicate comedy with which these ordinary dealings with the "outside" are handled marks the self's truce with the alien externality. The self's points of opening (doors and windows) remain guarded as an inside from which the other world can be focalized, the threshold at which that world can appear ("An ancient crone appeared at the window"). The creation of a fragile autonomous self in Mexico is dramatized thereby, after Kate takes leave of her American companions and escapes the city. The first trip to Ramón's hacienda then marks the moment of an initial, favorable step into an other collectivity and a transformation in the self that has hitherto been a shelter against a horrific "Mexico." On returning, "Her own house seemed empty, banal, vulgar" (PS 211). The novel makes much of this emerging contrast between the deracinated emptiness of "white" world and self and the possibility of rediscovering cultural energy in the precolonial subaltern. In order to figure the entry into another collective formation, *The Plumed Serpent* employs the prior textual model of Joseph Conrad's *Heart of Darkness*, as well as the popular romance *The Sheik* by E. M. Hull (1919).

❖ ❖ ❖

Kate's entry into an alien collectivity in *The Plumed Serpent* is, as critics have noted, an elaboration of a key aspect of Joseph Conrad's *Heart of Darkness*. *The Plumed Serpent* explores the pattern of epistemic change in the self through an attempt to represent a displacement of affective value between these works.

The fate of Kate's "conversion" signals a stalling of the vanguard's and the text's parallel desires to embrace and restore a dead subaltern voice. *The Plumed Serpent* activates this stalling by transposing intertextually the inversion of natural significations in Conrad's *Heart of Darkness*. The textual model of *Heart of Darkness* is constantly evoked by *The Plumed Serpent*, as critics such as Tony Pinkney, Brett Nielson, Deborah Castillo, and Eunyoung Oh have observed; and variants of the phrase "heart of darkness" even appear twice (PS 337, 382). As Pinkney shows, Kate's itinerary from metropolitan to distant rural space allusively recapitulates Marlow's trajectory into the Congo in Conrad's novel.[44] However, as Oh has pointed out, there is no one-to-one correspondence between the protagonists of *The Plumed Serpent* and those of *Heart of Darkness*.[45] The phantasmatic and allegorical scene of proxies and doubles between the two novels makes substitutions between various functions of the protagonists possible and plausible. Yet beyond noting the obvious textual allusions to *Heart of Darkness*, critics have not explored the specific ways in which Lawrence transposes and rewrites Conrad's rhetorical values.

The undoing of Kurtz, in the verdict of the narrator of *Heart of Darkness*, is the trembling of his stiff upper lip, the failure of his "restraint": "Mr. Kurtz lacked restraint in the gratification of his various lusts."[46] A "soul that knew no restraint," Kurtz enters the space of a "horror" that is how the novel imagines close contact with the African (HD 108, 112). As Gayatri Spivak has put it, "Do not 'go native,' become obliterated in another collectivity. . . . If you lack such restraint, you will discover how horrible it is to be truly uncivilized."[47] "Good" colonizers are restrained, avoiding both personal and collective horror; but Kurtz's intimate relationship with the African woman signifies the depth of horror to which he has sunk. It is this horror that justifies the "lie" told to Kurtz's Intended back in Europe so that civilization may continue (HD 118–23). Here, the figure of the European woman describes the paradox of an innocence that must be protected with a lie. In *Heart of Darkness*, the possible humanity of the African induces such an anxiety that, as Spivak continues, "the text must reverse the values of nature, turn 'natural' semiotics around as the backdrop of this uncanny humanity" (DD 78). What causes nature to appear perverted in the novel is not the absolute alienness of the Africans, but the possibility of their human commonality with the white imperialists:

"No, they were not inhuman. Well, you know, that was the worst of it—this suspicion of their not being inhuman" (HD 106). Chinua Achebe's renowned point about *Heart of Darkness* turns precisely around the paradox written into this double negative. The terrifying and guilt-inducing possibility that Africans *are* human leads the text figuratively to "dehumanize" them and set them in an environment where nature itself is threatening and unnatural.[48]

The Plumed Serpent works to imagine a "going native" that reverses the signs of "horror" constituting the surface of the text's negative primitivism. The extensive play between the words *horror* and *hope* in the text—along with its representation of the corresponding affects—gives rise to the movements of "ambivalence," "attraction/repulsion," "hesitation," "essential ambivalence," and so forth noted by numerous critics.[49] It is as if *The Plumed Serpent* wished to produce a transgressive reading of the colonial "horror" of *Heart of Darkness* by finding grounds for a postcolonial "hope" in the effort to resurrect what was killed by colonization. The most vivid staging of this occurs in a climactic passage of free indirect discourse signaling Kate's thought world, where the syntax of Kurtz's last words is reiterated with an inverted content: "The hope! The hope! Would it ever be possible to revive the hope in these black souls, and achieve the marriage which is the only step to the new world of man?" (PS 416).

The Plumed Serpent does not depict the fulfillment of the "hope" that would be the compensatory cure for Kurtz's (and Kate's) "horror." Rather, it manifests a chain of displacements between hope and horror, such that each appearance of hope in the text immediately reverts to horror; the more hope, the more horror, in an autoimmune system sustaining and self-destructive for the protagonist, and both ruinous and generative for the narrative.

Each scene of hope gives way to a scene of horror, which in turn engenders a yet more exaggerated hope and a more abject horror. The pattern is sustained throughout, with hope and horror converging on the ambiguous humanity of the Indian: " 'I would like to give them hope' " says Kate in the early tea party scene. " 'If they had hope, they wouldn't be so sad, and they would be cleaner, and not have vermin' " (PS 39). Far from this naive and banal metropolitan benevolence, the hope and horror are juxtaposed by the end of the novel as hyperbolical hope at entering into a fusion with "the old, antediluvian blood-male" and abject horror at having blood in common with an alien, quasi-human being:

> She knew more or less what Ramón was trying to effect: this fusion!. . . And for this, without her knowing, her innermost blood had been thudding all the time . . . The hope! The hope! Would it ever be possible to revive the hope in these black souls, and achieve the marriage which is the only step to the new world of man? But meanwhile, a strange, almost torn nausea would come over Kate, and she felt she must go away, to spare herself. The strange, reptilian insistence of her very servants: *Blood is one blood. We are all one blood-stream.* Something aboriginal and tribal, and almost worse than death to the white individual. . . . Sometimes it made her feel physically sick: this overbearing blood-familiarity.
>
> (PS 415–16)

The thought of a possible commonality of blood induces the horror of a physical repulsion, which is itself followed by a lengthy return to the register of hope in a full page of free indirect discourse: "He [Ramón] was human as Kate was human. . . . He was the Living Quetzalcoatl" (PS 418).

Appearing as both affective and epistemological shifts within the individual subject, the oscillations between hope and horror are not resolved in the novel's development, but hyperbolized. Rather than becoming a better "reader" of the (social) text as Pinkney has argued, Kate remains locked within an ever more intensely phantasmatic vacillation between the two initial terms, hope and horror.[50] The narrative tracks "change" from anxiety to full-blown paranoiac/ecstatic delusions of copulation with gods and incorporation by evil, swarming demons, akin to the canonical case of psychosis that bears the name of Daniel Paul Schreber.[51] Overwhelming in their figurative violence as these passages may be, they are the sign that the reader must step outside Kate Leslie's mental theater and look for other accounts of epistemic change.

Walter Benn Michaels's reading of the "blood" passage cited earlier is that "Kate is made to lose any sense of her difference from her Indian servant" and that this figures a "primitivist universalism . . . that transcends the boundaries of race and nationality."[52] However, it is precisely here that "blood"-commonality is denegated by racism and classism, not accepted, a denegation signified by the nausea that marks a threatened boundary and that the novel stages as engendering the fantasy of commonality with a god/master. *The Plumed Serpent* uses the boundaries of "race" to suggest an international collectivity based on *class*, or on aristocratic lineage (i.e., a precapitalist concept of classified difference). As the Quetzalcoatl movement seeks to take over the State, the trajectory of its story is that of a reversal of modernity's great self-justifying narrative of emergence from feudalism. *The Plumed Serpent* depicts Ramón's movement as dreaming of a return from State to lineage. It is Ramón as godlike leader who is "human as Kate was human," and their collectivity, whose felicitousness is itself suspended in question until the very end of the novel, is ultimately a solidarity of class-as-breeding. This ideology of community, lineage, *Geschlecht*, the one the novel comes closest explicitly to endorsing, is expressed in Ramón's speech to Cipriano before they confront the Bishop:

> Every country its own Saviour, Cipriano: or every people its own Saviour. And the First Men of every people, forming a Natural Aristocracy of the World. One must have aristocrats, that we know. But natural ones, not artificial. And in some way the world must be organically united: the world of man. But in the concrete, not in the abstract. Leagues and Covenants and International Programmes: Ah! Cipriano! it's like an international pestilence. The leaves of one great tree can't hang on the boughs of another great tree. The races of the earth are like trees; in the end they neither mix nor mingle. They stand out of each other's way, like trees. Or else they crowd on one another, and their roots grapple, and it is the fight to the death.—Only from the flowers there is commingling. And the flowers of every race are the natural aristocrats of that race. And the spirit of the world can fly from flower to flower, like a hummingbird, and slowly fertilize the great trees in their blossoms.—Only the Natural Aristocrats can rise above their nation; and even then they do not rise beyond their race. Only the Natural Aristocrats of the World can be international, or cosmopolitan, or cosmic. It has always been so. The peoples are no more capable of it than the leaves of the mango tree are capable of attaching themselves to the pine.
>
> (PS 248)

Class before class: it is paradoxically the European's aristocratic solidarity with Ramón that makes the gulf between vanguard and subaltern tangible. Cipriano, Lawrence's Indian General, comes eventually to give Kate the indigenous name "Malintizi" (PS 370), inaugurating the narrative's final sequence of tropological movements and its difficult attempt to project a proxy or representative that can mark this solidarity.

◆ ◆ ◆

Most critics of *The Plumed Serpent* note that the name "Malintizi" is one version of the name of the indigenous woman who was the consort, translator, negotiator, and intelligence officer for Hernan Cortés during the Conquest.[53] Historically subject to a host of differing and incompatible interpretations, the figure of La Malinche, as "Malintzi" is now usually known, has one constant aspect in the modern era: as the indigenous woman who gave birth to the colonizer's children, she is the symbolic vessel or medium of the specifically Mexican "racial" mixture. In the novel's logic, the granting of this name signifies the Quetzalcoatl leadership's attempt to mark Kate's entry into its space as a valid actor. By this point she has "married" Cipriano in a Quetzalcoatl ceremony but remains resistant to the name "Malintzi," hovering on the cusp of what the novel codes as responsibility in the vanguard movement (PS 371). The three female figures associated with the Quetzalcoatl faction, Kate, Carlota, and Teresa, graph positions of female involvement. These range from Carlota's suicidal rejection, through Kate as the key figure of the text's self-resistance, to the primitivist fantasy of Teresa as the "dark female" with a "hidden secretive power" who spontaneously repeats the movement's patriarchal ideology of reproduction and woman's function (PS 399, 412).

In *The Plumed Serpent*, Malintizi is just a name. There is not even a minimal textual outline of the overdetermined Malinche figure even as the fictive Kate/Cipriano pair clearly stands as an inversion (and therefore a symbolic cancelation) of the historical Cortés/Malinche pair. Moreover, it is the nonfecundity of the new couple, failing to complete the anticipated romance plot structure of marriage and reproduction (and therefore an implied future for the Quetzalcoatl movement's mestizo vanguard), that, once more, signals the stalling of the fiction's counterfactual history and its suspension between the terms of hope and horror.

As the mytho-historical Malinches engendered a new kind of collective formation through cooperation, sex, and marriage with the Spanish, so Kate's cooperation, sex, and marriage in the Quetzalcoatl movement are supposed to graph her educative transformation from tourist-observer into participant. It is the narrative form of romance that structures these textual moves, and the affect of heteronormative erotic passion is the means by which the novel figures forth entry into relation with the other's collectivity. The particular thematic material mobilized by *The Plumed Serpent* to fill out this textual structure has provided much for critics (rightly) to object to: the seeming endorsement of a self-abnegating, non-clitoral kind of sexual intercourse (PS 422); the horrific signifier finally switching from "Mexico" to the repulsive "grimalkin" figures of emancipated, sexually active, older white women (PS 438–39); and the apparent acquiescence of Kate to the priapic rituals and beliefs of the Quetzalcoatl movement.

It is this last list of items that the novel offers as the contents of Kate's reeducation, Kate's new "knowledge" (PS 422), and the sign of a re-education of her desire: "'I ought to *want* to be limited'" (PS 439). Her reeducation succeeds to the extent that the "horror" of Mexico has been displaced onto the figure of her *semblable*, or double self: "Horror! Of all the horrors, perhaps the grimalkin women, her contemporaries, were the most repellant to her" (PS 439). Thus, the novel's subterranean task will have been to displace the signifier "horror" from the signified "Mexico" to the signified "white women," to track this conversion as a process of reeducation of the emancipated white woman, and also, importantly, to sign the trace of a resistance with a "perhaps." The represented epistemic change is itself an effect of the text's play of voices as *The Plumed Serpent*'s politics of voice aligns the narrator's present diagnosis of the problems of womanhood with the represented script of Kate's mental theater. Lawrence stages this alignment by deploying an exterior voice quoted by the narrator. He uses the words of a fictitious "woman writer" as the foil against which Kate's transformation can be measured: "Kate was a wise woman, wise enough to take a lesson," says the narrator, marking the point at which Mexico has instructed the protagonist how to learn that her emancipated contemporaries are in fact "horrifying" (PS 438). "It is all very well for a woman to cultivate her ego" continues the narrator with a violent shift into the diagnostic present tense mode, which in the following sentences moves yet more aggressively into an imperative: "'Woman has suffered far more from the suppression of her ego than from sex suppression,' says a woman writer, and it may well be true. But look, only look at the modern women of fifty and fifty-five who have cultivated their ego to the top of their bent! Usually, they are grimalkins to fill one with pity or with repulsion" (PS 438). It is only by contrast with the ficted, quoted "voice" of an unnamed (unnamable) "woman writer," itself embedded in the narrator's diagnostic present tense and hectoring imperatives, that epistemic change within Kate can attain representation. These layers of mediation testify to the immense textual effort and war of self-resistance enacted by the novel's attempt to depict "change."

Moreover, the torturous phrase of psychonarration ("I ought to *want* to be limited") discloses the novel's other desire, which is the desire that such an education not fully "take" in its subject. The problem and limit that *The Plumed Serpent*'s depiction of the European protagonist's learning hits, therefore, are a false dilemma between the alienated (sexual) individualism of the metropole and collectivity as sexual submission in the new postcolony. The troping of an educative entry into a new collective formation is rendered as a change of sexual and sexed positions, a diagram that will ultimately open up the narrative possibilities of *Lady Chatterley's Lover* (1928). E. M. Hull's "desert romance" *The Sheik*, published in 1919, well known as a pop-cultural model for *The Plumed Serpent*, had already crudely dramatized a kind of coercive reeducation of desire in a relation leading from kidnap-rape to love.[54] It is perhaps difficult to represent entry into solidarity outside the pervasive fictional means of its structuring in terms of eroticized passions, hence the well-known homoerotic encounter at the heart of the two male leaders' relationship in *The Plumed Serpent* (PS 367–69).

As we see, two important models for *The Plumed Serpent* are variations on the theme of the erotic as portal into the other's social and cultural text. *Heart of Darkness* codes this negatively, as lack of restraint leading to a fatal downfall of civilization in entering the other's space; Kurtz's "horror" is the product of this collectivity-as-sex (or vice versa). In *The Sheik*'s negative romance, marriage (along with the sexual knowledge that comes with it) is "a thing of horror and disgust" to Diana Mayo, the asexual, masculine, English protagonist, before her kidnap and rape in the desert. "Horror" is the main signifier of affect during her incarceration by the sheik. In *The Sheik*, therefore, the narrative task is to turn "horror" to "love" through the harsh pedagogy of rape, the coercive rearrangement of desire: "I never lived until you taught me what life was, here in the desert," says Diana Mayo when she finally declares her love for the sheik.[55] Yet marital union and sexual reproduction are precisely the points at which the articulation of white and dark fails in *The Plumed Serpent*. Malintzi/La Malinche may symbolically have mothered the Mexican mestizo, but the Quetzalcoatl movement does not accede to "this fusion!" (PS 415).

While the name "Malintzi" remains mysterious in the text of *The Plumed Serpent*, this very mysteriousness allows us to transgress the text's own protocol of leaving the signifier unelaborated. The levers that open up "Malintzi" to the Mexican social text are the invocations of "fusion" and the "cosmic" race quoted earlier (PS 415, 248). The shadowy figure of "Malintizi" brings us to the pedagogy of the subaltern in postrevolutionary Mexico, linking the "reproduction" of subjects through education to the biological (re)production of a racially specific Mexican.

❖ ❖ ❖

In 1923, on his first visit to Mexico, Lawrence tried and failed to meet José Vasconcelos, Mexico's secretary of education from 1921 to 1924. Lawrence was apparently intrigued by Vasconcelos's attempt to link social transformation to indigenized values.[56] It was Vasconcelos and his colleague Manuel Gamio who developed the theoretical formulations that constituted the official discourse of *indigenismo* for the revolutionary period: "According to the emerging orthodoxy of the Revolution, the old Indian/European thesis/antithesis had now given rise to a higher synthesis, the mestizo, which was neither Indian nor European, but quintessentially Mexican."[57] It is this "cult of the mestizo" to which the paradoxical name *indigenismo* is attached during the revolutionary period.[58] As we have already seen, the figure of the mestizo was by this time ambivalently coded through the body of La Malinche. The racialized discourse of *mestizaje* emerged in order to manage the crisis of "Indian" participation in the Revolution. If the war was "fought on the basis of considerable Indian participation," it was also "in the absence of any self-consciously Indian project."[59] Into the abyss between the perceived lack of "self-consciousness" of the Indian and the developmental agenda of the national State stepped the vanguard with its overtly educative program.

As an argument for how the difference of the Indian can be absorbed and set to work for the sake of the nation, Gamio's *Forjando patria (pro nacionalismo)* (Forging fatherland [for nationalism], 1916) "sets the terms of the debate for decades to come."[60] In Gamio's account, it is only through racial mixing that the Indian can accede to the sphere of properly national culture. Indianness is the (re)source of the nation, but on its own it cannot constitute nationality. According to Maria Saldaña-Portillo, Gamio's theory proposes the Indian as a kind of national homeopathy (a *pharmakon*) whose function is to protect the nation from Indianness. The mestizo absorption of Indianness will homeopathically "inoculate the modern Mexican nation, . . . prevent the nation of minority rule from becoming Indianized by the majority" (*Revolutionary Imagination* 211–12). The early postrevolutionary formulations of *mestizaje* such as Gamio's were explicitly developmentalist (*Forjando patria*, indeed), and national education was a main plank of this emergent State, which had inherited a deeply fragmented social landscape. However, even if the rural schools promoted nationalism and linguistic (Spanish) homogeneity, the other choices faced by the State in the 1920s were surely rather limited (322). Saldaña-Portillo is no doubt correct that the eventual dominance of the Gamio-type *mestizaje* discourse "had devastating effects for the indigenous population" because it obliterated other identities and brought "mestizaje as a process of identification" to the fore (322). Yet I am here less interested in processes of self-identification (claims to Indian or mestizo identity) than in the vanguardist instrumentalization of "Indiannness" as an alibi for development within a racialized double bind. That is, attention must be paid to the discursive structures upstream from identity that appear to compel a loaded choice between one *racially* defined identity and another. The definition of "identity" in terms of race (whether "pure" or "mixed") is itself "the triumph of [a] rationalist's modern idea," the imposition of a single discursive category as identity-horizon.[61]

In 1925, Vasconcelos published an essay titled "La raza cósmica" (The cosmic race), a summary of his high race theory, in which Mexican *mestizaje* opens the door to the future of the world because it represents "the multiple and rich plasma of future humanity."[62] The American continent has a "predestination" to be "the cradle of a fifth race into which all nations will fuse with each other" as "the definitive race, . . . the first synthetic race of the earth" (CR 18, 20, 23). Vasconcelos compares Spanish colonialism in the Americas favorably with British colonialism because while the British preached race segregation and practiced ethnocide, the Spanish began the long process of race mixing that will win out in the long run. The Anglo Saxons "*committed the sin of destroying those races, while we assimilated them, and this gives us new rights and hopes for a mission without precedent in History,"* writes Vasconcelos; "this mandate from History is first noticed in that abundance of love [*amor*] that allowed the Spaniard to create a new race with the Indian and the Black, profusely spreading white ancestry through the soldier who begat a native family" (CR 17, original emphases).

In Vasconcelos's argument, the hybrid will not be one race among many, but will be *the* race, the universal and definitive human race, a kind of cosmopolis of flesh and blood. Vasconcelos's celebration of the "love" that has reigned in Latin America, allowing Indian and black women to give birth to the children of Spanish men, is certainly a striking interpretation of several hundred years of colonial history. By contrast with other contemporary colonial narratives that deal with sexual relations in Lawrence's immediate Anglophone context (narratives from or about British India), Vasconcelos's assessment is remarkably positive. In *Heart of Darkness*, as we have seen, or in the historical and fictional narratives that for a century followed the Indian Mutiny of 1857, sexual relations between colonizer and colonized of either gender seem only representable in terms of horror and rape, or, in the case of a Kipling, as comedy.[63] In North America, the figure of the "tragic mulatta/mulatto" invests miscegenation with a predestined tragedy and, in the inverse mode to the Latin American mestizo, embodies an "excuse for 'other/otherness' that the dominant culture could not . . . appropriate or wish away."[64] In the British context, the permissible narratives of sexual relations between races allow an E. M. Forster in 1922 to write *A Passage to India*, a queer novel also deeply constrained by—yet also critical of—the post-Mutiny construction of the Indian man as rapist of white women. Three years later, Vasconcelos's earnest essay in racial science fiction can, on another continent with a different colonial history, celebrate interracial "love" as "a work of art" (*obra de arte*) determined by the "mysterious eugenics of aesthetic taste" (CR 31, 30). However much Vasconcelos's sanguine account occludes the gendered violence of colonial history in New Spain and Mexico, such a statement would have been unutterable in the context of British India in 1925. Vasconcelos lays claim to the heritage of an Enlightenment, to be written in the future flesh of a new *Geschlecht*, an Enlightenment that he regards as having been betrayed by white "arrogance," "conquests," "materialism and social injustice" (CR 25).

My point here is not to criticize the shortcomings or exclusions of Vasconcelos's discourse, postrevolutionary *indigenismo* in general, or Lawence's mediations of either. Rather, I wish to underline two related issues. First, the insistent *raciality* of the entire discursive field, from Gamio's anthropology to Lawrence's fictive counterhistory. Lawrence, trying to create the counternarrative to a baleful modern story of abstraction and rationality, repeats that story by embedding the counternarrative in a modernized and abstract discourse of race. *The Plumed Serpent* depicts the recoding of the horror of difference as the horror of the other *race*, and then attempts to displace this racial horror onto the figure of the emancipated white woman. That this displacement remains suspended is confirmed by the novel's last few lines, which reinstate once again the physical horror of "blood" (hence, race/ism), thereby leaving the novel's autoimmune, self-resistant rhetorical system in play (PS 444). If the vanguard's premodern counter to the deathly abstractions of modernity is itself the wholly "modern" abstraction of a racial solution, a "fusion" of white and black, then the novel ends arrested on a note of gendering between race and racism.

Second, Lawrence explores in more imaginative depth than Vasconcelos the centrality of the reproductive woman as the vehicle of these figurations of cultural transformation. In Vasconcelos, the woman is occluded by being mentioned: "the Indian and the Black" (women, presumably) are partners to "the [Spanish] soldier who begat a native family" (CR 17). The celebration of mixing—an inversion of the North American taboo on miscegenation—forgets every other dynamic and complexity of this relationship, sealing them under the aestheticized heading of "love." In Lawrence, the historical "Malintzi" is occluded by being mentioned, but the figure of woman as reproductive vehicle for a redemptive new mestizo race is brought into the foreground as a strange corrective to Vasconcelos.

The significations of La Malinche as victim/traitor were powerfully established by Lawrence's time, instantiated in the postindependence period (after 1821) mainly in literary works, according to Sandra Messinger Cypess.[65] In a famous essay of 1950 that "synthesizes the most representative aspects of the modern attitude towards the Malinche legend," Octavio Paz identified La Malinche as "La Chingada," literally "the fuckee," and the Mexican people/nation as thereby the child of a colonial rape.[66] Paz diagnoses the psychosubjective pathologies of the Mexican subject by recourse to this analysis of archetypes. The narrative of La Malinche (and, by metonymy, Mexico) as "fucked" prescribes a series of gendered positions ranging from the violently inverted male (the macho *gran chingón*, or great fucker) to the abject and unlivable female position ("she does not resist violence, but is an inert heap of bones, blood and dust," writes Paz).[67] Paz emphasizes one side of the dual signification of the Malinche figure that had come into prominence during the nineteenth century: Malinche as rape victim, the metaphorical mother of the mestizo Mexican.

The other determination of this figure, which again seems to have been emphasized only with the nineteenth century's particular mode of nationalism, is the connotation of treachery: La Malinche betrayed the precolonial social order and the indigenous race, playing an active and willing role in their destruction by the colonizers. In this context Jean Franco has pointed out that while Paz's interpretation "restores the violence of the conquest" occluded in revisionist accounts (that emphasize La Malinche's role as translator and intermediary), it also "hides the fact that she collaborated."[68] For Franco, the story of La Malinche complicates the scene of *mestizaje* in another way. It is not a simple and brutal story of colonization-as-rape. It is also the story of a change in the signs of (sexual) economy from gift to sexual contract. In other words, it is a narrative that tells the transition from "the cruelty of the indigenous" gifting of slaves to a colonial, heterosexual contractuality, a complicitous relation that leaves the woman still subordinate but "freed" into a kind of upward mobility.[69] It is a story of "modernization" in which La Malinche is cast as privileged collaborator of Cortés, and it does not let the precolonial formation off the hook as a golden age destroyed by colonialism.

In changing the colors of the Malinche narrative, Lawrence appears to steer outside both of the positions of victim and traitor for his "Malintzi," veering closer to a depiction of a renegotiation of the sexual contract described by Franco. This aspect of the counterfactual narrative of revolutionary Mexico is once more, therefore, arrested by the same modernity that the novel aspires to contest. If this stalling now appears to be the novel's subject, elaborately and painstakingly staged as the epistemic (non)transformation of a single European protagonist into a postcolonial vanguardist, then what of the subaltern?

❖ ❖ ❖

"The great script of modern socialism" is writ large across the urban landscape of *The Plumed Serpent*'s opening scenes, exemplified by the frescoes of "Ribera" and other muralists on display at the University (PS 52). "All the major, and even many of the minor, murals of the first few years—from 1922 up to around 1928—were located in key educational institutions," writes David Craven.[70] The scene in the university is the first link the text makes between the Revolution's great didactic projects and the subaltern Indians instrumentalized therein. The novel's narration, focalized by Kate, casts a baleful eye on this pedagogy of contemporary socialism: "In the many frescoes of the Indians, there was sympathy with the Indian, but always from the ideal, social point of view. Never the spontaneous answer of the blood. These flat Indians were symbols in the great script of modern socialism, . . . symbols in the weary script of socialism and anarchy" (PS 52). This paragraph, once more rendered in free indirect speech, enacts the novel's dislocated confusion of voices such that protagonist and narrator apparently "see" and narrate the murals together. It enables the text to level a charge against the Revolution—the charge that it has turned the Indian into a flattened and abstract sign—without an assignation of responsibility for the statement.

Inside the university, the students exemplify for the protagonist the sign-perversions symptomatic of the modernized disorder wrought by socialist revolution and its educational projects: "On the corridors of the University, young misses in bobbed hair and boys' jumpers were going smartly around, their chins pushed forward with the characteristic, deliberate youth-and-eagerness of our day. . . . And very American" (PS 52). The earnest young female subjects of a metropolitan, "socialist" Mexican education are focalized through Kate as cross-dressers, mixing the signs of sexual difference and national specificity as Americanized parallels of the New Women who appear in Lawrence's earlier novels. Indeed, Mexico had its own New Women, the *"chicas modernas* (modern girls) who popped up all over Mexico City in the 1920s, sporting bobbed haircuts and short, flowing dresses."[71] As Anne Rubenstein has shown, bobbed hair was an ambiguously provocative signifier in Mexico City during the early 1920s.[72] Hostility toward *las pelonas* (the haircut women) came to a head early in 1924, exactly between Lawrence's two visits to Mexico, with a series of physical assaults on bob-haired university students. The attacks were carried out by upper-class male students fighting a symbolic loss of privilege and status with the entry of larger numbers of middle-class female students into higher education ("War" 70–72). Gender and class rage in education once again. These attacks and the bob phenomenon received widespread attention in newspapers and popular culture for at least a decade. Moreover, the "masculinity" and "international modernity" connoted by short hair and its attendant fashions also signified an affiliation to the Revolution's modernizing didactic and social engineering endeavors (not only school teaching, but mass spectacle and mass physical training). While the "pelona style" marked a particular metropolitan, class-fixed affiliation to "society women and international celebrities," it also signified an association with "the revolution and its gendered educational projects" ("War" 71). Rubenstein sees the *pelonas* as a virtual emblem for the SEP (Secretaría de Educación Pública), at least in terms of metropolitan spectacle ("War" 71–75). How far this extended into the backwaters of rural education is unclear; in the 1920s, the eventually extensive SEP rural schools program was still being developed, but women teachers were certainly on the move from the city to the country at this time.

Mexico's extension of formal education into its own peripheries was an avowedly rational nation-building process: "Postrevolutionary educators participated in an international milieu of developmentalist thinking and social engineering designed to nationalize citizens in the interest of order, production, and military defense."[73] The new State implemented an extensive program of rural education in the 1920s and 1930s, and "revolutionary educators focused on poor women in their response to the general social upheaval of the day."[74] This effort ultimately included "sending thousands of women teachers into the countryside," a "vanguard of the school movement" with the "missionary" assignment of "effectively inculcating habits of work and making more productive the relation between school and economy."[75] All of the statements on rural education analyzed by Mary Kay Vaughan, the historian of Mexican education, concern bringing the subaltern into functional productivity through education: "The Indians form over one half of the Mexican population. They will be an important factor of production when they emerge from their present conditions," writes the *Boletín de la Secretaría de Educación Pública* in 1924.[76] Mexico was pioneering in applying Deweyan principles to State education. However, the "learning by doing" philosophy in practice laid emphasis on social conformity and vocational instruction, putting onto one side training in the disinterested capability to analyze. More pitilessly expressed, in *La educación rural en México* (1927) the Deweyan Moisés Sáenz, who became the secretary for public education in 1928, wrote that "the school has to teach these creatures how to live."[77] We should not simply leap to condemn such pitilessness: a normalized subalternity calls forth a double bind, one knot of which is emphasized in Sáenz's statement. The violence of the notion of teaching "creatures how to live" at least has the virtue of avoiding the false piety of declarations that subaltern and vanguardist metropolitan are somehow already on equal terms and may without further difficulty enter into dialogue with each other. Yet it clearly stresses the class-fractured, assimilationist, developmentalist side of education at the expense of working for other kinds of mind-change in subaltern and metropole alike. The developmentalism of this period traced a line of progress leading from the country to the city, and sedimented class contempt and separation between the urban schoolteachers and their rustic constituencies.[78] It is true, as Elsie Rockwell observes, that policies expressed in the metropolis are not always practiced in the distant classroom, and thus the rural schools should not simply be identified with statements of State policy.[79] Moreover, the school renewal program came up against prevailing structures of rural society that ran interference with any simple application of the metropolitan doctrines.

Consequently, although it is impossible to generalize about rural education in the early 1920s because of its embryonic character, due to pronounced regional differences, and because of the variegated quasi-feudal character of the rural zones, Lawrence would have been aware in broad strokes of the emerging discourses of rural education in Mexico through his metropolitan contacts.[80] As we have seen, he attempted to meet José Vasconcelos, the education minister, in 1923.

The theater of *The Plumed Serpent* expresses skeptical contempt for the postcolonial and postrevolutionary efforts at pedagogical reform in Mexico in the 1920s by projecting them in the negatively coded image of a Mexican simulacrum of the "flat Indian" and the emancipated Anglo-U.S. woman. The metropolitan, rationalist, and "socialist" pedagogy emblematized by the bob-headed university students is an experiment with modernization that the narrative warns will go horribly wrong. After viewing the murals, Kate protests to a young socialist professor at the university that the "twelve million poor—mostly Indians— . . . don't understand the very words capital and socialism. They are Mexico, really, and nobody ever looks at them except to make a *casus belli* of them" (PS 54). Pedagogy instrumentalizes the Indian, just as "perhaps the automobile will make roads even through the inaccessible soul of the Indian" (PS 116).

Lawrence's warnings about a developmentalist, instrumentalizing, and rationalist education program predict that it will turn its subjects into modernized or Americanized monsters—creating the conditions where they will greedily insert themselves into the same chaotic realm of self-interest he had earlier diagnosed as the disease afflicting Europe. Yet it is on a pedagogical terrain that he poses the counterfactual narrative of the Quetzalcoatl movement, suggesting that socialist education will not be able replace religion with something powerful enough to mold a people: "without a religion that will connect them with the universe, they will all perish. Only religion will serve: not socialism, nor education, nor anything," says Ramón to the Bishop (PS 264). Modernity's Indians are two-dimensional socialist murals in the city university, and the novel undertakes to imagine a different arena for the sentimental education of the subaltern.

The scene of formal rural education is marginal in *The Plumed Serpent*, as it surely still was in the Oaxaca of Lawrence's time. *The Plumed Serpent* traces a gulf between the formal program and actual practice of institutionalized rural education by having the new vanguard movement step into this abyss. Kate's servant Juana "could not read nor write" (PS 142–43) and "as soon as possible she shooed her girls away to school. Sometimes they went: mostly they didn't" (PS 142). The rural school is almost an absence in the novel's world; nonmetropolitan space is portrayed as still insulated from the deathly horrors of socialist pedagogy, and therefore open to the alternative teachings of the Quetzalcoatl vanguard. Between the Quetzalcoatl manuscript and *The Plumed Serpent*, some of Lawrence's most significant revisions turn on the question of literacy and reading. In the Quetzalcoatl manuscript, "The two girls could read a little. . . . The boys couldn't read at all" (Q 138). The "hymns" by which the movement spreads its message are not written on paper but transmitted orally, mnemically scripted, composed by Ramón and orally transmitted through the country by "trained singers" (Q 187). In *The Plumed Serpent*, on the other hand, not only are the hymns augmented and much further elaborated, but it is the teenage son of Kate's subaltern servant who is literate and who reads aloud "The *Written* Hymns of Quetzalcoatl" to Kate and the assembled family. The hymns are also distributed in pamphlet form and read out in public gatherings "in all the towns and villages" by "the slow voice of some

Reader" (PS 260). Listening to reading is now equated with the presence of a political authority: "in the Songs and Hymns of Quetzalcoatl, there spoke a new voice, the voice of a master and an authority" (PS 261). The modern political semiotic of State and representative is displaced onto the premodern system of master and subject as the vanguard's words are ventriloquized by the subaltern. The European subject-focalizer takes the performance of this ventriloquism as the "strange dumb people of Mexico . . . opening its voice at last" (PS 350), in a political allegory of complete misunderstanding. This aspect of *The Plumed Serpent*'s narrative exemplifies the postcolonial and developmentalist fantasy of people "speaking for themselves," as if an articulate and recognizable subaltern voice preexisted and only required the "key-word to the Mexican soul," the right sign-combination, to unlock "the tongues of their own blood" (PS 264, 248). The narrator gives voice to the vanguard fantasy of the peoples' desires: "there was a strange, submerged desire in the people for things beyond the world. They were weary of events, and weary of news and the newspapers, weary even of the things that are taught in education" (PS 260).

Lawrence establishes with clarity the texture of a didactic vanguard relation between the movement's leadership and its subjects. The leadership is split into two figures, reminiscent of contemporary political "pairs" such as Lenin and Trotsky or Gandhi and Nehru, and the movement's style is depicted as having a theatricalized element of cross-dressing, which can be compared with the Gandhian rustic masquerade. In any case, the fact that the novel takes such changes of costume seriously is indicated by the way it places a superficial criticism of mere dressing up in the words of Ramón's first wife, Carlota. She is portrayed as a diehard adherent of a sentimental and deathly Catholicism, and says to Kate of the vanguardist transvestism that "You didn't know my husband had become one of the people—a real *peon*—a *Señor Peón*, like Count Tolstoy became a *Señor Moujik*?" (PS 168). The power of such masquerade, as Marx and Gandhi knew, cannot be undone merely by exposing the wearer of the costume as not of the group whose vestments she or he wears.[81]

The Quetzalcoatl movement is also defined by its feudally organized handicraft manufactures producing indigenized insignia and clothing at Ramón's hacienda; the "Written Hymns of Quetzalcoatl" composed by Ramón, which combine lyric invocations of the gods with narratives of the fallen condition of Mexico and the gods' return; a military wing headed by General

Cipriano Viedma, the depiction of which evokes the deployment of Indian rituals and dances as martial training; ritualized destruction of the signs and idols of the Catholic church, in scenes clearly drawn from Lawrence's knowledge of the anticlerical purges by the Mexican State during the period; and all manner of new rituals, songs, and dances overseen by the leadership, in combination with a newly institutionalized series of divisions of the day as an alternative to clock time. Lawrence's counterfactual counterstate is portrayed as teaching its "creatures how to live" in a mode that fantasizes *indigenismo* as a revivalism based on a neofeudal artisanal manufactory.

Ramón is an aristocrat, an "eminent historian and archaeologist," and a "great scholar" who "graduated in Columbia University" (PS 56, 30, 68), as well as being the master of a rural hacienda. Cipriano's class formation is of the upper peasantry. His father "was one of the overseers on the hacienda," and Cipriano is the figure of a bright Indian boy, plucked up by the English bishop of Oaxaca and sent to school in London and Oxford University. The narrative of the church producing colonial subjects by educating them to become priests is typical of several European colonialisms, with the Jesuits as the best-known model of a Eurocentric church reproducing itself in and through the native population. As Cipriano says of the bishop, " 'He hoped I should be a priest. He always said that the one hope for Mexico was if she had really fine native priests' " (PS 69). The figures of Ramón and Cipriano thus offer the taxonomic outline of two kinds of Mexican colonial subject produced in ultimate solidarity from different class locations. I differentiate the figure of the colonial subject here from that of the subaltern, the colonial subject being the indigenous subject whose lines of mobility are opened up in a restricted way by colonialism and who is, in certain ways, a complicit "beneficiary" of colonialism even as she or he may be virulently opposed to it.[82] The revolutionary uprising in New Spain in 1810 (which led to independence in 1821) may be seen as a revolt of colonial subjects. Subalternity is the condition in which institutionalized lines of social mobility are closed: in the nineteenth and twentieth centuries, the general name for the subaltern in Mexico has been "Indian." The Indian Cipriano, son of an overseer rather than a lowly peon, is precisely the figure of the exception that proves the rule. One of the unexpected lessons of *The Plumed Serpent* is that not all Indians in Mexico are or were subaltern.[83]

Although colonial subjects, the figures of Ramón and Cipriano are not simply a Mexican equivalent of the "class of persons Indian in blood and color, but English in tastes, in opinions, in morals and in intellect" called for by Lord Macaulay in British India to mediate between English rulers and Indian subjects.[84] The multilayered imperialistic internationalization of nominally independent Mexico involved the internationalism of both the Catholic church and the modern intelligentsia; massive foreign investment in and ownership of the oil industry, railroads, mines, and plantations; rivalry among foreign powers for influence in Mexico; and the consequent transformation of Mexico into a proxy political theater in a Latin American version of the Great Game. As it narrates Ramón's self-"conversion," the earlier Quetzalcoatl manuscript sets itself within this geopolitical scenario: "The 'liberal' government of the moment was just wavering helplessly between the Scylla of bolshevism and the Charybdis of industrialism and exploitation" (Q 113). Like Antonio Gramsci's Italy, Mexico in the 1920s was hampered by having been both fragmented in the colonial era and prematurely internationalized by church, capital, and the cosmopolitan affiliations of its intelligentsia.[85]

Thus in Mexico, as in Italy, "an effective *Jacobin* force was always missing and could not be constituted" to represent and organize a general will.[86] Jacobin-like groups there were in revolutionary Mexico, but the power to represent a general will remained elusive. Historical studies of the Revolution show how its complex patchwork of elements and the legacy of colonial history made the emergence of either a constitutionally or an institutionally resilient *national* formation or public sphere all the more difficult, and left its borders open to transnational economic forces without robust State protections. It was under the Porfiriato (the nineteenth-century dictatorship of Porfirio Diaz) that the policy of "tying Mexico more strongly to the 'developed' industrial nations, principally France, Germany, the United States, and Britain" both increased the overall mass of the Mexican State and hollowed it out because of the unrestricted movement of foreign capital.[87] In spite of some of the extraordinary social reforms brought about by the Revolution, in the 1920s "Mexico functioned as just one more dependent country within the larger global capitalist network."[88] Or as Alan Knight has put it, "it is true that Mexico's economy had not been revolutionized by the Revolution," though its "social and political life was dramatically changed."[89] In other words, while the ideological and cultural work of nation-building went on in the rural schools program, for example, behind the scenes in the economic realm the State was being deeply compromised. Thus, in addition to the still powerful Spanish colonial heritage, the British and U.S. imperial links to Mexico are also reflected in the backgrounds of Ramón and Cipriano ("Columbia University" and "Oxford"). "On the eve of the revolution," writes Friedrich Katz, "Great Britain was by far the dominant European power in Mexico, the only one that constituted a serious challenge to U.S. economic domination."[90]

The Plumed Serpent's counterfactual narrative imagines what could come in the place of the impossible Jacobin force in Mexico, and the shape of the general will so created. The vanguard, produced out of colonial semifeudalism, thinks to enact a vast historical short circuit of the precolonial and the postcolonial, constructing the subaltern of the present as having preserved the precolonial culture intact but dormant. Lawrence prefigures Antonin Artaud's sense that "the Mexican soul has never lost, at its base, contact with the telluric forces of the earth" and that these "living sources" may be "turn[ed] into resurrection" by the *researcher*.[91] "Feeble as my contribution may be, I ask merely that it permit me to this search [*recherche*] for living sources, search that one day will turn into resurrection."[92] "I had not come to visit the Tarahumara as a tourist [*en curieux*] but to regain a Truth which the world of Europe is losing [*qui échappe au monde de l'Europe*] and which his Race has preserved," writes Artaud in *Les Tarahumaras* (1955).[93] Both Lawrence and Artaud imagine that an insurgent, antediluvian cultural secret may be accessed in the Mexican subaltern, but the way each of them thinks its "resurrection" is radically different.[94]

Lawrence finally opts to depict this cultural secret as the echo of an external cultural script prepared by a pedagogic vanguard, while Artaud, by self-conscious contrast with Lawrence's notions of vanguardism, invokes the possibility of an unmediated—or almost so—"re-ignition" [*rallumer*] of the "magical reality of a culture . . . lost in the castings of volcanic lava, vibrating in Indian blood."[95] "Lawrence has had his idea," writes Artaud, "nothing stops us from putting forward our own" as a "hypothetical dream" ("La Mexique," 129, 128). While this is not the place for an extended comparison of Artaud and Lawrence on Mexico, the contrast between Lawrence's emphasis on script and Artaud's criticism of it remains instructive. In spite of Lawrence and Artaud's shared diagnosis of the current decay of Europe and North America, Lawrence's acknowledgment of the role of the vanguard in the process of catalyzing the image of subaltern voice is oddly clearer in identifying the problem of the agent of "change." Artaud systematically finesses the question of the agent, writing of how "modern Mexico is in the process of realizing . . . this task of epic dimensions. . . . Modern Mexico can give us this lesson."[96] The proper name "Mexico" covers over a more precise assignment of the power that might "realize" this task, even as Artaud surreptitiously claims it for himself, the researcher. It is thus as if Lawrence had anticipated a kind of Artaud in the figure of Ramón the "researcher." Lawrence, for better or worse, portrays the naked speech of the subaltern as a vanguardist fantasy, and depicts the nature of the vanguard's development of this fantasy in some detail.

◆　◆　◆

The Plumed Serpent portrays epistemic change in the subaltern as a matter of learning and echoing the vanguard script. The "Huitzilopochtli's Night" chapter is a focal point here, depicting the sacrificial execution of some peons who attempt to assassinate Ramón. There the exchange between Cipriano, the guards, and Ramón abruptly and unexpectedly takes on the form of a dramatic script, a call and response couched in the form of questions and formulaic answers (PS 377–86):

CIPRIANO: Who are these four?
GUARDS: Four who came to kill Don Ramón.
CIPRIANO: Four men, against one man?
GUARDS: They were more than four, my Lord.
CIPRIANO: When many men come against one, what is the name of the many?
GUARDS: Cowards, my Lord.

(PS 379)

The novel represents subaltern participation in the vanguard movement *as* the performance of a dramatic prescript—but this is a drama on the page of a novel that is destined never to be read aloud. Lawrence thoroughly embeds this work within the modern protocols of "silent reading" as, according to V. N. Vološinov, the free indirect discourse so heavily relied on by the author is only technically possible as a *silent* play of voices.[97] This silence is both ruptured and reaffirmed by the extreme stylistic break that switches to the format of dramatic script, and by representations of the singing of hymns and invocations of ritual formulae. *The Plumed Serpent* thereby both invokes the phonic presence of a restored subaltern voice and acknowledges the impossibility of realizing this *in the text*. The text is not, cannot be, a realization of the desire it so powerfully expresses.

Shortly before this, the vanguard fantasy of a naked subaltern speech has been focalized through Kate as having been realized: "This strange dumb people of Mexico was opening its voice at last. It was as if a stone had been rolled off them all, and she heard their voice for the first time, deep, wild, with a certain exultance and menace" (PS 350). These sentences are followed by lines from the hymn "Welcome to Quetzalcoatl," which Kate (along with the reader) is reading as it is sung by the peons: "The naked one climbed in. / *Quetzalcoatl has come!*" (PS 350, original emphasis). The male collective voicing these lines is followed by a single female voice singing the response, and then a verdict in free indirect discourse, "the people had opened their hearts at last. . . . A new world had begun" (PS 350). As we have seen, *The Plumed Serpent* clearly cannot *be* the fulfillment of its own express desire to revive the precolonial by releasing its audible voice. Indeed, in the representation of the hymn, a phonic intensification is even suggested by the italicization of the words announcing (or claiming to enact?) the key event, the arrival of Quetzalcoatl. Yet this representation of the hymns printed on the page to be "read" along with Kate's reading of them—as well as the textual alignment of this moment with the opening of the Indian peon's "voice"—declares that the faculty of expressing this desire for subaltern speech is the very faculty that frustrates the realization of that speech as naked or unmediated.

Lawrence imagines the interface between intellectual vanguard leadership and subaltern subject in a dual mode that combines modern literacy and distribution networks with feudal leadership style. Thus his counterfactual narrative envisions the failures of State and revolution as they leave space for a neofeudalism to emerge. In the ruins of a struggling State, a self-appointed nonstate agency speaking in a religious idiom can appear as savior. The peon is not granted the potential for analytical capability in this scenario, but is conceived as a rote learner of "voice" until the "voice" returns from the peon: "by a sort of far-away note in the voice, and by the slow monotony of repetition, the thing would drift darkly into the consciousness of the listeners" (PS 261).

The notion that an "image" such as the "key word" could be the object around which a revolutionary general will can be made to congeal is a powerful Sorelian theorization of the task and limit of vanguardist activity. Marx and Sorel, as well as contemporary politics itself, showed this much to Lawrence, and from these elements Lawrence attempts to give Sorel's General Strike a Mexican signifier.

Yet Lawrence, having no experience of or commitment to any sort of activism, can allow his imagination to move unconstrained by the practical limits of activism when depicting the shape and development of a political movement in modern Mexico. It is here that I would introduce the question of the biographical in a reading of The Plumed Serpent, rather than searching for the various proxies and mouthpieces of "Lawrence" in the novel's protagonists. It is the limitations of the Lawrence life and his minimal empirical experience of political work that enable him to produce such an expanded fantasy of the actions of a social movement and its relationship with its followers. It is this very lack in the Lawrence "life" that allows him to depict the workings of a political movement in such a way. The fantasy of an unmediated causal line between vocalization, awakened spirit, and successful action is not an uncommon political fantasy, but it is constantly displaced in actual politics. Lawrence's virtue here is that he deploys the resources of literary fiction to stage this fantasy and also to make visible its internal self-resistance. It is thus best to read The Plumed Serpent as staging a cautionary, counterfactual fantasia of feudalistic identitarian vanguardism occupying the space where State and revolution have left ruin or incompletion. In this space of modern ruins spring up metropolitan desires to occupy the precolonial past, projected as surviving unscathed within the subaltern. As with Artaud's fantasy of "resurrection," the "key word"—the right combination of signs—will call forth in the present the voice of this past and its curative energy.

Lawrence weaves the fantasia of The Plumed Serpent from a contemporary Mexican landscape that he takes as the ruined traces from which new signs can be spun. The allegory of this production is contained in the novel as the obscure story of how the Quetzalcoatl movement began. The movement is first introduced when Kate Leslie is reading a newspaper and comes across an article headlined "The Gods of Antiquity Return to Mexico" (PS 56). The report is presented in the novel as a direct citation. It tells of the apparition, to a group of "humble and superstitious" Indian washerwomen, of a figure from the Saylua lake (PS 56). The figure clothes himself in peasant clothing belonging to one of the women's husbands and speaks to the women of the imminent return of "the old gods . . . to their own home" (PS 57). A second apparition concerns the peasant husband of the woman whose laundry was taken. He is led by the figure to a chamber where "a small light was burning, revealing a great basin of gold, into which four little men smaller than children were pouring sweet-scented water" (PS 57). Clothed in new garments by the "dwarfs," the man is told to deliver the message that "*Quetzalcoatl is young again*" (PS 58, original emphasis). While the fantastical imagery borrows from messianic subaltern movements, the novel here allegorizes its own obscure source as an unverifiable and highly mediated subaltern space. The passage introduces the idea of authoring a movement—or a novel—by reterritorializing (or by conspiratorially inventing, we cannot know) a constellation of signs emanating from the space of the subaltern in crisis; yet it depicts this account of crisis in the reportage of the modern mediatic vehicle of the daily newspaper and its commercial/ideological journalistic apparatus.

In the article's concluding paragraph, we read along with Kate that "Don Ramón Carrasco, our eminent historian and archaeologist, whose hacienda lies in the vicinity, has announced his intention of proceeding as soon as possible to the spot, to examine the origin of this new legend" (PS 58). It is this newspaper report—already at least doubly removed from the testimony of the source—that offers the reader the most proximate account of the movement's emergence. Compare this with chapter 7 of the Quetzalcoatl manuscript, which is titled "Conversion" and actually refers to the dual "conversions" of Ramón and Cipriano to their own cause. They are there depicted as conspiratorially deciding to invent a religious movement so as to control the people (Q 109–28). In *The Plumed Serpent* on the other hand, in a barely noticed textual detail, Lawrence keeps open ended the double bind between the notion of conspiratorial manipulation by the vanguard and that of a "spontaneous" emergence from religion to messianic militancy on the part of the subaltern. In any case, *The Plumed Serpent* depicts a reterritorialization by the vanguard of the subaltern's messianic impulse; yet it does leave a space in which the trace of different kinds of subaltern activity can be read.

The staging of the newspaper report interweaves several modes of narration in its testimonial account: "These humble and superstitious women were astonished to see a man of great stature rise naked from the lake. . . . His face, they said, was dark and bearded. . . . As if unaware of any watchful eyes, he advanced calmly. . . . The stranger turned his dark face upon them, and said in a quiet voice: Why are you crying? Be quiet!" (PS 57–58). The agent and character of the "event" told here are obscured by these multiple mediations (direct reported speech of the apparition, indirect reported speech of the women, journalistic prose, and the fictive newspaper report itself). Further circuits of gossip, report, and rumor leave the confusion of agency in place: for the German hotel manager in Orilla, the movement is a further twist in the conspiratorial politics of revolution, "another dodge for national-socialism. . . . They say Don Ramón Carrasco is at the back of it" (PS 103). The source of the political actions whose elaboration *The Plumed Serpent* describes is shakily located by the novel in a millenarian indigenous vision. Neither the complex testimonial structure of the report nor the fact that an apparition is staged as announcing the return of the old gods offers a securely locatable agency for the new revolution. In the first instance, it cannot be described as a willed act: its coming is merely announced by the (at least) threefold proxy structure of apparition, peasant witnesses, and newspaper report.

This is an important moment because the motif of the washerwomen recurs throughout the novel as the trace of a task left undone. If, when it comes to the (anti-)*Bildung* of Kate, the novel undertakes to track the stalled conversion from the signs and affects of horror to those of hope, the parallel mission for the novel's subaltern figures is to be ordered into the regimented signs of obedience with a "key word." " 'Women must go down the centre, and cover their faces. And they may sit upon the floor. But men must stand erect' " is the vanguard command of order in the new rituals (PS 337–38). Thus "around the low dark shrubs of the crouching women stood a forest of erect, upthrusting men" (PS 339). The vanguard's script for the subaltern turns out to be the inscription of an abject sign of obedient gendered segregation. Yet the transformation remains incomplete and the novel's subaltern women remain as the image of an incomplete assignment, a peculiar kind of blemish on the colorfulness and erectness of the Quetzalcoatl movement. The novel constellates a pattern of such blemishes or "lumps" (PS 218), microcollectivities of subaltern women or lone female figures doing "normal" gendered activities that remain on one side from the ordered rectitude of the militants.

These emblems of that which is not integrated into the rigid verticality of the Quetzalcoatl movement are centered on women's activity by the lake, on actions of bathing and laundry that are everyday events of bodily main-tenance not raised to a militaristic principle like the actions performed by men. A partial reconstruction of the constellation in its sequence would be as follows: "the women sat in the shallows of the lake, isolated in them-selves like moor-fowl, pouring water over their heads and over their ruddy arms from a gourd scoop" (PS 151); "a cluster of women were busily washing clothes" (160); "In the shallows of the lake itself two women sat bathing, their black hair hanging dense and wet" (160); "In the near distance, some dark women were kneeling on the edge of the lake, dressed only in their long wet chemises in which they had bathed" (214); "Lumps of women were by the water's edge" (218); "Outside her window the women were passing quietly, the red water-jar on one shoulder, going to the lake for water" (239); "Women were kneeling on the stones, filling red jars" (243); "women wash-ing, kneeling on stones at the lake side" (327); "Two women, tiny as birds, were kneeling on the water's edge, washing" (334).[98]

Such "lumps of women" occupying public space obviously fall prey to the tourist gaze—both Lawrence's and his protagonist's—but their inclu-sion here also speaks of the subalternity left untouched by the militant fantasy of opening the subaltern voice and unleashing the secrets of the subaltern soul. The blurred, withheld utterance of a lone, elderly Indian woman is depicted in explicit contrast with the zesty colorfulness of the vanguard movement, not even acceding to the thirdhand representation of the reported messianic visions of the newspaper article's women by the lake: "He [Cipriano's horseman] rode the Arab slanting through the water, to where an old woman, sitting in her own silence and almost invisible before, was squatted in the water with brown bare shoulders emerging, ladling water from a half gourd-shell over her matted grey head. The horse splashed and danced, the old woman rose with her rag of chemise clinging to her, scolding in a quiet voice and bending forward with her calabash cup" (PS 325). This figure of a silent, "almost invisible" old woman "scolding in a quiet voice" does not demand of the reader a pathos-ridden or celebra-tory reconstruction or restoration of what the voice says as some kind of "resistance." That is precisely the dream that *The Plumed Serpent* has been staging throughout, with results that it seems to question. Rather, what *The Plumed Serpent* brings to the reader's attention with these imaged female microgroupings is the limit of a vanguardist fantasy. The prancing horseman and the lone, stooped, scolding woman are the emblem of this impasse. To "hear," to be able to understand, or to be able to represent the "quiet voice" of the old woman would be an entirely different project that the novel suggests is beyond its capability.

The final view of the subaltern women as an orchestrated group does depict their playing the prescribed role, manikins in an activist's fantasy theater. The entire passage is worth quoting, as it stages the role of fantasy particularly well:

> Ramón was coming down towards the boat, the blue symbol of Quetzalcoatl in his hat. And at that moment the drums began to sound for midday, and there came the mid-day call, clear and distinct, from the tower. All the men on the shore stood erect, and shot up their right hands to the sky. The women spread both palms to the light. Everything was motionless, save the moving animals. Then Ramón went on to the boat, the men saluting him with the Quetzalcoatl salute as he came near. "It is wonderful, really," said Kate, as they rowed over the water, "how—how splendid one can feel in this country! As if one were still genuinely of the nobility."
>
> (PS 436)

Lawrence himself clearly realized the limits of this (fascist) fantasy and, in his usual extremist manner, now denying completely the role of a vanguard reduced to a parody of its most radical form, expressed his awareness of these limits two years after the publication of *The Plumed Serpent*: "The hero is obsolete and the leader of men is a back number. After all, at the back of the hero is the militant ideal: and the militant ideal, or the ideal militant, seems to me also a cold egg. We're sort of sick of all forms of militarism and militantism, and *Miles* is a name no more, for a man. On the whole I agree with you, the leader-cum-follower relationship is a bore."[99]

My argument in this book is that the double bind of the indigenous vanguard should not be reduced to the single bind of either of its knots. Neither the rejection of the role of the vanguard by privileging the fantasy of a fully formed subaltern, indigenized spontaneity nor the disavowal of subaltern political impulses because they are unrecognizable within the prevailing institutional frameworks. *The Plumed Serpent* explores the shape of this double bind by inventing a counterfactual history of the Mexican Revolution. In doing so, it brings us again to the limits of an investigation into Modernism and its supposedly alternative avatars.

5

INDIA OUTSIDE INDIA

Gandhi, Fiction, and the Pedagogy of Violence

andhi vs. Lenin: this is the name of an English-language pamphlet from 1921 by the Marathi communist organizer and trade unionist S. A. Dange. *Gandhi vs. Lenin* is probably the first published comparison of what these two names stand for.[1] This extraordinary and ambivalent document prefigures many of the coordinates by which these two names, Gandhi and Lenin, came to metonymize and translate figures of the strike, of revolution, of law and justice, and of questions of emancipatory and State violence in colonial India. This double metonymy cannot of course exhaust all the possibilities for subcontinental political figures in the first half of the twentieth century, but I will treat them, Gandhi and Lenin, as especially intensified nodal points, sites of multiple condensations and displacements, because they have appeared as such in the subcontinent and beyond for a century or more.

In 1921, with restricted access to authentic Leninist or Bolshevik literature due to censorship and surveillance by the colonial State, the twenty-two-year-old Dange cannot decide the contest between Gandhi and Lenin announced in his title. He presents each of them as confronting a modernity that means, predominantly, capitalism and the forms of social organization that are both its condition and its effect (including, therefore, imperialism). For Dange it is in terms of both means and, ultimately, ends that the two figures differ, even if the antagonist is the same. Where Lenin stands for the homeopathic turning of capitalist modernity to social ends, Gandhi stands for the destruction of that modernity and its civilizational forms. The former will remake human society from without, consciously deploying vanguard violence to change the political structure and afterward to effect sociocultural change for the majority subjects of that structure; the latter attempts to change minds and habits first, engendering a nonviolent and ultimately generally transformative withdrawal from the imperatives of modernity as such.

From this point, synthesizing the previously opposed figures of Lenin and Gandhi, Dange concludes his pamphlet by picturing something resembling a compromise between them. He proposes the deployment of Gandhian *tactics* (nonviolent noncooperation) resonant with sociocultural conditions in India so as to attain emancipation from imperialism and arrive at a broadly socialist outcome: a kind of agrarian socialism plus nationalized industry that looks rather like the Congress Party of that epoch. However, it is interesting that the strategic mode of struggle Dange advocates as the means of emancipation has a distinctly ambivalent relation to Gandhian strike tactics. Dange supplements the latter with the reintroduction of all the "evils" of civilization that are in tension with the Gandhian ethics of relinquishing or rejecting them as ways of enacting a renunciation or sacrifice of the sovereignty of others (and others' hold over ourselves) that they represent. Dange: "railways, mines and vast factory plants [that] may be nationalized and controlled by the State . . . [the willing devotion] of the surplus to the State to be utilized for common good" (GL 60). Gandhi: with railways, the more mobility you have, the faster and further plagues and contaminations spread; the faster and further people will move in search of markets for grain, spreading famine in their own locales; the more divisions will become sedimented as people become estranged from one another through amplified travel. With factories, the more you produce, the more you will want to consume to baleful excess. With doctors, the more you cure, the more unlimited the diseases *to* cure will become. The more lawyers there are, the more legalistic domination and laws there will be. And so on, in a diagnosis of the autoimmune ills of modernity.[2]

Supplementing Gandhi's tactics of a general strike or "sabotage" in a series of ramified withdrawals from the control of the colonial State and economy, the colonized, writes Dange, "must build up their own State within the State," an "inner State" (GL 54–58, Dange's emphasis). The practices of withdrawal and boycott described by Dange resemble closely the contemporary Gandhian tactics of Congress's Non-Cooperation movement (1920–22), which was an attempt to foment a general strike on a subcontinental scale. "Educational and Legal Institutions" were "moral" mainstays of State authority (55). Exodus from these institutions and an economic boycott of foreign goods would reveal the violent spectral essence of colonial State power in its "military basis" (55). Dange clearly knew that a number of national schools and colleges were being founded as part of the Non-Cooperation "sabotage," such that education becomes a way of laying the subjective groundwork for the development of the general strike's "extreme moment [when] Indian labor refuses to work."[3] Dange thus envisages the education and legal systems as being the infrastructure of the "inner State": "The Congress must evolve its own ministries of Education, Law and Order" (56). If this calls forth "terrorism" from the remaining functional colonial State apparatus, the educational work already done by the "inner State" will have prepared India's workers and peasants for the collective withdrawal from its military and communications machinery (sustained by them) such that "the outer [State] crumbles completely" (56–58). Gandhi would envisage a rather different kind of "Constructive Program."

Dange's notion of the "inner State" is comparable to Lenin's formulation in a Pravda article of 1917 titled "On the Dual Power."[4] It is almost certain that Dange did not know about this article in 1921. Dange quotes directly from Trotsky's *History of the Russian Revolution to Brest-Litovsk* (English translation, 1919), which describes, without naming as such, the (dual) power struggles between the Soviets and the Government during 1917.[5] Dual power (*dvoyvlastjie*), a "supplementary and parallel government" structure that comes from below, puts itself outside the laws instituted by a "centralized state power" and does away with its institutions such as the police and military. It is, for Lenin, a *"transitional"* figure that is a scandal for political sovereignty.[6] Remarking its originality he writes: "*Nobody* previously thought, or could have thought, of a dual power" ("Dual Power," 38, Lenin's emphasis). Why does he say this? Because it is unthinkable within classical (and modern bourgeois) theories of sovereignty in which sovereign power must be one and indivisible. It cannot be shared. The revolutionary event has brought about an unprecedented political form, but it is a monstrous and almost unrecognizable figure.[7]

Dange's sketch of the Indian general strike proposes that education and law will be the areas of organizational and epistemological preparation, in terms both of withdrawal from the colonial constructs and of retrenchment outside them (much of the Indian political intelligentsia was trained in law and practiced it professionally, and the independence movement also attracted massive student support). The movement will defend itself from militaristic "terrorism" by *satyagraha*, a Gandhian term usually translated as "passive resistance" (GL 58): that is, not by building a countermilitary as such but by inaction that will paralyze the workings of the colonial army's instruments of communication and military maneuver. Since the army will be the only functioning remnant of the colonial State in this situation, passive resistance will be the instrument that effectively neutralizes it.

Dange and Gandhi, and indeed the collective organization and practice of Non-Cooperation in India, give an Indic signifier (or signifiers) to the general strike, an originary translation within a *longue durée* of mass movements under the specific social, political, and cultural conditions of colonial India. Gandhi, like Lenin, appears as a kind of *figure* in Dange's account, in the sense in which, as Étienne Balibar has put it, these figures raise the question of "the nature, the mode of constitution, of the transindividual *collective link* that makes possible the emergence of a political subject."[8] Within the political field so defined, Gandhi appears as a "leader as an object of common love and a subject endowed with a quasi-maternal love that would benefit all the participants of the struggle, and that helps them endure the sacrifices it involves":[9] that is, the "affective investments, or processes of subjective identification" in what Dange, in the concluding remarks to *Gandhi vs. Lenin*, repeatedly—and defensively—names the "dream" of action, the future, *Swaraj*.[10]

Dange, referring to his image of the State within a State as a kind of "dream" of the future, seceding through the founding of a new Law and an independent educative power, brings his interpretation of Gandho-Leninist activism close to the overall framework of the Sorelian general strike as a political form. Unwitting association of Dange's or not, this is a compelling linkage that invites inquiry into how each of them, Gandhi and Dange, in different but connected ways, gives the general strike an Indic signifier, an originary translation for colonial India.

In spite of asserting that the insurgents should "*calculate* upon the worst first" and thus begin "with a clear idea of it," Dange knows that the structure of wish and dream will also determine the constitution of the acting political subject (GL 59, my emphasis). Thus, too, did Georges Sorel account for the general strike as a political form, structured by dreams and images, that exceeds a conscious calculative logic. The general strike as an event of crisis and break is the object of Sorel's *Reflections on Violence* (1908).[11] Sorel's political theory of myth underscores the importance of aesthetic, imaginative, and figurative work in the formation of a revolutionary subject: the general strike is the "mythic" figure at the center of his theory. Sorel conceives myth as the vehicle by which societies pass through transformation, but in each case the impending change figured and promised by myth is entirely without guarantees. Myth is the transitional mediator of desire and act that gives onto an unforeseeable future and is a necessary blind spot in relation to any actual future.

A work stoppage imagined as a cataclysmic ending of the prevailing order, the general strike myth involves a "proletariat . . . separating itself from the other parts of the nation, and regarding itself as the great motive power of history . . . [with a] feeling [*sentiment*] of the glory which will be attached to its historical role" (RV 161). Thus, the proletariat must both act in a vanguard way and desire and envision itself in this exemplary and elevated role. In other words, the general strike is also the work of constructing subjectivity and changing desire through aesthetic, figural means that supplement the reasoned, enlightening spread of class consciousness characteristic of social democracy. In Antonio Gramsci's words, the Sorelian myth is "the creation of a concrete phantasy which acts on a dispersed and shattered people to arouse and organize its collective will."[12] The resultant act, according to Gramsci, would actually be a "passive activity" characterized by a withdrawal that may be seen as violent inasmuch as it challenges and indeed undoes the order of legality monopolized by the State (SPN 127).

The general strike as myth is a pedagogical instrument of sorts. To have its full "educational value" socialist organization toward the strike must maintain the following: "Socialists must be convinced that the work to which they are devoting themselves is a *serious, formidable, and sublime work*; it is only on this condition that they will be able to bear the innumerable sacrifices imposed on them by a propaganda which can produce neither honors, profits nor even immediate intellectual satisfaction" (RV 130, original emphasis). It is not the specific content of the general strike that is important (its set of practical objectives or its vision of the future), but its mobilizing power, the "myth" of an apocalyptic or catastrophic end to the present order. The violent event may, like the Reformation or the French Revolution, produce effects absolutely unexpected and unintended by the actors; but the point is that the workers' desiring machines would not have cathected, and they would not have acted, without an aesthetic *tableau* of revolt, a combine that must arouse "in the depth of the soul a sentiment of the sublime" that will quash those parts of the subject driven to rebellion by mere *ressentiment* (159).

> The first Christians expected the return of Christ and the total ruin of the pagan world, with the inauguration of the kingdom of the saints, at the end of the first generation. The catastrophe did not come to pass, but Christian thought profited so greatly from the apocalyptic myth that certain contemporary scholars maintain that the whole preaching of Christ referred solely to this one point. The hopes that Luther and Calvin had formed of the religious exaltation of Europe were by no means realized.... Must we for that reason deny the immense result which came from their dreams [*rêves*] of Christian renovation? It must be admitted that the real developments of the Revolution did not in any way resemble the enchanting pictures [*tableaux*] which created the enthusiasm of its first adepts; but without those pictures would the Revolution have been victorious?... These Utopias came to nothing; but it may be asked whether the Revolution was not a much more profound transformation than those dreamed [*rêvées*] of by the people who in the eighteenth century had invented social utopias.
>
> (RV 115–16)

The general strike is myth, a dreamwork, imagery directed at the imagining, desiring, and ethical faculties of the subject—to make that subject (want to) act because the action is sublime even if it will involve suffering. Because the general strike is also the form of appearance of actual social antagonisms (a *war* of classes) at the surface of society, Sorel analogizes with the sentimental education of the Greek citizen: "the institutions of the Greek republics had as their basis the organization of armies of citizens. . . . Philosophers conceived of no other possible form of education than that which fostered in youth the heroic tradition" (160).

Sorel's epistemological intervention proposes that (collective) subjective preparation for a noncapitalist epoch is other than a matter of theoretical-intellectual, analytic, progressivist argument as to the superior rationality of socialism; and it is also more than the cultivation of a sensibility of *ressentiment*, jealousy, and immiserated (vengeful) victimhood on the part of the working class. In the moral element of Sorel's argument, the aesthetic category of the sublime plays a role, raising the working class above affects of "jealousy and vengeance" (158). "The notion of the proletarian general strike ... awakens in the depth of the soul a sentiment of the sublime proportionate to the conditions of a gigantic struggle; it forces the desire to satisfy jealousy by malice into the background" (159). How will these new values and desires be instilled? And where do they come from? These remain open questions.

The general strike as image/myth is a short circuit to the working-class "soul." Sorel's terminology of soul and spirit indicates that he is thinking a supplement to the narrowly intellectual and cognitive faculties of the subject. While his theory of the subject is not highly developed, Sorel does indicate that his epistemological intervention is directed to capturing—or indeed reeducating—the desiring machines of the working class. The educative image-politics of the general strike are prereflective, given to sensory immediacy, not analyzed but intuited en bloc: "the movements of the revolting masses are represented so as to make a fully overwhelming impression [*impression pleinement maitrisante*] on the soul of the rebels" (112).

> The general strike is indeed what I have said: the *myth* in which socialism is wholly comprised, i.e. a body of images [*organisation d'images*] capable of evoking instinctively all the sentiments which correspond to the different manifestations of the war undertaken by socialism against modern society. Strikes have engendered in the proletariat the noblest, the deepest and the most moving [*les plus moteurs*, i.e., that impart the most physical motion] sentiments that they possess; the general strike groups them all in a coordinated picture [*tableau d'ensemble*] and, by bringing them together, gives to each one its maximum intensity; appealing to their painful memories of particular conflicts, it colors with an intense life all the details of the composition presented to consciousness. We thus obtain that intuition of socialism

which language cannot give us with perfect clearness—and we obtain it as a whole, perceived instantaneously.

(118)

Even though language cannot articulate the general strike in the force of its *generality*—and Sorel posits a kind of bypassing of language and reading for a supposed immediacy and unity of the image—the process is nevertheless accounted for as an imprint, an *impression* on the soul, locating the general strike in a figurative and textualized field. Repeatedly referring to Henri Bergson as the philosophical infrastructure of his position, Sorel argues that this nonlinguistic, sensory representation is nevertheless an unmediated "intuition" and an "integral knowledge" (*connaissance totale*) as opposed to the partitions of analysis.

There is a paradox in this theory of pedagogy that intersects with a general ambiguity in education. On the one hand, the working class *knows* already. Sorel argues that the worker's structural place in the system determines that already-knowing, short-circuiting the requirement of a Party vanguard to raise its consciousness as to its true condition. It is an argument for the suspension of a certain kind of political pedagogy. To this extent, it does not matter if the general strike "is simply a product of the popular imagination" (117). The point is rather that it may well be this. Sorel is trying to imagine (or at least arguing the necessity of imagining) how the syndicats—the activists in the working-class movement who are closest to the general experiences, realities, and structures of the capitalist workplace for the exploited—themselves conceive of political change. Get into the presuppositions and epistemo-epistemological space of the exploited and oppressed, he argues, so as to move (with) them, to see what affects them and how they can be affected. This point also applies to Gandhi and the different epistemo-epistemological cultural scripts of the subcontinent. Gandhi's incomparable political success as a channel of popular desire is surely his ability to resonate with what he knows and has learned of everyday Hinduism, as well as Jainism, Buddhism, Christianity, and up to a point Islam in the subcontinent, to define the broad strokes of his ethico-political teaching. In this context it is important to acknowledge that one of Gandhi's main and almost obsessive points of reference is the sliver of the epic *Mahabharata* known separately as the *Bhagavad Gita*. The ethics of war and killing, and the conception of a nonhuman time that enfolds human temporalities, are central to this excerpt. Additionally, many episodes from the rest of the epic, and also the *Rama-yana*, animate Gandhi's writings and speeches.[13] We also see Gandhi reso-nating with what else he has learned from everyday Hinduism, Jainism, Buddhism, and Christianity in the broad strokes of his ethical teaching.)

The short circuit represented by Sorel works as a condensation or super-imposition of two linked but different claims. One is that the general strike expresses the truth of working-class desires and conceptions that remain unknown to the parliamentary and Party leaderships that seek to guide the workers in generally reformist ways. This knowledge-gap is short-circuited in the strike itself, which can happen beyond the control and direction of an official Party. On the other hand, Sorel's use of a pas-sive impersonal knots the paradox: "the movements of the revolting masses are represented [*on représentera*] so as to make a fully overwhelming impres-sion on the soul of the rebels" (RV 112). Who and what does this represent-ing, this imprinting or inscribing on the soul; who *teaches*, and by what authority? These are questions that resonate in this political theory, and they too will bring us back to Gandhi and Dange.

Dange and Gandhi enter this field of problems by another path. It is not a completely independent path inasmuch as many "sources" (both textual and practical) for Sorel, Lenin, and Benjamin were also inherited by Dange and Gandhi, and so many others, in their own ways. Neither dependent nor independent, the path is original because it responds to and intervenes in the problems of a different region, situation, and set of cul-tural, historical, linguistic, and epistemo-epistemological frameworks. All these writings and political acts thus "read" one another in ways that still remain to be grasped.

As is well known, and as was important for Walter Benjamin's later deliberations on the topic, *Reflections on Violence* theorizes a distinction between two types of general strike: the proletarian general strike and the general political strike. It is from this distinction that Benjamin, in his "Critique of Violence," published in 1921, adapts his own differentiation between a general political strike (that works to refound and thus preserve law and State) and a general proletarian strike (that works to destroy both law and State).[14] The political general strike represents an incorporation of the force of the proletarian strike in a reform or reestablishment of the existing parliamentary or State law-and-order that the proletarian strike seeks to dissolve. In Sorel's words: "the State would lose nothing of its strength. . . . The transmission of power from one privileged class to another would take place. . . . The mass of the producers would merely change masters" (RV 171).

Dange projects the "inner State" as a State of education and law. His account of its educational aspect is far from elaborated, but this notion of an educational secession preparing the epistemo-epistemological ground for social change builds upon a very substantial history of unusually extensive and manifold experiments in the reform and indigenization of education in the subcontinent. Even just looking at one region, Bengal, on which the remainder of this chapter will be focused, we can trace such a history at least into the early nineteenth century. This history would take us from the work of Rammohun Roy (1774–1833) through Ishwarchandra Vidyasagar (1820–91) to Bhudev Mukhopadhyay (1827–94), Keshab Chandra Sen (1838–84), Rabindranath Tagore (1861–1941), Swami Vivekananda (1863–1902) and Sister Nivedita (1867–1911), and Rokeya Sakhawat Hossein (1880–1932), to name just a few of the best-known individuals.[15] I do not propose to enter into the detail of that history here, but merely to underline that the imagining of an educational-legal "inner State" is built of original historico-cultural elements that make thinking its withdrawn noncooperation possible. The educational projects metonymized by these names are not necessarily insurgent or resistant, and indeed many of them were quite compatible with the running of the colonial State. The point is rather that they can also represent unguaranteed openings toward a "strike" or "sabotage," to put it in vivid terms. How so? As we have seen from the introduction to the present volume, a peculiar aspect of educational institutions and processes is that they work on forming the capability to construct objects of knowledge and produce cathexes in a singular but collective way, where the objects of knowing and desiring are open to negotiated change, without guarantees. Thus, as I have reiterated many times quoting Althusser, school is both the site and the stake of (class) struggle.[16]

It is striking that in altering Sorel in his "Critique of Violence," Benjamin must posit a "divine violence" (*göttliche Gewalt*) as the alternative to the coimplication of foundational and preservative violence: that is, as an alternative to two forms of power or force (also possible meanings of *Gewalt* for which Benjamin allows a lot of leeway) that, respectively, found laws or preserve them. This "divine *Gewalt*" is "law-destroying" (*rechtsvernich-tend*), destructive of boundaries, and also, most importantly, unlike the "mythic" *Gewalt* that it opposes, neither "guilt-inducing" (*verschuldend*) nor "retributive" (*sühnend*) ("Critique" 150–51). "Divine power is de-retributive" (*entsühnend*); it *takes away* the guilt-trip of an arbitrary punishment that lays down the law. As Gayatri Spivak has indicated, Benjamin is convinced that "contemporary life" occasions a "manifestation" of this power: "That which stands outside the law as the educative power [*erzieherische Gewalt*] in its perfected form is one of its forms of appearance [*Erscheinungsfor-men*]."[17] This is so, in Benjamin's argument at least, because—at least in its "perfected form"—the space of education resembles the Mosaic Command-ment: there is no enforcement, no coercion. You can take it or leave it because (apparently) it is a "bloodless" violence that does not seek to found anything. No guarantees.

Space does not permit me to formalize the Gandhian political vocabu-lary in order to explore in detail the analogies and differences here with its many key terms and their traditional translations, such as *ahimsa* (non-violence), *satyagraha* (passive resistance), *atmabal* (soul-force), *Ramarajya* (the kingdom of Rama, Gandhi's figure of an alternative and just ethico-political order), and so forth. It is certain that the Gandhian positions will not turn out to be fully compatible with those of Benjamin, and mere com-patibility is not the point. Ajay Skaria has in the last few years produced an exciting body of readings of these and other important Gandhian terms and their rhetorical play across the Gujurati and English of Gandhi's writ-ings.[18] I do want to suggest, though, borrowing from Skaria's interpreta-tion, that the central doctrine of *ahimsa*, or nonviolence, shares with the Benjaminian formulation a double edge that secretes a certain violence within nonviolence whose significance will thereby become highly equiv-ocal and even terrifying.

The Sanskrit-derived term *himsa* (violence) is by no means an equivalent for the German *Gewalt*. *Gewalt* contains a sense of legitimate force or insti-tuted power that *himsa*, also accommodating hurt, injury, wrongdoing, destruction, or killing, does not. *Himsa* is much more unambiguously nega-tive word than *Gewalt*, and so its grammatical suspension with a privative a- prefix, *ahimsa* (un- or non*himsa*), cannot immediately translate Benjamin's *gewaltlos*, without-*Gewalt* nonviolent, which he uses to characterize the "pure means" of the proletarian general strike on the way to divine violence.

This figure of withdrawal and "passive activity" repeats in an originary way in the Gandhian logic of struggle. The puzzle and paradox of the *satyagrahi* (the "passive resister" in Gandhi's translation of the term) are that he or she does not recognize the law, yet must practice, in Skaria's words, a "resistant submission to it."[19] Gandhi writes in his manifesto *Hind Swaraj*, published in 1909, that "the real meaning of the statement that we are a law-abiding nation is that we are passive resisters" (*Hind Swaraj* 91). The *satyagrahi* must both defy the laws of the State and obey them: obey, or at least defer to the instituted laws, because *satyagraha* dreams of a suspension of the existing, calculable, and knowable order of laws and the installation of an ethics ungrounded by a calculus of justice. It questions the laws but does not seek to lay down the law. This relinquishment of sovereignty, as self-surrender, does not register or remains illegible in the necessarily legal, calculative domain of politics. Passive surrender to its laws (or to oppression, arrest, imprisonment, beatings, and the like, even death) can only appear in that calculable domain as bizarre and self-defeating. If, as Balibar has put it, for Gandhi "all political struggle must involve *a moment of opening to the adversary* that conditions the transformation of his point of view," then the "gift" of equality that this offers the oppressor is unrecognizable as such.[20]

Thus, Gandhi can, without contradiction, inhabit the calculative political space of laws, can lend support to all manner of legal-political reforms, negotiate for formal independence, direct a "mass" movement, and even (and quite innovatively) advocate for Hindi as a "universal language for India . . . with the option of writing it in Persian or Nagri characters" (*Hind Swaraj* 105). This last proposal was ultimately to become the basis of subsequent Congress education policy. At the limit, *ahimsa* remains the most difficult issue, with the highest stakes. "God alone knows what is *himsa* and what is *ahimsa*," says Gandhi on several occasions.[21] This *cannot* be calculated, and it is precisely our inability to know (only God can know) that counts.

If *ahimsa* is a radical project of giving up on the effort to know and calculate ends and means because only God can do that, this opens the door to the mutual contamination or even indistinguishability of *himsa* and *ahimsa* in the human domain. It is from within this supposition that Gandhi can write in 1918 "that all killing is not *himsa*, that, sometimes, practice of *ahimsa* may even necessitate killing and that we as a nation have lost the true power of killing. It is clear that he who has lost the power [shakti] to kill cannot practice non-killing. *Ahimsa* is a renunciation [a *tyaag*, a giving-up or abdication] of the highest type."[22] Please note that I am not saying Gandhi advocates killing people. It is rather that he acknowledges there cannot be a line of pure opposition between *himsa* and *ahimsa* because such a line would require an order of calculating comparative judgment that the *ahimsa-satyagraha* complex is specifically designed to question. Thus, if it is impossible to know whether killing is violence or nonviolence, this is also the biggest test of what it is to renounce or submit, to give in to the incalculable. Perhaps this frightening Gandhian logic (and by all accounts Gandhi was himself deeply alarmed and disturbed by it) can also bring us back to rethink the disturbing logic of "bloodless" violence in Benjamin as it was once questioned by Jacques Derrida.[23] Allowing Gandhi and Benjamin to be read in this complicit way may open a space for the acknowledgment and discussion of the benign violence in education, not a killing, but what we analyzed in the introduction as "discipline" (Kant), "suffering" (Gramsci), or "neutralization of motor-functions" (Stiegler): not divine, or even necessarily bloodless, but the *pharmaka* of education that displace retributive, guilt-tripping power and open the responsibility of "not knowing in advance" or even of "ignoring" the pedagogical commandments ("Critique" 152).

I now bring us to the space of literary history in order to show that this complex and perhaps even quite confusing space of reterritorialization, translations, and untranslatabilities plays out in several other areas. I will look first at the bizarre play of "Gandhi" as a mythic dream-figure in relation to Lenin and Leninism and simultaneously in relation to the practical founding of a significant Indian educational institution (a highly interested and ends-orientated fundraising literary tour). At the same time, in spite of the counterintuitive complexity of Gandhi's *philosophy* of "unconditional equality" (but perhaps in a sense also possibilized by it), this scenography is interrupted and turned to other ends by assertions of Gandhi's name "from below," in terms that posit and dizzyingly multiply that very name as the announcement of the arrival of a new kind of *rajya* or State.

❖ ❖ ❖

If it is plausible today to speak of the "Gandhi novel" as a subgenre of modern Indian fiction, as many now do, then it must also be acknowledged that the initial coinage of this term was a misnomer. Shortly before he published the monumental *History and Class Consciousness* in 1923, Georg Lukács wrote a short and polemical piece on the Bengali poet and novelist Rabindranath Tagore for *Die rote Fahne*, the official daily newspaper of the German Communist Party (KPD). "Tagores Ghandi-Roman" (Tagore's Gandhi novel) is a review of Tagore's *Ghare Baire* (literally, "inside [and] outside," translated as *The Home and the World* in English).[24] This novel was published in Bengali in India in 1915–16 and translated into English in 1919.[25] The English version, which has in its way become a freestanding work, was a partial translation by Rabindranath's nephew Surendranath Tagore. The novel was then translated from Surendranath's English into German as *Das Heim und die Welt* by Helene Meyer-Franck, and published by Kurt Wolff Verlag in 1920.[26] It is this German version that Lukács reviewed in 1922. Thus did Lukács inadvertently occasion a subgeneric category, a category that does not seem to have registered in literary criticism until Lukács's article was, in turn, translated into English in 1983. After this moment, and with the rise of postcolonial literary criticism, we witness the growing production of studies that refer to "the Gandhi novel" in categoric terms, a curious instance of a circuitous and *nachträgliche* conferral of originarity upon an apparently minor piece of journalism.[27]

The article's voice is in keeping with the strident, polemical mode of contemporary writers of the political vanguard. Founded by Rosa Luxemburg and Karl Liebknecht as an organ of the Spartakusbund, *Die rote Fahne* was an avowedly partisan publication, providing the KPD's general viewpoint on political and economic events of the day. Additionally, it printed a smaller amount of cultural analysis such as Lukács's article, which was the first of a series he wrote for the paper that year. Lukács's differences with Luxemburg are well known (there is a whole chapter of them in *History and Class Consciousness*).[28] In this period following the Russian Revolution Lukács acts out a desire to be a proxy and mouthpiece for Lenin and for a certain interpretation of the specific energy and directedness of the Leninist *Gewalt*.[29]

As if to compensate for the "tediousness and want of spirit" that he perceives in Tagore's novel, Lukács writes in what he calls "sharp" (*schroff*) prose, violently repudiating what he regards as Tagore's rejection of the anticolonial "use of violence" (*Gewaltanwendung*) (9). In other words, Lukács understands Sandip, the *violent* "patriots' leader" of Tagore's novel, as a "worthless [*nichtswürdige*] caricature of Gandhi" (10). This itself should give us pause, as by the 1920s Gandhi was indelibly associated with a doctrine of nonviolence. The question of violence or force (*Gewalt*) loomed large over European Communists in the wake of Sorel's *Reflections on Violence*, the syndicalist movement, the Russian Revolution and civil war, the recent world war, and the unsuccessful attempt to carry out a revolution in Germany in 1919. It is no coincidence that Walter Benjamin, engaging with this deep point of concern, had published his "Critique of Violence" (*Kritik der Gewalt*) in the *Archiv für Sozialwissenschaft und Sozialpolitik* in 1921; and the sixth chapter of Lukács's *History and Class Consciousness*, dated 1920, is also devoted to the question of *Gewalt*, legality, and illegality as it concerns the Bolshevik movement.

Lukács's specific criticism of *The Home and the World* is that it offers an alibi for British imperialism, playing the role of a propagandist "pamphlet" (9) against the nationalist movement in general and caricaturing Gandhi in particular. In the name of a spurious "universally human" (*allgemein Menschlichen*), says Lukács, Tagore warns against the violence necessary for a national liberation movement to succeed and thereby preaches the "*ideology of the eternal subjection of India*" (9, original emphasis). There is a plausible point in this criticism, even though the vehicle of Tagore's novel is an inappropriate one with which to make it. If a major front of Tagore's intellectual activism was to deconstitute the rigidity of a system of binary oppositions between "East" and "West," then this includes the polarization that more narrowly defines relations between colonizer and colonized. The protagonist of Tagore's earlier novel *Gora* (1907–09) is an identitarian Bengali Hindu who discovers himself to be a white adoptee into a Bengali family.[30] If one were to generalize the ethics of hospitality staged in *Gora*, then, as Spivak has pointed out, the opposition between imperialism and independence would be completely undone.[31] Unconditional hospitality would welcome the colonizer as guest who becomes domineering host. Lukács charges Tagore with urging the colonized to live this kind of unconditional hospitality under the banner of the "universally human" because it is ethically worse to be violent than to suffer violence.

In posing a general question about the ethics and politics of violence, Lukács may make a fair point; but how far Tagore's work actually endorses an overall attempt to realize unconditional hospitality in conditions of imperial occupation is another issue altogether. The imagined universe of

The Home and the World is the Swadeshi movement in Bengal of 1905–08, which took place before Gandhi returned to India. As Lukács describes it (without apparently knowing quite what and when it was), Swadeshi represents "the beginnings of the national movement: the struggle to boycott British goods, to squeeze them out of the native market and to replace them with native products" (9). It is by this national, indigenist logic, more or less correctly characterized by Lukács, that the movement came to be named Swadeshi, "of one's own land."[32] To be sure, Gandhi would later pick up the term *Swadeshi* and couple it with *Swaraj*, meaning self-rule; but Tagore's novel depicts, precisely, a *pre*-Gandhian political scene led by a small, agrarian intellectual elite. For various reasons the Bengal Swadeshi movement did not succeed in mobilizing the mass of the rural population, though in Sumit Sarkar's estimation it anticipates much of the Gandhian constructive, village-oriented politics of the 1920s and 1930s as a small-scale prototype.[33] *The Home and the World* represents an internal critique of the dilemma of indigenous vanguardism in two of the main currents of the Swadeshi movement: elite, aristocratic feudal-benevolent patronage versus self-servingly populist, feudal-demagogic organization. These two styles of indigenous vanguardism—apparently in conflict—are by the end of the novel shown to be complicit both in terms of their quasi-feudal nature and in terms of their gender politics. *The Home and the World* is thus at one level a warning about the distance that Indian vanguards must travel in order to close the gap between their phantasms of resistance and the people they seek to mobilize as well as the women they seek to modernize.[34]

The paradox of Lukács's article is thus that, due to his own parochialism, he is obliged to misread a critique of *pre-Gandhian* indigenous Indian vanguards as applying unmediatedly to the Gandhi of the 1920s. By then Gandhi's brilliant strategy of rural masquerade actually seemed, for the time being, to have solved the problems of benevolent versus demagogic feudal political leadership depicted by Tagore. Lukács is moreover led to dismiss Tagore's warning as leading the potential intellectual vanguard of Germany astray into a weak and ersatz Orientalism and a rejection of Bolshevik revolutionary violence. By 1922, when Lukács wrote his review, Gandhi had already staged the first of his *Satyagraha* mobilizations in India (in Champaran in 1917 and in Kheda in 1918). The Non-Cooperation Movement of 1920–22 had, uncannily, just ended in the deadly violence of the

Chauri Chaura incident, where after a police shooting twenty-three offi-
cers had been killed by demonstrators at a police station.[35] Gandhi took
the step of publicly fasting so as to halt a movement he perceived as having gone out of control.

Two months before Lukács's article appeared, therefore, Gandhi was
struggling to restrain violence, to eject it from the movement he stood for.
If the violence of Chauri Chaura might be a "poison" in the movement's
social body, Gandhi himself could expel it: "I must undergo personal cleans-
ing. I must become a fitter instrument able to register the slightest variation in the moral atmosphere about me," he wrote days after the rioting.[36]
Gandhi as measuring-instrument *and* representative condemns the pro-
fane mouthing of his own name by the protestors: "Probably they hacked
the constables—their countrymen and fellow beings—with my name on
their lips. . . . I would . . . suffer every humiliation, every torture, absolute
ostracism and death itself to prevent the movement from becoming violent or a precursor of violence" ("Crime of Chauri Chaura" 182).

"They hacked the constables . . . with my name on their lips." Perhaps
they did. Testimony from a witness at the subsequent trial reads as follows:
"I asked why they were calling out 'Gandhi Maharaj' and they said the *thana*
[police station] of Chaura had been burnt and razed to the ground [by them]
and the Maharaj's swaraj had come."[37] If we turn to such subaltern imag-
inings of Gandhi, utterance of his name and projections of the content of
his speech sanction the very acts that Gandhi himself worked so hard to
discipline and control. If the Gandhian movement spectacularly "included"
the variegated rural masses as a representation and political weapon, it
correlatively tried to ensure their instrumentalized nonparticipation. Just
as peasants were appropriating his name, Gandhi's most effective political
maneuver was to cross-dress in class terms, in peasants' clothing.[38]

Yet in a persistently recurring pattern, movements nominally headed
by Gandhi countersigned his name in transgressive actions: "What did he
[Gandhi] tell everybody? Just this much: 'Fucking hell! take back your
raj, turn out these mother-fuckers; kick out the Englishman!' "[39] These
confused scenes of violence and voicing disclose a capillary multiplication of Gandhis that is also reflected in the explosion of literary representations of Gandhi from the late 1920s. As Gyanendra Pandey observes,
every "popular nationalist upsurge that occurred in the name of Gandhi . . .
went substantially beyond any confines that Gandhi may have envisaged."[40]

In their studies of Gandhism during the 1920s, both Shahid Amin and Pandey have shown that the terms *Gandhi Raj* or *Gandi Swaraj* were key components of how Gandhi as a figure "registered in peasant conscious-ness."[41] Although "there was ... no single authorized version of the Mahatma," both authors agree that the figure of Gandhi Raj in this con-text combines the idea of a millennial or messianic arrival of a regime of justice and the sense that the current system of law, of modes of authority, has been miraculously suspended (or may be suspended by direct action by the peasants, legitimated by the arrival of Gandhi Raj).[42] This of course exceeded the bounds of actual Congress Party activity at the time, and indeed of Gandhi's express instructions, which were often propagated in an attempt to quell or control peasant movements. Yet we have also seen that at another level the Gandhian discourse prefigures such transgres-sions of disciplined mobilization.[43]

◆ ◆ ◆

In spite of his problem with accurately situating Gandhi, Lukács may be seen as a strangely anticipatory observer in another sense. Judging by the extensive bibliography of "Gandhian Literature" in fifteen Indian languages in the Sahitya Akademi's *Encyclopaedia of Indian Literature* (1988), there were very few literary depictions of Gandhi in 1921. Those that did exist would have been inaccessible to Lukács. The *Encyclopaedia* also testi-fies to the fact that the figure of Gandhi subsequently captured modern Indian literary representation in a particularly powerful way.[44] This is not restricted merely to thematic depictions of Gandhi or rural India in mod-ern novels, poems, and plays, but extends to works that are held to voice Gandhian discourse by miming Gandhi's own role as a spokesman or ven-triloquist of a vast, unspoken colonized collectivity. Priyamvada Gopal, for instance, has suggested that Gandhi's opening lines in *Hind Swaraj* (Indian Home Rule, 1909), describing the function of newspaper media as "to under-stand popular feeling and give expression to it, ... to arouse among the people certain desirable sentiments; and ... fearlessly to expose popular defects," became a "literary manifesto" for a certain modernism in India.[45] The tasks of voicing, disseminating, producing, and surveilling the "pop-ular" are expressed in very general terms at this point in the text, but are nevertheless immediately reflexively turned upon *Hind Swaraj* itself: "The exercise of these three functions is involved in answering your question," says the book's "Editor" to the "Reader" (*Hind Swaraj* 13). The fact that *Hind Swaraj* is staged in the form of a dialogue between a "Reader" and an "Editor" formally suggests that the message's voice is more than one. A self-staging, self-interrogating formal structure; a critical proximity to the spaces and discourses of modern media and communications; a certain "primitivism"; the staking of a forceful claim to national autonomy: even this preliminary catalog of *Hind Swaraj*'s surface features helps illustrate why it became an irresistible modernist literary manifesto in India.

Within a few years more technically sophisticated, differentiated, and apparently effective modalities of voice-representation, dissemination, production, and surveillance were available to both the Gandhian vanguard and the literary practitioners of the 1930s and 1940s. Yet as I have already indicated, *Hind Swaraj* represents an early attempt to give the general strike an Indic signifier, presenting its tableaux of resistance under the indigenized heading of "Swaraj" and in the mode of a fully modernized, mediatized Upanishadic question-and-answer session.[46] We have already glimpsed what Gandhian "nonviolence" does with the dreams of violence imaged in the Sorelian text in its originary translation of the general strike. In the passage from the potential "literary manifesto" of *Hind Swaraj* to actual works of fiction, *Hind Swaraj* will turn out to be an odder kind of manifesto than would immediately appear.

Returning to Lukács and his defense of a violent vanguardism: it should at this point be clear that the term *Gandhi novel* is an expression that emerges via a different route of Gandhian references, from a web of more than usually problematic translation questions. Lukács was undoubtedly aware that the German translation of Tagore's *Ghare Baire* had been made from English, as the copyright page of *Das Heim und die Welt* reads "translated from the English by Helene Meyer-Franck." Although several translations were made from English, nothing of Tagore's was directly translated from Bengali to German until 1926 (some short extracts from the prose-poems collected in *Lipika* [Notes]), and nothing more substantial until 1930. The well-known problems with the plangent Edwardian prose of the English translation inevitably carry over into the German *Das Heim und die Welt*. Very few Europeans, for instance, were prepared to read Tagore's fiction and poetry, in translation or not, in ways that could begin to grasp his own presuppositions and frame of reference.[47] Thus, in spite of Lukács's lack of intellectual scruple in this instance, it can be argued that the real object of his critique is a German intelligentsia as uninformed as himself about both literary and political milieus in colonial India.

For Lukács, then, an apparent critique of violent resistance as such must be subjected to a ferocious denunciation and a rooting out of "intellectual-spiritual substitutes" (*geistiger Ersatzwaare*) (8). And Lukács is not wrong-headed in his assessment of what the use made of Tagore by his German admirers meant. "Whatever was said and done about India in the 1920s," writes Dietmar Rothermund, "was more or less a pale reflection of the German idealist quest for India."[48] We must acknowledge the effects of a certain German Orientalism on the reception of Tagore in Germany, and on the counterrevolutionary impulses of a bourgeoisie seeking alternatives to perceived crises of parliamentary democracy and even of the spirit of European civilization itself.[49] Giving a general impression of Tagore reception in the 1920s, Martin Kämpchen writes that "in Germany as elsewhere in Europe there existed little curiosity to discover the *Bengali* poet. Although Tagore loved to recite his poems in the original, the public took them rather as exotic curios appreciated for their melodious qualities. . . . Very few among German intellectuals and scholars felt they were unable to 'savor' the entire Tagore through his German translations from the English."[50]

A love of the sonority of the voice aloud, regarded as meaninglessly (or indeed -fully) "melodious" or admired as an expression of a higher-level spirituality, legitimates by reversal the protoracist slight of *barbarophônos*, which holds "foreign" languages to be mere noise. Such representations of Tagore's voice as a nice-sounding noise are a displaced repetition, in the mode of benevolence, of the ancient category of the barbarian, a word whose origin and function were to mark the foreigner (non-Greek, with the strong sense of inferior) through a supposed onomatopoeia of the meaningless clamor of their talk: *barbaros, barbarophônos*. Lukács does not of course celebrate the meaninglessness of Tagorean vocalization. He sees all too much meaning in and beyond the text, meaning that must be subjected to a ferocious denunciation and a rooting out of "intellectual[/spiritual] substitutes" (*geistiger Ersatzwaare*) (8).

In addition to the new Tagore translation, therefore, Lukács was responding to the Indian poet's visit to Germany in 1921. This visit had seen the peak of what Martin Kämpchen calls a "Tagore cult" in Germany that Lukács was keen to denounce as a symptom of the "total cultural dissolution" of the intellectual elite.[51] Tagore was on the last leg of a European and

US tour to raise funds for, and attract participants to, the university he was founding at Santiniketan in Bengal.[52] His main German patron, Count Hermann Keyserling, put Tagore on display at a "Tagore Week" organized at Keyserling's recently founded Schule der Weisheit (School of Wisdom) in Darmstadt. Keyserling was a participant in the interwar European crisis-thinking that looked to a phantasmatic Orient to heal the wounds of Western civilization. "Europe has nothing more to give me," he writes in his *Travel Diary of a Philosopher* (1919); "the whole of Europe is essentially of one spirit. I wish to go to latitudes . . . where I will be forced to forget that which up to now I knew. . . . I want to let the climate of the tropics, the Indian mode of consciousness, the Chinese code of life and many other factors . . . work their spell upon me . . . and then watch what will become of me."[53] The narcissistic self-transformation of the European subject-in-crisis will be effected through a journey that will re-create *him* by engendering "an inwardly conceived and inwardly coherent work of fiction" (9).

On the other side of a shared debate about the fate of Europe and its vanguard place in the world, the protofascist Henri Massis critically observes in 1920 that "it is in Germany that the East has found new pioneers."[54] Participating in a widespread diagnostic and polemical discourse of European crisis, Massis cites with approval Ernst Robert Curtius's identification of the causes of this eastward turn: "the collapse of the old régime, . . . the Treaty of Versailles and the setback of the Wilson programme," and a sense of "the worn-out ideals of Western civilization."[55] In either case, it is a matter of the preservation of a *European* subject that either will try to rediscover itself in the East or must labor to resist dilution into "cross-breedings of cultures . . . mixed systems . . . monstrous unions" (Massis 131). In such a scenario, the signifier "Tagore" plays the role of designating a savior or a destructive seducer: "Tagore's idealism covers a desire for vengeance."[56]

More broadly, after being awarded the Nobel Prize for Literature in 1913, "Tagore" had already become a contested signifier in Europe. Again, this did not take place through any substantive engagement with his writings in their idiomaticity, but rather as an intra-European debate about Europe's own condition of civilization, its purported "decline." In the British Vorticist group's first issue of their journal *BLAST* (1914), edited by Wyndham Lewis, the opening section of the first "Manifesto" comprises pages that charge the reader to "blast," "curse," "damn," and "wring the neck of" a large number of items that make up a wild taxonomy of what this new avant-garde defines itself against. The closing page of the section is dotted with regularly spaced names, a constellation of people, products ("Codliver oil"), and institutions to be blasted, violently expunged from the universe of the avant-garde. Among those names is a certain "Rhabindraneth Tagore." BLAST, with its imperative to a purgatory violence, brings a Sorelian tone into the British avant-garde that prefigures the well-known atmosphere of "destruction" that followed in the interwar period. Furthermore, the paranoia about an undermining "Indian" attack on the Western subject that Lewis later reflected in Paleface (1929) finds its precursors in Massis and Halévy, and also in a number of contemporary German commentators.[57]

In such contested circumstances, Tagore was stage-managed by the orientalist Keyserling so as to convey "a *quasi-mythological atmosphere*. Sensitive to symbols and heightened meanings, [Keyserling] saw to it that Tagore appeared in a setting which tended to mythologize his appearance and personality."[58] Kämpchen emphasizes the Christlike manner in which Tagore's appearance and physical positioning were arranged, an effect confirmed by contemporary accounts of these events. Symptomatic of the argument about voice and meaning made earlier is this contemporary description of a thank-you speech Tagore made in Bengali: "When Count Keyserling wanted to translate his words the whole crowd called out: Don't translate, we have understood everything. This spontaneous understanding was perhaps the greatest homage that the people could pay to Tagore, and he knew it."[59] Thus, if the Tagore-admirers were satisfied with their knowledge in the translation—and indeed the nontranslation—that was available to them, then so was the severe critic Lukács; and this shared ground, opened up by the practice of translation, undoes the opposition between Lukács and his enemies. They are both equally satisfied with the same Tagore but ascribe opposing values to what they find there.

This underlying complicity between lovers and haters of Tagore embodies a displaced repetition of a rather older "blinding and misrecognized symptom of the crisis of European consciousness."[60] Coemergent with a certain European modernity, the investigation of the history of writing in the seventeenth century produced three "prejudices," two of which demonstrate a subterranean complicity between an expulsive "ethnocentric scorn" and an assimilative "hyperbolical admiration." Two figures of modern racism. In Derrida's words:

The concept of Chinese writing thus functioned as a sort of European hallucination. . . . And the hallucination translated less an ignorance than
a misrecognition [*méconnaissance*]. It was not disturbed by the knowledge
of Chinese script, limited but real, which was then available. At the same
time . . . a *"hieroglyphist prejudice"* had produced the same effect of interested blindness. The occultation, far from proceeding . . . from ethnocentric scorn, takes the form of an hyperbolical admiration. We have not
ceased verifying the necessity of this schema. Our century is not free
from it: each time that ethnocentrism is precipitately and ostentatiously
reversed, some effort silently hides behind all the spectacular effects to
consolidate an inside and to draw from it some domestic benefit.[61]

As I emphasized, our pattern does not map exactly onto Derrida's coordinates here; it displaces them in an altered repetition that generates, on the
one hand, laudatory "misrecognition by assimilation" (80) of Tagore, and
on the other hand a scornful dismissal from the Marxist critic. In each
case, the "Tagore" at stake is a token in a game of accumulating "domestic
benefit," a game that harbors worries about conserving some European
leading edge. Reflecting an intra-European obsession with its own vanguardism, these positions of assimilation and expulsion remain complicit
upon a shaky ground of translation.[62]

❖ ❖ ❖

Important subsequent readings of Lukács's Tagore essay have mischarac-
terized the Marxist critic's review of Tagore as transposing the contemporary official doctrine of the Communist International concerning
Gandhi onto Tagore himself. Kalyan Chatterjee, in what is perhaps the
first significant scholarly discussion of the Lukács piece, writes that
Lukács's "position on Tagore echoes audibly the Comintern thesis on
Indian nationalism as declared in its Congress in Moscow (September
1920)."[63] Ashis Nandy reiterates the same point, accompanying it with
the following quotation from a Comintern communiqué that also appears
in Chatterjee:

Tendencies like *Gandhi-ism* in India, thoroughly imbued with religious
conceptions, idealize the most backward and economically most reactionary forms of social life, see the solution of the social problem not in

proletarian socialism, but in a reversion to these backward forms, preach passivity and repudiate the class struggle, and in the process of the development of the revolution become transformed into an openly reactionary force. Gandhi-ism is more and more becoming an ideology directed against mass revolution. It must be strongly combated by Communism.[64]

This quotation is in fact from the program adopted by the Sixth Comintern Congress of 1928, six years *after* Lukács published his essay. Its criticism of Gandhi reflects the minimal and abstract statement of the Comintern's later position against what the program calls one of the "ideologies among the working class inimical to communism" (including Anarchism, Austro-Marxism, Garveyism, and "Sun Yat-Senism"). The Congress had in fact developed a sustained and complex analysis of imperialism that is not done justice by this quotation critical of Gandhi.[65] Now, I am not here simply making a correction of a chronological error for which a footnote would suffice. If anything, there might be a peculiar *prefiguration* of the Comintern's later statement on Gandhi in Lukács's tirade against Tagore. In this scene of ghosts and proxies of past, present, and future, Lukács makes the Tagore of 1916 into the Comintern's Gandhi of 1928; and the forcefully non-violent Gandhi of 1922, whom he appears concerned to defend as a proponent of revolutionary violence, is misrecognized in the Sandip of *The Home and the World*'s imaginatively projected turn-of-the-century Swadeshi leader.

The situation discloses an allegory of reading from which no one is immune: I am not interested in Lukács just because he supposedly makes a "mistake" concerning Gandhi, but because in the literary text and in the sociopolitical text such aberrations are systemic. Lukács is one of "us," as it were. Entering a perilous scene of linguistic and cultural translation, Lukács "fails" in a manner symptomatic of many variants of transnational criticism. As he reads the names "Gandhi" and "Tagore" he makes these things merely continuous with his own local concerns. If Lukács's use or misuse inadvertently parallels the unauthorized mouthing of Gandhi's name by subaltern activists in India who were turning him into a mythic figure of their general strike, does this not reveal a specific space of both complicity and fissure between "literature" and "politics" around the name of the Mahatma? Not a collapse of the one into the other, but an asymmetrical activation of literary effects in the field of the political and political effects in the field of the literary?

❖ ❖ ❖

I turn now to a literary representation of the Gandhian general strike in colonial India, a representation that takes the problematic of the general strike and of a critique of violence to be a matter of formal significance as well as constituting thematic material. Satinath Bhaduri's first novel, *Jagori* (1946), was composed in the early 1940s at the height and during the aftermath of the last great (and most violent) anticolonial movement nominally headed by Gandhi: the Quit India movement.[66] *Jagori* is an adjective meaning wakeful, watchful, vigilant, or a noun meaning one who is sleepless, wakeful, or vigilant. This dual adjective/noun function is already quite interesting as the adjective can be taken as a predicate or descriptor of the novel itself—a reflexive claim that might assign it or us the task of being watchful or vigilant over or bearing witness to the exemplary and extreme violence of the colonial State's legal system as both instantiated and maintained in the death penalty. For *Jagori* is set in a colonial jail in May 1943, and it orbits around two extradiegetic events of violence: an unspecified act of sabotage on the part of a young man, Bilu; and his execution, as punishment for this crime, that awaits him at dawn. Citing the exceptionality of wartime conditions, and having declared India a hostile power in the war, the colonial State in the early 1940s introduced ordinances that imposed the death penalty for non-deadly acts of sabotage on infrastructure such as rail lines, telegraph communications, highways, and administrative facilities.

Quit India was one of the greatest counterpublic manifestations of the official nationalist movement. Recapitulating the practice of dual power as a transitional suspension of the colonial State, Congress in fact established parallel "national administration" in many areas. For example, in areas of Bengal "civil administration completely collapsed" and there were pockets of Congress-run parallel government established across eastern India.[67] The historian Hitesranjan Sanyal has shown that the militant activities of Quit India were focused on symbols of State authority located in the country towns (especially *thanas*, police stations) and communication lines, and were led by student, Congress, or other urban activists with "peasants [taking] a prominent part" ("Quit India" 66). This is, in a sense, the displaced repetition of Non-Cooperation—a situation in which the "inner State" dreamed of by Dange was much closer to being a reality than in 1920–22. Yet while it is undoubtedly the case that large numbers of adivasis and peasants did participate in the movements of 1942, the insurgency of these subaltern figures was organizationally constrained from above, a fact attested to by the novel *Jagori* as it undoes the difference between the metonymic signifiers "Gandhi" and "Lenin" and marks fissures between activists and "people."

Sleeplessness or wakefulness—*jagori*—also defines the theme of the book's four sections, each of which is focalized by a different member of Bilu's family, who, physically separated from one another in different parts of the jail, await his death the night before he is to be hanged on the prison gallows: Bilu himself in the condemned cell; his father in the upper-division ward for political prisoners; his mother in the women's section; and his free brother Nilu at the jail gates. It is on the testimony of Nilu, out of an impersonal party loyalty that the novel questions, that Bilu has been convicted of his capital crime against the colonial State. The two sons, Bilu and Nilu, brought up in a "Gandhi ashram" (*Jagori* 11) according to their father's will, have departed from his Gandhian affiliation and joined the socialists. Not only is the putative "interiority" of the family eviscerated by its cellular parcellization in the spatial segregation of prison; it already has been turned inside out by the practices of the ashram, where, following Gandhi's own precepts, nothing was to be "hidden from public gaze. Everything was open to observation and narration."[68] As Dipesh Chakrabarty has pointed out, Gandhian modernity keeps the narratability of the private strictly impossible, precisely so that everything else, including the intimate habits of the body, may be laid open. Its line between public and private is significantly different from that grounding legality in European modernity. The Bilu section of *Jagori* denies that it could be a written testimony by the condemned man, because the writing materials that his brother pays the guards to deliver to him never reach him. Instead, the novel's questioning of the testimonial as making the private public emerges through focalization particularly clearly because the novel seems to flatten, without entirely eradicating, idiomatic distinctions between the diction of the represented "voices" of its four first-person narratives of persons of different genders and generations. If through the techniques of internal monologue and free indirect discourse fiction can stage "everything . . . open to observation and narration," this is a simulation of transparency that is necessarily organized by cuts and elisions. Analogously, the panoptic ashram-jail in which everything is as if already seen must be read in terms of the ways it structures figurative visibility. In the novel, a tendentially unifying narrative voice ventriloquizes the focalizing figures who paradoxically often appear to address an interlocutor. Yet the presentation of the text surface seems deliberately normalized, with an extensive system of ellipses between sentences that further stages the impression of a bureaucratically redacted transcript. The ellipses and the novel's overall pattern of parataxis ask the question of disconnection and representability, and invite a work of reconnection that can only be performed in acts of reading.

Contributing to these effects is a series of explanatory footnotes that gloss the terms of the local Hindi dialect and explain certain technical bits of prison vocabulary. *Jagori* is set in Purnea Central Jail in the Hindi-speaking region of Bihar; and the first written inscription staged in the novel is as follows: "You can also see the top story of the jail *'gumati'*—on its wall English writing in huge letters—'Purnea Central Jail, Bihar.'" I leave the word *gumati* untranslated because it is in quotation marks and footnoted in the text. It marks the specific lexical difference of Bihari Hindi from the focalizer's Bengali. The footnote reads in English "Central Tower" and then in Bengali, *jeler bhitorer kormokendro*, "the jail's inner center of operations" (1–2).

As I suggested earlier, *Jagori* establishes a tentative comparison between the space of the ashram and that of the jail. The jail is predictably panoptic, dominated by that central tower covered in English writing overlooking all the cells, and run by a ramified hierarchy of overseers and watchers. The ashram, on the other hand, provides a kind of mutual transparency (so that, for example, everyone can see Nilu, who, "just where the boundary edge of the ashram stops, measured right to the inch, will cook meat, eat" [109]). Nilu, then, apparently breaking the rules of nonviolence as vegetarianism, figures the precarious frontier between *ahimsa* and *himsa*, the autotransgression that permits violence to be enacted in the name of Gandhi. "One day what did he do, he was about this tall—killed bedbug after bedbug and wrote up like a signboard in the blood—'Nonviolence is the best religion' [*ahimsa poromodharma*, also: highest ethics]" (109). What kind of a pedagogy is this, where the instructive signwriting is precisely not bloodless but stages a kind of complicity with violence and even possibly vengeance on the parasitic bedbugs? No alibi here for what potential cruelties "teaching" must negotiate with and use as its material, especially perhaps where the thought of the transcendental is at stake ("the best *dharma*, the highest ethics").

The point on which I shall rest is that, in addition to *Jagori*'s carefully staged distinctions between its Gandhian and Leninist or socialist figures and positions, which might offer the materials for a particular political interpretation of the work, it also dramatizes their complicity in terms of the very question that is at the center of a State's legal monopoly of violence: the death penalty. The novel ends with an apparent deus ex machina: *gobhornmenter chithi eseche je, phanshir ordar to ekhon mulobi thakbe;* "A government letter has arrived saying hanging orders are now suspended. . . . Excepting military areas, all those condemned to death for sabotage anywhere in India during the August movement have had their executions indefinitely postponed" (163). This ending, with an indefinite suspension of the death sentence, also permits the metonymic transfer of the power over life and death to the emergent nation-state of India that was around the corner when Satinath wrote *Jagori*. However, what the novel has also taught us is the separation of classes of prisoners: political and ordinary, where Gandhians and Leninists alike are segregated from the ordinary prison population. The situation of Bilu, the condemned man, is exceptional, perhaps because capital. His ward mates in the other condemned cells are two "bomb case" revolutionary terrorists and two "ordinary" prisoners: a "madman" whose words are incomprehensible, and a murderer who sings *bhajans* (hymns) all day long. One of the "ordinary" condemned prisoners is executed in Bilu's place: "I heard noise, a groaning sound like someone trying to speak. Really pathetic, stricken, helpless agony!" (54). Amid the fractured yet extensive discourse of the political prisoners is the mere sound of an attempt at speech that remains inarticulate, where no words can be heard. Just as Tagore warned the post-Swadeshi Indian vanguard about the fissures between activists and those for whom they act, so this death of an inarticulate ordinary prisoner marks the coimplication of "Gandhi" and "Lenin" in a scene where the "ordinary," whose message cannot be understood, drops out, or down through the gallows hatch.

❖ ❖ ❖

To end: three scenes of teaching. Three scenes in each of which the phar-makon of education receives a singular *Erscheinungsform*, as Benjamin might have put it.

Beside depicting in fiction an ambiguous process of gendered senti-mental education in *The Home and the World*, Rabindranath Tagore wrote regularly and extensively on the topic of common education for almost his entire literary career. In many ways, his educational philosophy remained consistent over almost fifty years of thinking and writing, though it became more informed and considerably less optimistic about the prospect of real educational change as he grew older. As is well known, Tagore founded a small school in rural Bengal in 1901 and a university that still exists in the same locale in 1921.[69] Santiniketan is the general name for the interlinked educational institutions founded by Tagore in the small town of that name in Birbhum, West Bengal. It pioneered an experimental arts and humanities-based educational program. Located away from the metropolis, in a district full of *adivasi*, or aboriginal, vil-lages, in the first half of the twentieth century, Santiniketan gathered a faculty that developed a unique and influential modernist aesthetic cel-ebrating the presence of aboriginal and rural culture and society in the region, especially in literature and the visual arts.[70]

I approach this complex of linked institutions and projects under the heading of a "Santiniketan Fraction," echoing Raymond Williams's essay "The Bloomsbury Fraction," which sets out some of the conditions by which one can study a cultural group that is not-quite-an-organized-vanguard (because it is a group by association rather than explicit program).[71] It is the self-representation of the cultural group as motivated by such struc-tures as friendship, aesthetic sensibility, and social conscience that marks it out as such, as a kind of liberalizing and modernizing force, a "fraction" of the middle class. As Williams says, the "point is not to question the intelligence or the cultivation of such self-defining groups," but to relate them to the wider conditions in which they make themselves intelligi-ble.[72] Santiniketan is a particularly interesting example, as the institu-tional structure of its university, Viswa-Bharati, has ensured it a lifetime far longer than cultural groups such as Bloomsbury, which was an essen-tially generational affair reaching back into the Godwin Circle and the Pre-Raphaelite Brotherhood, and forward into the New Left. The San-tiniketan Fraction reaches back into currents of the nineteenth century

Bengal Renaissance and forward to the present. In terms of general class formation, or of ideological reach, Santiniketan is perhaps less of a tiny *fraction* of the Bengali middle class than the Bloomsburies were a fraction of their own class. Its structure of feeling accommodates a bigger group than was formally educated there. The admirable aspects of the Santiniketan Fraction's structure of feeling could be sketched as an ideological subject of humanistic, secular rationalism, a universalist humanism, love of the tribals, love and preservation of the folk arts, concern for those on the wrong side of the barriers of caste and class, the valuing of compassionate social service, and care for the environment—all values that appear increasingly embattled today. Tagore knew very well the persistent and *longue durée* force of what Spivak has called the "class apartheid" that divides education everywhere, and which has been extensively outlined in this book.[73] In a speech delivered at Calcutta University in late 1932 or early 1933, Tagore pointed to a class divide in education in these terms: "The widest caste division of all in the country is right here— untouchability between classes" (*desher shokoler ceye boro jatibhed eikhanei srenite srenite asprisyata*).[74] Tagore is here specifically referring to the way in which English education means that the minds of the class so educated cannot meet the minds of the "majority" (*sarbasadharan*), but the point extends further than this ("Bikiran" 330). Given what it had to work against, it is hardly surprising that a "fraction" emerged in spite of the best efforts within this small island of an experimental university. It is for similar reasons of overwhelming difficulty working against such divisions that other efforts to change children's education turned (often reluctantly or resignedly) to the urban middle and lower-middle classes.[75]

Our first scene brings us to 1892, when Tagore has not yet founded a school or seriously experimented with formal educative work. This was a decade after the establishment of a major Education Commission presided over by W. W. Hunter, which had nominally given support to the structuring of "indigenous" primary schooling in "vernacular" languages. In practice, a limited support for infrastructural development coupled with the absence of a formal policy of "compulsory and free" primary education seems to have exacerbated a general rural/urban and rich/poor system of schooling differences in terms of both quality and quantity.[76] Tagore's "Shiksar Herpher" (Education's Aberrance), first delivered as a speech at the Rajshahi Association, is a more general critique of the disjunction that he would later describe as determining ongoing caste-separation in 1933: the cultural and epistemic alienation that is produced by an education of Bengalis in the English language.[77] Education is a supplement that can help release the human spirit from imprisonment in sheer necessity (*atyaba-shayak... kararuddha*) ("Herpher" 565). Education through the alien medium of English actually exacerbates the very imprisonment that education promises to loosen; and worse, it produces the wound of a disjunction in the subject between language (*bhasha*) and *bhab* (an untranslatable word that accommodates "thought," "affect/mood," and "sensibility" in a relational way). Not English as such, but the social and structural conditions of its pedagogy: badly taught teachers who know not what they teach and are thus unable to teach the relation between *education* (*shiksa*) and *life* (*jiban*), because the *language* of education has no connection to the *bhab* of those who are being educated. This ruins children's minds, argues Tagore, because they are forced to expend so much effort just to be functional in an alien language that their thinking-power (*cintashakti*) remains unexercised. The performance of learning without understanding is memorization: we do the absolute minimum of this so as to qualify for job and career, and this produces both an artificial immaturity and an inability actually to construct anything with the epistemological materials at hand (568). Again, memory-power (*smaranshakti*) is developed at the expense of thinking-power (*cintashakti*) and power of imagination (*kalpanashakti*) (568). This results in a terrible and autoimmune vicious circle in which the more (foreign) *bhasha* there is the less indigenous *bhab*, a disjointedness that is the engine of its own development (572). If a certain modernity represented by Bankim Chandra Chatterjee and especially his Bengali journal *Bangadarshan* has indicated one way of beginning to effect a "union" (*milan, samanjasya*) between education and life, language and *bhab*, the problem requires more than the publication of a journal.

As with Léopold Senghor (discussed in chapter 2), Tagore presupposes that the child bathes in the mother tongue of his or her place and that this should provide an epistemic and elementary epistemological rooting that continues the rich cultural texture of that place. This ideally entails an articulation between *bhasha* and *bhab* from childhood, and a specific orientation of these things to the child's "life" that, if not carefully attended to, will result in painful (and sometimes absurd) pathologies in the gap between "theory and practice" (*bidya ebang byabahar*) (570). Otherwise,

the self-divided subject can "preach the shining ideal of liberty (or independence)" (*swadhinatar ujjwal adarsha*) while allowing itself to remain
dependent (*adhin*), enjoy a diverse literary culture while actually being
busy with wealth accumulation and business development (570).

This entire baleful scene engenders unconscious *ressentiment* within
the subject against itself (against an internalized education severed from
its life), against "European thought [*bhab*]," and against the Bengali language that has now suffered a great injury. As part of the rich metaphorical weave of his essay, Tagore figures the language as a young bride-to-be
insulted and disgraced by an arrogant young man. A more extended analysis would have to take into account all the figures of (normatively gendered) union, injury and disgrace, as well as food, digestion, and agricultural cultivation that vehiculate and indeed construct Tagore's argument.
Tagore here diagnoses a problem that is class-specific and as yet unfixed.
Epistemic *and* epistemological repair needs to work in the epistemic space
where the child is primarily immersed. A better articulation of *bhasha*
and *bhab* will pharmakontically attenuate if not finally cure the aberrant
vicious circle of autounderdevelopment. But so far this "disgraced and
wounded language" (*abhimaniya bhasha*), the starting point of this larger
work of repair, has itself not yet been allowed to heal (571–72).

❖ ❖ ❖

Almost forty years later, Tagore delivered another talk at Calcutta University where he addressed the topic of common education. The talk,
which I quoted from earlier, was titled "Shiksar Bikiran," which refers to
the radiation, the radiating and illuminating rays of education across a
wide social field. The title indicates, and the lecture directly invokes, the
question of Enlightenment. Tagore's emphasis has changed considerably since "Shiksar Herpher": though he remains concerned with rifts
and fissures within the individual, he is now also thinking of division on
a social scale. The initial but determining question is that of number, the
"number of people invited" to the feast ("Bikiran" 327). How far, to how
many, will the light of "enlightenment" reach? The essay diagnoses a
divided modernity, a "modernity [*adhunikata*] . . . divided, half in light,
half in darkness" (329). This condition of modernity, argues Tagore, is
complicit in destroying indigenous traditions of education that once had
a very wide social reach. At the same time, infrastructural access for a

primarily urban minority has produced a situation in which this minority appears to represent the commonality. Underlining his concern with infrastructure, Tagore uses the metaphor of the water supply: "in the villages, drinking water sank to the level of sludge, but in the towns, in every home, piped water ran" (328). Urban development takes place at the cost of rural stagnation. The vicious circle identified in this later talk is that the more enlightenment there is for the lucky few, the more darkness there is for the majority: "This foreign education system is like lights in a railcar. The car itself is bright, but the miles on miles it hurtles through are obliterated in darkness. As if only the factory-made car is real, and the whole country filled with agonized life is immaterial" (328–29). The price of the "enlightened" (*enlaitend, alokito*) few is the eclipse of the many (329). The light of Enlightenment is blinding: "in the blinding light of education, they mistake educated society for the whole country" (329). The very light cast by a certain modernity, which largely remains the restricted modernity of "English education," throws a shadow larger than the light source itself; and this metaphorics of light and darkness figures a social divide that supplements the cultural alienation outlined in "Shiksar Herpher."

Tagore is perhaps too idealistic about a precolonial system of education that, as he imagines it, trickled down a general epistemo-epistemological formation across a social body much less divided than the present one.[78] But he underlines that it is only by being in step first with the *language* of the rural poor that effecting epistemo-epistemological change will be possible. Obviously, this involves such changes on the part of the educators as well. The contemporary political situation was saturated with the Round Table negotiations toward political independence and with the talk of swadeshi and swaraj. Political freedom, he argues, will be meaningless without a wider and transformed educational work. Haggling over political rights at high-level negotiations is one thing; but "right now we have to fix the bottom of the boat where the seals have come loose" (332). "We are prepared to work in intense misery in the political sphere to get *swaraj*, but it would be an understatement to say that we have not aroused any enthusiasm for *swaraj* in the educational field" (333). The idea of a "general" or "common" (*sarbasadharan*) education remains one of infrastructural invention: not bringing "pipes to where they will not reach," but setting up a practice for the "water of education" by other means, there where work in the "mother tongue" is the only hope that something more than "what will gather in a cow's hoofprint" will remain (333).

❖ ❖ ❖

The third scene of education, and the final part of this chapter, brings us to a novel written by Tarashankar Bandyopadhay, erstwhile president of the Comintern-aligned Anti-Fascist Writers' and Artists' Association. Although produced by a man who was also a Gandhi-sympathizing author, it is a novel that attests to the fictionalities that allowed the Mahatma's own modes of subaltern representation to be acted out in history. It thereby also returns us to the open question of *swaraj* (adding *swadeshi* and also *Gandhi Raj*) that Tagore left us with.

Set, like *Jagori*, during the Quit India movement, the most intense period of the anticolonial struggle in the early 1940s, Tarashankar Bandyopadhay's *The Tale of Hansuli Turn* (*Hansuli Banker Upakatha*, 1946–51) confronts the reader with a teaching scene across the uneven rifts of class and caste partitions in modern India.[79] *The Tale of Hansuli Turn* maps its representation and simulation of a learning drill onto language differences of "standard" and creolized Bengali. In so doing, it also dramatizes a problem of literary representation—how to tell the "tale" of a subaltern group—as a reflection on the transformation of "tale" (*upakatha*) into written novel (*upanyasa*) across an abyssal social divide. The mechanisms of this dramatization involve mutations of syntax, semantics, and rhetoric that make *Hansuli Turn* an unusual example for postcolonial political interpretations. It embarks upon the project of depicting aspects of the predicament of India's poorest subalterns as colony fights to become an independent nation-state; and the alternative future suggested by the novel's teaching apparatus subsists in its rhetorical staging of a call-and-response, a staging of a teaching "from below" across social lines.

Tarashankar himself dramatizes the plan in the rhetorical form of an almost-denial in the dedication of *Hansuli Turn* from 1948. "I don't know how the subject of these people will go down in educated society," he writes (dedication page). "These people" are the Kahars, a so-called Criminal Tribe who live on the river bend named in the novel's title. The dedication, made to the poet Kalidas Ray, alerts the reader more than once to what will take place at the level of the novel's language. "The earth of that place, its people and their aberrant language [*apabhrangsa bhasha*]—

all these things are very familiar to you," says Tarashankar. I use "aberrant" to translate Tarashankar's Bengali *apabhrangsa*, which means fallen-away, collapsed, disintegrated. In the great sixth to twelfth century CE Sanskrit treatises on language and literature, *apabhramsha* appears as a name for corrupt, or at least "derivative," language, "*speech fallen off (from the norm), vulgar speech.*"[80] That is, language that differs in some significant ways from Sanskrit, usually in the direction of a perceived incorrectness, and is often associated with rustic, non-Brahmin groups.[81] Historical linguistics tells us that the language-forms known as *apabhramsha*s by the Indian intelligentsia in the fifth to seventh centuries were a phase in the development of a new norm, the "vernacular" languages of modern India. Thus, "the modern representatives of Magadhi Apabhransa are Bengali, Assamese, Oriya, Magahi, Maithili and Bhojpuriya."[82]

In the present context I call what Tarashankar refers to as *apabhrangsa* language "Creole," after Edouard Glissant's definition: "a language whose lexicon and syntax belong to two heterogeneous linguistic masses: Creole is a compromise."[83] The Bengali Creole of *Hansuli Turn* is not a Creole in a strict technical sense, nor is it unconditionally "aberrant." Here, its "aberrant" or *apabhrangsa* status refers to its literary elaboration in the novel, marked as a relational, differenced mix, like the "hinduized aborigines" who use it, positioned in the lowest strata of class and caste.[84]

Tarashankar's use of the historically sedimented word *apabhrangsa* signals *Hansuli Turn*'s relation to a complex and extensive literary and linguistic debate in South Asia. The classic Sanskrit dramas, for example, had always used differences of linguistic register between Sanskrit and multiple "vernacular" Prakrits to encode hierarchies of gender, class, and caste.[85] While, strictly speaking, a Creole comes after the event of the "cultured" languages it mixes, the Prakrits represent "nature" to Sanskrit's "culture." *Hansuli Turn* revisits the relation between Sanskrit and its others, revising that story through the mechanism of a "Creole glossary" that is distributed *within* the main body of the narrative. Structured as an erratic yet persistent shifting of the narrative into a teacherly, explanatory mode, the glossary enacts the task of responding to an other, "aberrant" scene of meaning, and of preserving the trace of that response.

In stressing his representation of an "aberrant language" to "educated society," Tarashankar underlines the work of glossing and commentary that unfolds in his novel. It is a work that goes *toward* educated society from a space marked as aberrant from its norms. And although the author is careful to locate his dedication in Labhpur, Birbhum (his birthplace in the region where the novel is set), he has already been a part of the space of educated society in Calcutta for many years. He knows this novel will have an impact there. At first critically lauded, *Hansuli Turn* was very quickly held to be obscene, antisocialist, reactionary, nihilistic, elitist, unrealistic.[86] It was an unwelcome lesson.

◆ ◆ ◆

Alongside the better-known discussions about India's Hindus and Muslims, the situation of tribals and untouchables in the emergent nation was fiercely debated, and not only by Gandhi and Ambedkar, during the 1930s and 1940s. As it related to the representation of an asserted indigeneity, at issue was the question of what the proper indigenous population of India was, who should represent that population, and how. A broad sketch of this debate about national indigeneity would place on the one hand the missionary-turned-anthropologist and advocate Verrier Elwin and on the other hand the social scientist G. S. Ghurye. Elwin vehemently claimed firstness for the aboriginals, emphasizing their autochthony to the extent of proposing a new name, *bhumijan* (soil-born), and famously concluding his pamphlet *The Aboriginals* (1943) by saying, "The aboriginals are the real swadeshi products of India, in whose presence everyone is foreign. These are the ancient people with moral claims and rights thousands of years old. They were here first: they should come first in our regard."[87] Strategically this was a brilliant argument, turning around the nationalist claim to be *swadeshi* (of one's own land) to define precisely the groups most neglected and marginalized by the nationalist construct. A claim to being "first" would evidently sit in some tension with the Congress/Gandhian claim to represent the *Swadeshis* (proper inhabitants) of India. Gandhi himself accepted this claim to firstness and was keen to assimilate adivasis into the national movement as "Indians" rather than see them press independent claims or become "de-Indianized" in the hands of Christian missionaries.[88] By contrast, Ghurye denied aboriginality or autochthony as an assertion of empirical priority because it can never be known who was really "original" in the millennia-long waves of nomadism, invasion, and assimilation to what he calls mainstream "Hindu society."[89] And in any case, as early as 1931, Gandhi claimed to represent all the marginalized groups of India "in my own person."[90] Gandhi made himself the very emblem of Swadeshi, the indigenous vanguard.

Gandhi staked his claim as representative through the extraordinarily effective political performance of a rustic cross-dressing designed, in Partha Chatterjee's words, to enable a political framework "in which the peasants are mobilized but do not participate."[91] *Hansuli Turn* finds a form in which to stage an unresolved tension between inclusion and exclusion as it pertains specifically to a subgroup of Chatterjee's peasants, the subaltern "Criminal Tribe."[92]

The plot of *Hansuli Turn* tells the story of one such Criminal Tribe, one of the many rural groups designated as inherently felonious by colonial law. The police periodically check up on these *dagi*-s (marked persons), though the Kahars have managed to shed their official criminal status and are now sharecroppers and palanquin carriers (19–21, 68–69). The novel's setting is a provincial hamlet on the bend of a river in the years 1941 to 1947, a period of war and anticolonial independence struggle in Eastern India. These two processes provide a broad dramatic backdrop for the novel's tracking of the disintegration and displacement of the Kahar community. When the villagers hear a terrifying sound coming from the jungle, differing interpretations of its meaning divide them. The elders see it as an apocalyptic warning from the old gods that they are abandoning their forest home, while a group of younger villagers led by Karali seeks a more rational explanation. The conflict between headman Bonwari and his adopted son Karali intensifies after Karali kills the snake making the sound, which the elders regard as the familiar of the local god. Following a violent dispute with Bonwari, Karali moves to the local town, begins systematically to attack all the symbols of the elders' world, and plans on modernizing the villagers by getting them all work in the town's wartime rail industry. War progresses, making increasingly visible the fault lines in the village. Meanwhile the Gandhian independence movement rages, but the Kahars are excluded because of their low social status. The interwoven sexual/generational conflict between Karali and Bonwari comes to a head in the aftermath of a devastating cyclone. Bonwari is mortally injured in a fight, and in the months he lies sick in bed Karali organizes the exodus of the villagers to the town and sells the surrounding jungle to a timber contractor for the war industries. When Bonwari awakens, his world is unrecognizable and he soon dies. The village is abandoned. Suchand, the female village elder and guardian of its narratives, lives on as a destitute in the town and retells the "Tale of Hansuli Turn."

The surface layer of the text is thus the archetypical story of a parregicidal father-son conflict as an allegory of primitive accumulation. The fatal intergenerational conflict between Bonwari and Karali articulates the narrative of the expropriation of the Kahars: their transformation from landless farm workers to an urban proletariat. At this level, the narrative aligns itself with mainstream history; the fate of the Kahars is to merge into the modernity of an independent India. History is subtended by masculine intergenerational struggle.

Karali is the figure of a subalternity brought into contact with the cutting edge of capitalist development—the war machine. Most of the novel is set during the war of 1939–45, when Eastern India was an Allied front against Japan, and the war's effects on the structures of rural Bengali life are vividly drawn. It is his entry into the colonial war machine that paradoxically offers Karali the resources to condemn the feudal humility and caste segregation of the Kahars. The horizons of rustic feudal hierarchy are ruptured by the world of wage labor and British military structure. Thus, as the war machine touches the subalternity of Karali, it causes that subalternity to exceed its own bounds into the mode of crisis, enabling a critique of the violence of feudality. Karali moves out of subalternity and becomes a *sardar*, a labor-gang leader and procurer of labor-power for the urban war-workshops, the one who brokers the ecologically devastating sale of the Kahars' ancestral bamboo forest to timber contractors and arranges for the villagers' final move to the town. This process is emblematized above all in Karali's vestiary metamorphosis from village boy to uncanny, militarized avatar in uniform, cap, and boots.

Taken in isolation, the plot presents an impossible double bind: to break feudal violence, complicity with the great structural violations of colonialism and war is necessary. *Hansuli Turn* codes the entire (narrative) process as one of a necessary and wrenching violence that will incorporate the primordial Kahars into the body of the new nation at the price of death, terror, and the loss of idiom. Yet in its rhetorical structure the novel cannot complete the process of mourning that this loss should entail. While *Hansuli Turn* is generally primitivist in its thematic treatment of the Kahars, who appear as "survivals" from a primordial epoch, "humans from the age before the discovery of fire!" (200), the task of the novel is to deal with this uncanny (un)familiarity as it persists and overflows into the present. The internal glossary dramatizes the ghostly presence of the unfamiliar within the familiar, of story within history, and vice versa. Refusing to undo the double bind, the novel's glossary represents an attempt to imagine the idiom's survival—as teachable—in the unfamiliar terrain of "educated society": a new literary/literate public sphere.

One of the earliest responses to *Hansuli Turn* from "educated society" is a letter of October 12, 1947, sent to Tarashankar by the great linguist and philologist Suniti Kumar Chatterjee. Chatterjee writes,

> In your book is something that I could not find anywhere else—you have given a flawless image of the mind of Bengal's archaic human beings. . . . The Bauris and Kahars of Hansuli Turn, whose portrait you have painted, have of course become detached from their ancestors' independence, autonomy and surrounding environment; a picture of a society living by the grace of others, forgetting itself, dissolving as a result of upper-caste, Brahminical, "Aryan" pressure. . . . Suchand and Bonwari . . . are situated in a mixed Aryan and non-Aryan context, but within that a pre-Aryan or even prehistoric epoch's human mindset and imagination are completely alive. And compared with the imaginative world of other classes of people there is no fundamental difference or defect. . . . In the clash between Bonwari and Karali . . . [is staged] an original or primary reality . . . possession and woman. . . . A language-enthusiast's thanks: I found out lots of useful bits and pieces about the Bauris' language.[93]

Chatterjee observes that the novel bears witness to a disintegrating premodern mind-set, that it records or preserves a society that is disappearing, and that it makes accessible a singular kind of language in a more general space. Yet the Kahars' *parole*, their speech, is not unmediatedly given. The novel provides a glossary, and Tarashankar's innovation was to make this glossary a key structure of the book itself by weaving it into the syntactic and semantic architecture. This glossary is not found at the end of the book or in footnotes, but is instead unevenly dispersed throughout the text of its pages, constantly interrupting the diegetic movement of plot with glosses of the meaning of words, a repetition-variation drill for teaching the educated reader. The Kahars' Creole Bengali is brought into the text under the two-way sign of a disappearing way of life and of a story to be learned so as to be newly animated in future elaborations of reading and writing. The alternative postcoloniality of *Hansuli Turn* thus consists in its near-invisible rhetorical structuring of the gift of a possible lesson from subaltern space.

❖ ❖ ❖

The glossary performs two main operations: First, quotation marks are often used to signal words deviating from the lexicon of received "colloquial Bengali" (*manya calit bhasha*). Second, words and phrases whose syntax or lexicon differs from the standard colloquial Bengali are glossed in the mainstream form. The difference or deviation here is always the swerve into the Creole of the Kahars, their "aberrant," *apabhrangsa* language.

The literary critic Pareschandra Majumdar writes that the narrator constantly steps in to give "an explanation of [the] meaning" of vernacular words. But *how* this glossary takes place is not explored further by any commentator.[94] The gloss is always announced with the word *arthāt*, from the Sanskrit ablative, which literally means "from its meaning" and colloquially means "that means," or "that's to say." *Arthāt* is used so often in the novel that it becomes a refrainlike signal of rapid shifting to the explanatory level. The commonest occurrence of *arthāt* in Sanskrit is in the extensive commentaries attached to the classical literary, legal, technical, and philosophical treatises. *Arthāt* is the didactic, explanatory pointer, constantly deployed to produce the meaning of the classical text: "This means *x*."

The word *arthāt* is colloquial in Bengali and is inconspicuously blended into the surface of the text of *Hansuli Turn*'s narrator. Yet that text is reconstellated by its scattering of *arthāt*-s, each one indicating a shift to an explicitly didactic level. It is there that the novel's glossary is to be found, dystactically disseminated throughout the work. The ablative *arthāt* from Sanskrit shades into the novel's Bengali by pointing to a *meaning*, indicating the "real meaning." Its function is not to suggest that the modern, standard Bengali of the narrator's text is the real meaning; rather, what is being pointed at with the didactic stick of the Sanskritic *arthāt* is an anterior substratum, decoded into the (implied) reader's derivative, "standard" idiom. Rather than "Creole" here representing a deviant fall from an original standard language form, the deracinated plurality of "Creoles" *underlies* the possibility of a generalized standard.

Here is a representative example from the novel. I have italicized the *arthāt*-s in the English and Bengali:

> Bonwari looked up at the sky. Yep, sure lookin' bad. Sky's took on the exact "you," *meaning* the hue, o' steel. Not like shadder's fallin', but like the light's gone "iskily," *meaning* sickly.
>
> (189)

> [Ākaser dike cāile Banwāri. Hān, gatik khārāpi bote. Ākās ekebāre ispāter "banna" *arthāt* barna dhāran kareche. Chāyā thik pare nāi, tabe rod jena "āmale" *arthāt* mlān haye eseche.]

From the first sentence to the second we shift from the unmarked narratorial voice into free indirect discourse, the mixed representation of Bonwari's thought-world and the narrator's voice. In the third and fourth sentences the idiomatic words *banna* and *āmole* (*barna* and *mlān*, "hue" and "sickly") are held in the sentence by quotation marks. These words and their punctuation simultaneously indicate the idiomaticity of the protagonist's (internal) utterance and enact a shift of levels that is completed by the narrator's gloss of the idiomatic term, commencing with "meaning," *arthāt*. The pattern is perfectly visible in this typical extract from a novel whose warp of glosses is held together by a weft of *arthāt*-s.

In the words of V. N. Vološinov, the work of the Creole glossary effects throughout the novel a "peculiar disfigurement of the semantic and syntactic physiognomy of the clause."[95] Vološinov is writing of free indirect discourse, a discourse that, he says, "serv[es] two masters, participat[es] simultaneously in two speech-acts" (137). *Hansuli Turn*'s autointerruptive and ironic system of free indirect discourse is itself interrupted by the glossary. Free indirect discourse remains forever suspended between the voice of the narrator and the voice of the protagonist, each inextricably superimposed upon the other. The operation that Vološinov identifies in free indirect discourse is a *"double-faced . . .* matter of *both* author *and* character speaking at the same time, a matter of a single linguistic construction within which the accents of two differently oriented voices are maintained."[96] The "author's accents and intonations [are] interrupted by these value-judgments of

another person" (155). In *Hansuli Turn*, the word *arthāt* announces the inter-
cession of an interruptive *glossarizing* mechanism, collapsing the simulta-
neity of free indirect discourse (or indeed the mimetic straightforward-
ness of direct speech) into a sequential expository mode: "Karali evil, Karali
th' incarnate 'deemo,' meaning demon" [*Karāli pāp, karāli saksāt 'dāno' arthāt
dānab*] (271). The voices now speak in turn, each reenunciating the "same"
word. Deemo and demon: the semantic/lexical/phonic excess of the Creole
word calls forth its redeployment in the standard form by the glossarizing
meaning-machine of *arthāt*, but this gives rise to a "disfigurement of the
semantic and syntactic physiognomy of the clause." Every time it happens,
the mechanical glossing of the Kahars' aberrant tongue produces a ruined
and aberrant semantics and syntax within the novel itself, gesturing
toward an unprecedented and unfigurable scene of teaching.

It is important to note that here, as for Vološinov, the speakers are not
regarded as psychological entities (in other words, as nonexistent "real
persons") but as carriers of a language, linguistic entities. In other words,
in *Hansuli Turn* as in any novel, the "persons" or voices are carriers of language seams or strata. The event we refer to is thus the encounter not of
two egos or psychological realities, but of two braided languages within
the "same" language.[97] The phonic and semantic overflow of subaltern Creole is used to generate a productive crisis in the narrator's language, both
interrupting the narrative and fleshing it out. It is here that this novel's
deepest modernist primitivism resides: its attempt to explore the disintegration of the representational sign by coding the Creole signifier as an
archaic sound prior to sense, and miming the process of meaning-making
whereby sound becomes sense. As the Creole signifier cuts into the semantic level as sound, so the machine of *arthāt* engages to turn it into public
meaning. Thereby, an imagined developmental trajectory from a Creole—
coded in the text as archaic—to a modern, public standard is repeated,
rememorated, over and over again by *Hansuli Turn*, a fantasmatic history
of the language, written and mimed in every clause of the glossary.[98]

The classical figure that names the semantic effect here is anacoluthon.
Anacoluthon describes a kind of shift in rhetorical register, a break in the
expectations set up by a syntactical or semantic pattern. Anacoluthon is
normal, it happens all the time: "It's a restaurant that I don't know whether
it will be any good." The shift in syntactic structure is easily visible here
as the sentence abruptly changes its subject in the middle, making a dras-

tic swerve from its implied course. Everyday language is full of such abysses. Anacoluthon wrenches narrative sequence out of joint by splitting the enunciating voice into (at least) two lines with alternative trajectories. In *Hansuli Turn* the turns of the anacoluthon are primarily semantic: "Bashanta understood what was going on. In a fearful voice she said—Dad 'ob? Meaning, ghost?" (*bābā or? arthāt bhut?*) (236). Through the repetition of this pattern, the novel becomes a story about the *making of meaning* and not just the telling of Bonwari and Karali's intergenerational fight as an allegory of modernization. Its system of semantic anacolutha cannot stabilize the relation between the Creole language seam and the "standard" of the narrator, and the system serves to highlight the repetitive pedagogical work of bringing the two into relation and of laying out the one in the format of the other. Creole cannot ultimately appear as a primitive ground zero of presemantic locutions. It is rather an *excess* of meaning—Vološinov's interruptive "value-judgments of another person"—that is staged and redeployed by the novel's anacoluthonic glossary system (*Marxism* 155). These two elements, Creole and the glossary, are locked into a productive tension that both splits *Hansuli Turn*'s language at the seams and engenders new narrative turns.

The novel's historical drama and all its fascinating anthropological details concerning the life of a Criminal Tribe on the cusp of postcoloniality thereby become the surface images of another scene of meanings secreted in the language of the novel itself. This scene of multiple meanings, both encrypted and elaborated in the very surface of the text, tells a different, counterfactual story about the relation between a Criminal Tribe and the postcolonial public sphere. It stages the dream (because it is no more and no less than its own *literary* institution) of an alternation, not a reversal, of the places assigned in the grim pedagogy of social structure.

Let us look at another example. In an important passage of direct speech, Suchand, the village's elder woman, is describing how the Kahars in the old days used to be *dacoits* (bandits). After a flood that washed away the plantation, they resorted to robbery in order to survive until they were reemployed as sharecroppers and farmhands by the landlord Chaudhury. We read:

> In the saheb masters' days the Kahars'd plant "lindijoe," meaning indigo,
> by force on the Sadgop masters' land; they cut the rice an' took it away,

jus' grabbed it. 'Sides that what did they know about farmin'? I mean, the Kahars didn' know "farmwork" well at all. Yet at Sire Chaudhury's word the boys an' lads was kept on as "herduns an' skinkers," meaning cowherds and servants.

(149–50)

[Kāhārerā sāyeb māshāyder āmale sadgop māshāyder jomite jor kare "leel" arthāt neel bunechhe dhān kete niye giyechhe, dhare niye giyechhe. Tā chhārā kāhārerā chāsheri bā jāne ki? Satyii kāhārerā "chāshkarma" bhāla kare jānta nā. Tabu chaudhuri māshāyer kathāy chhelechokrāke "bāgāl mānder" arthāt rākhāl māhindār rākhle.]

Herein lies a microhistory of the fate of a Criminal Tribe under colonial semifeudalism. The Kahars go from being armed muscle for the colonial planters to being farmhands for the colonial-era Bengali landlord once the planters have gone. The Creole glossary is again at work, this time within the direct speech of Suchand. The effect of one voice being elaborated by another is intensified because Suchand cannot be imagined as glossing her own utterances. The explanatory shift is operated once more by the disposition of *arthāt*. While the rustic Creole of *leel* (lindijoe) or *bāgāl mānder* (herduns an' skinkers) does indeed retain a trace of meaning within mainstream "standard" Bengali, an elaboration nevertheless takes place. This represents the pervasive texture of the entire novel, exemplifying the glossary-pattern that can be found on almost every page.

❖ ❖ ❖

In subcontinental Anglophone (post)colonial writing, the glossaries to be found at the end of some (but by no means all) novels often mark their quasi-anthropological authenticity at the same time as bracketing off the non-English idioms.[99] It is generally true to say that the glossary is a fraught textual prosthesis that creates an odd dynamic of marginality and centrality. Tarashankar's innovation in this regard has been to disperse the glossary throughout the text so as to try to activate the relationship between the two language-fields, to elaborate each by means of the other. His novel's positive gloss, then, subsists in its counterfactual effort to imagine the possibility of the subaltern Creole speaker as the catalyzing agent of the glossary's elaboration as a public mechanism of meaning-making.

The subaltern Creole speaker *is not* yet such an agent in real history, and though the novel does not presume to offer the reader—educated society—an image of the "subaltern point of view" or "subaltern identity," it offers an other scene of meaning to be thought, a scene that cannot be depicted as such. The novel's pervasive glossary-texture is the dispersed site of this other scene of meaning, which finds unexpected textual support at the end. In the closing moments, the possibility of another scene of meaning is powerfully staged and the glossary is retrospectively reframed.

At the end, a dramatic *après coup* reveals the preceding several hundred pages as a framed narrative, knotting the text around itself. The entire preceding narrative is shown to have been the *stake* of another narrative whose revelation now reveals itself as the key event of the novel. This key event is the injunction to preserve the very story (*upakathā*) that has just been narrated: the story of the disintegration of the Kahar community under the pressures of modernity; the story that contains the account of the Kahars' past and present; the story punctuated by the Creole glossary.

This wager is finally revealed near the very end, when the Kahars have been uprooted from their village and displaced to the town. Suchand, the protagonist mentioned here, is the village's elder woman, and the keeper and teller of its story. She is now reduced to being a marginal urban beggar:

> Sitting under a tree, Suchand tells the tale of Hansuli Turn. Some listeners hear the beginning, some the middle, and some the end. Meaning they hear a bit then get up and leave. The old woman tells it to herself. At the end of the story she says—Sonny, 'eard it when I were a kid. 'S'an 'eart thing, ya know—keep it in yer 'ead, lice'll eat it; bury it in earth, termites'll geddit; 'old it in yer 'and an' yer nails'll mark it, or sweat-stains; so I've 'eld it in me 'eart. If ya keep an 'eart thing in the 'eart—it stays there. None took this 'un, nor kept it. This tale's gonna end wi' me, yeh. But if ya can, keep it in writin'. Ah!—Hansuli Turn's done—I'm done too— story's done.
>
> (371–72)

[Suchānd gāchhtalāy bose bole jāy hānsuli bānker upakathā. Srotārā keu sone gorātā, keu mājhkhāntā, keu bā seshtā. Arthāt khānikta sone tārpar uthe chole jāy. Buri āpan mane bole jāy. Galpa sesh kore bole—bābā, chhelebelāy sunechhi hiyer jinis jā—tā māthāy rākhle ukune khāy, mātite rākhle pinpure dhore, hāte rākhle nakher dāg bose, ghāmer chop lāge; tāi hiyete rekhechhi. Hiyer jinis niye hiyete jadi keu rākhto—tobe thākto. Tā to keu nile nā rākhle nā. Āmār sāthe sāthei e upakathār sesh. Tabe pāro to nike rekho. Ah!— Hansuli bānko sesh—āmio sesh—kothāo sesh.]

For the first time in the novel, on its penultimate page, a central Kahar protagonist addresses the narrator or the reader directly.[100] The narrator has so far been extradiegetic, absent from the story, and the entire preceding sequence—which has led us to this point—is thus suddenly reframed as an embedded narrative. The passage establishes an infinitesimally condensed retrospective frame narrative that stages the inheritance of the tale itself by the narrator/reader who only appears inside the diegesis at this moment, reflected in another's imperative statement. The novel's allegory of reading opens onto a scene of writing in which the novel attempts to grasp the figure of its own originating impulse: a call for response across the divisions of class and caste, Suchand's demand.

"If ya can, keep it in writin' ": I read this demand for preservation in writing as staging a demand for inscription into history and the public sphere. An oblique demand for the institution of an education, if we can hear it. The narrator/reader is invited to enter into the performance of the tale and thereby to engender future performances elsewhere: the space of literacy, of "educated society" and the mainstream public sphere. History and the public sphere are what "writing" in the narrow sense is made to mean in *Hansuli Turn*. In the logic of the novel's rhetoric, Suchand's telling of the tale becomes a performative, a speech act whose event produces an effect; and in this case the effect appears as a perform*ance*, as the novel itself. The performative necessarily engenders, as it transgresses, an institutional setting, a collectivity of some kind. The injunction from the ancient subaltern woman figures the invitation to enter a collectivity and become a part of a tale-machine, but a tale-machine that will make possible a new performance of the tale in another time and place.[101] As the staging of a post hoc rewriting of Suchand's "tale" in another voice, *Hansuli Turn* registers the force of this other scene of writing every time its glossary-machine kicks into effect. The trace of an authorial responsibility might be found in this post hoc, prosthetic "repetition" of a figural "original," where the mechanical tic of the glossary subverts any simple ventriloquism or reproduction of the subaltern voice on the part of author or narrator.

Suchand's demand of the narrator may be read as an attempt, in Barthes's terms, to "contaminate" the other with her narrative. It is as if the main event or primary fabula of the novel is, in fact, "Suchand asks someone to write down the *upakathā*—the story—she has been telling." Its dramatic change of subject shifts the earlier pattern of anacoluthon onto a higher structural plane as the novel takes a sudden swerve out of its expected trajectory. What "happens" is the possibility that *upakathā* will be passed on to an indefinite future by being set out in another frame, another story-form as glossary-structure. *Hansuli Turn* thereby allegorizes the elusive source of its own fictive work as the subaltern desire to contaminate (to enter) the inaccessible literary public sphere by elaborating the tale within it. If read characterologically, Suchand's attempt to pass on the tale is not a moment of quiet heroism or a cause for celebration: it is clearly staged as the last resort of a desperate individual calling to an unknown future in terrible circumstances. If taken as part of a rhetorical reading, the act dramatizes the tension between the subject that wants the tale of Hansuli Turn to be preserved, written, and therefore generalized for (unknown) others, and the novel itself, whose title is *The Tale of Hansuli Turn*. In the productive tension between Suchand's "tale of Hansuli Turn" and the novel *The Tale of Hansuli Turn* is posed the question of a possible survival as reelaboration. It is manifested as a formal tic, an interruptive and perhaps even irritating simulacrum of a grammatological classroom-type practice drill.

❖ ❖ ❖

Debate over the "place of these peoples [tribals and untouchables] within the emerging nation" and its public sphere was at its height during the 1940s, and though a political-legal form for its resolution was reached in the Indian Constitution's Articles on Scheduled Castes and Scheduled Tribes, the debate has persisted "as the quality of life of the large majority of Adivasis continued to deteriorate in post-independence India."[102] I cannot here go into the complex legislative and political history that led up to the official representation of the subaltern in the constitutional form it finally took.[103] In *Hansuli Turn* it is the Kahars' *distance* from such political space that is most noticeable, for example, when the Quit India movement of 1942 erupts.

As we already saw with *Jagori*, Quit India was one of the greatest counterpublic manifestations of the official nationalist movement, a "popular nationalist upsurge that occurred in the name of Gandhi but went substantially beyond any confines that Gandhi may have envisaged" (Pandey 5). As we have seen in their studies of Gandhism during the 1920s, both Shahid Amin and Gyan Pandey have shown that the terms *Gandhi Raj* or *Gandi Swaraj* were key components of how Gandhi as a figure "registered in peasant consciousness."[104] In one sense, this was a subaltern assumption of something emerging toward the "inner State" or "State within a State" of Dange. Although "there was . . . no single authorized version of the Mahatma" (Amin 53), both authors agree that the figure of Gandhi Raj in this context combines the idea of a millennial or messianic arrival of a regime of justice and the sense that current modes of authority have been miraculously suspended (or may be suspended by direct action by the peasants, legitimated by the arrival of Gandhi Raj). Thus, what follows suspension and withdrawal of the old State is a new *Raj*: a subaltern *claim* to infrastructural access rather than the luxury of its renunciation. This of course exceeded even the bounds of actual Congress Party activity at the time, and indeed of Gandhi's express instructions, which were often propagated in an attempt to quell or control peasant movements.

The space of a Gandhian/nationalist political collectivity can be registered but not occupied by the subaltern in *Hansuli Turn*. The active political factions do not permeate down to their subaltern space as locus of an active and participatory constituency: "overhead, like great swarms of hornets, squadrons of airplanes fly with a droning noise; then everyone throws their work aside and stands to look. Even Bonwari looks. Ah my, wartime, Father! There in Channanpur, and in every gentry 'villidge' and town, they've started up all that weird Gandhi Raja stuff. Pulling up rail lines, burning government buildings; police-military shooting bullets, they're hit by bullets, dying, yet no fear, no dread" (328). The passage articulates in free indirect discourse an awareness of Gandhian politics seen from a distance of nonparticipation and exclusion: a mix of detachment and admiration for the courage of the "gentry sires" in the country town.

Yet echoes of the militant rustic appropriation of "Gandhi" appear in the term *Gandhi Raja*. The one other appearance of this word in the novel places it in the context of "new types of song" (for example, songs about the war) performed by Karali's music group. As with the tale, song is presented in *Hansuli Turn* as a flexible and incorporative medium that can take on news and commentary as much as generically proverbial moral wisdom or didacticism. The "new" songs of Karali's group are composed by a townsman, the confectioner Mukunda Moyra who reads the gazette that arrives by train (108–9) (already a metonymic chain here to imperialism and mainstream nationalist politics): "He's also seen Mukunda reading the gazette. Mukunda has put a lot of things into the songs. There's even stuff about Gandhi the Raja" (109). The narrator notes Bonwari's approval of this subject, as against other "horrible stuff" picked up in town for their songs by Karali's group, yet by contrast with Amin's and Pandey's studies of actual manifestations of an insurgent claim to the word *Gandhi*, the stress here is on a group *separated* as agents from an appropriative or autonomous access to the name as an enabler of struggle. While it is demonstrably the case that large numbers of adivasis and peasants did participate in the movements of 1942, the word *Gandhiraja* in *Hansuli Turn* is a referential pointer to a specific political and historical space marked as occurring elsewhere.[105] The subaltern perhaps did not leave a lasting mark on the movement of the 1940s. Besides marking a subaltern disconnection from nationalist politics, it is as if the word signals that "history" is what takes place beyond the covers of fiction. Yet the political appropriation of "Gandhi Raja" was an attempt to call a just future into the present, the performative employment of a fiction (there was no presently existent Kingdom or State of Gandhi) in order to act in or on history, to make a claim on the State.

If the Gandhian movement spectacularly "included" the variegated rural masses as a representation and political weapon, it correlatively tried to ensure their instrumentalized nonparticipation. Just as peasants were appropriating his name, Gandhi's most effective political maneuver was to become a class cross-dresser in peasants' clothing. In spite of Tarashankar's own committed Gandhism, *Hansuli Turn* discloses this relation. The novel's teaching exercises, little grammatized drills in the interstices of a big national story, imagine the loosening of such historically frozen relations.

NOTES

Introduction

The epigraph by the anonymous schoolteacher comes from a letter published in *Narodnoe Prosveshchenie* (weekly), 1921, cited in Sheila Fitzpatrick, *The Commissariat of Enlightenment: Soviet Organization of Education and the Arts Under Lunacharsky, October 1917–1921* (Cambridge: Cambridge University Press, 1970), 164.

1. The Congress of the League Against Imperialism of 1927 (held in Brussels) is a symbolic or metonymic instance of the tangledness and also the fragility of the threads linking international communism and national liberation movements in the interwar period. Organized from Berlin under the aegis of the Comintern, the Congress brought together anticolonial organizers and intellectual allies from all over the colonial world (China and East Asia, India, the Middle East, Africa, and the Americas). The many delegates included Jawaharlal Nehru, José Vasconcelos, Lamine Senghor, George Lansbury, Sen Katayama, Henri Barbusse, and J. T. Gumede. A summary of its proceedings may be found in *Das Flammenzeichen vom Palais Egmont: Offizielles Protokoll des Kongresses gegen koloniale Unterdrückung und Imperialismus* (Berlin: Neuer Deutscher Verlag, 1927). Fredrik Petersson, *Willi Münzenberg, the League Against Imperialism, and the Comintern, 1925–1933* (New York: Edwin Mellen, 2014) is an exhaustive documentation of the vicissitudes of this organization. There are some excellent studies of the Comintern's fluid debates and policies on "the Colonial Question," in particular Sobhanlal Datta Gupta, *Comintern, India and the Colonial Question, 1920–37* (Calcutta: Centre for Studies in Social Sciences, Calcutta/K. P. Bagchi, 1980); Datta Gupta, *Comintern and the Destiny of Communism in India, 1919–1943: Dialectics of Real and a Possible History* (Bakhrahat: Seribaan, 2006); Hakim Adi, *Pan-Africanism and Communism: The Communist International, Africa and the Diaspora, 1919–1939* (Trenton: Africa World Press, 2013); Holger Weiss, *Framing a Radical African Atlantic: African-American Agency, West African Intellectuals and the International Trade Union Committee of Negro Workers* (Leiden: Brill, 2014).

2. Frantz Fanon, *Les damnés de la terre* (Paris, Maspero, 1961). Hereafter parenthetically cited in the text as *Damnés*. Fanon's critical account of anticolonial violence in the book is also legible as a critical reading of the revolutionary syndicalist Georges Sorel's *Reflections on Violence*. Fanon recognizes that because of its "national-bourgeois" class leadership, twentieth-century national liberation bears some resemblance to the French and American Revolutions while short-circuiting the historical development and "role" of a "genuine bourgeoisie." Fanon, *The Wretched of the Earth*, trans. Richard Philcox (New York: Grove, 2004), 97–144. Hereafter cited parenthetically in the text as *Wretched*. I have silently modified translations where necessary.

3. George Padmore, *How Russia Transformed Her Colonial Empire: A Challenge to the Imperialist Powers* (London: Dennis Dobson, 1946) gives a participant's account of the Soviet Union as a kind of postcolonial formation avant la lettre.

4. Gayatri Chakravorty Spivak, *An Aesthetic Education in the Era of Globalization* (Cambridge, MA: Harvard University Press, 2012), 430. This is Spivak's generative and rarefied definition of the subaltern, a position at which "social lines of mobility, being elsewhere, do not permit the formation of a recognizable basis of action" (431). In a differently oriented analysis for which I do not have the training, one could examine more deeply the predicament of the Soviet Union in related terms.

5. Antonio Gramsci, *Selections from the Prison Notebooks*, trans. Quintin Hoare and Geoffrey Nowell-Smith (London: International, 1971), 54–55. Hereafter cited parenthetically in the text as SPN. The twenty-fifth of Gramsci's published prison notebooks (from 1934) is titled "At the Margins of History (History of Subaltern Social Groups)."

6. Michel Foucault, "A Preface to Transgression," in *Language, Counter-Memory, Practice*, ed. and trans. Donald F. Bouchard and Sherry Simon (Ithaca: Cornell University Press, 1977), 29–52.

7. Foucault, 35. Further, "The limit and transgression depend on each other for whatever density of being they possess: a limit could not exist if it were absolutely uncrossable and, reciprocally, transgression would be pointless if it merely crossed a limit composed of illusions and shadows" (34).

8. T. J. Clark, "Clement Greenberg's Theory of Art," *Critical Inquiry* 9, no. 1 (September 1982): 139–56. "Negation is the sign inside art of this wider decomposition: it is an attempt to *capture* the lack of consistent and repeatable meanings in the culture—to capture the lack and make it over into form" (154).

9. Declaration of Human Rights, Art. 26, United Nations, (1989); Convention on the Rights of the Child, General Assembly resolution 44/25 of 20 November 1989; entry into force 2 September 1990: www.unhchr.ch/html/menu3/b/k2crc.htm. "Universal Declaration of Human Rights, 1948," in *Documents on Human Rights*, ed. Ian Brownlie and Guy S. Goodwin-Gill (New York: Oxford University Press, 2010), 39–44. Also at www.unhchr.ch/udhr/.

10. Bernard Stiegler, *Technics and Time*, vol. 3, *Cinematic Time and the Question of Malaise*, trans. Stephen Barker (Stanford: Stanford University Press, 2011), 145; Stiegler, *La technique et le temps*, vol. 3, *Le temps du cinéma et la question du mal-être* (Paris: Galilée, 2001), 219, translation modified.

11. Bernard Stiegler, *Taking Care of Youth and the Generations*, trans. Stephen Barker (Stanford: Stanford University Press, 2010), 60. Hereafter cited parenthetically in the text as TC followed by page number.

12. Theodor Adorno, *Erziehung zur Mündigkeit: Vorträge und Gespräche mit Hellmut Becker, 1959-1969* (Frankfurt: Suhrkamp, 1970), 140; Theodor Adorno and Hellmut Becker, "Education for Maturity and Responsibility," trans. Robert French, Jem Thomas, and Dorothee Weymann, *History of the Human Sciences* 12, no. 3 (1999): 21, translation modified.

13. The ramifying question of the *"mise-en-abyme . . .* [an] indefinite series of mutual reflections" is clearly formulated by Gregory Bateson in *Steps to an Ecology of Mind*, and illuminatingly discussed by Spivak whose description I have quoted. See Spivak, *Aesthetic Education*, 4–5. It summarizes the question of "aesthetic education," training the imagination, in the sense that it captures the supplementary chain of "solutions" without guarantees, as the "premises" (for Adorno, that which is "presupposed") of each position are continually reexamined.

14. Especially Homi Bhabha, *The Location of Culture* (London: Routledge, 1994); and Gayatri Spivak, *A Critique of Postcolonial Reason: Toward a History of the Vanishing Present* (Cambridge, MA: Harvard University Press, 1999).

15. Partha Chatterjee, "Our Modernity," in *The Present History of West Bengal: Essays in Political Criticism* (New Delhi: Oxford University Press, 1998), 193–210. Hereafter cited parenthetically in the text as "Modernity."

16. Aamir Mufti has correspondingly written of "a slow but cumulatively massive Orientalizing of culture in the colonized society itself. . . . Orientalist theories of cultural difference are grounded in *a notion of indigeneity as the condition of culture*—a chronotope, properly speaking, of deep habitation in time—and that therefore *nationalism is a fundamentally Orientalist cultural impulse.*" Mufti illustrates his point with the example of Jawaharlal Nehru's *Discovery of India* (1946), "in which the nationalist consciousness and imagination emerge at the end of a long arc of development out of Indic civilizational roots." Mufti, *Forget English! Orientalisms and World Literatures* (Cambridge, MA: Harvard University Press, 2016), 37.

17. "Soul-making," a term I borrow from Spivak, accommodates the desire to "humanize" through education in a manner larger than the outlines of instilling rational and technical knowledge. Neither intrinsically good nor bad, "soul-making" is an intrinsic part of education, a *pharmakon*, a homeopathy that can act as poison or medicine. Spivak, *A Critique of Postcolonial Reason: Toward a History of the Vanishing Present* (Cambridge, MA: Harvard University Press, 1999), 116–28. In the colonial frame Spivak uses the term to name a class-specific engendering of a special intimacy with and willing surrender to an "alien" cultural formation though its literary idiom. Given her training and field of reference in this essay, I imagine that Spivak adapted this notion from John Keats's famous letter of February 1819 on "the vale of soul-making," where he writes of schooling the intelligence to make it a soul. John Strachan, ed., *The Poems of John Keats: A Literary Sourcebook* (London: Routledge, 2003), 19–20. Gauri Viswanathan, *Masks of Conquest: Literary Study and British Rule in India* (New York: Columbia University Press, 1989) is a pathbreaking study of the literary curriculum in colonial higher education as a soul-making program. Chapter 2 of Sangeeta Ray, *Gayatri Chakravorty Spivak: In Other Words* (Malden, MA: Wiley-Blackwell, 2009) contains an informative outline of the theme of soul-making in Spivak.

18. Immanuel Kant, *Kant on Education*, trans. Annette Churton (Boston: Heath, 1900), 1–2. Kant, *Immanuel Kant über Pädagogik*, in *Werkausgabe* (Frankfurt: Suhrkamp, 1977), 12:697. Hereafter parenthetically referenced in the text as *Education* with English followed by German page numbers. I have altered the translation where necessary.

This is the most obviously programmatic discussion of pedagogical principles and practice by Kant, but as Derrida has observed, "Kantian critique and metaphysics are inseparable from modern teaching"; there is a more or less explicit pedagogy running through Kant's philosophy as such. Derrida, *Who's Afraid of Philosophy? Right to Philosophy I*, trans. Jan Plug (Stanford: Stanford University Press, 2002), 51 and passim. Derrida's point is greatly elaborated in his full collection, Derrida, *Du droit à la philosophie* (Paris: Galilée, 1990).

19. Gramsci, *Prison Notebooks*, 298.

20. Kant, *Education*, 3/698: "*Wildheit ist die unabhängigkeit von Gesetzen.*"

21. Antonio Gramsci, *Further Selections from the Prison Notebooks*, ed. and trans. Derek Boothman (Minneapolis: University of Minnesota Press, 1995), 51.

22. Jacques Lacan, "The Mirror Stage as Formative of the *I* Function as Revealed in Psychoanalytic Experience," in *Écrits*, trans. Bruce Fink (New York: Norton, 2006), 78, 76.

23. I discuss this in terms of its classic Kantian expression in "What Is Enlightenment?" in chapter 1.

24. Louis Althusser, "Ideology and Ideological State Apparatuses (Notes Towards an Investigation)," in *Lenin and Philosophy*, trans. Ben Brewster (New York: Monthly Review, 1971), 176, my emphasis. Hereafter cited parenthetically in the text as "Ideology." It goes without saying that being well born (middle- or upper-class) does not guarantee a successful insertion into "maturity" (and vice versa).

25. Adorno, *Erziehung*, 148; Gramsci, *Prison Notebooks*, 55, translation altered: "*I gruppi subalterni subiscono sempre l'iniziativa dei gruppi dominanti.*" It is not an accident that Spivak framed her initial (and now classic) formulation of the question of subalternity in terms of speech-agency: "Can the Subaltern Speak?"

26. Spivak, *Critique of Postcolonial Reason*, chap. 1. Hereafter parenthetically referenced in the text as CPR.

27. *Groundwork of the Metaphysics of Morals* was published in 1785, and the *Critique of Judgment* in 1790.

28. Not able to be admitted or represented (symbolized) on the "inside." J. Laplanche and J.-B. Pontalis, *The Language of Psychoanalysis*, trans. Donald Nicholson-Smith (New York: Norton, 1973), 166–69; Spivak, *Critique of Postcolonial Reason*, 1–6.

29. Dipesh Chakrabarty, *Provincializing Europe: Postcolonial Thought and Historical Difference* (Princeton: Princeton University Press, 2000), 8. Hereafter cited parenthetically in the text as PE. If political modernity is assumed under a single metropolitan metric, then "it could always be said with reason that some people were less modern than others, and that the former needed a period of preparation and waiting before they could be recognized as full participants in political modernity" (9).

30. Ranajit Guha, *Elementary Aspects of Peasant Insurgency in Colonial India* (New Delhi: Oxford University Press, 1983) provides massive documentation and thorough analysis of this fact.

31. Spivak, *Aesthetic Education*, 431. This bursting out is without guarantees, as in Spivak's example of Bhubaneswari Bhaduri, where the subaltern attempt to speak through the suicided body was misconstrued as signifying an "illicit love affair." Spivak, *Critique of Postcolonial Reason*, 308.

32. Fanon, *Wretched*, 138. *La politisation* is education that is specifically directed toward knowledge of principles of the workings of the polity, and thus an aspect of the making of citizens who can in principle legislate.

33. Frantz Fanon, *Toward the African Revolution*, trans. Haakon Chevalier (New York: Grove, 1967), 171: "The African peoples must likewise remember that they have had to face a form of Nazism, a form of exploitation of man, of physical and spiritual [*spirituelle*] liquidation."

34. Fanon, *Wretched*, 199–201. The dossier of psychiatric case studies that constitutes the book's final main section represents the "raw material" that makes possible the critique of violence developed in the preceding four chapters.

35. Fanon, *Wretched*, 2. The Bible passage is Matthew 20:16: *houtōs esontai hoi eskhatoi prōtoi kai hoi prōtoi eskhatoi.* Fanon repeats variations of the phrase twice more in the text.

36. Fanon, *Wretched*, 238. Fanon's resort to the biological "brain" here (and perhaps the associated senses of consciousness and cognition rather than soul and spirit) merits further analysis. As a psychiatrist, the physiological and organic aspects of human brain development would certainly have been of interest in his understanding of how "souls" are made. As is well known, Fanon was ruthlessly critical of the colonial psychiatry that claimed Africans had different patterns of brain-formation and specific pathologies that develop from this.

37. I mean mainly primary school and high school, though this does not at all preclude other instances. Fanon was interested in the entire sequence, from the familial environment through primary and up. Rabindranath Tagore (discussed in chapter 5) founded a famous university; but it is important to note that before he did so, he founded a children's school in Santiniketan. It is also important to note and to take account of the fact that so many instances of anticolonial organization have emerged from university students and young teachers fighting for reforms at the tertiary and posttertiary level.

38. Althusser, "Ideology"; Christian Baudelot and Roger Establet, *L'école capitaliste en France* (Paris: Maspero, 1972).

39. Étienne Balibar, "The Nation Form," in *Race, Nation Class: Ambiguous Identities*, by Étienne Balibar and Immanuel Wallerstein (New York: Verso, 1991), 92. Hereafter cited parenthetically in the text as "Nation Form."

40. This is part of the substance of Partha Chatterjee's dispute with Benedict Anderson's "modular" account of nationalism in Chatterjee, *Nationalist Thought and the Colonial World: A Derivative Discourse?* (Minneapolis: University of Minnesota Press, 1993).

41. Balibar, "Nation Form," 94. It is important to note that the processes described here are neither some sort of brainwashing or indoctrination, nor the result of primordial forces of group identification.

42. Balibar, 98. The institution of a national language is no simple affair, as the massive modern history of struggles around this question demonstrates.

43. Stiegler, *Technics and Time*, 3:144, translation modified. Hereafter parenthetically referenced in the text as TT3.

44. "Tertiary" because in theory derived from humanly conscious time as anticipated and retained flux ("primary") and whatever is retained of this flux in individual memory threads "secondary." This third stage exteriorizes, records, and begins to analyze the first two, and this analytic spatialization of time gives rise to writing and numeration systems, logos, and history. Stiegler, *For a New Critique of Political Economy*, trans. Daniel Ross (Cambridge: Polity, 2010), 8–10, hereafter parenthetically cited as CPE. Stiegler systematizes somewhat the account of writing in the general and narrow senses developed in the early Derrida, especially *Of Grammatology* and *Voice and Phenomenon*.

45. As will be clear, I am following Stiegler's reading and deconstructive augmentation of the Kantian "Transcendental Deduction"—that which must be assumed without evidentiary backup so that experience itself may be possible. The argument unfolds across all the *Technics and Time* volumes, but the closest engagement with the *Critique of Pure Reason* comes in volume 3. Stiegler should be read in conjunction with Spivak's analysis of Kant in *Aesthetic Education*, which outlines the "transcendental gap" and "intended mistake" (14–23).

46. Fanon, *Wretched*, 179.

47. This is the summary view of Ferry taken by Stiegler, *Taking Care*, 59; Stiegler, *Prendre soin de la jeunesse et des générations* (Paris: Flammarion, 2008), 11. Ferry's reforms were both condition and effect of a series of other developments in media and communications as well as economy (the industrialization of printed publishing, rail, road, and telegraphic networks).

48. The relevant arguments are set out in Jules Ferry, *Discours et opinions de Jules Ferry*, 7 vols. (Paris: A. Colin, 1893–98), vols. 4 and 5, passim.

49. Stiegler, *Taking Care*, 66; *Prendre soin*, 124. For government evidence of this as deployed in the critical analysis of capitalism, one need only look at the passages in Marx's *Capital* (vol. 1) on the prevention of development and the mental destruction of children working in factories. See especially the chapters "The Working Day" and "The General Law of Accumulation."

50. Spivak, *Aesthetic Education*, 38. The chapter I am quoting, "The Burden of English," addresses the question of English literary education in India.

51. I translate *Mensch* freely between "man" and "human" in the following passages, acknowledging the sexism, endemic to Kant's epoch and our own, of having sometimes to use a gender-specific noun to designate generic humanity.

52. These questions about writing are discussed in great detail in Jacques Derrida, *Of Grammatology*, trans. Gayatri Chakravorty Spivak (Baltimore: Johns Hopkins University Press, 1976). For Derrida's analysis of a certain underside of the Kantian position, where "writing" is seen as a fall into exploitation, political power, and hierarchy, see the chapter "The Violence of the Letter."

53. Edgar Landgraf, "The Education of Humankind: Perfectibility and Discipline in Kant's Lectures *Über Pädagogik*," *Goethe Yearbook* 12 (2007): 43.

54. Étienne Balibar, *Citizen Subject: Foundations for Philosophical Anthropology*, trans. Steven Miller (New York: Fordham University Press, 2017), 378. Kant states that morality must be instilled into children through maxims, 83/740.

55. Stiegler, *Taking Care*, 65; *Prendre soin*, 123.

56. Thus, as Kant elaborates the subsequent development of understanding he contends that the child must be able to reconstruct the "rules" of knowledge, that it be able to "abstract" rules such that it is not "merely mechanically" following them (75/734).

57. Manfred Kuehn, *Kant: A Biography* (Cambridge: Cambridge University Press, 2001), 45. According to James Van Horn Melton, the introduction of compulsory common education in Prussia and Austria between the late seventeenth and eighteenth centuries was condition and effect of a shift in the technologies of power and governance toward an "internalized" model of self-discipline. The Pietist school of the epoch left a structural legacy of (primary) education that we still to some extent inhabit (State-approved and standardized textbooks, certification and professionalization of instructors, practices such as children raising their hands before speaking). The arc of Melton's study

illustrates once more the incalculable and unpredictable effects of general schooling. Melton, *Absolutism and the Eighteenth Century Origins of Compulsory Schooling in Prussia and Austria* (Cambridge: Cambridge University Press, 1988). Kant's own primary education had been "private" in two senses, first within the home, as was normal for the petit-bourgeois of his time, at the small private Hospitalschule, and from the age of ten at the Pietist Collegium Fridericianum. A detailed account of what Kant's early formal education might have been like may be found in Heiner F. Klemme, ed., *Die Schule Immanuel Kants* (Hamburg: Felix Meiner, 1994).

58. *On Education* posits the public school as a necessary supplement to private education, supplementarity once more expressed as the former "perfecting" the latter. The school thus "completes" familial rearing in a process of felicitous supplementation, ironically anticipating Althusser's observation that the "School-Family couple" is modernity's dominant ideological complex ("Ideology" 154).

59. Friedrich Kittler, *Discourse Networks 1800/1900*, trans. Michael Metteer (Stanford: Stanford University Press, 1990), gives an interesting critical account of Prussian State pedagogy and its breakdown, especially in terms of the system's annihilation of women through their apparently benevolent mobilization. The *Schulstaat* (180) will enlighten humanity by making men into pedagogical civil servants and women into the vehicles of their formation. Kittler does not mention Kant's account of pedagogy, which offers a significantly different prognosis than his own.

60. Althusser, "Ideology," 147. Althusser's pairing of stake and site, *enjeu* and *lieu*, offers a richer intellectual and political field of intervention than the now impoverished-seeming utopias that posit peer-to-peer networking as "alternatives" to a to-be-abolished-school such as Ivan Illich's "deschooling" model, which has in fact become a kind of nightmare reality. Ivan Illich, *Deschooling Society* (New York: Harper and Row, 1971).

61. N. K. Krupskaya, "K voprosu sotsialisticheskoj shkole [On the Question of Socialist Schools]," in *Pedagogicheskij sochineniia v desiati tomakh*, ed. N. K. Goncharova, I. A. Kairova, and N. A. Konstantinova (Moscow: Izdatel'stvo akademii pedagogicheskikh nauk, 1958), 2:18. Translation available as "Concerning the Question of Socialist Schools" in Krupskaya, *On Labour-Oriented Education and Instruction* (Moscow: Progress, 1985), 47–54. Krupskaya was involved in the founding and administration of the Soviet educational experiment right from its inception and was a key member of Narkompros (The People's Commissariat of Education/Enlightenment) between 1918 and her death in 1939. I am exceptionally grateful to Cate Reilly for discussion of, and help with, this and all the Russian-language materials I cite in the following pages.

62. Baudelot and Establet, *L'école capitaliste*, 10–40 and passim.

63. Paul Willis, *Learning to Labor: How Working Class Kids Get Working-Class Jobs* (New York: Columbia University Press, 1981). " 'The lads' culture, for instance, is involved in making its own realistic bets about its best chances in a class society and about how best to approach an impoverished future in manual work. Meanwhile, their advisors are tying themselves up in humanistic, developmental knots which bear very little relation to the actual laboring future of their pupils. This suggests just how far liberal, humanistic, generally 'left' illusions can be from the reality of the oppressed and the real possibilities facing them." The book reveals "the complex and surprising ways in which intellectual 'backwardness' can be associated with worldly precocity so as to plunge people forwards into adult relations of exploitation" (205–6).

64. The quotation is from Krupskaya, "Socialist Schools," 48. Andrew Donson, *Youth in the Fatherless Land: War Pedagogy, Nationalism, and Authority in Germany, 1914–1918* (Cambridge, MA: Harvard University Press, 2010).

65. Karl Marx, "Thesen über Feuerbach," in *Marx-Engels Werke* (Berlin: Dietz, 1958), 3:5–7. English translation my own. The standard translation is Marx, "Theses on Feuerbach," in *Marx and Engels Collected Works* (New York: International, 1976), 5:3–8. The "theses" are notes-to-self (and indeed notes addressed "to" [*ad*] Feuerbach) that have been monumentalized as "theses." A reading protocol for them must take this into account. I have tried to sketch an outline of a reading protocol in "Schiz-Ability," *PMLA* 29, no. 3 (2014): 484–90.

66. I rely here on Georges Labica's detailed reading of the "theses," which I summarize and rephrase. Labica's specific examples of the Enlightenment philosophy that he sees Marx responding to are Helvetius and Holbach, more or less contemporaries of Kant. Georges Labica, *Karl Marx, "Les thèses sur Feuerbach"* (Paris: Presses universitaires de France, 1987).

67. Gramsci, *Prison Notebooks*, 9, 40, 30, 32. Gramsci is imagining a future public education only vestigially emergent in his era that would offer a general "humanistic" education to all social classes such that with maturity citizens have the imaginative resources to use the specialist skills and rational knowledges they later acquire. His emphasis on a certain "discipline" and "conformism" echoes Kant inasmuch as it is a discipline that can structure subsequent sharable independent thinking.

68. Derrida, *Rogues: Two Essays on Reason*, trans. Pascale-Anne Brault and Michael Naas (Stanford: Stanford University Press, 2005), gives a sense of the torturous political and philosophical dimensions of this question. "How far is democracy to be extended? The *people* of democracy, and the 'each' one" of democracy? To the dead, to animals, to trees and rocks?" (54).

69. Recognizing of course that the actual history of enfranchisement or suffrage has been a highly differentiated process fraught with struggles over inclusion and exclusion coded around signs of the acceptable (normative) corporeal form (sexual difference), social class, mental capacity, age of maturity, place of birth or naturalization, parentage, and so on. I examine the situational specificities of some of these realities in the following chapters.

70. Condorcet, *Cinq mémoires sur l'instruction publique* (Paris: Flammarion, 1994), 326, 78. The first quotation is from Condorcet's "Essai sur les Assemblées provinciales, 1788." The five *mémoires* were published in 1791, while Condorcet was a member of the Legislative Assembly. Condorcet's philosophy of public education is too complex to do justice to here. A good overview may be found in Charles Coutel and Catherine Kintzler's introduction to *Cinq mémoires*, and in Kintzler, *Condorcet: L'instruction publique et la naissance du citoyen* (Paris: Le Sycomore, 1984). Coutel and Kintzler acknowledge that what became of French public education in practice was rather different from Condorcet's ideal.

71. An overview of the situation as concerns the British Empire may be found in Judith M. Brown and Wm. Roger Lewis, eds., *The Oxford History of the British Empire*, vol. 4, *The Twentieth Century* (Oxford: Oxford University Press, 1999), esp. 306–702, dealing with the political vicissitudes of the former colonies as they became independent nation-states.

72. Lenin, *Collected Works* (Moscow: Progress, 1964), 26:113. The pamphlet from which the quotation is taken is "Can the Bolsheviks Retain State Power?" (October 1917). Lars

T. Lih has observed that Lenin's invocation of a (female) cook, *kukharka*, is an allusion to a Tsarist circular of 1887 from the Minister of Public Education "that discouraged the education of the children of cooks and similar persons." Lih, *Lenin* (London: Reaktion, 2011), 138. See also 23.

73. Althusser, "Ideology," 100.

74. N. K. Krupskaya, "Proydenny put' [The Road Traveled]," in *Pedagogicheskij sochineniia v desiati tomakh*, ed. N. K. Goncharova, I. A. Kairova, N. A. Konstantinova (Moscow: Izdatel'stvo akademii pedagogicheskikh nauk, 1959), 3:291–96.

75. Krupskaya, 295. Krupskaya quotes from Lenin's long, extremely interesting, and painfully equivocal speech "The Tasks of the Youth Leagues" (1920), in Lenin, *Collected Works* (Moscow: Progress, 1966), 31:283–299, and from "Report at the Second All-Russia Trade Union Congress" (1919) in Lenin, *Collected Works* (Moscow: Progress, 1978), 28:412–28. The watchword of the "Youth Leagues" speech is "learn" (*uchit'sya*), but also "learn what and learn how?" Lenin, for understandable reasons, is overly confident about the teaching and learning process (283–84).

76. An overview of the incredible turbulence of early Soviet educational theory and practice, encompassing elementary to tertiary, may be found in Sheila Fitzpatrick, *Education and Social Mobility in the Soviet Union, 1921-1934* (Cambridge: Cambridge University Press, 1979).

77. Gramsci, *Prison Notebooks*, 329. One of the most moving literary stagings of the unraveling of the soviet experiment as a chance for a future epoch of intellectual change in worker and subaltern is Andrey Platonov, *Kotlovan* (written around 1930 but not published in Russia until the late 1980s). In English as Platonov, *The Foundation Pit*, trans. Robert Chandler, Elizbeth Chandler, and Olga Meerson (New York: NYRB, 2009).

78. The quotation from 1917 is from Lenin's *Pravda* article of April 16, 1917, "Congress of Peasants' Deputies," in Lenin, *Collected Works* (Moscow: Progress, 1964), 24:170: "Democracy must be built at once, from below [*snizu*], through the initiative of the masses themselves, through their effective participation in all fields of state activity, without "supervision" from above, without the bureaucracy" (169). In this article, Lenin outlines a complex double task—to immediately try to bring the differentiated "lowest" rural classes into the running of the State, while educating them and learning from them "teach the people, down to the very bottom, the art of government not only in theory but in practice" (170). In 1920, highlighting the question of working with desires, Lenin had written about the preconditions of revolution: "Only when the '*lowers*' [nizy] *do not want* to go on in the old way and the '*uppers*' *cannot go on in the old way* is the revolution able to win out." Lenin, " 'Left-Wing Communism'—an Infantile Disorder," in *Collected Works* (Moscow: Progress, 1966), 31:85, Lenin's emphases, translation modified. Notice here the cognate *snizu* (from below) and *nizy* (lowers). Lenin's terminology for social groups is looser than in the standard translation ("lowers" and "uppers" rather than lower and upper *classes*), allowing the sense that the structure of desire for change (*khotet'*, "to want or desire") may not be exactly continuous with the class-conscious set of workers. This permits us to think a difference between subaltern and working class undoubtedly important for Lenin's conjuncture.

79. Lih, *Lenin*, 181–88.

80. Lenin, "Better Fewer, but Better," in *Lenin's Final Fight: Speeches and Writings, 1922-23*, ed. George Fyson (New York: Pathfinder, 1995), 238, translation modified.

81. Lenin, 237–38.

82. Lenin, 251; and Lenin, "Our Revolution (Apropos of N. Sukhanov's Notes)," in *Lenin's Final Fight*, 222.

83. The historical and critical literature on *byt* (the sedimented everyday) in the Soviet Union is extensive and I cannot enter its detail here, nor on *Proletkult*, which sought a more immediate implementation of a "proletarian culture." However, this cannot be passed over without mentioning Leon Trotsky's *Problems of Everyday Life* (1923), which intensified the soviet discussion of *byt* and cultural change. Trotsky, *Problems of Everyday Life, and Other Writings on Culture and Science* (New York: Monad, 1973). Trotsky regards paraschool structures as supplements to the school as a specific institution, ways of supplying the "cultural deficit." He is especially interested in the potentialities of media such as the newspaper and the map. Much less familiar than Krupskaya in particular with the infrastructural details of the education of the young, Trotsky tends toward the mechanical and semiregimented in these areas (understandable, given his main role after the Revolution). After all, the use of map, newspaper, and the like also need to be learned. Among many recent analyses, good discussions of cultural transformation in the interwar Soviet era are Michael David-Fox, *Crossing Borders: Modernity, Ideology, and Culture in Russia and the Soviet Union* (Pittsburgh: University of Pittsburgh Press, 2015); Christina Kiaer and Eric Naiman, eds., *Everyday Life in Soviet Russia: Taking the Revolution Inside* (Bloomington: Indiana University Press, 2006).

84. Spivak, *Aesthetic Education*, 29.

85. Lars Lih discusses the "dream" in his *Lenin Rediscovered: What Is to Be Done? In Context* (Chicago: Haymarket, 2008), 415.

86. George Padmore, "A Guide to Pan-African Socialism," in *African Socialism*, ed. William Friedman and Carl G. Rosberg, Jr. (Stanford: Stanford University Press, 1964), 231. Hereafter cited parenthetically in the text as AS.

87. George Padmore, letter from George Padmore to W. E. B. Du Bois, January 12, 1955. W. E. B. Du Bois Papers (MS 312). Special Collections and University Archives, University of Massachusetts Amherst Libraries.

88. Louis Althusser, *Philosophy and the Spontaneous Philosophy of the Scientists*, ed. and intro. Gregory Elliott, trans. Ben Brewster (London: Verso, 1990), 90.

89. "To understand the humanities, we must seek out the meaning of the 'culture' they dispense in the norms of the forms of behavior that are dominant in the society under consideration: religious, moral, juridical, political, etc., ideology—in short, in *practical ideologies*. With this implication: the literary culture dispensed by the teaching that goes on in schools *is not a purely academic phenomenon*; it is one moment in the ideological 'education' of the popular masses." Althusser, 90.

90. Michel Foucault, *Discipline and Punish: The Birth of the Prison*, trans. Alan Sheridan (New York: Vintage, 1995), 135–69.

91. Derrida, *Of Grammatology*, 153–78. It is no accident that Jean-Jacques Rousseau was captured by the supplement and the substitute as he wrote a treatise on education, *Émile*. The supplement brings the danger of the incalculable. Whereas the schooling system is set up to try to manage the future, it also and inevitably opens onto the future's incalculability. The supplement is "dangerous" because the very supplementary systems set up to fill a lack are incalculable as to their effects and the further supplements they will call forth.

92. Jacques Derrida and Derek Attridge, "This Strange Institution Called Literature," in *Acts of Literature*, ed. Derek Attridge (New York: Routledge, 1992), 74. The last, difficult-to-

translate phrase reads, "elle apparaît dans un champ institutionnel préparé pour qu'elles s'y découpe et enlève." Derrida and Attridge, "Cette étrange institution qu'on appelle la littérature," in *Derrida d'ici, Derrida de là*, ed. Thomas Dutoit and Philippe Romanski (Paris: Galilée, 2009), 291. This seems to carry the paradox that the institutional field of appearance for the work is so structured as to both absorb the new work and allow it to cut itself out of that field and outline a new one. (This might be another description of supplementarity.) The point about literature's articulation of a dream-desire to educate the reader is so central to advanced literary-theoretical writing of the past half-century or more that additional references are perhaps redundant. A field in which it is at least presupposed would take us from Wittgenstein's *Philosophical Investigations* through the works of Iser and Jauss; Barthes, Derrida, and Kristeva; de Man, Riffaterre, Genette, Raymond Williams, Fredric Jameson, Mieke Bal, Jacqueline Rose, Gayatri Spivak, and many others. The writings of these critics are far from continuous with one another; but, I contend, they do work on a presupposition about literature's desire to educate or train its reader in new competencies even as it remains bound by certain old, generic ones. (That is, the literary work "fails" in instructive ways, each time anew. Fail again, fail better?)

93. Laura Doyle and Laura Winkiel, ed., *Geomodernisms: Race, Modernism, Modernity* (Bloomington: Indiana University Press, 2005); Peter Kalliney, *Modernism in a Global Context* (London: Bloomsbury, 2016); David Damrosch, *What Is World Literature?* (Princeton: Princeton University Press, 2003); Susan Stanford Friedman, *Planetary Modernisms: Provocations on Modernity Across Time* (New York: Columbia University Press, 2015); Mufti, *Forget English!*, to name a few recent landmarks in this discussion.

94. Raymond Williams, *The Politics of Modernism: Against the New Conformists* (London: Verso, 1989), 45.

1 Harlem/Berlin

The epigraph is from Folder 3, Box 164–162, Series F, Alain L. Locke Papers, Moorland-Spingarn Research Center. I am not entirely convinced that this scrap is filed in the right place. It is currently among the materials from Berlin. Further down the same bit of paper—in what looks to be the same mode of the same hand and in the same ink (i.e., probably written at the same time)—is a humorous note about lunch with a certain "McKay," presumably Claude McKay. There is a queer jokiness about it. Since Claude McKay did not leave Jamaica until 1912 and must have first met Locke rather later than that, it is unlikely that the note is from the Berlin days if the lunch anecdote refers to him.

1. Alain LeRoy Locke, *The New Negro: An Interpretation* (New York: A. and C. Boni, 1925). Hereafter referenced parenthetically in the text as NN. Later editions have inexplicably dropped the important subtitle, *An Interpretation*. The collection also plays a representative role in such accounts of black internationalism as Brent Hayes Edwards, *The Practice of Diaspora: Literature, Translation, and the Rise of Black Internationalism* (Cambridge, MA: Harvard University Press, 2003). As Edwards indicates, a request came from Paris for permission to translate the book into French as early as 1927 (see 16–17). Largely via *The New Negro*, the Harlem Renaissance came profoundly to influence the Francophone Négritude writers in Paris in the 1920s and 1930s. Edwards's account of

the practice of diaspora demonstrates the generally class-fixed and restricted cosmopolitan transnationalism of the vanguard intellectual circles he describes (see 116–17
for a specific statement of this, though the overall point is germane to the book). Here,
I too examine the limits of the metropolitan vanguard.

2. *The New Negro* has remained a contested document, a testimony to its importance.
Good accounts of contemporary and subsequent contestations of its position, inclu-
sions, and exclusions can be found in, for example, in Venetria K. Patton and Maureen
Honey, *Double-Take: A Revisionist Harlem Renaissance Anthology* (New Brunswick, NJ: Rut-
gers University Press, 2001), in Henry Louis Gates and Gene Jarrett, *The New Negro: Readings on Race, Representation, and African American Culture, 1892–1938* (Princeton: Princeton
University Press, 2007), and in most of the related scholarship cited here in subsequent
notes. A much more encyclopedic and international collection, in a different mode of
"Modernism," would emerge almost a decade later with the publication of Nancy
Cunard's *Negro* (London: Wishart, 1934). The collection- or anthology-form as it relates
specifically to *The New Negro* is illuminatingly discussed in Jeremy Braddock, *Collecting
as Modernist Practice* (Baltimore: Johns Hopkins University Press, 2012), 156–208. For
modernism, it seems that the manifesto *is* a collection.

3. Barbara Foley, *Spectres of 1919: Class and Nation in the Making of the New Negro* (Urbana:
University of Illinois Press, 2003), 3, 70–121; William M. Tuttle, *Race Riot: Chicago in the
Red Summer of 1919* (New York: Atheneum, 1970). See both Edwards, *Practice of Diaspora*,
and Anthony Dawahare, *Nationalism, Marxism, and African American Literature Between the
Wars: A New Pandora's Box* (Jackson: University Press of Mississippi, 2003), for further
commentary on the fragility of internationalism and the power of nationalism in this
context.

4. Foley, *Spectres of 1919*, 198.

5. "The ease with which Locke's version of the New Negro became hegemonic is attrib-
utable in no small measure to the Left's prior accession to Locke's nationalist premise," Foley, 6.

6. Jacques Derrida, "Onto-Theology of National-Humanism (Prolegomena to a Hypothesis)," *Oxford Literary Review* 14, no. 1 (July 1, 1992): 10.

7. Compare it with, for example, A. Philip Randolph, *The New Negro: What Is He?* (New York:
Messenger, 1920) published in *The Messenger* in 1920; reprinted in Patton and Honey,
Double-Take, 7–9. This short militant text—a response to a newspaper debate on the
topic—emphasizes social justice and political organization. Locke's anthology is
firmly culturalist.

8. Rampersad, introduction to *The New Negro: Voices of the Harlem Renaissance*, by Alain
Locke (New York: Touchstone, 1999), xii; Anthony Appiah, *Lines of Descent: W. E. B. Du Bois
and the Emergence of Identity* (Cambridge, MA: Harvard University Press, 2014); F. Abiola Irele, "'What Is Africa to Me?': Africa in the Black Diasporic Imagination," *Souls: A
Critical Journal of Black Politics, Culture and Society: Critical Perspectives on W. E. B. DuBois* 7,
nos. 3/4: 26–27.

9. Locke, "Beauty Instead of Ashes" (1928), in *The Works of Alain Locke*, ed. Charles Molesworth and Henry Louis Gates (Oxford: Oxford University Press, 2012), 218. Herder is usually held to argue that a *Volk* is a *Volk* because it has its national *Bildung* through a
(single) language. In *Imagined Communities: Reflections on the Origin and Spread of Nationalism* (London: Verso, 1983) Benedict Anderson criticizes Herder's reductive formulation of the relation between national formation and a single language (a nation is only

imaginable on the basis of a single shared language; nation = a language because European nation-states modernized themselves on the basis of the nationalization of their vernaculars, claiming the "rights" of these language-culture-people complexes). For Anderson (a) the nation's outline is *not* fundamentally linguistic, and (b) the Herderian version does not account for the different way the nation-form had previously emerged in the Americas; see 46, 67. Fichte's odd place here is useful to Locke, as we shall see.

10. For Fichte's reception within Zionist intellectual circles, see Manfred Voigts, "Fichte as 'Jew-Hater' and Prophet of the Zionists," *Leo Baeck Institute Yearbook* 45, no. 1 (2000): 81–91. For the Chinese context, see Joachim Kurtz, "Selbstbehauptung mit geliehener Stimme: J. G. Fichte als Redner an die chinesischer Nation," in *Selbstbehauptungsdiskurse in Asien: China—Japan—Korea*, ed. Iwo Amelung et al. (Munich: Iudicium, 2003), 219–42. Sati al-Husri, a key intellectual figure in the turn from "Ottomanism" to Arab Nationalism in the interwar period, adapted Fichtean theses to his conjuncture. For discussion, see William L. Cleveland, *The Making of an Arab Nationalist: Ottomanism and Arabism in the Life and Thought of Sati' Al-Husri* (Princeton: Princeton University Press, 1972); Sylvia Haim, "Islam and the Theory of Arab Nationalism," in *The Middle East in Transition*, ed. Walter Z. Lacqueur (New York: Praeger, 1958), and also Haim, *Arab Nationalism: An Anthology* (Berkeley: University of California Press, 1974). According to John Breuilly, al-Husri was even known as "the Arab Fichte." Quotation from Breuilly, *Nationalism and the State* (Chicago: University of Chicago Press, 1994), 149.

11. For instance, Martin Buber, "On the [Jewish] Renaissance (1903)," in *The Martin Buber Reader: Essential Writings*, ed. Asher D Biemann (New York: Palgrave Macmillan, 2002), 139–44. Buber's article thus translated is the first section of a longer essay, "The Jewish Culture-Problem and Zionism." While "renaissance" does not actually appear in the title section (it is added in the translation), the first sentence reads, "We speak of the Jewish renaissance" (*Wir sprechen von der jüdischen Renaissance*). Buber, "Das jüdische Kulturproblem und der Zionismus," in *Die Stimme der Wahrheit: Jahrbuch für wissenschaftlichen Zionismus*, ed. Lazar Schön (Würzburg: N. Philippi, 1905), 205–17. Locke did not coin the term *Harlem Renaissance*, referring rather to a "Negro Renaissance" in his collection.

12. The phrase "Harlem . . . is the home of the negro's 'Zionism'" occurs in Locke's essays in both *Survey Graphic* (New York: Black Classic Press, 1925), 633, and *The New Negro* (14). The *Survey Graphic* cover, however, reads "Harlem Mecca of the New Negro," though "Mecca" in this conjuncture would have connoted any locus of pilgrimage rather than a specifically Islamic alternative to the Zionism analogy. Indeed, the references to Zion in Locke's writing can be seen as a competitive bid against Garveyite discourse that had more than a whiff of Zionism about it. The UNIA boasted members such as Rabbi Mordecai Herman, reformer in 1921 of the Moorish Zionist Temple in Harlem, and Arnold J. Ford, who in 1923 became the rabbi of the Beth B'nai Abraham congregation in Harlem. Ford would later attempt to found a black Jewish homeland in Ethiopia. More detailed accounts, and the longer view in its great complexity, may be found in Yvonne Patricia Chireau and Nathaniel Deutsch, *Black Zion African American Religious Encounters with Judaism* (New York: Oxford University Press, 2000); Elias Farajajé-Jones, *In Search of Zion: The Spiritual Significance of Africa in Black Religious Movements* (New York: Peter Lang, 1990); I. K. Sundiata, *Brothers and Strangers: Black Zion, Black Slavery, 1914-1940* (Durham: Duke University Press, 2003).

13. In the early 1900s at least, Buber emphasized cultural activism as "the most signifi-cant means [eines der wesentlichsten Mittel, one of the most essential means] to reach ter-ritorial goals—to win the land." Buber, "On the [Jewish] Renaissance (1903)," 143. He sees cultural work as a long-term means to the territorial end, rather than as an alter-native to the conquering of territory. Anson Rabinbach, In the Shadow of Catastrophe Ger-man Intellectuals Between Apocalypse and Enlightenment (Berkeley: University of Cali-fornia Press, 1997), outlines the turn toward a Jewish messianism and apocalypticism after World War I; see 27–65. Perhaps inevitably, given the period of his intellectual formation in the 1910s, Locke's position remains more consonant with that of the gen-eration of Georg Simmel and Hermann Cohen.

14. Beside Buber, some of Locke's near-contemporaries in Germany who were involved in the philosophical and political debates about Zionism included Franz Rosenzweig, Wal-ter Benjamin, and Gershom Scholem. I discuss the older Hermann Cohen later in this chapter.

15. See Molesworth and Gates, The Works of Alain Locke, 391–92. This includes Locke's inter-chapters from When Peoples Meet, a Study in Race and Culture Contacts, by Alain Locke and Bernhard Joseph Stern (New York: Committee on Workshops, Progressive Education Association, 1942). For example, "The Predicaments of Minorities": "Wirth points out how the culturally snubbed Jew has often become the apostle of nationalism and racial consciousness, and shows the extent to which anti-Semitism has been responsible for the development of Zionism. There are close analogies in other minority experi-ence, particularly the Negro." Molesworth and Gates, Works of Alain Locke, 391.With Garveyism particularly in mind, Locke goes on to warn of the extremes that can be generated in such reactive movements.

16. Pheng Cheah, Spectral Nationality: Passages of Freedom from Kant to Postcolonial Literatures of Liberation (New York: Columbia University Press, 2003), 121. Bildung is the central con-cept for Cheah's book. He refers specifically to the Angola of Amilcar Cabral, the Alge-ria of Frantz Fanon, the Indonesia of Pramoedya Ananta Toer, and the Kenya of Ngũgi wa Th'iong'o.

17. Cheah, 129.

18. Locke slightly predates discussions that identify a U.S. "internal colonialism," and his writing uses the terms of a liberal version of enlightenment rather than the more mili-tant language of colonialism and imperialism that characterized communist discus-sions of black predicaments later in the 1920s. A detailed account of the vicissitudes of the latter can be found in Mark Solomon, The Cry Was Unity: Communists and African Ameri-cans, 1917–36 (Jackson: University Press of Mississippi, 1998). There is further discussion of this conjuncture in Erik S. McDuffie, Sojourning for Freedom: Black Women, American Communism, and the Making of Black Left Feminism (Durham: Duke University Press, 2011), 1–58; and Mark Naison, Communists in Harlem During the Depression (Urbana: University of Illinois Press, 1983), 3–25.

19. Johann Gottlieb Fichte, Addresses to the German Nation, trans. Gregory Moore (New York: Cambridge University Press, 2008); Fichte, Reden an die deutsche Nation (Hamburg: Felix Meiner, 2008). Hereafter referred to in the text parenthetically as AG with English page references followed by German. I have silently modified translations where necessary.

20. Fichte was forced by the censor to change the word Staat (State) to das gemeine Wesen (commonwealth) in these passages.

21. As I have tried to indicate in the text, *Erziehung* has a slightly broader sense than education narrowly or institutionally conceived. It can take on notions of upbringing or rearing outside the school, and thus implicates broader familial and sociocultural spaces and forces. Uncannily anticipating rather later vanguard notions of childrearing (e.g., some versions of early Soviet imagining), Fichte proposes that children be entirely extracted from the biological familial space for the term of their upbringing.

22. Gayatri Spivak has addressed some of these questions from a different perspective in "Nationalism and the Imagination," in *An Aesthetic Education in the Era of Globalization* (Cambridge, MA: Harvard University Press, 2013), 275–300. Other situations and idioms will have their own names for the border and what it delineates and protects.

23. Hegel, who took over Fichte's chair at the University of Berlin after the latter's death, published his *Phenomenology of Spirit* (*Phänomenologie des Geistes*) in the same year Fichte delivered his lectures. Georg Wilhelm Friedrich Hegel, *Die Phänomenologie des Geistes* (Bamberg: Joseph Anton Goebhardt, 1807).

24. Etienne Balibar, "Fichte and the Internal Border," in *Masses, Classes, Ideas: Studies on Politics and Philosophy Before and After Marx* (New York: Routledge, 1994), 66–68. Perhaps this is why Balibar in conclusion refers to the "infinitely plastic" nature of the national idea in Fichte's formulation (84).

25. "Philosophy of the Last Century (from Fichte to Nietzsche and Bergson)." "Verzeichnis Der Vorlesungen an Der Königlichen Friedrich-Wilhems-Universität," 1911–1910, Folder 8, Box 164–162, Series F, Alain L. Locke Papers, Morland-Spingarn Research Center. In spring 1911 Locke also took "Grundbegriff der Wissenschaften" and "Probleme der Moderne Kultur" with Simmel. Other classes taken by Locke include "Idealistische Weltanschauung" (Prof. Münsterberg), and "Geschichteder Philosophie: Kant und Idealismus" and "Seminar: Kantischen Antinomie" (both Prof. Riehl). See Locke, "List of Courses Taken" and "Grade Book" 1910–11, Folder 4 and Folder 5, Box 164–162, Series F, Alain L. Locke Papers, MSRC. Specific material from Simmel's teachings can be found in Angela Rammstedt and Cécile Rol, eds., *Georg Simmel Gesamtausgabe*, vol. 21 (Berlin: Suhrkamp, 2010). This volume contains transcripts of Simmel's class notes for two classes for the academic year 1913–14, and class notes from a range of students in his classes between 1897 and 1914. Simmel taught similar classes from year to year, though no class notes for the classes Locke took in the years he took them are reproduced there. Of the similarly named classes that Locke did take, we have detailed notes from students on "Philosophie des 19. Jahrhunderts," 1902–03, 1903–04, 1907–08 and 1911–12; and "Ethik und Probleme der Moderne Kultur," 1913. Among Simmel's other students during the period represented by this volume were Ernst Robert Curtius, Adolf Löwe, Georg Lukács, and Robert Ezra Park. For the standard biographical account, see Leonard Harris and Charles Molesworth, *Alain L. Locke: Biography of a Philosopher* (Chicago: University of Chicago Press, 2008), 59–106. Placing the emphasis on Locke's sexual psychobiography, Anne Pochmara makes some interesting connections to early-twentieth-century homoerotic German youth movements such as the Wandervogel. She suggests that a concern with emergent youth combines here with Locke's fantasy of male (pre) creativity into a "pedagogical Eros"—and that this German example also linked a homosexualized *Jugend* collective with the notion of national renewal. Pochmara inexplicably assigns Locke to Berlin for four years between 1907 and 1911, when he was in fact at Oxford from 1907 to 1910 and Berlin from 1910 to 1911. Anna Pochmara, *The Making of*

the New Negro Black Authorship, Masculinity, and Sexuality in the Harlem Renaissance (Amsterdam: Amsterdam University Press, 2011), 57–93.

26. The notes from Rudolf Pannwitz (1903–04) and Herman Schmalenbach (1907–08) are particularly extensive and useful. One must of course exercise caution when relying on student notes to gauge the content of a great teacher's lecture series (the case of Saussure's *Cours de linguistique générale* comes to mind). However, the student notes on Simmel's lecture series can usefully be compared with the brief sections on Fichte in his books *Hauptprobleme der Philosophie* (Leipzig: Göschensche, 1910) and *Schopenhauer und Nietzsche: Ein Vortragszyklus* (Leipzig: Duncker und Humblot, 1907), in which some of the material of that series is worked into book form.

27. Georg Simmel, *Schopenhauer and Nietzsche*, trans. Helmut Loiskandl et al. (Amherst: University of Massachusetts Press, 1986), 151.

28. Simmel, *Gesamtausgabe*, 21:367: "das vernünftige Denken Herr werden soll über die Zufälligkeit des Daseins." Both Pannwitz and Schmalenbach's notes record Simmel's understanding of Fichte as the first German socialist. Fichte's work of philosophical political economy, *The Closed Commercial State* (1800; Albany: State University of New York Press, 2012), is also perhaps compatible with emergent national socialist positions before national(ist) socialism became Nazism.

29. For the intellectual connection between Simmel and Cohen via their student Ernst Cassirer, see Gregory B. Moynahan, *Ernst Cassirer and the Critical Science of Germany, 1899–1919* (New York: Anthem, 2013), esp. 33–35. Simmel's reading of Kant seems indebted to Cohen.

30. Hermann Cohen "Deutschtum und Judentum" (1915), in *Hermann Cohen: Werke* (Hildesheim: G. Olms, 1998), 16:535. Cohen emphasizes the phrase "Das soziale Ich hat er als das nationale Ich entdeckt."

31. Jacques Derrida, *Psyche: Inventions of the Other* (Stanford: Stanford University Press, 2007), 2:283.

32. Paul de Man, *Aesthetic Ideology* (Minneapolis: University of Minnesota Press, 1996), 172–73.

33. See Harris and Molesworth, *Alain L. Locke: Biography of a Philosopher*, and David S. Marriott, *Haunted Life: Visual Culture and Black Modernity* (New Brunswick, NJ: Rutgers University Press, 2007), chap. 5.

34. "He seldom separated this commitment [to what he saw as his 'race tradition'] from the other concern that motivated much of his thought and effort, namely the German sense of education and self-discipline—conveyed by the word *Bildung*—which he absorbed at Harvard and even more so at Oxford and Berlin." Harris and Molesworth, *Alain L. Locke*, 46.

35. Locke demonstrates his familiarity with the trajectory of modern German philosophy and intellectual history at many other points in his published writings and unpublished student papers. For a general sense of this, see the collection by Molesworth and Gates, *The Works of Alain Locke*.

36. Fichte, *Addresses to the German Nation*, 45–46. Steve Pinkerton is surely correct to remind us of the biblical and Christian framework not only of Locke's language and imagining of emancipation, but of the *New Negro*'s contributors in general. Steve Pinkerton, "'New Negro' v. 'Niggeratti': Defining and Defiling the Black Messiah," *Modernism/Modernity* 20, no. 3 (2013): 539–55, esp. 540–45. This is inevitable, given the history of African American liberation theology. Here I am establishing that it is also fully com-

patible with Fichte's messianic, revelatory, testamentary mode. Seeing only the narrowly religious "sacred" in Locke's evocations of spirit, Pinkerton misses its intersections with the philosophical seam therein. In *The Rhetoric of Romantic Prophecy* (Stanford: Stanford University Press, 2002), 48–51, Ian Balfour brings out clearly the (biblical) prophetic dimension of Fichte's *Addresses*, where the testament is the transmission of a call for a (dismembered) nation to become what it (originally) is. Hence the combination of institutional futurity (education) and spiritual entreaty.

37. See, for example, David Kenosian, "Sound Reasoning: Fichtean Elements in Wilhelm von Humboldt's Philosophy of Language," and Claude Piché, "Fichte, Schleiermacher and W. von Humboldt on the Foundation of the University of Berlin," in *Fichte, German Idealism, and Early Romanticism*, ed. Daniel Breazeale and Tom Rockmore (Amsterdam: Brill/Rodopi, 2010). For a philosophical defense of Fichte's concrete plans for higher education, see Theodor W. Adorno, *Critical Models: Interventions and Catchwords*, trans. Henry W. Pickford (New York: Columbia University Press, 1998), 21–22. The global effects of the Humboldtian university system have of course been incalculable, but they have reproduced aspects of the very class fissures Fichte criticized.

38. Derrida, "Onto-Theology," 13.

39. Fichte, *Addresses to the German Nation*, 97/124, my emphasis.

40. Fichte, 97/124.

41. David Farrell Krell, *Phantoms of the Other: Four Generations of Derrida's Geschlecht* (Albany: State University of New York Press, 2015), 48.

42. A sense of the overwhelming complexity of the question of *Geschlecht* in the context of modern literature and philosophy, and to which I am indebted in the following, can be gained from Derrida, "Geschlecht I" and "Geschlecht II," in *Psyche: Inventions of the Other*, ed. Peggy Kamuf and Elizabeth Rottenberg (Stanford: Stanford University Press, 2008), 27–86; "Geschlecht," in *The Dictionary of Untranslatables*, ed. Barbara Cassin et al. (Princeton: Princeton University Press, 2014), 394–96; Krell, *Phantoms of the Other*.

43. This deracinated "origin" of course goes for the dominant white United States too, as a comparatively recent settler-colony with a genocidal relation to the indigenes. However, as I suggested earlier, Locke's subversive turn is to name as nationally exemplary subject the descendants of slaves forcibly brought to the country and lacking full civil rights.

44. Nikhil Pal Singh, *Black Is a Country: Race and the Unfinished Struggle for Democracy* (Cambridge, MA: Harvard University Press, 2004), 21.

45. Singh, 38, 44.

46. Locke, *The New Negro*, xxvii, 51. The language of "generation" is pronounced in the section "Negro Youth Speaks," from which the latter quotation is drawn.

47. There are echoes here of Frederick Douglass, "What to the Slave Is the Fourth of July?" (1852), in *Frederick Douglass: Selected Speeches and Writings*, ed. Philip Sheldon Foner and Yuval Taylor (Chicago: Lawrence Hill, 1999), 188–206. See Singh, *Black is a Country*, 44–45 for relevant discussion.

48. Fichte, *Addresses to the German Nation*, 186, 195, my emphasis. *Vollkommenheit* was the German translation of the French *perfectibilité*, with *Vervollkommnung* as the name for the state supposedly thereby approached. The different valences of the French and German suffixes -ité and -heit must be taken into account here, as must the difference between *Vollkommen* and *perfect*. An excellent overview and bibliography of the eighteenth-century debates surrounding the translation of Rousseau's *perfectibilité* into

both German and English may be found in Cassin et al., *Dictionary of Untranslatables*, 769–72. For further discussion, see Koepke, "Mephisto and Aesthetic Nihilism," in *Subversive Sublimities: Undercurrents of the German Enlightenment*, ed. Eitel Friedrich Timm (Columbia, SC: Camden House, 1992), 38; Edgar Landgraf, "The Education of Humankind: Perfectibility and Discipline in Kant's Lectures *Über Pädagogik*," *Goethe Yearbook* 12 (2007): 43.

49. See again Edwards's *The Practice of Diaspora* for an account of the practical dimensions of the cosmopolitanism and internationalism evoked in outline by Locke.

50. Antonio Gramsci, "The Different Position of Urban and Rural-Type Intellectuals," in *Selections from the Prison Notebooks*, trans. Quintin Hoare and Geoffrey Nowell-Smith (London: International, 1971), 21. The entire passage is worth quoting in spite of Gramsci's lack of empirical detail, as it almost appears as a reading of Locke: "One further phenomenon in the United States is worth studying, and that is the formation of a surprising number of negro intellectuals who absorb American culture and technology. It is worth bearing in mind the indirect influence that these negro intellectuals could exercise on the backward masses in Africa, and indeed direct influence if one or other of these hypotheses were ever to be verified: 1. that American expansionism should use American negroes as its agents in the conquest of the African market and the extension of American civilization (something of the kind has already happened, but I don't know to what extent); 2. that the struggle for the unification of the American people should intensify in such a way as to provoke a negro exodus and the return to Africa of the most independent and energetic intellectual elements, the ones, in other words, who would be least inclined to submit to some possible future legislation that was even more humiliating than are the present widespread social customs. This development would give rise to two fundamental questions: 1. linguistic: whether English could become the educated language of Africa, bringing unity in the place of the existing swarm of dialects? 2. whether this intellectual stratum could have sufficient assimilating and organizing capacity to give a 'national' character to the present primitive sentiment of being a despised race, thus giving the African continent a mythic function as the common fatherland of all the negro peoples? It seems to me that, for the moment, American negroes have a national and racial spirit which is negative rather than positive, one which is a product of the struggle carried on by the whites in order to isolate and depress them. But was not this the case with the Jews up to and throughout the eighteenth century? Liberia, already Americanized and with English as its official language, could become the Zion of American negroes, with a tendency to set itself up as an African Piedmont."

51. See in particular "The Legacy of the Ancestral Arts," an essay penned by Locke himself, but also the entire containing section, "The Negro Digs Up His Past."

52. The manifesto is the exemplary document of both political and cultural vanguardism. Janet Lyon writes that the conventional understanding of the manifesto is as "the testimony of a historical present tense spoken in the impassioned voice of its participants," a "speaking voice" or "speech-like genre." Janet Lyon, *Manifestoes: Provocations of the Modern* (Ithaca: Cornell University Press, 1999), 9, 36. I follow Lyon in questioning the apparent transparency of the manifesto form and its voice(s).

53. Lyon, 10. Lyon sets the twentieth-century manifesto-form into a genealogy that goes as far back as seventeenth-century revolutionary tracts by Diggers and Levellers (couched in eschatological discourses of religious prophecy). This enriches and expands

studies of *The New Negro* such as Pinkerton's that highlight its biblical or (new) testamentary character, though what clearly connects the two is the apocalyptic or revelatory mode, of which the manifesto-form seems to be a modernized derivation. See
Jacques Derrida, "Of An Apocalyptic Tone Recently Adopted in Philosophy," *Oxford Literary Review* 6, no. 2 (1984): 3–37.

54. Lyon, *Manifestoes*, 9.

55. Locke refers to himself as a "philosophical mid-wife to a generation of younger poets,
writers, artists" in his "Values and Imperatives" (1935), and as having the "avocation
of mid-wifery to younger Negro poets" in his "Class Report" of 1933. Marriott, *Haunted
Life*, 152, 154. Marriott reminds us of the Socratic philosophical maieutics that bring
together same-sex eroticism and intellectual procreation (144–44).

56. Marriott's reading rightly emphasizes the homoeroticism and homosexuality of Locke's
imagined relationship to the fecundity of male cultural procreation. In some sense,
these figurative births circumvent the question of sexual difference by appearing phan-
tasmatically for Locke as the autoprocreation of men. The midwife role, as that played
by an individual (Locke), "ruins" his own narrative of a collective "descendence by not
being part of but nonetheless central to the racial reproduction of the manly 'succession of spirit.' " Marriott, *Haunted Life*, 149. Surprisingly, Marriott does not mention the
"Brown Madonna" image discussed later.

57. www.nga.gov/content/ngaweb/Collection/art-object-page.33254.html.

58. Julia Kristeva, "Motherhood According to Giovanni Bellini," in *Desire in Language: A Semiotic Approach to Literature and Art*, trans. Leon S Roudiez, Thomas Gora, and Alice
Jardine (New York: Columbia University Press, 1980), 238; the French is Julia Kristeva,
Polylogue (Paris: Seuil, 1977), 410. Kristeva sees in the work of Bellini a sequential taxonomy of depictions of (an ideology of) maternal jouissance staged in terms of struggles
and splits between mother and child. Marcia Ian has interestingly connected the fantasy of the phallic mother to the aesthetics of Modernism in Ian, *Remembering the Phallic
Mother: Psychoanalysis, Modernism, and the Fetish* (Ithaca: Cornell University Press, 1993).

59. Lena M. Hill, *Visualizing Blackness and the Creation of the African American Literary Tradition*
(New York: Cambridge University Press, 2014), 101. See also the general argument of
Pinkerton, " 'New Negro vs. 'Niggeratti.' " Anne Stavney writes trenchantly that "Locke's
literary text and Reiss's graphic text circulate a homologous sexual topography of
geographic and vocational space: woman as birthing body, man as birthing mind."
Anne Stavney, "Mothers of Tomorrow," *African American Review* 32, no. 4 (Winter 1998):
546–47.

60. This is a modern displacement from ancient definitions of the slave. As Marx notes in
Capital, the Roman slave was considered an *instrumentum vocale* (speaking implement);
the domesticated animal an *instrumentum semi-vocale* (semispeaking implement); and
the tool an *instrumentum mutum* (mute implement). Karl Marx, *Capital*, trans. Ben
Fowkes, vol. 1 (Harmondsworth: Penguin, 1992), 303. By this reckoning, the "modern"
slave system, itself not homogenous, can perhaps be considered a regression from the
more differentiated modes of slavery in the premodern world.

61. Frederick Douglass, *Narrative of the Life of Frederick Douglass, an American Slave* (New York:
Penguin, 1982), 62.

62. I have no direct evidence that Locke read this piece. However, its argument and presuppositions had worked themselves thoroughly into the post-Kantian philosophy
studied by him. Some of Locke's philosophical relation to Kant is sketched in Johnny

Washington, *A Journey Into the Philosophy of Alain Locke* (Westport, CT: Greenwood Press, 1994). Washington emphasizes in particular Locke's attempt to pluralize the Kantian categorical imperative (9–10, 179–89).

63. Michel Foucault, "What Is Enlightenment?," in *The Foucault Reader*, ed. Paul Rabinow (Harmondsworth: Penguin, 1984), 38 and passim. I do not believe that the Enlightenment should be held up as some fixed moment of inauguration for whatever gets called "modernity." Its particular playing-out of emancipatory claims is, however, especially significant in the context of postcoloniality, and that is why it receives a special emphasis here. One example among very many relevant to this study is Frantz Fanon's repeated gesture toward repairing the colonial betrayal of Enlightenment humanism. Questions of the relationship between slavery, race, and Enlightenment are addressed in thought-provoking ways in Fred Moten, "Knowledge of Freedom," *CR: The New Centennial Review* 4, no. 2 (2004): 269–310; and Simon Gikandi, *Slavery and the Culture of Taste* (Princeton: Princeton University Press, 2011).

64. Immanuel Kant, *Perpetual Peace, and Other Essays on Politics, History, and Morals* (Indianapolis: Hackett, 1983), 41. Kant and then Fichte are developing the translation and transposition of terms from Roman law in precursors such as Christian Wolff, who gives a detailed legal definition of the function of the "Vormund" in the *Grundsätze des Natur- und Völckerrechts* (1769). In the section on "Patriarchal Authority" (*väterlicher Gewalt*) Wolff defines the "Vormünder (tutores)" as those responsible for the bringing up (*Erziehung*) of unreared children. The "waifs," "*Wäifen* (pupilli *Mündel*)," are the fatherless wards of the *Vormünder*. See §898 and §§898–912 for the entire discussion of the *Vormund*. James Schmidt, ed., *What Is Enlightenment?: Eighteenth-Century Answers and Twentieth-Century Questions* (Berkeley: University of California Press, 1996), 63, has a brief note on these terms.

65. Locke refers to the *Survey Graphic* issue as "the nucleus of this book" in *The New Negro*, xxvi. The following quotation is from Locke's prefatory "Harlem" in the *Survey Graphic* 6, no. 6 (March 1925): 630.

66. Manfred Sommer, *Identität Im Übergang: Kant* (Frankfurt: Suhrkamp, 1988), 137. Sommer draws his etymology from the Grimm Brothers: in old high-German *Munt* (*manus*) is "hand," "force," "shield." A more specifically Foucauldian discussion of the relationship between *Mündigkeit*, speech, and subjectivation toward the end of the nineteenth century may be found in Brigitta Bernet, "Mündigkeit Und Mündlichkeit: Sprachliche Vergesellschaftung Um 1900," *Figurationen: Gender, Literatur, Kultur* (2008): 47–60.

67. See Sommer, *Identität*, 117–21, on the use of the term in legal discourse.

68. According to Sommer, this "contamination" was at play, and a possible source of the punning generation of meaning, as early as Martin Luther's writings. Sommer, *Identität*, 137–39.

69. Adorno, *Critical Models*, 281; Theodor Adorno, *Gesammelte Schriften*, 20 vols. (Frankfurt: Suhrkamp, 1997), 10.2:785. Adorno's German translator ascribes the derivation to *Mund* (mouth) in his notes on Adorno's "Critique," in *Critical Models*, 383. Adorno has more to say about *Mündigkeit* in *Erziehung zur Mündigkeit: Vorträge und Gespräche mit Hellmut Becker, 1959–1969* (Frankfurt: Suhrkamp, 1970). See the introduction to this volume for commentary.

70. Immanuel Kant, *Anthropology from a Pragmatic Point of View*, trans. Robert B. Louden (Cambridge: Cambridge University Press, 2006), 103; Immanuel Kant, *Werke*, 12 vols. (Frankfurt: Suhrkamp, 1968), 12:522.

71. A crude but real example: as anticolonial nationalist independence movements mutate into postcolonial State formations, the demands of women in decolonization can be strategically deferred in the name of national unity, until freedom is achieved, until the new nation is built up, and so on ad infinitum, having a "deleterious effect on their emergence as full-fledged citizens." Deniz Kandiyoti, "Identity and Its Discontents: Women and the Nation," *Millenium: Journal of International Studies* 20, no. 3 (1991): 440–41.

72. The groundwork for an investigation of this terrain may be found in Cheryl A. Wall, *Women of the Harlem Renaissance* (Bloomington: Indiana University Press, 1995); Hazel V. Carby, *Reconstructing Womanhood: The Emergence of the Afro-American Woman Novelist* (New York: Oxford University Press, 1987).

73. It should be noted that the public debate on *Aufklärung* in the pages of the *Berlinische Monatsschrift* beginning in 1783 started as a discussion about the clerical validation of the institution of marriage. The footnote that asked "What is enlightenment?" was in an article whose topic was "Is it advisable no longer to have marriage ceremonies sanctified by religion?" J. F. Zöllner, "Ist es Rathsam, das Ehebündniß nicht ferner durch die Religion zu Sancieren?," *Berlinische Monatsschrift* 2 (1783): 516. As James Schmidt puts it, "Zöllner was troubled by the article's claim that much of the population found the presence of clergy at weddings 'ridiculous.' Such an attitude, he suggested, testified to the corruption of public morals and confusion that had been wrought 'in the name of enlightenment' in the hearts and minds of the citizenry." James Schmidt, "Misunderstanding the Question: 'What Is Enlightenment?': Venturi, Habermas, and Foucault," *History of European Ideas* 37 (2011): 43–52, 43. Thus a certain emergent mutation in the very institution that makes of man the "proxy" (*Stellvertreter*) or "curator" (*Kurator*) of woman (to use Kant's terms from the *Anthropology*) gives rise to a far more ramified debate about other types of social dependency, while the already shadowy "woman question" disappears. See also Schmidt's introduction to *What Is Enlightenment?* and Robin May Schott's essay in that volume, "The Gender of Enlightenment."

74. In *Readings*, Gayatri Chakravorty Spivak has commented briefly on the "almost" in the spirit I do here. Spivak, *Readings* (Calcutta: Seagull, 2014), 50.

75. Kant, "An Answer to the Question: What Is Enlightenment?" in Schmidt, *What Is Enlightenment?*, 62.

76. Bernard Stiegler, *Taking Care of Youth and the Generations*, trans. Stephen Barker (Stanford: Stanford University Press, 2010), 26, Stiegler's emphasis, translation modified.

77. Stiegler, 24, translation modified.

78. The radicalism or avant-gardism of the Fichtean national upbringing can be elaborated by developing the way his adaptation of Pestalozzi's experimental pedagogy necessitates a step away from familial structures into a mode of rearing that is determined by a collective organization with an alternative morality. For Fichte, the collectivity is called "national," though this must be taken in the eccentric way he presents it. Its broad outlines prefigure, for instance, early Soviet discussions and representations of, and experiments with, alternative practices of childrearing defined socially rather than nationally. The relation of Fichte's nationality (of spirit) to Soviet understandings of the "social" is obviously not straightforward, but relevant comparisons would be the Soviet feminist theorist and politician Alexandra Kollontai's essays, especially "Theses on Communist Morality in the Sphere of Marital Relations" (1921) and "Soon (in 48 Years' Time)" (1922), among many other works, in *Selected Writings of Alexandra Kollontai*, ed. Alix Holt (New York: Norton, 1980). A fuller discussion would

inevitably have to account for the place of Rousseau's *Émile* in revolutionary experiments in childrearing.

79. The classic reference is Marx writing on modes of production in the preface to *A Contribution to the Critique of Political Economy* (1859). Karl Marx and Friedrich Engels, *Karl Marx, Frederick Engels: Collected Works*, vol. 29 (New York: International, 1975). Raymond Williams, *The Country and the City* (New York: Oxford University Press, 1975), develops this narrative as it is reflected in literary representations. Fredric Jameson, *The Political Unconscious: Narrative as a Socially Symbolic Act* (Ithaca: Cornell University Press, 1981), moves the model in a more theoretical direction. Barbara Foley tells us that Locke, in the *Survey Graphic* version of his essay from 1925, merely "gestured toward a Marxist modes of production narrative." Foley, *Spectres of 1919*, 219. The possible irony of Locke's applying this narrative to code U.S. history is lost in Foley's account. Nicholls suggests that the "historical schematic" of African American history "profoundly disrupts and reshapes the transition narrative provided by the European Enlightenment, . . . retrofitting Eurocentric notions." David Nicholls, *Conjuring the Folk: Forms of Modernity in African America* (Ann Arbor: University of Michigan, 2000), 133–34.

80. Locke's use of the category "folk" was doubtless determined by both Du Bois's practice in *The Souls of Black Folk* and his own studies in German philosophy. It seems clear that Locke, like Du Bois, was transforming, in translation, the Germanic term and category of *das Volk*. For preliminary discussion of these matters, see Arnold Rampersad's introduction to the edition from 1992 of *The New Negro* and Ronald R. Sundstrom, "Douglass and Du Bois's *Der Schwarze Volksgeist*," in *Race and Racism in Continental Philosophy*, ed. Robert Bernasconi and Sybol Cook (Bloomington: Indiana University Press, 2003), 32–52.

81. Again, the general overview and bibliography for the translation questions here is found in Cassin et al., *Dictionary of Untranslatables*, 751–64 (People/Race/Nation).

82. The term *folk* was not the exclusive property of Du Bois and Locke or of "black folk" in general in the early-twentieth-century United States. As in Europe, the study and preservation of folk forms and folklore were in the process of being institutionalized for a variety of endeavors, nationalist, linguistic, narratological, and so forth.

83. Foley, *Spectres of 1919*, 51, 160. Many subsequent critics of Locke have observed that this positing of continuity between cultural avant-garde and people through a phantasmatic figure of the earthy folk has further effects. It makes of the New Negro a figure of U.S. nationalism; it occludes the history of black militant socialism after World War I; and ultimately it exchanges "transnational black solidarity" for "a certain kind of national currency, an anti-racism in one country." Edwards, *The Practice of Diaspora*, 6. An extensive critical discussion of *The New Negro* on these lines has been pursued in the following works: *The New Negro*; William J. Maxwell, *New Negro, Old Left: African-American Writing and Communism Between the Wars* (New York: Columbia University Press, 1999); Foley, *Spectres of 1919*; Dawahare, *Nationalism, Marxism, and African American Literature Between the Wars*; Houston A. Baker, *Modernism and the Harlem Renaissance* (Chicago: University of Chicago Press, 1987); George Hutchinson, *The Harlem Renaissance in Black and White* (Cambridge, MA: Belknap Press of Harvard University Press, 1995).

84. Luce Irigaray's *Speculum of the Other Woman* is, among other things, an extended meditation on the (non)place of this matrix in Western discourse on sexual difference and representation. Luce Irigaray, *Speculum of the Other Woman*, trans. Gillian C. Gill (Ithaca: Cornell University Press, 1985).

85. A very general account can be found in Peter Geschiere, *The Perils of Belonging: Autochthony, Citizenship, and Exclusion in Africa and Europe* (Chicago: University of Chicago Press, 2009), 1–38.

86. Carter Godwin Woodson, *The Rural Negro* (Washington, DC: Association for the Study of Negro Life and History, 1930), xv.

87. "Peasantry" was a generally used term for the Southern rural population in this period. Another important study, for example, is Arthur Franklin Raper, *Preface to Peasantry: A Tale of Two Black Belt Counties* (Chapel Hill: University of North Carolina Press, 1936).

88. Valerie Grim, "African American Rural Culture, 1900–1950," in *African American Life in the Rural South, 1900–1950*, ed. Hurt R. Douglas (Columbia: University of Missouri Press, 2003), 109. Woodson, *The Rural Negro*. Citations hereafter given parenthetically as RN. It is worth noting that *The Rural Negro* is a sort of photobook, part of a kind of genre of such in the South, replete with artless and often candid photographic illustrations that contrast with the more expert and professional documentary later produced by the photography team of the Farm Security Administration. Raper's *Preface to Peasantry* also contains several photographs similar in style to those of *The Rural Negro*. Due to its wealth of illustrations, *The Rural Negro* is further comparable to *The New Negro* as an illustrated book, but I cannot go further with that analysis here. In her essay, Grim is concerned to re-present black rural life in terms of a listing of somewhat cozy positive images of community activities and religious observance because Woodson's depictions appear to her too "negative" (108). While the textured habitations of normal life in the rural South should not of course be left out of history, correcting Woodson by positive reversal risks occluding processes of subalternization in favor of presentist celebrations of cultural identity. This is precisely the gesture of Locke updated.

89. William P. Browne, "Benign Public Policies, Malignant Consequences, and the Demise of African American Agriculture," in *African American Life in the Rural South, 1900–1950*, ed. Hurt R. Douglas (Columbia: University of Missouri Press, 2003), 132, 135. Browne's article gives empirical substantiation to the argument that subalternity is a remnant of development in conditions where processes of redress are minimized: the more development, the more subalternity. *The Rural Negro* is in fact more positive about the USDA's effects than is Browne, who has the benefit of hindsight.

90. Woodson, *Rural Negro*, 26. "The year 1910 . . . represented the peak year of black land ownership" according to a report by the Black Economic Research Center, *Only Six Million Acres: The Decline of Black Owned Land in the Rural South* (New York: Black Economic Research Center, 1970), 19.

91. Woodson, *Rural Negro*, 67. Peonage as a term for debt bondage is loaned from colonial Mexico. But a peon is a footsoldier—the word is etymologically linked with the foot. The term's doubleness spells out a cruel irony: the footsoldier's characteristic is mobility; he must move by foot. But the foot has a metonymic link with the earth (and thus staying in place), which is the essence of the peon as indentured servant. The peon is both movable at will and tied to wherever the employer wants him or her to be: a pawn, a thumbnail definition of subalternity.

92. Marx, *Capital*, 1:873–940.

93. Woodson himself makes the argument that U.S. South-North migration is primarily an economically determined process. Woodson, *Rural Negro* 25, 43–44. See also his more detailed analysis of the World War I-era migration in *A Century of Negro Migration* (Washington, DC: Association for the Study of Negro Life and History, 1918), 167–92.

94. See "Floor Was Her Pallet, Girl Wails," *Chicago Defender*, June 30, 1923; "Fifteen-Year-Old Girl Rescued from Peonage," *Pittsburgh Courier*, June 23, 1923; "Saved from Peonage in Jersey City," *NY Amsterdam News*, June 20, 1923; "Released from Peonage," *Afro-American*, June 22, 1923. I thank Jill Jarvis for inspired research assistance tracking down this material.

95. See Woodson's astonishing story of the complicity of Red Cross and National Guard disaster relief workers after the Mississippi flood in 1927, in which the relief workers ensured the return of peons to their "owners" from Red Cross camps set up to house refugees from the flooding. Woodson, *The Rural Negro*, 86–89. *Plus ça change . . .*

96. Derrida, "Of an Apocalyptic Tone," 27–35.

97. Pinkerton, "'New Negro' v. 'Niggeratti,'" 542–44.

98. Harris and Molesworth, *Alain L. Locke*, 318. See Pinkerton, "'New Negro' v. 'Niggeratti,'" 544, for comment on Locke's statement.

99. Pinkerton, "'New Negro' v. 'Niggeratti,'" 544. The full reference can be found in Pinkerton's note 20. The five extant draft sections of "Worlds of Color" from around April 1924 are located in the W. E. B. Du Bois Papers, Special Collections and University Archives, University of Massachusetts Amherst Libraries.

100. W. E. B. Du Bois, "The Negro Mind Reaches Out," in *The New Negro*, 385–414. A first version was published as "Worlds of Color," *Foreign Affairs* 3, no. 3 (April 1925): 423–44. It should be noted that one of Alain Locke's key essays in *The New Negro*, "The Legacy of the Ancestral Arts," also sounded a cautionary note of distance and nonidentity between the positions of African and African-American.

101. Frantz Fanon, *The Wretched of the Earth*, trans. Richard Philcox (New York: Grove, 2004), 58; Frantz Fanon, *Les Damnés de la terre* (Paris: La Découverte, 2002), 99. Fanon is primarily speaking of the economic plundering of the "underdeveloped" postcolonial world (i.e., neocolonialism and the discourse of aid in the post–World War II period). Du Bois's essay was written thirty years before the concept of the Third World was embodied institutionally at the Afro-Asian Conference in Bandung, 1955.

102. That is, a competitive ranking of civilizations on a qualitative scale, where civilizations are regarded as relatively homogenous entities based on a single principle (or a small set of principles). The term *civilizationism* has gained some currency in recent years; see, for example, Derrick P. Alridge, "Of Victorianism, Civilizationism, and Progressivism: The Educational Ideas of Anna Julia Cooper and W. E. B. Du Bois, 1892–1940," *History of Education Quarterly* 47, no. 4 (November 1, 2007): 416–46.

103. An excellent example is Bill Mullen, *Afro-Orientalism* (Minneapolis: University of Minnesota Press, 2004). The book gives an instructive overview of this aspect of Du Bois's work; see 1–41.

104. W. E. B. Du Bois, "What Is Civilization? Africa's Answer," in *W. E. B. Du Bois: A Reader*, ed. Meyer Weinberg (New York: Harper and Row, 1970). Du Bois fleshes out what "laziness" signifies: "In Africa the 'lazy' survive and live. This African laziness is several things: It is shelter from the penetrating rain; it is defense from malaria. And it brings with it leisure and dreams and human intercourse" (379). A way of living in the environment and a mode of sociability, then. In his pamphlet *Africa, Its Place in Modern History* (Girard, KS: Haldeman-Julius, 1930), Du Bois gives a striking account of organized resistance to colonialism and enslavement in Africa. My emphasis on laziness here is in the interest of showing an acknowledgment of what detaches from or

interrupts the moment of vanguardism, even as vanguard formations are a necessary—and irreducible—element.

105. W. E. B. Du Bois, *Dark Princess: A Romance* (Oxford: Oxford University Press, 2007). Driven of course by its constraining genre of romance, the novel stages the unity of the Afro(-American) and Asian worlds as happy reproductive marriage between an American black man and an Indian princess. A eugenic solution to the problem of international and interracial solidarity?

106. Du Bois, "Negro Mind," in Locke, *The New Negro*, 408, 411. Two pages on, Du Bois writes, "We face, then, in the *modern* black American, the black West Indian, the black French-man, the black Portuguese, the black Spaniard, and the black African a man *gaining in knowledge and power* and in the definite aim to end color slavery and give black folk a *knowledge of modern culture*" (413, emphases added).

107. Du Bois, "Worlds of Color," ca. April 1924. W. E. B. Du Bois Papers (MS 312). Special Collections and University Archives, University of Massachusetts Amherst Libraries, 15.

108. Du Bois of course more directly refers to Euro-American capitalism, imperialism, and its culture with this last phrase. "Laziness" evokes the famous pamphlet from 1883 by Marx's son-in-law Paul Lafargue, "The Right to be Lazy" (*Le droit à la paresse*), which was published in more than one translation in the United States in the period. Lafargue criticizes the Left's adoption of the slogan of the "right to work" to the extent that he sees the Left as trivially seduced by the development power of capitalist industry. Given Du Bois's growing interest in socialism at this time, it is plausible that he would have been aware of this widely read work. Paul Lafargue, *The Right to Be Lazy Being a Refu-tation of the "Right to Work" of 1848*, trans. Harriet E. Lothrop (New York: International, 1898; Chicago: Charles H. Kerr, 1907). This may indeed be connected to Du Bois's implicit argument a decade later in *Black Reconstruction* (1935) that certain aspects of the post-Marx, post-Sorel theory of the general strike need to be revised in the light of black slave activism. "This was not merely the desire to stop work. It was a strike on a wide basis against the conditions of work. It was a general strike that involved directly in the end perhaps a half million people. They wanted to stop the economy of the plantation system, and to do that they left the plantations." W. E. B. Du Bois, *Black Reconstruction in America, 1860–1880* (New York: Free Press, 1998), 67.

109. Du Bois's biographer believes that Du Bois was virtually delusional about Liberia: "Judg-ment and Liberia were like oil and water in Du Bois's optic," writes David Levering Lewis, *W. E. B. Du Bois—the Fight for Equality and the American Century, 1919–1963* (New York: Holt, 2000), 125. Levering Lewis perhaps judges with the benefit of hindsight, even as it is surprising that Du Bois does not seem to perceive the tremendous rapaciousness of U.S. capitalism at this time. The unique and complex situation of Liberia may have led Du Bois to imagine early on that a "good imperialism" could occasion a benign and socially general development.

110. Some sense of the complexity involved can be gleaned from Monday B. Abasiattai, *Afri-can Resistance in Liberia: The Vai and the Gola-Bandi* (Bremen: Liberia Working Group, 1988); and Yekutiel Gershoni, *Black Colonialism: The Americo-Liberian Scramble for the Hinterland* (Boulder, CO: Westview, 1985). I. K Sundiata, *Black Scandal: America and the Libe-rian Labor Crisis, 1929–1936* (Philadelphia: Institute for the Study of Human Issues, 1980) and Sundiata, *Brothers and Strangers*, are judicious analyses of the insoluble political paradox of using protection of the indigenes as a stick with which to beat Africa's sole black republic of the epoch.

111. Through the Firestone Plantations Company. Du Bois wrote to Harvey Firestone in October 1925 and received a brief reply from the Office of the President in November. See Herbert Aptheker, ed., *The Correspondence of W. E. B. DuBois* (Amherst: University of Massachusetts Press, 1976), 1:320–23.

112. Du Bois, "Letter to Firestone," in Aptheker, *Correspondence of W. E. B. Du Bois*, 323. For a brief overview of the prefiguration, see Samir Amin, "Underdevelopment and Dependence in Black Africa-Origins and Contemporary Forms," *Journal of Modern African Studies* 10, no. 4 (December 1, 1972): 503–24; Charles Johnson, *Bitter Canaan: The Story of the Negro Republic* (New Brunswick, NJ: Transaction, 1987); Sundiata, *Black Scandal*.

113. Du Bois, "Liberia and Rubber," in Aptheker, *Correspondence of W. E. B. Du Bois*, 329. See also Du Bois, "The Wide Wide World," editorial in *The Crisis* 34 (March 1927).

114. George Padmore, *The Life and Struggles of Negro Toilers* (London: RILU Magazine, 1931), 68–69.

115. Du Bois, letter from W. E. B. Du Bois to the Federal Council of Churches of Christ in America, August 4, 1933. W. E. B. Du Bois Papers (MS 312). Special Collections and University Archives, University of Massachusetts Amherst Libraries. Du Bois, *Liberia, the League, and the United States* (New York: Council on Foreign Relations, 1933).

Z Négritude (Slight Return)

1. Renée Riese Hubert, *Surrealism and the Book* (Berkeley: University of California Press, 1988); Andrée Chédid and Pierre Torreilles, *Guy Lévis Mano* (Paris: Seghers, 1974).

2. For instance, Luca Signorelli's fifteenth-century "Martyrdom of Saint Stephen" (Cassa Risparmio, Perugia).

3. The occlusion of the signs of a female-sexed body well-nigh allegorizes the situation discussed by Brent Edwards with regard to pervasive accounts of the emergence of Négritude as a male self-birth. Edwards restores to some extent the context of the women intellectuals who made Négritude possible in Brent Hayes Edwards, *The Practice of Diaspora: Literature, Translation, and the Rise of Black Internationalism* (Cambridge, MA: Harvard University Press, 2003), chap. 3.

4. Léon Gontran-Damas, *Pigments* (Paris: Présence Africaine, 1962); Noland, *Voices of Negritude in Modernist Print: Aesthetic Subjectivity, Diaspora, and the Lyric Regime* (New York: Columbia University Press, 2015), 65.

5. Edwards, *Practice of Diaspora*, 20.

6. V. Y. Mudimbe, "A Meeting with L. G. Damas," in *The Mudimbe Reader*, ed. Pierre-Philippe Fraiture and Daniel Orrells (Charlottesville: University of Virginia Press, 2016), 38.

7. Albert S. Gérard, ed., *A Comparative History of Literatures in European Languages*, vol. 6, *European-Language Writing in Sub-Saharan Africa* (Amsterdam: John Benjamins, 1986), 341.

8. It has become something of an academic ritual to put Négritude in its place by underlining a lack of political radicalism. Christopher Miller writes that Négritude is "less radical, more descriptive, and more essentialist" than the anticolonial and worker-oriented Comité de Défense de la Race Nègre (which published the newspaper *La voix des nègres*). Miller, *Nationalists and Nomads: Essays on Francophone African Literature* (Chicago: University of Chicago Press, 1998), 37. See also the presentation of Négritude in Martin Steins, "Black Migrants in Paris," in *European Language-Writing in Sub-Saharan Africa*, ed. Albert Gérard (Budapest: Akadémiai Kiadó, 1986), 365–78; and Edwards, *Practice of Diaspora*, 178–80. While much of this has been of corrective use by showing what

was occluded by the rise to political power and literary celebrity of Senghor and Cés-aire in particular, it has also too often resulted in a lack of detailed critical readings of their work.

9. I borrow "gnostic" from V. Y. Mudimbe, *The Invention of Africa: Gnosis, Philosophy, and the Order of Knowledge* (Bloomington: Indiana University Press, 1988). It contrasts with *episteme* to the extent of being "structured, common, and conventional knowledge . . . under the control of specific procedures for its use as well as transmission," but neither *"doxa* or opinion," nor *"episteme,* understood as both science and general intellectual configuration" (ix). What is at stake in the distinction is the possible specificity of African knowing-conditions *"upstream"* of the existing "results" within the epistemological constructs of anthropology, history, and so on. (x). This remains a productively open question and puzzle for Mudimbe throughout.

10. Jacques Derrida, *Monolingualism of the Other; or, The Prosthesis of Origin,* trans. Patrick Mensah (Stanford: Stanford University Press, 1998), 49; Derrida, *Le monolinguisme de l'autre, ou, la prothèse d'origine* (Paris: Galilée, 1996), 82–83. English translation hereafter cited parenthetically in the text as *Monolingualism.*

11. Léopold Senghor, *Ce que je crois: Négritude, francité et civilisation de l'universel* (Paris: B. Grasset, 1998), 9.

12. Damas, *Retour de Guyane* (1937; Paris: Jean-Michel Place, 2003).

13. To give a sense of how this worked within the hexagon, M. Martin Guiney contends that the institutionalization of instruction in "French literature," displacing Latin in the Third Republic, stood for "the overcoming of the 'foreign' within the national literary tradition." This is because while, "during the Revolution, French was indeed a foreign language to the majority of potential citizens, in the Third Republic it retained a figurative 'foreignness' that made it the perfect model for the foundational principle of assimilation: to be French one had to be 'born again' into the nation, and the school was the site and the instrument of that rebirth." Guiney, *Teaching the Cult of Literature in the French Third Republic* (New York: Palgrave Macmillan, 2004), 208. See also 113–37. I discuss in more detail the process of French-language nationalization in the following chapter. The classic reference point remains Michel de Certeau, Dominique Julia, and Jacques Revel, *Une politique de la langue: La revolution française et les patois* (Paris: Gallimard, 1975).

14. Ralph J. Bunche, "French Educational Policy in Togoland and Dahomey" (1934), in *Selected Speeches and Writings,* ed. Charles P. Henry (Ann Arbor: University of Michigan Press, 1995), 137.

15. These vicissitudes are well described and theorized in Gary Wilder, *The French Imperial Nation-State: Negritude and Colonial Humanism Between the Two World Wars* (Chicago: University of Chicago Press, 2005). See also Alice Conklin, *A Mission to Civilize: The Republican Idea of Empire in France and West Africa, 1895-1930* (Stanford: Stanford University Press, 1997).

16. Jules Ferry, *Discours et opinions de Jules Ferry,* ed. Paul Robiquet (Paris: A. Colin, 1893), 5:156. As I have discussed in the introduction, it is perhaps no accident that Jules Ferry, the minister who oversaw the expansion of French overseas colonial policy in the 1880s, also in that decade instituted the modernization of the French primary education system.

17. Georges Hardy, *Nos grands problèmes coloniaux* (Paris: Armand Colin, 1933), 142. Hardy is writing in the context of "individual naturalization" (i.e., citizenship), which is

precisely the exception that proves the rule: citizenship for the mass would mean admission of people who, when "viewed politically, leave infancy behind with difficulty" (142). Even the "exceptional individuals" from colonies where citizenship is not conferred at birth must also somehow display *more* signs than the "adoption of European habits or university degrees" to be eligible for consideration as full citizens (142). The stratified and differentiated educational program envisioned for French West Africa by Hardy and subsequent "humanist" educational reformers was designed to leave the great mass of "indigenous culture"—as understood by colonial anthropology—relatively untouched. This included subaltern strata. Once more, an abstract registration of the diverse subaltern strata in colonial discourse. The small naturalized class will, through "endosmosis," be the operatives of "fusion" between the "tutor-society" and the "pupil-society" (142).

18. Jules Brévié, *Discours prononcé par M. J. Brévié, gouverneur général de l'AOF à l'ouverture de la session du conseil de gouvernement, décembre 1930* (Gorée: Imprimerie du Gouverneur Général, 1930); citation from Wilder, *French Imperial Nation-State*, 119.

19. Senghor uses this phrase (*humanisme colonial*) in a somewhat mysterious formulation in one of his first published articles: Léopold Senghor, "Le problème culturel en A.O.F.," in *Liberté I: Négritude et Humanisme* (Paris: Éditions du Seuil, 1964), 17. Hereafter cited parenthetically in the text as *Liberté*. He seems to be criticizing the "humanist" notion that France's colonies could be smoothly integrated into France's own imaginary picture of its evolution toward "enlightenment and liberty." Wilder, *French Imperial Nation-State*, 43–145, develops the "colonial humanism" concept as an epistemological category for understanding the specificity of French policy in AOF in the interwar period.

20. This does not preclude an entire field of two-way narcissism-effects, wherein the making and self-making of a *semblable* are enacted in the play of desire between student and teacher. But this can also be likened to the push and pull of transference, ever unfixing the game of self-consolidation. Teaching has to work with and against these effects, thus becoming, in a philosophically and politically ideal sense, the process of producing or nurturing the unlike that can yet occupy the educative position.

21. Antonio Gramsci, *Selections from the Prison Notebooks*, trans. Quintin Hoare and Geoffrey Nowell-Smith (London: International, 1971), 350. Hereafter cited parenthetically in the text as SPN.

22. Gramsci, 350, my emphasis. Gramsci's sense of (quasi-colonial) racialized differences of class is most vividly captured in his "Some Aspects of the Southern Question" (1926) in Gramsci, *Selections from Political Writings, 1921–26*, ed. Quintin Hoare, trans. John Mathews (New York: International, 1978). Gramsci summarizes the popular racial ideology of class: "the Southerners are biologically inferior beings, semi-barbarians or total barbarians, by natural destiny; if the South is backward, the fault does not lie with the capitalist system or with any other historical cause, but with Nature, which has made the Southerners lazy, incapable, criminal and barbaric" (444). Education (hegemony) conducted by the "leading" Northern working class must work on both sides of this constructed division.

23. Louis Althusser, "Ideology and Ideological State Apparatuses (Notes Towards an Investigation)," in *Lenin and Philosophy* (New York: Monthly Review, 1971), 152–53. Hereafter cited parenthetically in the text as "Ideology."

24. Robert Delavignette, "Pour le paysannat noir; pour l'esprit africain," *Esprit* 4, no. 39 (December 1, 1935): 387. Much of Delavignette's picture of the rural popular school

echoes that of Georges Hardy, who had written perhaps the most systematic and influ-ential projection of African education almost twenty years before. See Georges Hardy, *Une conquête morale: L'enseignement en A.O.F.* (Paris: Librarie Armand Colin, 1917). Hardy was at that time Education Inspector of French West Africa. Compare especially Delavi-gnette with the "Écoles de village" section of Hardy's second chapter, especially 51–55. Hardy emphasizes "moralization and loyalism," French patriotism and progressivism in a way that is attenuated in Delavignette because of the intervening anthropologiza-tion of the teaching system. Delavignette was also Hardy's successor as director of the École Nationale de la France d'Outre-Mer.

25. Althusser underlines repeatedly the "imaginary *form* of ideology," that the "*formal struc-ture* of all ideology is always the same" ("Ideology," 162–63, 177, my emphases). Like the value-form, it is empty and can therefore accommodate any worldly content so as to represent an imaginary relation to the real.

26. Following Althusser, though, I think we have to understand all hegemonic struggle as remaining within the ideological realm: that is, within the field of subject-reproducing practices.

27. Kojo Touvalou-Houéno, "Doctrines et doctrinaires de l'école coloniale," *Les Continents* (July 18, 1924). He was responding to the publication of Louis Verlaine, *Notre colonie: Con-tribution à la recherche de la méthode de colonisation* (Bruxelles: Eugène Denis, 1923), and to the positive reception of the book by Maurice Delafosse.

28. Jules Brévié, circular of August 18, 1932, in *Circulaires de M. le Gouverneur Général J. Brévié sur la politique et l'administration Indigènes en Afrique Occidentale Française* (Gorée, 1935), 7. Hereafter cited parenthetically in the text as *Circulaires*.

29. Laurent Dubreuil, *Empire of Language: Toward a Critique of (Post)Colonial Expression*, trans. David Fieney (Ithaca: Cornell University Press, 2013), 40, 48.

30. Brévié, circular of August 18, 1932, 30.

31. Historical documentation and theorization of this may be found inter alia in Conklin, *Mission to Civilize*; Wilder, *French Imperial Nation-State*; Edwards, *Practice of Diaspora*; and Dubreuil, *Empire of Language*.

32. The question "how many are we?" (*combien sommes nous?*) is a key and varied refrain in Jacques Derrida, *Politics of Friendship*, trans. George Collins (New York: Verso, 1997). The question inaugurates the question of political collectivity on the basis of the dif-ficulty of knowing something as apparently proximate as the friend or the classroom group. Derrida interrogates the basis for friendship, politics, citizenship in identity, the common, *semblance*, and resemblance, political figures that are key to all the move-ments considered here, including Négritude.

33. Dewitte, *Mouvements*, 24–44.

34. See Dewitte, *Mouvements*, 251–75; Edwards, *Practice of Diaspora*, 119–86 and passim; T. Denean Sharpley-Whiting, *Negritude Women* (Minneapolis: University of Minnesota Press, 2002); Michael Richardson, ed., *Refusal of the Shadow: Surrealism and the Caribbean* (New York: Verso, 1996), 1–65.

35. Dewitte, *Mouvements*, remains the standard account. See also Miller, *Nationalists and Nomads*; Martin Steins, "Les antécédents et la genèse de la négritude senghorienne" (PhD diss., University of Paris III, 1981); Steins, "Black Migrants in Paris," in Gérard, *A Comparative History of Literatures in European Languages*, vol. 6; Edwards, *Practice of Dias-pora*; Wilder, *French Imperial Nation-State*; Lamine Senghor, *La violation d'un pays et autres écrits anticolonialistes* (Paris: L'Harmattan, 2012).

36. *Hypokhâgne* is the name for the first year of study at the great Lycées, the year before the *khâgne*, which is the preparatory courses and examinations for entry into ENS. For details of Senghor's education, see Janet G. Vaillant, *Black, French, and African: A Life of Léopold Senghor* (Cambridge, MA: Harvard University Press, 1990); Jacques Louis Hymans, *Léopold Senghor: An Intellectual Biography* (Edinburgh: Edinburgh University Press, 1991). For Césaire's itinerary, see Georges Ngal, *Aimé Césaire: Un homme à la recherche d'une patrie* (Paris: Présence Africaine, 1994).

37. Cream-of-the-cream schools such as Lycée Louis-le-Grand, which Césaire and Senghor attended, are machines for reproducing the political and intellectual ranks of the French ruling class. Senghor, as is well known, became a friend of Georges Pompidou at Louis-le-Grand, and the list of its alumni is almost a roster of the modern French intelligentsia and political leadership. For an analysis of this general field, see Pierre Bourdieu, *The State Nobility: Elite Schools in the Field of Power*, trans. Loretta C. Clough (Stanford: Stanford University Press, 1998). Senghor and Césaire went on to become politicians and heads of State after World War II, enacting a symbolic displacement from cultural (poetic and literary) avant-gardism to political leadership, though they continued to practice as literary artists. Senghor eventually became the first president of independent Senegal, while Césaire became mayor of Fort de France and deputy to the French National Assembly for Martinique. Damas and other writers in their milieu, such as Ousmane Socé, also went on to enter politics. I would contend that the early, intensive aesthetic-political work done on education as a fundamental organ of the State was a determining factor in the future political ascendance and policies of these figures.

38. Emily Musil Church, "In Search of Seven Sisters: A Biography of the Nardal Sisters of Martinique," *Callaloo* 36, no. 2 (Spring 2013): 378–79, 382. Paulette Nardal had also received a diplôme d'études supérieures (equivalent to an MA) for her thesis on Harriet Beecher Stowe.

39. Olivier Sagna, "*Des pionniers méconnus de l'indépendance: Africains, Antillais et luttes anti-colonialistes dans la France de l'entre-deux-guerres (1919–1939),*" (PhD diss., Paris 7, 1986), 305–6. Dewitte, *Mouvements*, 127–70; Guy O. Midiohouan, "Lamine Senghor (1889–1927), Precurseur de la Prose Nationaliste Negro-Africaine," in *The Growth of African Literature: Twenty-Five Years After Dakar and Fourah Bay*, ed. Edris Makward et al. (Trenton, NJ: Africa World Press, 1998), 69–78; Edwards, *Practice of Diaspora*, 28–29.

40. Lamine Senghor, *La violation d'un pays*. For this connection, see David Murphy, "Child's Play? Storytelling and Ideology in 1920s Francophone Sub-Saharan Africa," *Francophone Postcolonial Studies* 7, no. 2 (2009): 73–88.

41. Abiola Irele, *The African Experience in Literature and Ideology* (London: Heinemann, 1981), 67–88. Léopold Sédar Senghor, ed., *Anthologie de la nouvelle poésie nègre et malgache de langue française* (Paris: Presses Universitaires de France, 1948).

42. Sudan, 1956; Ghana, 1957; Congo, 1960; Mali, 1960; Nigeria, 1960; Chad, 1960; Algeria, 1962; Kenya, 1963.

43. *L'Étudiant Martiniquais*, new series, no. 1 (May 1934): 2.

44. The most vivid deflation of exaggerated claims for the unificatory, originating, and political significance of *L'Étudiant Noir* is Edward O. Ako, "*L'Étudiant Noir* and the Myth of the Genesis of the Négritude Movement," *Research in African Literatures* 15, no. 3 (Autumn 1984): 341–53. Ako's position must be revised slightly with the discovery of the third issue of the newsletter, but much of his argument remains relevant. *L'Étudiant Noir* was

still subtitled the monthly journal of the Association des Étudiants Martiniquais en France. Césaire was voted president of the Martinican Students' Association in December 1934, and under his presidency the group's organizing committee moved to rename the journal (Ngal, *Aimé Césaire*, 69–70). Damas was the editorial secretary. As Edwards has remarked, while this grouping may have brought together many of the Antilleans, Léopold Senghor was the sole African contributor to the first issue (the only one available to Edwards at the time). Edwards, *Practice of Diaspora*, 179. In issue three of *L'Étudiant Noir*, recently discovered, there is a review of Senegalese writer Osmane Socé Diop's novel *Karim* (1935) by Sadio Teranga, as well as a notice for the formation of a committee of solidarity with Ethiopia. *L'Étudiant Noir*, no. 3, May–June 1935; reproduced in Christian Filostrat, *Negritude Agonistes, Assimilation Against Nationalism in the French-Speaking Caribbean and Guyane* (Cherry Hill, NJ: Africana Homestead, 2008). Nevertheless, the heterogeneity and sometimes mutual incompatibility of the contributions to *L'Étudiant Noir* remain marked. Not that this is a bad thing.

45. Jules Brévié, circular of August 18, 1932, 9. See also Wilder, *French Imperial Nation-State*, 128.
46. Wilder, *French Imperial Nation-State*, 143, my emphasis.
47. Irele, *African Experience*, 203.
48. Vaillant, *Black, French*, 148.
49. Senghor, "Le problème culturel en A.O.F.," *Paris-Dakar* (September 6–11, 1937). It is also reprinted in a significantly edited version in Senghor's collected works, *Liberté I*, 11–21. According to *Paris-Dakar* of September 6, 1937, the speech was delivered on August 4, but this was a Wednesday; and the report on the speech in *Paris-Dakar* of September 7 says the meeting was held on "Saturday evening," which was September 4. On September 4, 1937, *Paris-Dakar* also advertised Senghor's speech as occurring "this evening" (it included a short interview with him). The August dating must be a typo. *Liberté* gives the delivery date as September 10, 1937, but this is also incorrect. All references in the text are to the *Paris-Dakar* version, cited parenthetically as PD with the date of the relevant article.
50. A list of the main dignitaries who attended may be found in *Paris-Dakar*, September 7, 1937. Vaillant reports that over a thousand people attended the lecture. Vaillant, *Black, French*, 151.
51. Wilder, *French Imperial Nation-State*, 221. At the same time Senghor was writing, Damas would remark on the "exceptional measure" of censorship taken by the Louis Rollin decree to suppress public opinion critical of the central government. This was an extension to nearly all French colonies of the Régnier decree of 1935 that initially applied to oppositional publicity in Algeria. Damas, *Retour de Guyane*, 121–25. See also Meredith Terretta, "'In the Colonies, Black Lives Don't Matter': Legalism and Rights Claims Across the French Empire," *Journal of Contemporary History* 53, no. 1 (January 2018): 1–26.
52. Wilder remarks that "Le problème" "envisions a . . . native vanguard" different from the class of "cooperative French-identified auxiliaries" that the colonial State relied upon. Wilder, *French Imperial Nation-State*, 238.
53. Recall that for Locke this ground level is a "peasant matrix" as it is aesthetically transfigured in a modernized "folk." See chapter 1, pp. 76–78.
54. See Vaillant, *Black, French*, 152; Wilder, *French Imperial Nation-State*, 238; Souleymane Bachir Diagne, *African Art as Philosophy: Senghor, Bergson, and the Idea of Negritude*, trans.

Chike Jeffers (New York: Seagull, 2011), 148–49. In an otherwise perceptive and interesting chapter section on "Le problème," Tsitsi Jaji also reads Senghor as "confessing . . . disingenuously . . . that he was going to speak as a peasant from the Sine." Jaji, *Africa in Stereo: Modernism, Music, and Pan-African Solidarity* (New York: Oxford University Press, 2014), 71.

55. Senghor establishes the link between peasants, agriculture, and culture by rhyming Samba Sène's query of culture with the observation that he "cultivates" the earth.

56. PD, September 6; for elaboration, see Souleymane Bachir Diagne, *Bergson postcolonial: L'élan vital dans la pensée de Léopold Sédar Sengor et de Mohamed Iqbal* (Paris: CNRS, 2011).

57. *Isogonía* comes from Plato's *Menexenus*. Natural equality of birth from the same soil/mother (hence brotherhood) linked to the search for legal equality. For relevant discussion in relation to my topic here, see Derrida, *Politics of Friendship*, 90–111.

58. I am indebted to Souleymane Bachir Diagne for discussion of the Wolof proverbs in this text.

59. PD, September 6. Senghor attributes the "different and together" (*différents et ensemble*) phrase to Robert Delavignette. It is from Delavignette, *Soudan-Paris-Bourgogne* (Paris: B. Grasset, 1935).

60. Derrida calls the first item the "phantasm" of the "genealogical tie," which does not make it less "real" in its effects: "All politics and all policies, all political discourses on 'birth,' misuse what can in this regard be only a belief some will say: what can only remain a belief; others: what can only tend towards an act of faith. Everything in political discourse that appeals to birth, to nature or to the nation—indeed, to nations or to the universal nation of human brotherhood—this entire familialism consists in a renaturalization of this 'fiction.' " Derrida, *Politics of Friendship*, 93.

61. Alain David, *Racisme et antisemitisme: Essai de philosophie sur l'envers de concepts* (Paris: Ellipses, 2001), is a remarkable discussion of the relationship between racism and a concern for form and formalization, racism as a mode of formalism.

62. Derrida, *Politics of Friendship*, 105. Derrida suggests that a "genealogical deconstruction" is not a way of pathologizing the figures that have filled out historical concepts of democracy with content ("national naturalness," origin, generation, familiality, fraternity, and so on). The point is "not to wage war on them and to see evil therein, but to think and live a politics, a friendship, a justice which begin by breaking with their naturalness or their homogeneity, with their alleged place of origin" (105).

63. "Afro-French" is Senghor's term.

64. In 1963, Senghor changed this word to "surviving" (*survivre*).

65. PD, September 7. The entire six-paragraph section on "active assimilation" in *Paris-Dakar* does not appear in the *Liberté* variant of the essay from 1963. In the newspaper version, Senghor frames it as a piece of self-citation from something he wrote "at the beginning of the year." The lines are in fact taken from his essay of January 6, 1937, in *Paris-Dakar*, "Réflexions sur l'éducation africaine: De l'assimilation." The article's second part appeared on January 9. This cluster of writings underlines how central the question of education was to the young Senghor. Senghor's essay "Vues sur l'Afrique noire ou assimiler, non être assimilés" (1945), in *Liberté I*, 39–69, develops and consolidates the *Paris-Dakar* argument empirically and theoretically. Criticizing Littré, which says that "to assimilate is to convert into the same [*convertir au semblable*]," Senghor asserts that "to assimilate is not to identify, to 'render identical.' . . . It will be objected that 'only the similar [*semblable*] can be assimilated.' But is this proposition not contra-

dictory? If to assimilate really means to 'convert into the same,' the same (*le semblable*) has no need of assimilation" (L 43). As in 1937, Senghor controls the dance of ipseity and difference at the level of civilizations.

66. Mamadou Diouf, "The French Colonial Policy of Assimilation and the Civility of the *Originaires* of the Four Communes (Senegal): A Nineteenth Century Globalization Project," *Development and Change* 29, no. 4 (October 1998): 671–72, reads this as a protest against the "loss of Black cultural values and the appropriation of French culture by the *originaires*."

67. In this area, one of the great cultural/anthropological resources for modernisms of all sorts was James Frazer, *The Golden Bough*, 12 vols. (London: Macmillan, 1906–15). Werner Hamacher, *Pleroma: Reading in Hegel*, trans. Nicholas Walker and Simon Jarvis (Stanford: Stanford University Press, 1998), is an extensive account of assimilation, incorporation, expulsion, and digestion in the philosophical structures of speculative idealism.

68. Thus at the First Congress of Black Writers and Artists in Paris, 1956, Césaire would deliver, in a typically grandiose and ferocious way, a speech implicitly challenging this aspect of Senghorian culturalism. Césaire, "Culture and Colonization," trans. Brent Hayes Edwards, *Social Text* 28, no. 2 (Summer 2010): 127–44. For example: "wherever there has been colonization, entire peoples have been emptied of their culture, emptied of all culture" (131); "there is not one bad colonization that destroys indigenous civilizations and attacks the 'moral health of the colonized people,' and another colonization, an enlightened colonization, a colonization backed up by ethnography that could harmoniously integrate the cultural elements of the colonizer within the body of the indigenous civilizations without risk to the 'moral health of the colonized people'" (133). Césaire calls the notion of hyphenated civilizations an "illusion" and adds that "it is inferred" (wrongly) "that as colonization puts two different civilizations into contact, the indigenous civilization will borrow cultural elements from the colonizer's civilization, and from this marriage there will result a new civilization, a mixed civilization [*une civilization métisse*]" (137). The French original is to be found in *Présence Africaine* (June–November 1956): 190–205. In the discussion following Césaire's speech, Senghor reiterates that even in the colonial situation, "we are, objectively, mixes [*des métis*]. . . . All the great civilizations are civilizations resulting from a mixing [*métissage*]. . . . This mixing is a necessity. It results from the contact between civilizations." He reiterates a variant of his great slogan, published for the first time in 1937, that "there is no need to be assimilated; one must assimilate [*il ne faut pas être assimilé; il faut assimiler*]" (216).

69. Drawing from a more rarefied academic sphere, consider the following: "colonizers founded Anthropology in order to know their subjects; Cultural Studies was founded by the colonized in order to question and correct their masters. Both disciplines study culture, the first the culture of others as static and determining, the second the culture of one's own group—as dynamic and evolving." Gayatri Spivak, *An Aesthetic Education in the Era of Globalization* (Cambridge, MA: Harvard University Press, 2012), 120. Senghor's position is a not-so-remote anticipation of disciplinary cultural studies.

70. Jacques Derrida, *Rogues: Two Essays on Reason*, trans. Pascale-Anne Brault and Michael Naas (Stanford: Stanford University Press, 2005), 34–35.

71. It is quite possible that Senghor introduced this ideal via the literary representation of the *samba linguère* in his friend Ousmane Socé's novel *Karim* (1935). *Karim* depicts the

failed, quixotic attempt to live by the values of an idealized aristocratic past, as a *samba linguère*, in the colonial present. I cannot do justice to the complexity of this innovative experimental fiction here, but it is worth noting that *Karim* is one of those works that offers its own idiomatic footnotes to the reader. When Karim is introduced as a *samba linguère*, a footnote glosses as follows: "Summarily, a '*samba linguère*' is a Noble in the sense this word had in France before 1789, because there was an aristocracy in Senegal before the arrival of the French." Socé, *Karim* (Paris: Nouvelles Éditions Latines, 1948), 23. For its place as a term in modern politics, see Jonathan S. Barker, "Political Factionalism in Senegal," *Canadian Journal of African Studies/Revue Canadienne des Études Africaines* 7, no. 2 (1973): 289.

72. In his philosophical reevaluation of Senghor, Souleymane Bachir Diagne writes that such gestures, "a tendency to negrify all that evokes for him the ontology of vital force, . . . racializing to the point of absurdity, to locate black influences (i.e. traces of blood) or 'characterological' affinities," do not "fail to irritate." Diagne, *African Art as Philosophy*, 93.

73. Derrida, *Monolingualism*, 24, 39. See also Senghor's essay "Le problème de la culture" (1950), in *Liberté* I, 93–97; and Dubreuil, *Empire of Language*, 45 for a discussion of the French debate about colony vs. possession.

74. Writing of human rights, Spivak says that "its so-called European provenance is for me in the same category as the 'enabling violation' of the production of the colonial subject. One cannot write off the righting of wrongs. The enablement must be used even as the violation is renegotiated." "Righting Wrongs," *South Atlantic Quarterly* 103, nos. 2/3 (Summer 2004): 524. Spivak's thinking of "access to the European Enlightenment through colonization as an enablement" (565) *and* violation (and thus as double bind) runs through her work of the last twenty-five years. See also Spivak, *Aesthetic Education*, 1–34. Gary Wilder, *Freedom Time: Negritude, Decolonization, and the Future of the World* (Durham: Duke University Press, 2015), is a sympathetic account of the postwar political praxis of Senghor and Césaire in light of this dilemma of enabling violation.

75. The classic representation is to be found in a novel by Robert Delavignette, *Les paysans noirs* (Paris: Delamain et Boutelleau, 1931). Senghor, as we know, allied himself intellectually with Delavignette, former colonial administrator and director of the École Coloniale from 1937 to 1946. Harry Gamble, "Peasants of the Empire: Rural Schools and the Colonial Imaginary in 1930s French West Africa," *Cahiers d'études africaines* 49, no. 3 (2009): 775–804, shows the surprising extent and power of this ideology of black peasantry.

76. Frederick Cooper, *Decolonization and African Society: The Labor Question in French and British Africa* (Cambridge: Cambridge University Press, 1996).

77. Véronique Dimier, "À l'origine de la politique européenne de développement durable: La doctrine colonial des paysans noirs," in *Appropriations du développement durable: Émergences, diffusions, traductions*, ed. Bruno Villalba (Villeneuve d'Ascq: Presses Universitaires du Septentrion, 2009), 145–68.

78. "Racisme? Non, mais Alliance Spirituelle," *L'Étudiant Noir* 3 (May–June 1935): 2. In "Le problème," Senghor revises that evaluation, seeing the most isolated African civilizations as also the most "stagnant" and in need of the "foodstuffs" of "foreign elements" (PD September 7).

79. The full picture of *originaire* status in its shifts and complexity is beyond the scope of this chapter and has been developed by many other scholars. A classic study is Michael

Crowder, *Senegal: A Study of French Assimilation Policy* (London: Methuen, 1967). See also Diouf, "French Colonial Policy"; Wesley Johnson, *The Emergence of Black Politics in Senegal: The Struggle for Power in the Four Communes, 1900-1920* (1971; Stanford: Stanford University Press, 1991).

80. For Senghor's early background, see Vaillant, *Black, French,* 5–33.

81. Senghor would discuss this hostility at more length in his speech to the International Congress on Cultural Evolution of Colonial Peoples. I discuss this later in the chapter.

82. There was also an earlier Africanized schoolbook called *Moussa et Gigla, histoire de deux petits noirs* (1916).

83. Senghor puts this even more explicitly in 1945, writing that the African elite will be educated in "the disciplines and knowledges that have formed the most developed [*évoluée*] nations of today. This is true for Mathematics and for the exact Sciences which, by definition, have no frontiers and appeal to reason, which is universal." This universality requires a supplement from the humanities based on the study of literature in an indigenous African language: " 'Modern Humanities' have been preached for decades. Why should there not be 'Negro-African Humanities'? Every language, by which I mean every civilization, can be material for the 'Humanities' because each civilization is the singularly charged expression of certain traits of Humanity [*l'expression singulièrement accusée de quelques traits de l'Humanité*]." Senghor, *Liberté I,* 67.

84. Senghor's anthropologically inflected civilizationalism, certainly far less virulent than what was generally on offer in the 1930s, is reflected in the following at this point: "without a written literature there is no civilization that could be more than an ethnographic curiosity." In the reprint from 1963 in *Liberté I* he again notes that he has since gone back on this too-summary judgment.

85. This epistemological structure is unfortunately reproduced throughout the "world literature" debate of the past decade or so in which, in practice, one or two big colonial languages are de facto general equivalents for all the other languages of the world.

86. George Padmore, *Pan Africanism or Communism?: The Coming Struggle for Africa* (London: D. Dobson, 1956), 288. We may not be comfortable with the way Padmore uses an outdated and somewhat paternalistic language of "tribalism" here, but it is of its time and certainly compatible with Senghor. Padmore's book concludes forcefully that "tribalism" is a much more dangerous threat to Africa's future than Soviet Communism.

87. Frantz Fanon, *The Wretched of the Earth,* trans. Richard Philcox (New York: Grove, 2004), 103, 126, translation altered.

88. C. L. R. James, *The Black Jacobins: Toussaint L'Ouverture and the San Domingo Revolution* (New York: Vintage, 1989), vii.

89. Senghor, "Ce que l'homme noir apporte" (1939; "What the Black Man Brings"), in *Liberté I,* 22–23. Senghor does acknowledge that the civilizational superstructure developed by the animating cultural spirit is "disappeared" and "forgotten"; but his point is that the cultural spirit survives its torments and exiles as the "Negro soul."

90. Jean Price-Mars, *Ainsi parla l'oncle* (Port-au-Prince, 1998). For Senghor's encounter with Price-Mars, see Hymans, *Léopold Senghor,* 60–63.

91. Noland, *Voices of Negritude,* 148. The Soutes version was titled "Fragment" and importantly included the repeated "MOI MOI MOI" that Senghor quotes and that was reduced to a single "MOI" in *Pigments.* Damas would restore the triple "MOI" in the revised edition of *Pigments* from 1972.

92. Spirit, in its philosophically inflected respiratory sense, is strongly associated for Senghor with the singular cultural rhythmicity of Africa, expressed most vividly in its plastic arts. "This ordering force that makes Negro style [*style nègre*] is rhythm. . . . It is the vital element par excellence . . . as respiration is of life; respiration that rises or falls, becomes regular or spasmodic. . . . Such is rhythm. . . . [The creation of oppositions] as inhalation is to exhalation. . . . This is how rhythm acts on what is least intellectual in us, despotically, to make us penetrate the spirituality of the object." Senghor, "Ce que l'homme noir apporte," 35, emphasis Senghor's. This essay from 1939, as well as much of Senghor's subsequent critical writing, substantiates the impression that drums and rhythmicity represent a claim to the persistence of the black spirit beyond the African continent. For the best philosophical account of this current, see Diagne, *African Art as Philosophy*, esp. the chapter "Rhythms." To relate Senghor's philosophy of spirit to the politics of the contemporary interwar philosophies of spirit in Europe, we should turn to Jacques Derrida, *Of Spirit: Heidegger and the Question*, trans. Geoffrey Bennington and Rachel Bowlby (Chicago: University of Chicago Press, 1989).

93. Noland, *Voices of Negritude*, 130–75.

94. Noland, *Voices of Negritude*: "Senghor later claimed [the poem] sounded like an African chant 'submitted' to 'un rythme de tam-tam instinctivement retrouvé'" (148); and the series of images evokes "violent invasion, . . . dead victims of assimilation," and the "violence of the colonial regime" (151).

95. Roland Barthes, "The Death of the Author," in *Image, Music, Text*, trans. Stephen Heath (New York: Hill and Wang, 1978), 142–48. We must always recall that this "death" also announces the birth of the reader in the final sentence.

96. Jacques Derrida, *Acts of Literature*, ed. Derek Attridge (New York: Routledge, 1992), 317–18. Up to a point, this is compatible with Noland's thesis that "Fragment" dissolves itself into a plurality of rhythmic anteriorities that scholarly research can track down and document.

97. Edwards notes another discrepancy between the French translation of *Banjo* and Senghor's quotation in "Le problème." He writes that in the collected and revised version from 1963 of "Le problème," the phrase "notre propre fonds" (our own funds or resources) appears as "notre profond fond" (our profound depths). Edwards, *Practice of Diaspora*, 362. But in *Paris-Dakar* the phrase appears as "notre propre fond" (singular: our own depths or resources or fund). In *Paris-Dakar* Senghor makes more ambiguous the play between "funds" and "depths" with the possibly accidental dropping of an "s," whereas in *Liberté* the sense of depth is further underlined through a more significant editorial decision or transcribing error. As is well known, McKay's novel *Banjo* (1929) had an incalculable impact upon diasporic black writers in Paris in the 1930s. Claude McKay, *Banjo: A Story Without a Plot* (New York: Harpers, 1929). Hereafter cited parenthetically in the text as *Banjo*.

98. Claude McKay, *Banjo*, trans. Ida Treat and Paul Vaillant-Couturier (Paris: Editions Rieder, 1931), 258.

99. Ernesto Laclau, *On Populist Reason* (New York: Verso, 2005); Stefan Jonsson, *A Brief History of the Masses (Three Revolutions)* (New York: Columbia University Press, 2008); Étienne Balibar, *Politics and the Other Scene*, trans. Chritine Jones et al. (London: Verso, 2002); Alain Badiou et al., *What Is a People?* (New York: Columbia University Press, 2016).

100. Jacques Derrida, *Of Grammatology*, trans. Gayatri Chakravorty Spivak (Baltimore: Johns Hopkins University Press, 1976), 101.

101. France's colonial territories were represented by thematized pavilion-like architectural clusters. Robert H. Kargon et al., *World's Fairs on the Eve of War: Science, Technology, and Modernity, 1937–42* (Pittsburgh: University of Pittsburgh Press, 2015).
102. Program outline in *Congrès international de l'évolution culturelle des peuples coloniaux (Rapports et compte rendu)* (Paris, 1938), 6. Hereafter cited parenthetically in the text as *Congrès.*
103. "Resolutions Adopted by the Congress," in *Congrès international*, 10–11. See also Vaillant, *Black, French*, 161–62 for brief commentary on the resolutions.
104. Senghor, "La résistance de la bourgeoisie sénégalaise à l'école rurale populaire," in *Congrès.* Hereafter referenced parenthetically in the text as RB. A general empirical account of the French policy of "adapting" its education system to African conditions may be found in Conklin, *A Mission to Civilize*, 130–41. More detail on the transition between the general concept of adaptation and the actual establishment of the "rural schools" in AOF from 1930 onward is given in Gamble, "Peasants of the Empire."
105. Gamble, "Peasants of the Empire"; Delavignette, *Les paysans noirs*; Delavignette, "Pour le paysannat noir," 367–90; Hardy, *Une conquête morale*; Hardy, *Nos grands problèmes coloniaux*, 19–23; Wilder, *French Imperial Nation-State*, 120–21.
106. Senghor, "Résistance," 42. Senghor is quoting from the weekly *Jeune Sénégal* (March 15, 1937), which, he says, "guards the most aged Senegalese spirit."
107. Vaillant, *Black, French*, 88–89. Senghor obtained his citizenship with the help of the deputy Blaise Diagne.
108. Fanon, *Wretched of the Earth*, 97, 99. His entire chapter on "The Misfortunes of National Consciousness" speaks to the problems that Senghor was delineating from the 1930s through the 1960s.
109. Gamble, "Peasants of the Empire," 793–94.
110. Gamble, 794. De Coppet's quoted words here are from a piece of official correspondence to Laborde (Inspector General of Education) of April 1938.
111. Discussed in Gamble, "La crise de l'enseignement en Afrique occidentale française (1944–1950)," *Histoire de l'éducation* 128 (October–December 2010): 129–62.

3 Négritude (Slight Return) II

1. Aimé Césaire, "Nègreries: Jeunesse noir et assimilation," in *Poesie, théâtre, essais et Discours*, ed. A. James Arnold (Paris: CNRS, 2013), 1293. "Jeunesse" was first published in *L'Étudiant Noir* 1 (March 1935): 3. Hereafter cited parenthetically in the text as JN.
2. Gary Wilder, *The French Imperial Nation-State Negritude and Colonial Humanism Between the Two World Wars* (Chicago: University of Chicago Press, 2005), 188. Hereafter cited parenthetically in the text as *French Imperial Nation-State.*
3. Césaire, "Conscience raciale et révolution sociale," *L'Étudiant Noir* 3 (May–June 1935): 1–2.
4. It is a book that begins with the derogation of books. On the surface at least, it posits the "simple" and the "child" as possessed of natural nobility of "instinct," as the source of renewal itself; "wise men" should "adjourn their studies, lock up their books,... and go quietly among mothers and nurses to unlearn" (at least so as to "reform" their wisdom); "In this book I have given a voice to [*j'ai fait parler*] those who as yet do not even know whether they have a right in the world [*au monde*]. All who groan or suffer in silence, all who are aspiring and struggling toward life, these are my people.

They are the people!" Michelet, *The People*, trans. John P. McKay (Urbana: University of Illinois Press, 1973), 120, 152.

5. Roland Barthes, *Michelet*, trans. Richard Howard (New York: Hill and Wang, 1987), 187. Barthes continues, "Michelet's entire speech—i.e., his entire work . . . bears him, lacerated, far from his paradise" (the People as redemption); "he is perhaps the first author of modernity able to utter only an impossible language" (187). Michelet knows he cannot enunciate the barbarian/savage/child/simple voice(s) of the People that he wishes to relay and claims as his own.

6. That is, the modern consolidation of racial difference under the heading of the biophysical heredity of species-groups, laws of Nature. See especially Colette Guillaumin, *Racism, Sexism, Power and Ideology* (London: Routledge, 1995), esp. chaps. 1–3; and Hannah Arendt, *Imperialism* (New York: Harcourt Brace, 1968), esp. 38–64.

7. This is also an allusion to an article by H.-M. Bernelot-Moens, "L'humanité peut-elle être humanisée?/Can Humanity Be Humanised?" published in the bilingual *Revue du monde noir* 3 (1931–32): 5–13; reprint in *La Revue du Monde Noir/The Review of the Black World: Collection complète* (Paris: Jean-Michel Place, 1992), 199–207. Although it adheres to a general scientific concept of racial distinction, the article is a liberal-rational criticism of the social hierarchization of racial difference. Bernelot-Moens discusses racial segregation in the United States and the illusory visuality of color-based racial segregation. As an illustration of this absurdity, the white Dutch author at one point passes for black in a segregated railcar. Bernelot-Moens's sense of the "humanization of humanity" is the perfectible civilizing of a universal human "brotherhood" (207). Edited by Paulette Nardal and Léo Sajous, the *Revue* was a major element of the international black cultural scene centered in Paris in the early 1930s. It was read closely by Césaire and his group, who themselves were closely associated with the *Revue*'s personnel and the Nardals' salon.

8. Étienne Balibar and Immanuel Wallerstein, *Race, Nation, Class: Ambiguous Identities* (New York: Verso, 1991), 59.

9. Carl Schmitt, *Der Begriff des Politischen: Text von 1932 mit einem Vorwort und drei Corollarien* (Berlin: Duncker und Humblot, 1963); Jacques Derrida, *Politics of Friendship*, trans. George Collins (New York: Verso, 1997), 89–90.

10. It is only remotely possible that Césaire knew of Carl Schmitt and his work in 1935. However, they swam in some of the same crosscurrents of interwar European culture and politics as Walter Benjamin, the Collège de Sociologie, the Surrealists, and many others. Derrida, *Politics of Friendship*, 91; Derrida is paraphrasing Plato's definition from the *Republic*. Schmitt in fact excludes *stasis* from the political. See also Aristotle, *Politics* 1301a 37–39.

11. Michelet, *Le peuple* (Paris: Hachette, 1846), 35; *The People*, 18, translation altered. *The People* has an entire chapter on "Bastard Classes"—upwardly mobile peasants who are the weirdly displaced antecedents of the *évolués* patterned in terms of a vulgar *nouveaux riches*. Michelet, *The People*, 115–18.

12. Césaire, *Jeunesse noir*, 1293. The term *grands enfants* returns us to Georges Hardy's *Nos grands problèmes coloniaux* (Paris: Armand Colin, 1933), discussed in the previous chapter, in which Hardy criticizes the "improvised psychology" in which "it is understood, for example, that the indigene is a 'big child' [*grand enfant*]" (196). Hardy sets himself against such doxa, to which he had previously subscribed. See Hardy, *Une conquête morale: L'enseignement en A.O.F.* (Paris: Librarie Armand Colin, 1917), passim. The double

bind is that Hardy, of course, now advocates a more systematic understanding of the indigenous psyche in its difference, for mutual understanding and forestalling "indigenous revolts"; and he reserves a special role for literature in "revealing to us the background of [the colonial population's] soul" (199–200).

13. George Meredith, *The Shaving of Shagpat: An Arabian Entertainment* (New York: Scribner, 1909).

14. *The Shaving of Shagpat* was translated into French in 1921 as *Shagpat rasé* by Hélène Boussinesq and René Galland (Paris: Éditions de la Nouvelle Revue française, 1921).

15. Paul de Man, "Literary History and Literary Modernity," in *Blindness and Insight* (London: Routledge, 1989), 142–65.

16. Leo Steinberg, *The Sexuality of Christ in Renaissance Art and in Modern Oblivion* (Chicago: University of Chicago, 1996), 3, 195. The wounds most often referred to the wounds of Christ.

17. Reprinted in Césaire, *Poesie, théâtre, essais*, 1298–300.

18. Christopher Miller, "The (Revised) Birth of Negritude: Communist Revolution and 'the Immanent Negro' in 1935," *PMLA* 125, no. 3 (May 2010): 743–49; Raisa Rexer, "Black and White and Re(a)d All Over: L'Étudiant Noir, Communism, and the Birth of Négritude," *Research in African Literatures* 44, no. 4 (Winter 2013): 1–14. The quotation is from Rexer, "Black and White and Re(a)d All Over," 1. In a sometimes triumphant exaggeration of Césaire's ability to either interrogate Marxism in racial terms or conjugate Marxism and black struggle, such commentators tend to conflate the "first" appearance of a word with the formed appearance of an identifiable vanguard movement as such. As I argued in the previous chapter, it took some years before Négritude became the proper name of an epistemological/aesthetic current or movement, and the first appearance of the word in print here does not necessarily coincide with the "birth" of Négritude as a distinct cluster of positions on the cultural politics of race and blackness in modernity. If asked to speculate further on this, I would venture the hypothesis (probably unverifiable) that Césaire coined *Négritude* in the context of his ENS thesis on the South in black American literature, and especially in the context of his intellectual and artistic association with the Nardals' salon. Christian Filostrat suggests Césaire "probably came upon the term in an American dictionary" in connection with his translation work on Langston Hughes. Christian Filostrat, *Negritude Agonistes: Assimilation Against Nationalism in the French-Speaking Caribbean and Guyane* (Cherry Hill, NJ: Africana Homestead, 2008), 119. Filostrat cites Webster's of 1934 and mentions the currency of *negritude* as a term during the American Civil War. Paulette Nardal had researched nineteenth-century American literature more thoroughly than anyone else in Césaire's milieu (for a diploma thesis on Harriet Beecher Stowe's *Uncle Tom's Cabin*), and she also had perhaps the strongest general knowledge of, and education in, English-language literature. If, as is likely, Nardal had researched the language of race in the nineteenth-century United States, she would almost inevitably have come across the not uncommon word *nigritude* as a general descriptor of blackness. The word *nigritude* appears under the entry for *negro* in the *Century Dictionary and Cyclopedia*, vol. 5 (New York: Century, 1904), 3960, and as early as the 1889 edition of the *Century Dictionary*. There is a copy of the 1899 edition of this dictionary in the Bibliothèque Nationale of Paris. The Supplement of 1910 (vol. 12) has an entry for "nigritudinous . . . having the character of nigritude," and also gives a Latin derivation of *nigritudo* (808). Césaire the classicist (and friend of sister Jane Nardal, also a classicist) would himself

have been able to make the link to the Latin *nigritudo* (blackness, e.g., in Pliny). For general context, Lloyd Thompson, *Romans and Blacks* (New York: Routledge, 1989), is a useful study of the semantic field of blackness (*nigritudo* and cognate terms, as well as others) in Roman antiquity. "Nigritude," as well as "negrohood," is used with reasonable frequency in the U.S. print media in the nineteenth century, also for nonracial kinds of darkness (seasonal darkness, or the darkness associated with soot deposits in urban areas). See, for example, an article on chimney sweeps in the Boston *Evening City Gazette* (July 6, 1822), widely syndicated in 1820s: "The Planter: A West India Story," *Baltimore Gazette and Daily Advertiser* (April 16, 1833), also syndicated; "The Gospel of Amalgamation," in *The World* (New York, May 14, 1863) (Civil War–era article on racial integration). Moreover, in a more obviously literary context *nigritude* appears around the mid-nineteenth century. See especially the poem "A Black Job" (1844) by the English late Romantic Thomas Hood (perhaps best known for "The Song of the Shirt"). Hood's "A Black Job" satirizes the racism of humanistic philanthropic benevolence, lampooning a philanthropic society established to wash blacks white so as to cure them of their social subordination (whiteness being the sign of common humanity). The penultimate line speaks of a "nigritude" that persists in spite of all the soap. Hood's poem was syndicated in several U.S. newspapers in the 1850s and 1860s, and it would be surprising if it had not been known to Paulette Nardal. See, for example, *Evening Star* (Washington, DC, June 28, 1862); and see for the original collection Thomas Hood, *Whimsicalities: A Periodical Gathering* (London: Henry Colburn, 1844), 1:215–24. What all this tells us, I think, is that the field of emergence of the *term négritude* in Césaire's coinage may well be extremely complex and entangled with the Nardals' cultural salon; with questions of translation, transcription, and what travels in literary/cultural space (and how); and in their shared discussion and work on blackness and literature in the United States of the nineteenth century.

   In a truly bizarre footnote to this footnote, it is worth mentioning that apparently reputable textbooks in clinical psychology and cultural history have incorrectly attributed the category of "negritude" to U.S. "founding father" Benjamin Rush, as the name for a pathology that causes the outward signs of racial difference in and as skin color. In *The Manufacture of Madness* (New York: Granada, 1973), Thomas Szaz writes of Benjamin Rush's "theory of Negritude." "Rush does not believe that God created the Negro black; nor that the Negro is black by nature. Instead, he believes that Negritude is a disease!" (154). In Szaz's argument, this "disease concept of Negritude" solves a double bind for a certain Enlightenment progressivism: how to acknowledge the human equality of blacks (Declaration of Independence) while at the same time recognizing and indeed justifying their separation and subjugation. Black pigmentation, according to Rush, was a symptom of congenital leprosy rather than essential racial difference. Given the supposedly voracious sexual appetite associated with leprosy, blacks ought to be segregated for the good of wider society until the condition disappears. Thus the double bind is kept in play: the common humanity of blacks is recognized (in keeping with enlightened sensibility), yet a benevolent reason for their being kept apart is also set in place (illness: a reason compatible with that enlightened sensibility). See Benjamin Rush, "Observations Intended to Favour a Supposition That the Black Color (as It Is Called) of the Negroes Is Derived from the Leprosy," *Transactions of the American Philosophical Society* 4 (1799): 289–97. Szaz uses the word *Negritude* innocently enough and does not explicitly ascribe it to Rush. However,

Szaz's formulations are also sufficiently ambiguous to make it seem as if Rush invented and named a condition called "Negritude" that was a specific mode of the disease leprosy. This is incorrect. Rush did not coin this term, and the more common "nigritude" was not a pathologizing descriptor at the time. This does not of course get Rush off the hook for trying to argue that black pigmentation was the symptom of a disease. However, a fuller analysis ought to be made of the legacy of the incredible contortions of Rush's paternalistic, benevolent humanism as he argues that the inherited disease of blackness is the blockage that prevents negroes from being accepted as equal members of the human race. If only this could be cured (and he thinks it can) and the blacks whitened, it would herald an end to slavery and an acceptance of the commonality of the entire human race. Thus: universalist humanist racism. As soon as blacks resemble whites (which they really want to do), they will be members of the human family and not objects of disgust and enforced exploitation. The overlap with the object of satire in Thomas Hood's poem is remarkable, especially as one of the donors to the philanthropic scheme in "A Black Job" is a certain "Master Rush." However, no one should claim that Rush made *Negritude* the proper name of a pathology. That was all Szaz; and a systematic misreading of his account of Rush has led a surprising number of commentators (including professional psychiatrists and cultural critics) to repeat the claim that Rush classified blackness as a disease called "Negritude," when in fact it was Szaz who introduced the term *Negritude* into the discussion. Some examples of the many works that have uncritically repeated the assertion that Benjamin Rush invented a disease called Negritude are Roy Porter, ed., *The Cambridge Illustrated History of Medicine* (Cambridge: Cambridge University Press, 2006), 104; James Aho and Kevin Aho, *Body Matters: A Phenomenology of Sickness, Disease and Illness* (Plymouth: Lexington, 2009), 56–57; Bridget Brereton, ed., *General History of the Caribbean*, vol. 5 (Paris: UNESCO/Macmillan, 2004), 246; Peter Conrad and Joseph W. Schneider, *Deviance and Medicalization: From Badness to Sickness* (Philadelphia: Temple University Press, 1992), 49; Maia Szalavitz, *Unbroken Brain: A Revolutionary New Way of Understanding Addiction* (New York: St. Martin's, 2016), 24; F. Bart Miller, *Rethinking Négritude Through Léon-Gontran Damas* (Amsterdam: Rodopi, 2014), 10n4. This is a small sample; the number of books that repeat the claim is large and interestingly symptomatic.

19. In Paul Morand, *Magie noire* (Paris: Grasset, 1928), 13–74.

20. "Nous autres, civilisations, nous savons maintenant que nous sommes mortelles." This is the resonant first sentence of "La Crise de l'esprit" (1919): "We others, civilizations, we now know that we are mortal." Valéry's epistolary address meditates on the "spiritual crisis" of Europe, diagnosing the spiritual (intellectual) ills that Europe's own vanguard powers have brought upon it in the face of the rise of world forces such as communism. Will Europe become a mere trace rather than the predominant giver of signs and meanings? "Will Europe become what she is in reality, that is, a little promontory of the continent of Asia? Or will Europe remain what she seems to be, that is, the precious part of the terrestrial universe, the pearl of the sphere, the brain of a vast body?" Valéry's "Letters from France" was first published in *The Athenaeum* (April 11, 1919): 183–84 and *The Athenaeum* (May 2, 1919): 279–80. It was published as "La crise de l'esprit" in *La nouvelle revue française* 6, no. 71 (August 1, 1919): 321–37.

21. Jacques Louis Hymans, *Léopold Senghor: An Intellectual Biography* (Edinburgh: Edinburgh University Press, 1991) gives a good accounting of this with more specific reference to Senghor. A literary touchstone for this thinking was Maurice Barrès, *Les déracinés*

(1897; Paris: Félix Juven, 1907). Subtitled "the novel of national energy," and part of a trilogy of these, the novel is importantly a critical dramatization of the dangers of modernized pedagogy uprooting subjects from their terrestrial locality—a localism or ethno-chauvinism that is ultimately also accorded a universalizable status. Discussion of Barrès may be found in Emily Apter, "Uprooted Subjects: Barrès and the Politics of Patrimoine," in Continental Drift: From National Characters to Virtual Subjects (Chicago: University of Chicago Press, 1999), 25–37.

22. Césaire, "Cahier d'un retour au pays natal," Volontés 20 (August 1939): 23–51. This version has now been published in a bilingual edition as The Original 1939 Notebook of a Return to the Native Land, trans. and ed. A. James Arnold and Clayton Eshleman (Middletown, CT: Wesleyan University Press, 2013). Cited parenthetically as Cahier, all page references in the text are to this edition unless otherwise noted. The mainly additive changes to the Cahier between the 1930s and the 1950s are aspects of an ongoing process of revision that Césaire conducted on many of his works. Nevertheless, this process of correction, revision, gap-filling, or elaboration should be taken seriously as an aspect of the work's play with form; read not just for the extra (thematic) content it adds (references to the Holocaust, to indentured Indian workers in the Caribbean, and to U.S. civil rights, for example), but also for what it might tell us about the poem as the dramatization of a scene of writing.

23. See for the first position A. James Arnold, "Beyond Postcolonial Césaire: Reading Cahier d'un Retour au Pays Natal Historically," Modern Language Studies 44, no. 3 (2008): 266; and for the second Ronnie Scharfman, Engagement and the Language of the Subject in the Poetry of Aimé Césaire (Gainesville: University Presses of Florida, 1980), 31.

24. For example, Scharfman, Engagement; Brent Hayes Edwards, "Aimé Césaire and the Syntax of Influence," Research in African Literatures 36, no. 2 (Summer 2005): 1–18; Noland, Voices of Negritude in Modernist Print: Aesthetic Subjectivity, Diaspora, and the Lyric Regime (New York: Columbia University Press, 2015).

25. See Nick Nesbitt, Voicing Memory: History and Subjectivity in French Caribbean Literature (Charlottesville: University of Virginia Press, 2003), 76–94, for an account of Césaire and fascism. A. James Arnold discusses the appearance of a Spenglerian word (pseudomorphosis, artificially distorted and externally determined cultural development) in the Cahier in his introduction to Original 1939 Notebook, xv–xvi. More interesting is the idea that intellectuals in the colonial world could read The Decline of the West in an alternative way—as heralding "the renaissance of cultures oppressed by the West." Arnold, Modernism and Negritude: The Poetry and Poetics of Aimé Césaire (Cambridge, MA: Harvard University Press, 1991), 21–23.

26. See also Césaire's poem-play "Et les chiens se taisaient" (And the dogs were silent). John Patrick Walsh, Free and French in the Caribbean: Toussaint L'Ouverture, Aimé Césaire, and Narratives of Loyal Opposition (Bloomington: Indiana University Press, 2013), develops these connections in relation to Césaire's political practice as the advocate of departmentalization.

27. "We have indicated the very often harmful role of the leader [du leader] many times. . . . People are no longer a herd and do not need to be driven." Frantz Fanon, The Wretched of the Earth, trans. Richard Philcox (New York: Grove, 2004), 127, translation modified. Fanon, Les damnés de la terre (Paris: Découverte, 2002), 176. Subsequent references given parenthetically in the text with WTE followed by English page numbers and then by French after the slash.

28. Fanon, *Wretched*, 138/187. Fanon's quotation points to one of Césaire's speeches from 1959, "The Man of Culture and His Responsibilities." Aimé Césaire, "L'homme de culture et ses responsabilités," *Présence Africaine, Deuxième Congrès des écrivains et artistes noirs* (Rome: March 26–April 1, 1959) 1, nos. 24–25, *L'unité des cultures négro-africaines* (February–May 1959): 118. Cited parenthetically in the text as *L'homme*. Fanon was present at the 1959 Congress of Black Writers and Artists where Césaire made this presentation, and he delivered the speech that would become the final section of the "National Culture" chapter of *Wretched* there. For comment on the Fanon/Césaire connection, see Matthieu Renault, " 'Des inventeurs d'âmes'—Fanon, lecteur de Césaire," *Rue Descartes* 83, no. 4 (2014): 22–35. Gary Wilder, *Freedom Time: Negritude, Decolonization, and the Future of the World* (Durham: Duke University Press, 2015), 181–82, situates Césaire's intervention in relation to his political practice of the period.

29. Césaire, "L'homme," 118. This phrase, quickly monumentalized as a Soviet cultural credo, was attributed to Stalin by Andrei Zhdanov in his keynote address at the First Congress of the Soviet Writers' Union (1934). "Writers are the engineers of the human soul" (*pisateli inzhenery chelovecheskikh dush*). John Garrard and Carol Garrard, *Inside the Soviet Writers' Union* (New York: Free Press, 1990), 34. *Dush* is usually translated as "soul," but it has a semantic range comparable in breadth to *Geist* or *esprit* as well. It is possible that the phrase originated with the poet Yury Olesha: Garrard and Garrard, *Soviet Writers' Union*, 256.

30. Fanon, *Wretched*, 88/133, my emphasis. The chain of displacement of the *sans transition* refrain should be followed in detail to here from page 1/39 through 14/53, 19/57, and 29/67.

31. Césaire, "L'homme," 119. "What would this event be then? Its exterior form would be that of a *rupture* and a *redoubling*. . . . The event, the rupture, the disruption . . . presumably would have come about when the structurality of structure had to begin to be thought, that is to say repeated, and this is why I said that disruption was repetition in every sense of the word." Jacques Derrida, "Structure, Sign, and Play in the Discourse of the Human Sciences," in *Writing and Difference*, trans. Alan Bass (Chicago: University of Chicago Press, 1978), 278, 280. There is room for a productive dialogue between Derrida and Césaire during this period, routed through the topoi of anthropology, structure, complicity, colonialism, and ethnocentrism.

32. Renée Larrier, "A Tradition of Literacy: Césaire in and out of the Classroom," *Research in African Literatures* 41, no. 1 (2010): 34.

33. Noland's reading of the *Cahier* develops a more complex understanding of literacy to argue for the poem staging "the primal experience of literacy acquisition, that strange and magical act by which letters of the alphabet morph into sounds." Noland, *Voices of Negritude* 43. Literacy as formally taught grammatization works the other way around, though: the timing-spacing of a sonic flow (speech) by cutting it up into discrete units to produce *writing* as narrowly understood.

34. Sartre, "Orphée noir," in *Anthologie de la nouvelle poésie nègre et malgache de langue française*, ed. Léopold Senghor (Paris: Presses Universitaires de France, 1948), ix–xliv. Translation: John MacCombie, "Black Orpheus," *Massachussetts Review* 6, no. 1 (Autumn 1964–Winter 1965): 13–52. Hereafter cited parenthetically as ON with French followed by English page numbers. I have altered the translation where appropriate.

35. Sartre, "Black Orpheus," xx/25. Sartre traces the modernist line from Mallarmé to Surrealism.

36. To be sure, the reversal is a dialectical passage for Sartre; the passage of negation that paves the way to the *Aufhebung* and universal humanity because its very assertion of blackness is supposed to lead to the radical (and tragic) act of négritude's self-abolition as particularity.

37. Lilyan Kesteloot, *Black Writers in French: A Literary History of Negritude*, trans. Ellen Conroy Kennedy (Philadelphia: Temple University Press, 1974), 173. A. James Arnold discusses the tripartite nature of the poem, a large-scale formal division that seems to be shared by almost every commentator, though not all agree on where the exact lines would be drawn. Arnold, *Modernism and Negritude*, 155–68.

38. James Clifford, *The Predicament of Culture: Twentieth-Century Ethnography, Literature, and Art* (Cambridge, MA: Harvard University Press, 1988), 176. Clayton and Eshleman gloss *verrition* from Césaire's explanation as "coined off the Latin verb 'verri,' meaning 'to sweep, to scrape a surface, to scan.'" Césaire, *Original 1939 Notebook*, 66.

39. See also Noland, *Voices of Negritude*, 39–40, for the avant-garde publication context of Césaire's coinage.

40. Edwards, "Aimé Césaire," 15.

41. See also Nesbitt, *Voicing Memory*, 94.

42. For example, Gervais Mendo Ze, *Cahier d'un retour au pays natal, Aimé Césaire: Approche Ethnostylistique* (Paris: Harmattan, 2010), 128. Ze gives a relentless statistical accounting of such patternings and repetitions. There are multiple critical readings of the anaphoric patterning of the *Cahier*. Patrice M. Somé develops Lilyan Kesteloot's observation that anaphora relates to ritual practice. Somé's suggestion that it figures patterns that evoke the oral formulaic is rich, and if followed up in detail would take my discussion in a rather different direction. See Somé, "The Anatomy of a Cosmogony: Ritual and Anaphora in Aimé Césaire's *Cahier d'un Retour au Pays Natal*," *Journal of Ritual Studies* 7, no. 2 (Fall 1993): esp. 37, 40–50.

43. Frédéric Godefroy, *Dictionnaire de l'ancienne langue française, et de tous ses dialectes du IXe au XVe siècle: Composé d'après le dépouillement de tous les plus importants documents, manuscrits ou imprimés, qui se trouvent dans les grands bibliothèques de la France et de l'Europe, et dans les principales archives départementales, municipales, hospitalières ou privées* (Paris: F. Vieweg, 1880). *Cahier* shares an etymology with *carnet*, though the semantic field of *carnet* seems to have accumulated a stronger sense of informality.

44. Maryse Condé, *Cahier d'un retour au pays natal: Césaire: Analyse Critique* (Paris: Hatier, 1978), 31–33.

45. Césaire, *Cahier*; Césaire, *Memorandum on My Martinique/Cahier d'un retour au pays natal*, trans. Lionel Abel and Yvan Goll (New York: Brentano's, 1947); Césaire, *Journal of a Homecoming*, trans. Gregson Davis (Durham: Duke University Press, 2017); see Davis, *Aimé Césaire* (New York: Cambridge University Press, 1997), 20–61; Césaire, *Return to My Native Land*, trans. John Berger and Anna Bostock (Baltimore: Penguin, 1969). Berger and Bostock's excision forecloses the possibility of reading the event of "return" as staged in a scene of writing that is perhaps also a scene of teaching/learning.

46. Aimé Césaire, *Notebook of a Return to the Native Land*, trans. and ed. Clayton Eshleman and Annette Smith (Middletown, CT: Wesleyan University Press, 2001), 55.

47. Davis, *Aimé Césaire*, 21.

48. Larrier, discussing the history of Césaire's activity as an *élève* and later as a schoolteacher, does not connect the poem's title to the exercise book, a key practical unit of

the classroom. Michel Hausser's promisingly titled "Césaire à l'école" is a discussion of the extracts from Césaire's works that have been published in school textbooks. Abiola Irele, who submitted almost every word of the *Cahier* to illuminating scrutiny, does not focus attention upon the title. Michel Hausser, "Césaire à l'école," in *Césaire 70*, ed. M. a M. Ngal and Martin Steins (Paris: Editions Silex, 1984), 203–27; Aimé Césaire and Abiola Irele, *Cahier d'un retour au pays natal* (Columbus: Ohio State University Press, 2000).

49. Robert Aldrich and John Connell, *France's Overseas Frontier: Départements et Territoires d'Outre-Mer* (Cambridge: Cambridge University Press, 2006), 6, 167.

50. Eugen Weber, *Peasants Into Frenchmen: The Modernization of Rural France, 1870–1914* (Stanford: Stanford University Press, 1976), 303.

51. A general account of the *instituteur* in rural society may be found in Theodore Zeldin, *France, 1848–1945: Intellect and Pride* (Oxford: Oxford University Press, 1980), 158–71.

52. Michel Foucault, *Discipline and Punish: The Birth of the Prison* (New York: Vintage, 1979).

53. It is likely that Foucault was steering clear of an area that appeared saturated by a certain Marxist analysis of "Ideological State Apparatuses" (Althusser) and by sociological critiques parallel to Althusser's analysis such as Pierre Bourdieu and Jean Claude Passeron, *La reproduction: Éléments pour une théorie du système d'enseignement* (Paris: Éditions de Minuit, 1970); Pierre Bourdieu and Jean Claude Passeron, *Reproduction in Education, Society and Culture*, trans. Richard Nice (London: Sage, 1977). Balibar writes that around 1970 the group around Althusser was planning "a collective work . . . on the theory of the school system in capitalist society" and indeed was developing theories of the "scholastic form" and "scholastic apparatus." Balibar, foreword to *On the Reproduction of Capitalism*, by Louis Althusser (New York: Verso, 2014), x. Other elements of this general project appeared in Christian Baudelot and Roger Establet, *L'école capitaliste en France* (Paris: Maspero, 1972); Renée Balibar, *Les français fictifs* (Paris: Hachette, 1974). The best-known intervention probably remains Althusser's "Ideology" essay. Nevertheless, *Surveillir et punir* often reads like an allegory of the modernized school system, and by the end of that book Foucault has included the school as part of a "carceral archipelago" (297/347).

54. Louis Althusser "Ideology and Ideological State Apparatuses (Notes Towards an Investigation)," in *Lenin and Philosophy*, trans. Ben Brewster (New York: Monthly Review, 1971), 154. Hereafter cited parenthetically in the text as "Ideology."

55. A significant study of the effectiveness of early literacy teaching in France is François Furet and Jacques Ozouf, *Lire et écrire: L'alphabétisation des Français de Calvin à Jules Ferry* (Paris: Éditions de Minuit, 1977). The classic general account of modern French education is Antoine Prost, *Histoire de l'enseignement en France, 1800–1967* (Paris: A. Colin, 1968).

56. Weber, *Peasants Into Frenchmen*, 67. A sense of the linguistic plurality of even mid-nineteenth-century France is given in the chapter "A Wealth of Tongues" on 67–94. A classic study is Michel de Certeau et al., *Une politique de la langue (la Révolution Française et les Patois)* (Paris: Gallimard, 1975). For the revolution, see also Patrice L.-R. Higgonet, "The Politics of Linguistic Terrorism and Grammatical Hegemony During the French Revolution," *Social History* 5, no. 1 (1980). A useful overview of the history and the scholarship on language in France is given in Pierre Achard, "History and the Politics of Language in France," trans. Michael Ignatieff and Susan Bullock, *History Workshop* 10 (Autumn 1980).

57. Jacques Derrida, "If There Is Cause to Translate I: Philosophy in Its National Language (Toward a 'Licterature en François')," in *Eyes of the University: Right to Philosophy 2* (Stanford: Stanford University Press, 2004), 1–42.

58. Derrida, 16.

59. Cited in Daniel Guérin, *La lutte de classes sous la Première République, 1793-1797* (Paris: Gallimard, 1968), 1:330.

60. Jullien cited in Guérin, 330.

61. This is the general argument of Cherval, *... et il fallut apprendre à écrire à tous les petits français: Histoire de la grammaire scolaire* (Paris: Payot, 1977). See also Furet and Ouzouf, *Lire et Écrire*.

62. Zeldin, *France*, 177–78.

63. Chervel, *... et il fallut*, 23. See also Baudelot and Establet, *L'école capitaliste*.

64. Gramsci, *Selections from the Prison Notebooks of Antonio Gramsci*, trans. Quintin Hoare and Geoffrey Nowell-Smith (London: International, 1971), 323–33. Common sense for Gramsci is the ideological *doxa* of everyday life. Its production and transmission are not simply a matter of the school, of course.

65. André Chervel, "Rhétorique et grammaire: Petite histoire du circonstanciel," *Langue française* 41 (1979): 18.

66. Chervel's remarks about the influence of Swiss pedagogue Père Grégoire Girard are important here. Girard's *Cours educatif de langue maternelle* (1845–48) played a key role in France's modernization to the extent that he influentially emphasized a shift of priorities in language instruction from abstract principles to self-expression. See Chervel, *... et il fallut*, 163–64.

67. Achard, "History and the Politics of Language in France: A Review Essay," 179.

68. Frantz Fanon, *Black Skin, White Masks,* trans. Richard Philcox (New York: Grove, 2008). What remains intriguing about Fanon's descriptions here is the extent to which he relies on analogies between the French provinces and the capital to think the relation between colony and metropolis. A further point of comparison could be made with studies such as Raymond Williams, *The Country and the City* (New York: Oxford University Press, 1975).

69. For key post-Fanon developments on the question of créolité in the Antillean context, see Édouard Glissant, *Le discours antillais* (Paris: Gallimard, 1997); Jean Bernabé, Patrick Chamoiseau, and Raphaël Confiant, *Éloge de la Créolité* [In praise of creoleness], trans. Mohamed Bouya Taleb-Khyar (Paris: Gallimard, 1993). Some criticisms of Fanon, such as that of Françoise Vergés, seem to conflate his pessimistic assessment of creole language with an assessment of creolité as such, as a social-cultural modality. See Vergés, "Where to Begin? 'Le commencement' in *Peau Noire, Masques Blancs* and in creolisation," in *Frantz Fanon's* Black Skin, White Masks: *New Interdisciplinary Essays*, ed. Max Silverman (Manchester: Manchester University Press, 2005), 32–45.

70. Jacques Derrida, *Monolingualism of the Other; or, The Prosthesis of Origin*, trans. Patrick Mensah (Stanford: Stanford University Press, 1998), 42; Jacques Derrida, *Le monolinguisme de l'autre; ou la prothèse d'origine* (Paris: Galilée, 1996), 74. Derrida does not mention Fanon's description of a similar analogy. A specific difference Derrida is addressing, however, is that of the metropolitan language as mother tongue rather than as a language that overwrites, as it were, a mother tongue such as Creole in the Antilles, or Arabic, Berber, and other languages in Algeria.

71. Chervel, *... et il fallut*, 26.

72. Aldrich and Connell, *France's Overseas Frontier*, 55.

73. André Lucrèce, *Civilisés et energumènes: de l'enseignement aux Antilles* (Paris: Editions Caribéennes/L'Harmattan, 1981), 80 In his fierce critique of educational practice in the Antilles, Lucrèce argues that the "Schoelcherist myth" of emancipation (through education) in the Antilles is that of the slaves being humanized by Schoelcher. In other words, the abolitionist deserves gratitude for having humanized the former slave population.

74. See the introduction to this volume for a more detailed discussion of common education with particular reference to France and Jules Ferry.

75. Sylvère Farraudière, *L'école aux Antilles françaises: Le rendez-vous manqué de la démocratie* (Paris: L'Harmattan, 2007); Joseph Jos, *La terre des gens sans terre: Petite histoire de l'école à la Martinique* (Paris: L'Harmattan, 2003).

76. Césaire, *Original 1939 Notebook*, 2–6.

77. Althusser, "Ideology," 151–53.

78. The translators give the dazzling "starvation has quicksanded his voice into the swamp of hunger" (7), with which I have no quarrel as it impressively sustains the semantic connection between *faim* and *inanition*, hunger and starvation. My flatter rendition simply serves to underline the link between the third strophe's *inanité* and *inanition*, the latter of which, more archaically, can also mean "emptiness," "void."

79. Césaire, *Original 1939 Notebook*, 6–7. Eshleman and Arnold translate "lumineusement obscur" as "chiaroscuro," which in its current sense does not capture the paradox of something luminously dark. In spite of its literal meaning of light-dark, chiaroscuro signifies in visual terms the theatrically contrastive play of light and dark that renders convincingly modeled shape, which is to say successful phenomenalization rather than resistance to it in linguistic paradox. Paradox, which resists empiricization by definition, is an important figure for this part of the poem: "insensé reveil" (senseless awakening) (2), "bavarde et muette" (chattering and mute) (4), "incendie contenu" (contained conflagration) (6), and so on. The Cahier's powerful images of scenes of colonial abjection are punctuated by figures of linguistic paradox that undermine their phenomenality.

80. Making an interesting connection with Fanon, Nesbitt calls this "phenomenology": "Cesaire's investigation, like Fanon's after him, is a phenomenology of consciousness par excellence." Nesbitt, *Voicing Memory*, 129.

81. Nesbitt's discussion specifically concerns the scene in the tram where the poem's speaker confesses to a shaming complicity with the mockery of a "COMICAL AND UGLY" black passenger. Nesbitt, *Voicing Memory*, 30.

82. This kind of representation is clearly not restricted to the realm of literature or art narrowly understood. Insurgency, street protest, the layout of a newspaper front page, an upheaval in everyday patterns of speech or action could all produce such moments. It is important to acknowledge that the possibility I am describing depends also on the attunement of a "reader," too, rather than being an exclusively immanent property of the "work" or statement.

83. For a certain empirical follow up, see André Thibault, "L'oeuvre d'Aimé Césaire et le français régional antillais," in *Aimé Césaire à l'oeuvre*, ed. Marc Cheymol and Philippe Ollé-Laprune (Paris: Archives Contemporaines, 2008), 47–85.

84. A certain current of Césaire scholarship justifiably seeks to pin down *verrition*—a word almost fiendishly designed to provoke and frustrate the desire for meaning and ori-

gin. Kesteloot, *Black Writers*; Clifford, *Predicament*; Edwards, "Syntax," among others. Noland makes an informative Joycean connection in *Voices*, connecting the *verrition* section to the contingencies of editorial policy in *Volontés* (37–60; see also 186–87). Noland's general impulse is to push meaning toward the trace-ness of sound or even noise. As both Noland and Arnold note, René Hénane discovered an actual prior instance of the word in Brillat-Savarin's *Physiologie du gout* (1825). See Hénane, *Glossaire des terms rares dans l'oeuvre d'Aimé Césaire* (Paris: Jean-Michel Place, 2004).

85. Charles Péguy is particularly significant. For follow-up, see the presentation of Césaire's and Péguy's poems in *Tropiques* 1 (April 1941): 39–50. For commentary, A. James Arnold and Scott T. Allen, "Césaire's 'Notebook' as Palimpsest: The Text Before, During, and After World War II," *Research in African Literatures* 35, no. 3 (Autumn 2004): 133–40.

86. Jacques Derrida, *Of Grammatology*, trans. Gayatri Chakravorty Spivak (Baltimore: Johns Hopkins University Press, 1976), 62; Jacques Derrida, *De la grammatologie* (Paris: Editions de Minuit, 1967), 92.

87. Jacques Derrida, *Rogues: Two Essays on Reason*, trans. Pascale-Anne Brault and Michael Naas (Stanford: Stanford University Press, 2005), 61.

88. Derrida, *Rogues: Two Essays on Reason*, trans. Pascale-Anne Brault and Michael Naas (Stanford: Stanford University Press, 2005), 61; Spivak, "Nationalism and the Imagination," in *An Aesthetic Education in the Era of Globalization* (Cambridge, MA: Harvard University Press, 2013), 279.

89. Julia Kristeva makes some of this connection in a work whose concerns overlap with some of mine here. "A 'lumpen-intelligentsia' thus delineated itself above countries [*pays*], refusing to belong to fantasmatic kingdoms and defeated countries [*pays*] (*pays* from *pagus*, from which also 'peasant' [*paysan*], 'pagan' [*païen*]." Kristeva, *Étrangers à nous-mêmes* (Paris: Fayard, 1988), 207. Kristeva's etymological excursion is inexplicably missing from the English translation. *Étrangers* concerns itself centrally with the psychic and political question of the *pays*.

90. Freud, "The Uncanny," in *The Standard Edition of the Complete Psychological Works of Sigmund Freud*, vol. 17, trans. James Strachey (London: Vintage, 2001), 217–56.

91. Freud, "Das Unheimliche," in *Gesammelte Werke*, vol. 12 (London: Imago, 1947), 259. As the poem develops its figures of erection, the speaker invokes the desire to fecundate or inseminate the ravaged body of the island across its final pages. See especially strophes 65 (*plonge dans la chair*, 36/7); 76 (*ensemencement*, 40/1); 92 (Onan ejaculating on the earth, 47). These are simply a few key instances of an insistent pattern.

92. It should be noted that "Das Unheimliche" was published in French in 1933 as "L'inquiétante étrangeté" (Disquieting Strangeness) in a translation by Marie Bonaparte and Mme. E. Marty in the volume *Essais de psychanalytique appliquée* (Paris: Gallimard, 1933). They note that the word *Unheimliche* is "untranslatable." I would add that the terminology of *pays* occurs in Bonaparte and Marty's translation, and when they are translating Freud's citations from the Grimms' dictionary they render "aus dem heimatlichen, häuslichen" as "du sentiment du pays natal." As we have seen, Marie Bonaparte was present at Senghor's lecture in Paris in 1937, though I am not aware of further connections between her and the Negritude group; nor do I know whether Césaire had read "L'inquiétante étrangeté." It is certain that there was some kind of engagement with the outlines of psychoanalysis through Surrealist connections and through the intellectual work of the radical black Parisian journal *Légitime Défense*.

René Ménil is an especially important figure here. Ranjana Khanna probably slightly overstates the case when she writes that the Tropiques group "formed a psychoanalysis of political resistance,... offered an interpretation of psychoanalysis quite distinct from Marxist surrealism and existentialism, ... posed questions concerning how to address the specificities of colonialism through both psychoanalysis and politics." Khanna, *Dark Continents: Psychoanalysis and Colonialism* (Durham: Duke University Press, 2003), 119. Any familiarity Césaire may have had with psychoanalytic writings does not come through in his critical work of the period, and intellectually he resonates much more with Jungian archetype theory than with Freud. See, for example, his "Poésie et connaissance," *Tropiques* 11 (May 1944): 168.

93. See previous chapter, p. 118.

94. Melanie Klein, "The Rôle of the School in the Libidinal Development of the Child," and "Early Analysis," in *Love, Guilt and Reparation, and Other Works, 1921-1945* (London: Vintage, 1988), 59–76 and 77–105. Hereafter cited parenthetically in the text as "School." The essays were written before Klein moved to London in 1926, and the originals are in German. Klein, "Die Rolle der Schule in der libidinösen Entwicklung des Kindes," *Internationale Zeitschrift für Psychoanalyse* 9, no. 3 (1923): 323–44; Klein, "Zur Frühanalyse," *Imago* 9, no. 2 (1923): 222–59.

95. As with any psychoanalytic work, the analyst's task would be to convert these traces into signs if she or he can, if they have become disabling symptoms. That would be the way of helping the analysand to resymbolize.

96. Klein, "Rôle of the School," 60, Klein's emphasis.

97. Klein, "Early Analysis," 96; but see the entire section from page 93 to page 105 for multiple elaborations and detailed additions to the Freudian argument.

98. Derrida, *Of Grammatology*, 88.

99. See once again the prodigious (long-winded) staging of this provincial dynamic for France in Barrès's incredibly influential *Les deracinées*, a book that both responded to and relayed the discourse of roots and rootedness.

100. Jacques Derrida, *Specters of Marx: The State of the Debt, the Work of Mourning, and the New International*, trans. Peggy Kamuf (New York: Routledge, 1994), 83.

੫ Educating Mexico

1. D. H. Lawrence, "Nottingham and the Mining Countryside," in *Phoenix: The Posthumous Papers of D. H. Lawrence*, ed. Edward D. McDonald (New York: Viking, 1936), 137. Hereafter cited parenthetically in the text as "Mining" with page number following.

2. In D. H. Lawrence, *D. H. Lawrence on Education*, ed. Joy Williams and Raymond Williams (Harmondsworth: Penguin Education, 1973), 7.

3. The best statement of this coding of differences as gendered hierarchies remains Hélène Cixous, "Sorties," in *The Newly Born Woman*, ed. Catherine Clément (Minneapolis: University of Minnesota Press, 1986), 63–131.

4. One example among many is Lawrence's essay "We Need One Another," in McDonald, *Phoenix*.

5. D. H. Lawrence, *Sons and Lovers* (Cambridge: Cambridge University Press, 1992), 185–86. Hereafter cited parenthetically in the text as SL, followed by a page reference.

6. Kate Millett, *Sexual Politics* (Garden City, NY: Doubleday, 1970) 253; hereafter cited parenthetically in text as SP, followed by a page reference.

7. As is well known, Jessie Chambers, the "real life" Miriam Leivers, had aspirations to be a writer like her friend David Lawrence. Lawrence learned to become "Lawrence" by destroying the possibility that Jessie Chambers could become a creative writer in her own right. Chambers's heartbreaking account of their friendship is a remarkable document of the formation of a male writer at the price of the deformation of a female writer, a not uncommon tale. Chambers destroyed her own manuscript and abandoned fiction writing after reading the literary representation of Paul and Miriam's relationship in *Sons and Lovers*. Lawrence should be neither accused nor excused for these events: they are common enough to be described as a general pattern of masculine authorship, and Lawrence was at least honest enough to recognize and record his own participation in this pattern. See Jessie Chambers, *D. H. Lawrence: A Personal Record by E. T. (Jessie Chambers)*, ed. J. D. Chambers (London: Cass, 1965).

8. D. H. Lawrence, *The Rainbow* (London: Penguin, 1995), esp. 334–82. Hereafter cited parenthetically in text as R, followed by a page reference.

9. It is curious that in his account of these motifs in *The Rainbow*, Tony Pinkney opposes the architectonic and the organic, when the very stake of the Gothic (in his own argument) is their articulation; see Tony Pinkney, *D. H. Lawrence and Modernism* (Iowa City: University of Iowa Press, 1990), 65–68. Developing Kate Millett's reading of the novel, he writes that "the building is a giant womb, . . . rainbows are cathedrals are wombs" (68). Earlier he writes that Lawrence's Gothic is thought within a Ruskinian framework: "the Gothic arch is a creaturely architecture" (65); "the Gothic cathedral itself is a body, and more specifically a female body, a womb" (67).

10. See, for example, Cornelia Nixon, *Lawrence's Leadership Politics and the Turn Against Women* (Berkeley: University of California Press, 1986); Judith Ruderman, *D. H. Lawrence and the Devouring Mother: The Search for a Patriarchal Ideal of Leadership* (Durham: Duke University Press, 1984); Eunyoung Oh, *D. H. Lawrence's Border Crossing: Colonialism in his Travel Writings and "Leadership" Novels* (New York: Routledge, 2007).

11. Whether either of these things are or were true is a different matter. The point is the experience or structure of feeling of art's homelessness or detachment from tradition, the experience of being subject to new kinds of social forces, and the new kinds of works that emerged from these experiences. These sentiments are everywhere to be found in modernist literature of the interwar period.

12. Frederic Jameson, *Fables of Aggression: Wyndham Lewis, the Modernist as Fascist* (Berkeley: University of California Press, 1979), 104; see also 87–121 for a more detailed discussion of the "break."

13. Ben Conisbee Baer and Gayatri Chakravorty Spivak, "Redoing Marxism at Gigi Café: A Conversation," *Rethinking Marxism* 20, no. 4 (2008): 637.

14. D. H. Lawrence, *Movements in European History* (Cambridge: Cambridge University Press, 1989), 256; hereafter cited parenthetically in the text as MEH, followed by a page reference. There is nothing more axiomatic than this statement, intended for publication in the edition of Lawrence's school textbook for adolescent readers from 1924. It is part of the epilogue, composed by Lawrence in Taos in 1924, and meant to bring the work into the present. The epilogue's polemic tone led to its being cut by the publishers, however.

15. D. H. Lawrence, *Sea and Sardinia* (London: Penguin, 1999), 9. Hereafter cited parenthetically in the text as SS with page reference. Neil Roberts, *D. H. Lawrence, Travel and Cultural Difference* (New York: Palgrave Macmillan, 2004).

16. Roberts, 53. Anthony Burgess described *Sea and Sardinia* as "the most charming work he ever wrote." Burgess, *Flame Into Being: The Life and Work of D. H. Lawrence* (New York: Arbor House, 1985), 143. Mark Kinkead-Weekes, one of the leading Lawrence scholars, has described it as "one of the most delightful of Lawrence's books." Weeks, *D. H. Lawrence: Triumph to Exile, 1912-1922: The Cambridge Biography of D. H. Lawrence*, 3 vols. (Cambridge: Cambridge University Press, 1996), 2:622.

17. Mary Louise Pratt, *Imperial Eyes: Travel Writing and Transculturation* (London: Routledge, 1992), 15–37.

18. D. H. Lawrence, *Fantasia of the Unconscious and Psychoanalysis and the Unconscious* (Harmondsworth: Penguin, 1977), 64; hereafter cited parenthetically in text as FU, followed by a page reference.

19. Lawrence, *Sea and Sardinia*, 67: "as if the intelligence lay deep within the cave." The allusion is to Plato, *Republic*, 7.514a.

20. Lawrence, *Sea and Sardinia*, 89; Lawrence, "Nottingham and the Mining Countryside," 137.

21. Julius Braunthal, *History of the International, 1864-1914*, trans. H. Collins and K. Mitchell (London: Nelson, 1966), 1–161. From here, the "national integration of the Socialist parties in the West" took place because "the spirit of international solidarity of the working classes [had been] superseded by a spirit of national solidarity between the proletariat and the ruling classes" (356, 355). His explanation is that mass affective attachments to the nation as community and culture overwrote the abstract collectivity of class. Braunthal subsequently gives a general account of the breakup of the Second International and the attempt to reconstruct some kind of operative international articulation in the Third.

22. D. H. Lawrence, "Democracy," in McDonald, *Phoenix*, 717; hereafter cited parenthetically in the text as D, followed by a page reference.

23. D. H. Lawrence, *The Plumed Serpent (Quetzalcoatl)*, ed. L. D. Clark (New York: Cambridge University Press, 1987). Hereafter cited parenthetically in the text as PS, followed by a page number.

24. "Quetzalcoatl" has since been published as a book: D. H. Lawrence, *Quetzalcoatl*, ed. Louis L. Martz (New York: New Directions, 1998); hereafter cited parenthetically in the text as Q, followed by a page reference.

25. Mary Kay Vaughan writes that Mexico had "one of the most consistent state commitments to the creation of national culture and the expansion of public education in the twentieth century." Vaughan, "Nationalizing the Countryside," in *The Eagle and the Virgin: Nation and Cultural Revolution in Mexico, 1920-1940* (Durham: Duke University Press, 2006), 157.

26. James F. Rinehart, *Revolution and the Millennium: China, Mexico, and Iran* (Westport, CT: Praeger, 1997); and Ilene V. O'Malley, *The Myth of the Revolution: Hero Cults and the Institutionalization of the Mexican State, 1920-1940* (New York: Greenwood, 1986).

27. Millett, *Sexual Politics*, 283.

28. In his *Flaubert: The Uses of Uncertainty* (Ithaca: Cornell University Press, 1974), Jonathan Culler has described *Sentimental Education* as "a *Bildungsroman* without *Bildung*" (152). This description would be appropriate for *The Plumed Serpent*, too.

29. Régis Debray, *Revolution dans la revolution?* Translated into English as Debray, *Revolution in the Revolution? Armed Struggle and Political Struggle in Latin America*, trans. Bobbye Ortiz (New York: Monthly Review Press, 1967).

30. Alan Knight writes that Mexico's Constitution of 1917, framed in the wake of the Bolshevik Revolution, was "one of the most radical of its time," particularly Articles 17 and 123, the former of which nationalized subsoil deposits and "asserted the nation's prior right to property which could justify expropriation (e.g. of latifundia) in the public interest." Article 123 placed limits on the working day and introduced a minimum wage and various other labor reforms. In spite of these historically significant innovations, the Constitution was, in Knight's view, "not even socialist," but "conferred powers on the state . . . to mitigate abuses and arbitrate between conflicting groups." Knight, *The Mexican Revolution*, 2 vols. (Cambridge: Cambridge University Press, 1986), 2:470–71. In other words, Knight sees the Constitution as enacting a crisis-management compromise between capital and socialist demands in a form that will contain the latter. Calling the glass half full though, it is arguable that such reforms opened up socialist possibilities, even if they were not carried through. Lawrence, of course, takes the counterfactual narrative in quite the opposite direction.

31. "*What they deterritorialize on one side, they reterritorialize on the other.* These neo-territorialities are often artificial, residual, archaic; only, they are archaisms with a completely contemporary function, our modern way of 'imbricating,' parceling off, reintroducing code fragments, resuscitating old ones, inventing pseudo-codes or jargons." Gilles Deleuze and Félix Guattari, *Anti-Oedipus: Capitalism and Schizophrenia*, trans. Robert Hurley, Mark Seem, and Helen R. Lane (Minneapolis: University of Minnesota Press, 1983), 257.

32. Gayatri Chakravorty Spivak, "Subaltern Studies: Deconstructing Historiography," in *Selected Subaltern Studies* (New York: Oxford University Press, 1988), 4.

33. Etienne Balibar, *Masses, Classes, Ideas: Studies on Politics and Philosophy Before and After Marx* (New York: Routledge, 1994), 3–38.

34. The so-called Cambridge Ritualists—a group of classical scholars centered on the figure of Margaret Jane Harrison—had begun to recode antiquity as primitive a decade earlier. This work had a great influence on primitivist art and literature, including Lawrence's. Before this, the nineteenth-century classicist Andrew Lang (whose translation of *The Odyssey* was the one used by James Joyce) wrote that the "revolting, . . . obscene" scenarios to be found in ancient Greek texts ("the beautiful sun-God makes love in the shape of a dog") represent "ugly scars" on the ideally flawless body of Greek culture. Lang, *Modern Mythology* (New York: AMS Press, 1968), v, 4–5. Anthropology and the Taylorian concept of the primitive "survival" in the present were deployed to explain these aberrations, these "fossils of rite and creed, ideas absolutely incongruous with the environing morality, philosophy, and science of Greece" (viii). Harrison's group attempted to recode Lang's horrors as evidence of a Bergsonian life-principle animating the ancient world. By the time of *The Plumed Serpent*, Lawrence had written out other textual links to the horror of the (possible) homosexuality figured by bull and horse. *Quetzalcoatl* depicts Owen and Villers, Kate's American traveling companions, as a campy, queer couple, in explicit contrast with the solemnly homoerotic, primitivized male bonding of Cipriano and Ramón. Thus, the safer homoerotic scene displaces the homo*sexual* signs at work in the earlier manuscript. A good discussion of these shifts in the representation of homosexuality in Lawrence can be found in Hugh Stevens, "*The Plumed Serpent* and the Erotics of Primitive Masculinity," in *Modernist Sexualities*, ed. Hugh Stevens and Caroline Howlett (Manchester: Manchester University Press, 2000).

35. Lawrence, "Democracy," 705–6. Lawrence continues, "We are all one, and therefore every bit partakes of all the rest. That is, the Whole is inherent in every fragment. That is, every human consciousness has the same intrinsic value as every other human consciousness, because each is an essential part of the Great Consciousness. This is the One Identity which identifies us all" (706).

36. Eric R. Wolf sees the Mexican revolution as the first in a constantly displacing chain of "peasant wars of the twentieth century" leading through Russia, China, Vietnam, and Algeria to Cuba. Wolf, *Peasant Wars of the Twentieth Century* (New York: Harper and Row, 1969). The chain could be extended, no doubt.

37. The classic study is Peter Hopkirk, *The Great Game: On Secret Service in High Asia* (London: Murray, 1990); see also Hopkirk, *Quest for Kim: In Search of Kipling's Great Game* (Ann Arbor: University of Michigan Press, 1997). For the way the high politics of the Great Game translates into the Mexican context, the indispensable resource is Friedrich Katz, *The Secret War in Mexico: Europe, the United States, and the Mexican Revolution* (Chicago: University of Chicago Press, 1981).

38. M. N. Roy, *Memoirs* (Bombay: Allied, 1964); Sibnarayan Ray, *In Freedom's Quest: A Study of the Life and Works of M. N. Roy, 1887-1954* (Calcutta: Minerva, 1998); Sobhanlal Datta Gupta, *Comintern, India and the Colonial Question*, 1920–37 (Calcutta: Centre for Studies in Social Sciences, Calcutta/K. P. Bagchi, 1980).

39. Barry Carr, "Marxism and Anarchism in the Formation of the Mexican Communist Party, 1910–19," *Hispanic American Historical Review* 63, no. 2 (May 1983): 277, 293.

40. According to the poet Witter Bynner, one of Lawrence's traveling companions, the Lawrences did meet with some of the metropolitan Mexican Communists, but "Lawrence has portrayed none of these figures in his writings." Bynner, *Journey with Genius: Recollections and Reflections Concerning the D. H. Lawrences* (New York: John Day, 1951), 22. In Bynner's words, the model for the Pole was "a middle-aged Polish professor of psychology . . . vacationing from some American university" (54). It is beyond my scope to explore the complex condensations and displacements between fiction and autobiography that enabled Lawrence to figure the Pole as a Bolshevik.

41. See Klaus Theweleit, *Male Fantasies* (Minneapolis: University of Minnesota Press, 1987), 229–49, for comparable protofascist German representations of the "Red flood" during the Weimar period. Carr has a fairly sober estimate of the size and influence of the party in Mexico in these years, as well as emphasizing its tenuous institutional links to the Comintern. Nevertheless, none of this mitigates its symbolic importance in our present context.

42. Evidence of an altogether different kind of link between Irish and Mexican revolutions can be found in this quotation from a memoir about the Easter Rising: "James Connolly also lectured us on Street Fighting, of which it was said he had had experience in Mexico." Frank Henderson, *Frank Henderson's Easter Rising: Recollections of a Dublin Volunteer* (Dublin: Cork University Press, 1998), 32. It is certainly possible that Connolly had visited Mexico during his years in the United States. In any case, the fact that the Mexican Revolution had become symbolically important for the Easter Rising is surely a further twist in the background of paranoia about internationalism in *The Plumed Serpent*.

43. Theweleit, *Male Fantasies*.

44. Pinkney, *D. H. Lawrence and Modernism*, 159–62.

45. Oh, *D. H. Lawrence's Border Crossing*, 129.

46. Joseph Conrad, *Heart of Darkness* (London: Penguin, 1999), 95. Hereafter cited parenthetically in the text as HD, followed by a page reference.

47. Gayatri Chakravorty Spivak, *Death of a Discipline* (New York: Columbia University Press, 2003), 54; hereafter cited parenthetically in the text as DD, followed by a page reference.

48. Chinua Achebe, "An Image of Africa," *Research in African Literatures* 9, no. 1 (April 1, 1978): 8–9.

49. L. D. Clark, *Dark Night of the Body: D. H. Lawrence's* The Plumed Serpent (Austin: University of Texas Press, 1964), is the book that first identified this pattern. See also Donna Przybylowicz, "D. H. Lawrence's *The Plumed Serpent*: The Dialectic of Ideology and Utopia," *Boundary 2* 13, nos. 2/3 (1985): 305; Deobrah Castillo, "Postmodern Indigenism: 'Quetzalcoatl and All That,'" *Modern Fiction Studies* 41, no. 1 (1995): 39; Pinkney, *D. H. Lawrence and Modernism*, 157; Oh, *Border Crossing*, 136–43.

50. Pinkney, *D. H. Lawrence and Modernism*, 154–59.

51. Daniel Paul Schreber, *Memoirs of My Nervous Illness* (New York: New York Review of Books, 2000); Sigmund Freud, "Psycho-Analytic Notes on an Autobiographical Account of a Case of Paranoia (Dementia Paranoides)" (1911), in *The Standard Edition of the Complete Psychological Works of Sigmund Freud*, trans. and ed. James Strachey, 24 vols. (London: Hogarth, 1958), 12:1–82; Samuel Weber, "Introduction to the 1988 Edition," in *Memoirs of My Nervous Illness* (Cambridge, MA: Harvard University Press, 1988), vii–liv.

52. Walter Benn Michaels, *Our America: Nativism, Modernism, and Pluralism* (Durham: Duke University Press, 1995), 100.

53. The documentary historical accounts of La Malinche are to be found in Bernal Díaz del Castillo, *The Conquest of New Spain*, trans. J. M Cohen (Baltimore: Penguin, 1963); Miguel León Portilla, *The Broken Spears: The Aztec Account of the Conquest of Mexico*, trans. Lysander Kemp (Boston: Beacon, 1962); Hernán Cortés, *Letters from Mexico*, trans. Anthony Pagden (New Haven: Yale University Press, 2001).

54. E. M. Hull, *The Sheik* (New York: Small, Maynard, 1921); Laura Frost, "The Romance of Cliché: E. M. Hull, D. H. Lawrence, and Interwar Erotic Fiction," in *Bad Modernisms*, ed. Douglas Mao and Rebecca Walkowitz (Durham: Duke University Press, 2006), 94–118.

55. Hull, *The Sheik*, 291.

56. Clark, *Dark Night of the Body*, 29, 32–33.

57. Alan Knight, "Racism, Revolution, and *Indigenismo*: Mexico, 1910–1940," in *The Idea of Race in Latin America*, ed. Richard Graham (Austin: University of Texas Press, 1990), 84–85.

58. Knight, 85. Paradoxical because the discourse of *mestizaje* regards the mix of Indian indigene and Spanish colonizer as that which is properly indigenous to the Mexican nation. The precolonial Indian is thus displaced in the same gesture as she or he is acknowledged. This is also why, as Jean Franco has pointed out, "it is *mestizaje* that separates Latin America from all other colonial ventures. It helps to explain why theories of postcolonialism never seem to approximate to the realities of the continent." Franco, "La Malinche: From Gift to Sexual Contract," in *Critical Passions: Selected Essays* (Durham: Duke University Press, 1999), 76. For useful summaries of the vicissitudes of *indigenismo* as it shifts from the nineteenth century to the twentieth, see Alexander S. Dawson, *Indian and Nation in Revolutionary Mexico* (Tucson: University of Arizona Press, 2004); Guillermo Bonfil Batalla, *México Profundo: Reclaiming a Civilization*, trans. Dennis

Adams (Austin: University of Texas Press, 1996); María Josefina Saldaña-Portillo, *The Revolutionary Imagination in the Americas and the Age of Development* (Durham: Duke University Press, 2003). The latter is hereafter referenced parenthetically in the text as *Revolutionary Imagination*.

59. Knight, "Racism," 76.

60. Manuel Gamio, *Forjando patria (pro nacionalismo)* (Mexico: Porrúa Hermanos, 1916). The description of *Forjando patria* is from Saldaña-Portillo, *Revolutionary Imagination*, 208.

61. Jack Forbes, *Africans and Native Americans: The Language of Race and the Evolution of Red-Black Peoples* (Urbana: University of Illinois Press, 1993), 128: "the early modern world placed greater stress on the religion, class, local origin, and culture, while the modern 'western' mind has selected so-called 'race' as an especially pertinent criterion." These prior, multiple codings of difference are not necessarily "better" than race (or racism), though they do indicate a less monolithic horizon than differences organized in rigidly polarized racial terms.

62. José Vasconcelos, *The Cosmic Race: A Bilingual Edition*, trans. Jaén Didier Tisdel (Baltimore: Johns Hopkins University Press, 1997), 17. Hereafter cited parenthetically in the text as CR, followed by a page reference.

63. See Jenny Sharpe, *Allegories of Empire: The Figure of Woman in the Colonial Text* (Minneapolis: University of Minnesota Press, 1993), passim. Sharpe is focused on narratives that take the Sepoy Rebellion (the Indian Mutiny of 1857) as the traumatically generative event, and such narratives are almost exclusively focused on the figure of the Indian man as rapist of white women. Her account gives us a sequence that stretches from the mid-nineteenth century to *A Passage to India*, *The Jewel in the Crown*, and beyond. The story of white men's sexual relations with Indian women—which would include Kipling's *Kim* and his short story "Lispeth"—is not dwelt upon. *Kim* imagines the hybrid as the "real" Indian; "Lispeth" is a comedy of conversion (and reversion) figured through the unrequited love of a tribal woman for a white man.

64. Hortense J. Spillers, "Notes on an Alternative Model—Neither/Nor," *Difference Within: Feminism and Critical Theory* 8 (1989): 166.

65. "The image we have of La Malinche has been produced largely through fiction." Sandra Messinger Cypess, *La Malinche in Mexican Literature from History to Myth* (Austin: University of Texas Press, 1991), 2.

66. Cypess, *La Malinche*, 10. Paz writes that the Mexicans (males) are "*el engendro de la violación*," or "the offspring of violation," as the translation has it. Octavio Paz, "The Sons of La Malinche," in *The Labyrinth of Solitude*, trans. Lysander Kemp (New York: Grove, 1994), 79. As Paz's essay suggests, this reading of La Malinche masculinizes the nation-subject (it engenders the macho sons of La Malinche) and leaves the place of woman as unlivable and abject. Paz's view is endorsed by at least one important feminist rereading of the Malinche figure, Frances Karttunen, "Rethinking Malinche," in *Indian Women of Early Mexico*, ed. Susan Schroeder, Stephanie Wood, and Robert Haskett (Norman: University of Oklahoma Press, 1997).

67. Paz, *Labyrinth*, 85.

68. Franco, "La Malinche," 77. The revisionist accounts specifically referred to are those of Todorov and Greenblatt.

69. Franco, 73.

70. David Craven, *Art and Revolution in Latin America, 1910-1990* (New Haven: Yale University Press, 2002), 33.

71. Mary Kay Vaughan, "Pancho Villa, the Daughters of Mary, and the Modern Woman: Gender in the Mexican Revolution," in *Sex in Revolution: Gender, Politics, and Power in Modern Mexico*, ed. Jocelyn H. Olcott, Mary Kay Vaughan, and Gabriela Cano (Durham: Duke University Press, 2006), 24.

72. Anne Rubenstein, "'The War on Las Pelonas': Modern Women and Their Enemies, Mexico City, 1924," in Olcott, Vaughn, and Cano, *Sex in Revolution*, 57–80; hereafter cited parenthetically in the text as "War," followed by a page number.

73. Mary Kay Vaughan, "Nationalizing the Countryside: Schools and Rural Communities in the 1930s," in *The Eagle and the Virgin: Nation and Cultural Revolution in Mexico, 1920–1940* (Durham: Duke University Press, 2006), 158.

74. Mary Kay Vaughan, "Women, Class, and Education in Mexico, 1880–1928," *Latin American Perspectives* 4, nos. 1/2 (Spring 1977): 145. See also Vaughan, *The State, Education, and Social Class in Mexico, 1880–1928* (DeKalb: Northern Illinois University Press, 1982).

75. Vaughan, "Rural Women's Literacy and Education," in *Women of the Mexican Countryside, 1850–1990: Creating Spaces, Shaping Transitions*, ed. Heather Fowler-Salamini and Mary Kay Vaughan (Tucson: University of Arizona Press, 1994), 107; Vaughan, *State, Education, and Social Class in Mexico*, 138–34.

76. *Boletín de la Secretaría de Educación Pública* 2, nos. 5/6 (1923–24): 606; cited in Vaughan, *State, Education, and Social Class in Mexico*, 180.

77. Cited in Vaughan, *The State, Education, and Social Class in Mexico*, 184.

78. Vaughan, "Nationalizing the Countryside," 158–59. There are of course exceptions to all this, but the singular texture of the rural school and its classroom in such instances during the 1920s has received little study.

79. Elsie Rockwell, "Schools of the Revolution," in *Everyday Forms of State Formation: Revolution and the Negotiation of Rule in Modern Mexico*, ed. Gilbert M. Joseph and Daniel Nugent (Durham: Duke University Press, 1994), 173–74.

80. For example, the introduction of "rational education" in the Yucatán. See Vaughan, *The State, Education, and Social Class in Mexico*, 98–115.

81. Karl Marx, "The Eighteenth Brumaire of Louis Bonaparte," in *Surveys from Exile*, ed. David Fernbach (Harmondsworth: Penguin, 1973).

82. Two studies that demonstrate the formation of such a subject in colonial India are Partha Chatterjee, *Nationalist Thought and the Colonial World: A Derivative Discourse* (Minneapolis: University of Minnesota Press, 1993); and Homi K. Bhabha, *The Location of Culture* (London: Routledge, 1994). These studies could be compared with Serge Gruzinski, *The Mestizo Mind: The Intellectual Dynamics of Colonization and Globalization* (New York: Routledge, 2002); and Bonfil Batalla, *México Profundo: Reclaiming a Civilization*.

83. The work of the Latin American Subaltern Studies Group began the project of outlining the character of the subaltern in this post/colonial space. See Ileana Rodríguez, ed., *The Latin American Subaltern Studies Reader* (Durham: Duke University Press, 2001); and José Rabasa, Javier Sanjinés, and Robert Carr, eds., *Dispositio/n on Subaltern Studies in the Americas* 46 (1996).

84. Thomas B. Macaulay, "Minute on Indian Education, February 2, 1835," in *Postcolonialisms: An Anthology of Cultural Theory and Criticism*, ed. Gajanan Desai and Supriya Nair (New Brunswick, NJ: Rutgers University Press, 2005), 121–31. In postcolonial studies, which generally grounds its thought too easily in the unquestioned example of the

British Empire as colonialism as such, the Macaulayan version of the colonial subject is the basic model.

85. Antonio Gramsci, "The Modern Prince," in *Selections from the Prison Notebooks of Antonio Gramsci*, trans. Quintin Hoare and Geoffrey Nowell-Smith (London: International, 1971); Jean Franco, *The Decline and Fall of the Lettered City* (Cambridge, MA: Harvard University Press, 2002).

86. Gramsci, *Prison Notebooks*, 131.

87. Wolf, *Peasant Wars*, 14–15.

88. Franco, *Critical Passions*, 447.

89. Alan Knight, "The Rise and Fall of Cardenismo," in *Mexico Since Independence*, ed. Leslie Bethell (New York: Cambridge University Press, 1991), 241.

90. Katz, *Secret War in Mexico*, 50.

91. "L'âme mexicaine n'a jamais perdu en son fond le contact avec la terre, avec les forces telluriques du sol." Antonin Artaud, "Les forces occulte du Mexique," in *Oeuvres complètes*, 20 vols. (Paris: Gallimard, 1956–84), 8:231. Artaud visited Mexico a decade after Lawrence, engaged intensely with Mexican revolutionary discourse, and wrote a number of articles that were translated into Spanish for the Mexican newspaper *El Nacional*. "Les forces occultes" appeared on August 9, 1936. The French original has been lost, and I cite the retranslation into French by Marie Dézon and Philippe Sollers.

92. Artaud, "Les forces occulte du Mexique," 231.

93. Artaud, *The Peyote Dance*, trans. Helen Weaver (New York: Farrar, Straus and Giroux, 1976), 34. The essays comprising *Les Tarahumaras* and translated as *The Peyote Dance* were composed and edited at different times during the 1940s, and mainly during Artaud's confinement at Rodez.

94. For a comparison between Lawrence and Artaud on Mexico, see J. G. Brotherston, "Revolution and the Ancient Literature of Mexico, for D. H. Lawrence and Antonin Artaud," *Twentieth Century Literature* 18, no. 3 (July 1, 1972): 181–89.

95. Artaud, "La Mexique et la civilisation," in *Oeuvres complètes*, 8:127, my translation; hereafter cited parenthetically in the text as "La Mexique," followed by a page number.

96. Artaud, "Ce que je suis venu faire au Mexique," in *Oeuvres complètes*, 8:212–13, my translation.

97. V. N. Voloshinov, *Marxism and the Philosophy of Language*, trans. Ladislav Matejka and I. R. Titunik (Cambridge, MA: Harvard University Press, 1986), 156.

98. It should be noted that many of these tableaux are of pairs of women, pairs that contrast interestingly with all the pairs comprising the vanguard group (Ramón and Cipriano, Kate and Carlota, Kate and Cipriano, Kate and Teresa, and so on). The pair of Kate and her maid Juana is a kind of mediator between the groups.

99. Letter to Witter Bynner, March 13, 1928. In *The Letters of D. H. Lawrence*, vol. 6, March 1927–November 1928, ed. James T. Boulton and Margaret Boulton with Gerald M. Lacy (Cambridge: Cambridge University Press, 1991), 321.

5 India Outside India

1. S. A. Dange, *Gandhi vs. Lenin* (Bombay: Liberty Literature, 1921). Hereafter cited parenthetically in the text as GL with page number following. In 1927, the Austro-Hungarian

journalist and cultural critic René Fülöp-Miller published the long book *Lenin und Gan-dhi* (Zurich: Amalthea, 1927), a study of the two figures that he regarded as representing "the spirit of the present age." Fülöp-Miller presents these two figures in a messianic framework as sharing the impulse of rescuing the oppressed from the specific conditions of a capitalist/imperialist modernity and technoscientific rationality European in origin. "In the faces of Lenin and Gandhi," he writes, "the physiognomy of the impersonal millionfold mass, which no one had ever looked at before, took on the form and austere features of two great personalities." *Lenin and Gandhi* in fact seeks partially to inoculate Europe against Lenin's and Gandhi's (valid) critiques by recognizing and promoting understanding of them. Quotations from the English translation by F. S. Flint and D. S. Tait (London: Putnam's, 1927), vii–x.

2. M. K. Gandhi, *Hind Swaraj, and Other Writings*, ed. Anthony Parel (Cambridge: Cambridge University Press, 2009), 46–65. Hereafter cited parenthetically in the text as *Hind Swaraj*.

3. Dange, *Gandhi vs. Lenin*, 56. Sumit Sarkar writes that during Non-Cooperation "a considerable number of national schools and colleges were also founded (like the Jamia Millia Islamia in Aligarh, . . . the Kasi Vidyapath at Banaras, and the Gujarat Vidyapith) with 442 institutions started in Bihar and Orissa, 190 in Bengal, 189 in Bombay, and 137 in U.P." Sarkar, *Modern India, 1885–1947* (Delhi: Macmillan, 1983), 207.

4. V. I. Lenin, "On the Dual Power," in *Collected Works* (Moscow: Progress, 1964), 24:38–41. The original was published in *Pravda* 28 (April 9, 1917). Hereafter cited parenthetically in the text as "Dual Power" with page number following.

5. Leon Trotsky, *History of the Russian Revolution to Brest-Litovsk* (London: George Allen and Unwin, 1919). It is noteworthy that this is the only Soviet literature directly cited by Dange, a possible index of what was available to Indian communists at this time. Dange quotes from Marx's *Capital*, vol. 1, in a passage taken from C. Delisle Burns, *The Principles of Revolution* (1920). Other citations are from Carlyle, Bertrand Russell, T. H. Green, Mazzini, Tolstoy, and Rousseau, as well as Tilak, the Bhagavad Gita, and of course Gandhi himself. Russell, *The Practice and Theory of Bolshevism* (London: George Allen and Unwin, 1920) is a decisive source of information, from which Dange directly quotes, for example, Lenin's "First Sketch of the Theses on National and Colonial Questions" from the second Comintern Congress (1920). Russell's own citation is translated by Russell himself from a French version.

6. Lenin, "The Tasks of the Proletariat in Our Revolution," in *Collected Works* (Moscow: Progress, 1964), 24:60. "Two powers *cannot exist* in a state. . . . The dual power merely expresses a *transitional* phase in the revolution's development" (61). The more Lenin analyzes dual power through 1917, the more he finds it to be an intolerable and unstable crisis-formation crying out for the reinstatement of undivided sovereignty in the peoples' soviets as "real democracy." Lenin, "Has Dual Power Disappeared?," *Collected Works*, 24:445–48.

7. In other words, the theory of the dual state is not the same as the early modern figure of *imperium in imperio* (state within a state), usually attributed to Spinoza, which tends to designate either an exclusive, self-selected group that has seceded from society or an inner force, secret society, or clique (nowadays the paranoid figure of the "deep State") that runs the State from within. Lenin's figure (and Dange's) posits a public and alternate counter-State that openly contests the prevailing governmental power and attempts to win popular support so as to replace it. For a discussion of the Spino-

zian usage, see Étienne Balibar, *Spinoza and Politics*, trans. Peter Snowdon (New York: Verso, 1998), 29–31. *Imperium in imperio* is also used by Alexander Hamilton in *The Federalist Papers* (number 15) to designate the "political monster" of the power contest between the states and the Union.

8. Balibar, "Lenin and Gandhi: A Missed Encounter?," trans. Knox Peden, *Radical Philosophy* 142 (March/April 2012): 14, Balibar's emphasis.

9. Balibar, 14.

10. Balibar, 14; Dange, *Lenin vs. Gandhi*, 59.

11. Georges Sorel, *Réflexions sur la violence* (Paris: Librairie des sciences politiques et sociales, 1936). Sorel's work was among the most influential upon important strands of the modernist intellectual, literary, and political elite of the early twentieth century. The first English translation, upon which the Cambridge edition cited later in this note is based, appeared in 1914. The English translator, the critic-philosopher T. E. Hulme, was a key influence on the Vorticist circle and on British avant-gardism in general in the prewar milieu (he was killed in 1917 in the First World War). Fanon makes a number of unambiguous references to it in *The Wretched of the Earth*. References here are to the revised English edition, Sorel, *Reflections on Violence*, ed. Jeremy Jennings (Cambridge: Cambridge University Press, 1999). Subsequent references parenthetically in the text as RV with page number following.

12. Antonio Gramsci, *Selections from the Prison Notebooks*, trans. Quintin Hoare and Geoffrey Nowell-Smith (London: International, 1971), 126. Hereafter cited parenthetically in the text as SPN.

13. Ajay Skaria, *Unconditional Equality: Gandhi's Religion of Resistance* (Minneapolis: University of Minnesota Press, 2016), 191–222.

14. "Zur Kritik der Gewalt." In English as "Critique of Violence," in Benjamin, *One-Way Street, and Other Writings*, trans. Edmund Jephcott and Kingsley Shorter (London: NLB, 1979), 132–54. Hereafter cited parenthetically in the text as "Critique" with page numbers following.

15. The work of the missionaries around William Carey associated with the Serampore Baptist Mission was also instrumental in mobilizing some of these tendencies because the missionaries were concerned with producing pedagogical and religious texts in indigenous languages. A somewhat dated but usefully documented account of the relation between English colonial education and the emergence of nationalist structures of feeling and organizational tendencies may be found in Bruce Tiebout McCully, *English Education and the Origins of Indian Nationalism* (New York: Columbia University Press, 1940). For a reading of this tendency as a "Calcutta Orientalism" centered on Fort William College, see Aamir Mufti, *Forget English! Orientalisms and World Literatures* (Cambridge, MA: Harvard University Press, 2016), 99–145. For an excellent account of the dense intersections of colonial and indigenous educational reforms in Bengal, see Sibaji Bandyopadhyay, *The Gopal-Rakhal Dialectic: Colonialism and Children's Literature in Bengal*, trans. Rani Ray and Nivedita Sen (New Delhi: Tulika, 2015), esp. 73–171. Brian Hatcher, *Idioms of Improvement: Vidyasagar and Cultural Encounter in Bengal* (Calcutta: Oxford University Press, 1996) is a focused study of Vidyasagar as educational reformer. An overview of the institution-building trends of the nineteenth century in Bengal may be found in Partha Chatterjee, "The Disciplines in Colonial Bengal," in *Texts of Power: Emerging Disciplines in Colonial Bengal*, ed. Partha Chatterjee (Minneapolis: University of Minnesota Press, 1995), 1–29. Parna Sengupta, *Pedagogy for Religion: Missionary*

Education and the Fashioning of Hindus and Muslims in Bengal (Berkeley: University of California Press, 2011) critically elaborates and moves on from the older postcolonial analyses of colonially imposed knowledge-forms such as that of Edward W. Said, *Orientalism* (New York: Vintage, 1978), and recent reprises of the Saidian position such as Mufti, *Forget English!* Thus, she argues that in the case of upper-class groups in colonial India, because "Western forms of schooling brought with them the foregrounding and standardizing of certain kinds of knowledge and forms of identity," the upper strata of religious communities began to demand and found separate schools for their own groups; but "the materials of modern schooling actually shaped the language and models of reform deployed by native leaders," and the epistemological presuppositions of the instruction provided by schools were formally identical. That is, at the same time that separate indigenous ethno-religious schools were set up for "the proper reproduction of particular religious and caste identities," the effective *forms* of instruction were becoming more and more standardized (1–5).

16. Louis Althusser, "Ideology and Ideological State Apparatuses (Notes Towards an Investigation)," in *Lenin and Philosophy*, trans. Ben Brewster (New York: Monthly Review, 1971), 147.

17. Benjamin "Critique," 151. Spivak, "Righting Wrongs," *South Atlantic Quarterly* 103, nos. 2/3 (Spring/Summer 2004): 570. For Spivak, "it breaks the crime/expiation chain that the law deals with" (570).

18. Most recently, Skaria, *Unconditional Equality*. Skaria's deconstructive reading places Gandhi in conversation with Derrida more than with Benjamin, but he does discuss the "Critique of Violence" and the term *pure means* (Gandhi: *swachh saadhan*; Benjamin: *reine Mittel*) on 197. I also refer in the following to Skaria, "The Strange Violence of *Satyagraha*: Gandhi, *Itihaas*, and History," in *Heterotopias: Nationalism and the Possibility of History in South Asia*, ed. Manu Bhagavan (New Delhi: Oxford University Press, 2010), 142–85; Skaria, "Gandhi's Politics: Liberalism and the Question of the Ashram," *South Atlantic Quarterly* 101, no. 4 (Fall 2002): 955–86; Skaria, "Relinquishing Republican Democracy: Gandhi's *Ramrajya*," *Postcolonial Studies* 14, no. 2 (2011): 203–29; Skaria, "Only One Word, Properly Altered: Gandhi and the Question of the *Veshya*," in *Rethinking Gandhi and Nonviolent Relationality*, ed. Debjani Ganguly and John Decker (London: Routledge, 2007), 115–37. There has been a significant resurgence of interest in Gandhian theory and practice of "nonviolence" in recent years. See especially the work of Leela Gandhi, Harish Trivedi, and Faisal Devji.

19. Skaria, "Relinquishing Republican Democracy," 226. It is important to note that a more literal translation of *satyagrahi* would be "one who grasps or is bent toward truth." Gandhi's translation has the very specific function of making it a figure of political action as passive action.

20. Balibar, "Lenin and Gandhi," 14.

21. Skaria, "The Strange Violence of *Satyagraha*," 172.

22. Gandhi, "Letter to Hanumantrao," July 17, 1918, in *Collected Works*, 17:131. Quoted in Skaria, *Unconditional Equality*, 136–37.

23. For this questioning, and also Derrida's commentary on the "differential contamination" between the two forms of violence and the argument that there can be no rigorous distinction (or the criteria for one) between them, see Jacques Derrida, "Force of Law: The Mystical Foundations of Authority," in *Acts of Religion*, ed. Gil Anidjar (New York: Routledge, 2002), 228–300. Skaria, *Unconditional Equality*, 136–37, elaborates the

development of this logic whereby "*ahimsa* might involve and even require killing and hurting" (139).

24. Georg Lukács, "Tagores Ghandi-Roman," *Die rote Fahne* (Berlin, April 23, 1922); Lukács, "Tagore's Gandhi Novel," in *Reviews and Articles from Die rote Fahne*, trans. Peter Palmer (London: Merlin, 1983), 8–11.
25. Rabindranath Tagore, *The Home and the World*, trans. Surendranath Tagore (London: Penguin, 2005).
26. Rabindranath Tagore, *Das Heim und die Welt: Roman*, trans. Helene Meyer-Franck (Munich: Kurt Wolff Verlag, 1920).
27. Harish Trivedi, "Literary and Visual Portrayals of Gandhi," in *The Cambridge Companion to Gandhi*, ed. Judith M. Brown and Anthony Parel (Cambridge: Cambridge University Press, 2010); Manmohan Krishna Bhatnagar, *New Insights Into the Novels of R. K. Narayan* (New Delhi: Atlantic, 2002), 119–26; Peter Morey and Alex Tickell, eds., *Alternative Indias: Writing, Nation and Communalism* (Amsterdam: Rodopi, 2005), 29; Radhika Mohanram and Rajan Gita, eds., *English Postcoloniality: Literatures from Around the World* (Westport: Greenwood, 1996), 100; Adam Barrows, *The Cosmic Time of Empire: Modern Britain and World Literature* (Berkeley: University of California Press, 2011), 3.
28. The chapter "Critical Observations on Rosa Luxemburg's 'Critique of the Russian Revolution'" hinges on the issue of vanguardism. Lukacs, *History and Class Consciousness: Studies in Marxist Dialectics*, trans. Rodney Livingstone (London: Merlin, 1971).
29. Lukács, *Lenin: A Study on the Unity of His Thought* (London: NLB, 1970).
30. Rabindranath Tagore, *Gora*, trans. Sujit Mukherjee (New Delhi: Sahitya Akademi, 1997); Tagore, *Gora*, in *Rabindra-Rachanabali*, 27 vols., vol. 6 (Kolkata: Visvabharati, 1957).
31. Gayatri Chakravorty Spivak, "Resident Alien," in *Relocating Postcolonialism*, ed. David Theo Goldberg and Ato Quayson (Oxford: Blackwell, 2002), 47–65.
32. The best history of the Swadeshi movement can be found in Sumit Sarkar, *The Swadeshi Movement in Bengal, 1903-1908* (New Delhi: People's Publishing House, 1973). Tagore, a major rural landholder and landlord himself, experimented with and wrote a good deal about the Swadeshi movement.
33. Sarkar, *Modern India*, 113.
34. The turn to "terrorism" in Bengal was the other way that this vanguardism played itself out. In Lukács's words, "Extremist propaganda took on aggressive Hindu colors and simultaneously veered towards terrorism—an almost inevitable development, as 'revolution' with the vast masses inert or hostile could mean in practice only action by an elite." Sarkar, 123. For a general outline of this radical strand, see Peter Heehs, *The Bomb in Bengal: The Rise of Revolutionary Terrorism in India, 1900-1910* (Delhi: Oxford University Press, 1993).
35. Sarkar, *Modern India, 1885-1947*, 225–26; Shahid Amin, *Event, Metaphor, Memory: Chauri Chaura, 1922-1992* (Delhi: Oxford University Press, 1996).
36. Gandhi, "The Crime of Chauri Chaura," *Young India*, February 16, 1922, in *The Collected Works of Mahatma Gandhi* (New Delhi: Ministry of Information and Broadcasting, Government of India, 2000), 26:179, 180. Cited parenthetically in the text as "Crime of Chauri Chaura" hereafter.
37. Testimony of Phenku Chamar as told to the sessions judge in August 1922; quoted in Amin, *Event, Metaphor, Memory*, 173.
38. A vivid sense of the simulacrum of rurality and of the astonishing political effectiveness achieved by Gandhi's cross-dressing can be found in "Gandhi and the Recreation

of Indian Dress" and "Is *Khadi* the Solution?," chapters 3 and 4 of Emma Tarlo, *Clothing Matters: Dress and Identity in India* (London: Hurst, 1996).

39. The words of Ramji Chamar, quoted in Amin, *Event, Metaphor, Memory*, 174. These words are from a more recent interview with the subject, who saw Gandhi's visit to Chauri Chaura in 1921. They illustrate the force of the subaltern borrowing of his name and mouth that we return to later in the chapter, and especially the notion that Gandhi is coresponsible for "violence."

40. Gyanendra Pandey, "Introduction," in *The Indian Nation in 1942*, ed. Gyanendra Pandey (Calcutta: CSSSC/K. P. Bagchi, 1988), 5.

41. Shahid Amin, "Gandhi as Mahatma," in *Subaltern Studies*, ed. Ranajit Guha (Delhi: Oxford University Press, 1984), 3:2, 51–55, hereafter parenthetically referenced in the text as Amin; Gyanendra Pandey, "Peasant Revolt and Indian Nationalism," in *Selected Subaltern Studies*, ed. Ranajit Guha and Gayatri Chakravorty Spivak (New York: Oxford University Press, 1988), 256. Hereafter parenthetically referenced in the text as Pandey. "Gandhiraja" means "lord/king Gandhi"; "Gandhi Raj," its cognate, means "the kingdom, or State, of Gandhi." Amin (51–52) has an interesting discussion of what some peasants in United Provinces understood by "Gandhi Swaraj" (Gandhi self-rule), for example, a utopian "world of free rents."

42. Amin, "Gandhi," 53.

43. Partha Chatterjee, *Nationalist Thought and the Colonial World: A Derivative Discourse?* (Minneapolis: University of Minnesota Press, 1993), 85–130; Ranajit Guha, *Dominance Without Hegemony: History and Power in Colonial India* (Cambridge, MA: Harvard University Press, 1997), 100–51.

44. Amaresh Datta, ed., *Encyclopaedia of Indian Literature*, 6 vols. (New Delhi: Sahitya Akademi, 1988), 2:347–1363.

45. Modernist "literary attempts to explore the nature of the self . . . to cleanse and regenerate Indian self and society." Priyamvada Gopal, *The Indian English Novel: Nation, History, and Narration* (Oxford: Oxford University Press, 2009), 45. Gopal looks exclusively at Anglophone examples, which she implicitly suggests are ultimately unrepresentative (46). The quotation from Gandhi is from *Hind Swaraj*, 13.

46. The "foreword" of *Hind Swaraj* is signed on the passenger cargo vessel *Kildonan Castle* (Union-Castle line, England to South Africa) and thus on the vehicle of a vital colonial communications and transportation route. The pamphlet was first published in *Indian Opinion*, a multilingual newspaper established by Gandhi as a transnational campaigning and informational medium. Hence, too, the figures of inquiring "Reader" and informing "Editor" that stage the voicing of Gandhi's insurrectionary dream-tableaux.

47. This is according to the information contained in Martin Kämpchen, *Rabindranath Tagore and Germany: A Bibliography* (Santiniketan: Visva-Bharati, 1997), 16, 18. Helene Meyer-Franck, who began translating Tagore from English, made an effort, heroic for its time and place, to learn Bengali well enough to translate it by 1930. See Martin Kämpchen, *Rabindranath Tagore in Germany: Four Responses to a Cultural Icon* (Shimla: Indian Institute of Advanced Study, 1999), 85–102; Rabindranath Tagore, *My Dear Master: Rabindranath Tagore and Helene Meyer-Franck/Heinrich Meyer-Benfey Correspondence, 1920-1938*, ed. Martin Kämpchen and Prasantkumar Pal (Santiniketan: Visva Bharati, 1999).

48. Dietmar Rothermund, *The German Intellectual Quest for India* (New Delhi: Manohar, 1986), 17.

49. An intellectual orientalism determined by Germany's "empire envy," perhaps, given that Germany had far fewer overseas colonial territories than the other great European powers. Other books that have dealt with these questions include Raymond Schwab, *The Oriental Renaissance: Europe's Rediscovery of India and the East, 1680-1880*, trans. Gene Patterson-Black and Victor Reinking (New York: Columbia University Press, 1984); Suzanne L. Marchand, *German Orientalism in the Age of Empire: Religion, Race, and Scholarship* (Washington, DC: German Historical Institute, 2009); Douglas T. McGetchin, Peter K. J. Park, and D. R. SarDesai, eds., *Sanskrit and "Orientalism": Indology and Comparative Linguistics in Germany, 1750-1958* (New Delhi: Manohar, 2004); Todd Curtis Kontje, *German Orientalisms* (Ann Arbor: University of Michigan Press, 2004); A. Leslie Willson, *A Mythical Image: The Ideal of India in German Romanticism* (Durham: Duke University Press, 1964); Douglas T. McGetchin, *Indology, Indomania, and Orientalism: Ancient India's Rebirth in Modern Germany* (Madison: Fairleigh Dickinson University Press, 2009).

50. Kämpchen, *Tagore in Germany*, 90, Kämpchen's emphasis.

51. Lukács, "Tagore's Gandhi Novel," 8. On the German "Tagore cult," see Kämpchen, *Tagore in Germany*.

52. An account of the itinerary of the tour may be found in Krishna Dutta and Andrew Robinson, *Rabindranath Tagore: The Myriad-Minded Man* (London: Bloomsbury, 1995), 219–36.

53. Hermann Keyserling, *The Travel Diary of a Philosopher*, trans. J. Holroyd-Reece (New York: Harcourt, Brace, 1925), 16–17; Keyserling, *Das Reisetagebuch eines Philosophen* (Munich: Duncker und Humblot, 1919).

54. "Asiatic Influences on the Intellectual Life of Contemporary Germany" (1920), appendix to Henri Massis, *Defence of the West*, trans. F. S. Flint (New York: Harcourt, Brace, 1928), 239.

55. Massis, "Asiatic Influences," 243. Tagore is one of the key exhibits in *Defence of the West*, and an additional appendix is devoted to criticizing him. Hereafter cited parenthetically in the text as Massis.

56. Daniel Halévy, quoted in Massis, 249. It should be noted that Massis's book is a tissue of quotations from other writers, such that it is sometimes very difficult to distinguish the author's voice from those he cites.

57. Wyndham Lewis, *Paleface: The Philosophy of the Melting-Pot* (London: Chatto and Windus, 1927). Besides Lukács, see Kämpchen, *Tagore in Germany*, 55–57, and Alex Aronson, *Rabindranath Through Western Eyes* (Calcutta: Rddhi India, 1978). Aronson documents the political uses to which the figure "Tagore" was put in Europe during the interwar period. With the ascendency of Nazism, Tagore's previously assumed originary Indic "Aryanness" was questioned and it was suggested that he might even be a crypto-Jew (62–63). Aronson quotes from a 1933 letter to the Calcutta *Statesman* that gives an account of a meeting in Germany where an audience member asserted that in fact his real name was "Rabbi Nathan" (63). Of course this is a letter to a newspaper, and thus hard to gauge as an index of general perception.

58. Kämpchen, *Tagore in Germany*, 54, emphasis Kämpchen's.

59. Alfred Bock, "Sanctified Days with Rabindranath Tagore," in *Rabindranath Tagore in Germany: A Cross-Section of Contemporary Reports*, ed. Dietmar Rothermund (New Delhi: Max Mueller Bhavan, German Cultural Institute, 1962). Cited in Kämpchen, *Tagore in Germany*, 52. Tagore himself was of course extremely skeptical about the "oriental fairy tale" being spun around him. Dutta and Robinson, *Rabindranath Tagore*, 235.

60. Jacques Derrida, *Of Grammatology*, trans. Gayatri Chakravorty Spivak (Baltimore: Johns Hopkins University Press, 1976), 75; Derrida, *De la grammatologie* (Paris: Editions de Minuit, 1967), 111–12. Cited hereafter with English and then French page numbers separated with a slash.

61. Derrida, *Of Grammatology*, 80/119. See also the comments on this passage in Spivak, *A Critique of Postcolonial Reason: Toward a History of the Vanishing Present* (Cambridge, MA: Harvard University Press, 1999), 280–81.

62. A more psychobiographical account would here discuss Lukács's status as an assimilated Hungarian Jew from the bourgeoisie of an inland empire recently dissolved. How might this have determined his perspective on India and Gandhi? A starting point can be found in Michael Löwy, *George Lukács: From Romanticism to Bolshevism*, trans. Patrick Camiller (London: NLB, 1979). Antonio Gramsci, who had a rather different geopolitical sensibility, wrote in 1930 that "India's political struggle against the English (and to a certain extent . . . that of Hungary against the Little Entente [of 1919]) knows three forms of war: war of movement, war of position, and underground warfare." The complexities of intraimperial struggle without open "military war" are at stake, and these colonial predicaments could open a different scene of comparison between the two figures. Gramsci, *Prison Notebooks*, 229.

63. Kalyan K. Chatterjee, "Lukács on Tagore: Ideology and Literary Criticism," *Indian Literature* 31, no. 3, no. 125 (June 1988): 156.

64. The quotation is from *The Programme of the Communist International: Comintern Sixth Congress 1928* (New York: Workers Library, 1929), 74–5. The paragraph on Gandhism is in section 6, "The Strategy and Tactics of the Communist International in the Struggle for the Dictatorship of the Proletariat. 1. Ideologies Among the Working Class Inimical to Communism."

65. The detail of these discussions is discussed in Sobhanlal Datta Gupta, *Comintern, India and the Colonial Question, 1920–37* (Calcutta: Centre for Studies in Social Sciences, Calcutta/K. P. Bagchi, 1980), 115–67; Gupta, *Comintern and the Destiny of Communism in India, 1919–1943: Dialectics of Real and a Possible History* (Bakhrahat: Seribaan, 2006).

66. Satinath Bhaduri, *Jagori* (Kolkata: Prakash Bhavan, 2010). In 1950, the novel won the first Rabindra Puraskar, the highest literary prize granted by the state of West Bengal. It was translated into English by Lila Ray as *The Vigil* (Bombay: Asia Publishing House, 1960). All translations in the present chapter are my own, cited parenthetically in the text as *Jagori*, with page references to the Prakash Bhavan edition.

67. Hitesranjan Sanyal, "The Quit India Movement in Medinipur District," in *The Indian Nation in 1942*, ed. Gyanendra Pandey (Calcutta: K. P. Bagchi, 1988), 41. Cited parenthetically in the text hereafter as "Quit India."

68. Dipesh Chakrabarty, *Habitations of Modernity: Essays in the Wake of Subaltern Studies* (Chicago: University of Chicago Press, 2002), 61.

69. The most comprehensive and informative English-language account of Tagore's educational institutions is Kathleen M. O'Connell, *Rabindranath Tagore: The Poet as Educator* (Kolkata: Visva-Bharati, 2012).

70. Partha Mitter, *The Triumph of Modernism: India's Artists and the Avant-Garde, 1922–1947* (London: Reaktion, 2007).

71. Raymond Williams, "The Bloomsbury Fraction," in *Problems in Materialism and Culture* (London: Verso, 1980), 148–68.

72. Williams, 150.

73. For example, Spivak, "Righting Wrongs," passim.
74. Rabindranath Tagore, "Shiksar Bikiran [Education's Radiation]," in *Rabindra Racanabali* (Kolkata: Visva-Bharati, 1993), 16:330. Hereafter referred to parenthetically in the text as "Bikiran."
75. Sister Nivedita more or less indicates that the plans that she and Swami Vivekananda had for children's education among the rural poorest would have to be put aside, and thus they founded urban schools for a different class formation. Sister Nivedita, "Hints on National Education in India," in *The Complete Works of Sister Nivedita* (Ramakrishna Sarada Mission, 1968), 4:329–446; Sister Nivedita, "The Master as I Saw Him," in *Complete Works*, 1:15–276. A brief account may also be found in Gopal Mukhopadhyay, *Mass Education in Bengal, 1882–1914* (Calcutta: National, 1984), 176–77. Mukhopadhyay gives an account of the class fix and the general short-lived-ness of experiments in common education in Bengal through much of the colonial era.
76. Gopal, *Mass Education in Bengal*, 68–69; Syed Nurullah and J. P. Naik, *A History of Education in India During the British Period* (Bombay: Macmillan, 1951), 346–73; J. M. Sen, *History of Elementary Education in India* (Calcutta: Book, 1933), 156–76.
77. Tagore, "Shiksar Herpher," in *Rabindra Racanabali*, 6:565–76. Hereafter referred to parenthetically in the text as "Herpher." *Herpher* means "alteration" or "modification," in the sense of creating differences or anomalies. I translate it perhaps too strongly as "aberrance" to catch the sense of out-of-jointness emphasized by Tagore, almost in the sense of a vicious circle or double bind.
78. It is doubtless the case that indigenous educational institutions were disrupted and destroyed during the colonial era. Tagore suggests that not only the old *pathsalas* and *tols* (teaching institutions) but a general extrainstitutional social effect of intellectual development has been obliterated by alien monoculture. For this argument—trees fertilizing the environment and being fed in turn—see especially Tagore, "Shiksar Swangikaran," in *Rabindra Racanabali*, 16:337–51. It is extremely difficult to gather detailed and specific material on precolonial educational structures and practices in India. Dharampal, *The Beautiful Tree: Indigenous Indian Education in the Eighteenth Century* (New Delhi: Biblia Impex, 1983) remains a useful resource, as do British colonial surveys such as William Adam, *Reports on the State of Education in Bengal, 1835 and 1838*, ed. Anathnath Basu (Calcutta: University of Calcutta, 1941), and Charles Trevelyan, *On the Education of the People of India* (Longman, 1838). The actual transformations of the colonial era are more amply documented, at least from the side of State archival sources, as witness the compendious volume by Nurullah and Naik, *A History of Education in India During the British Period*. The vicissitudes of East India Company work, missionary activity, and the "Anglo-Oriental Controversy" are described in D. P. Sinha, *The Educational Policy of the East India Company in Bengal to 1854* (Calcutta: Punthi Pastak, 1964). Paramesh Acharya, *Bangalir Shikshachinta* (Kolkata: Dey's, 2011) gives an overview of the modern period's educational theory with more extensive reference to Bengali theory and reform practices. It seems to me that Tagore's account of the precolonial educational situation is rather idealized, but this idealization is in part a rhetorical foil to illustrate the specific class divisions that have been institutionalized as modernity and Enlightenment.
79. Tarashankar Bandyopadhyay, *The Tale of Hansuli Turn*, trans. Ben Conisbee Baer (New York: Columbia University Press, 2011). Hereafter parenthetically referenced in the text as *Hansuli* with page numbers following. I refer throughout to the author as

Tarashankar, the way he is invariably respectfully known in the subcontinent. All other translations from Bengali are mine. Some of the following is drawn from my essay on *The Tale of Hansuli Turn*: Baer, "Creole Glossary: Tarashankar Bandyopadhyay's *Hansuli Banker Upakatha*," PMLA 125, no. 3 (May 2010): 622–39.

80. Suniti Kumar Chatterjee, *The Origin and Development of the Bengali Language* (1926; New Delhi: Rupa, 2002), 89.

81. Chatterjee, *Origin and Development*, 79–117, has an important and detailed discussion of *apabhrangsa*. More discussion may be found in Aloka Parasher, *Mlecchas in Early India: A Study in Attitudes Towards Outsiders up to AD 600* (New Delhi: Munshiram Manoharlal, 1991); and Sheldon Pollock, *The Language of the Gods in the World of Men: Sanskrit, Culture, and Power in Premodern India* (Berkeley: University of California, 2006).

82. Chatterjee, *Origin and Development*, 91.

83. Édouard Glissant, *Poetics of Relation*, trans. Betsy Wing (Ann Arbor: University of Michigan Press, 1997), 118.

84. I here use the term *Creole* loosely so as to relate it to Glissant's work on creolity, and I differentiate the trajectory of my inquiry from the trend in positivist linguistics that attempts to mine literary representations for verifiable information about dialect distribution, variation, or authorial linguistic competence. Representative examples of the latter would be Sumner Ives, "A Theory of Literary Dialect," in *A Various Language: Perspectives on American Dialects*, ed. Juanita V. Williamson and Virginia M. Burke (1950; New York: Holt, Rinehart and Winston, 1971); and E. W. Schneider and C. Wagner, "The Variability of Literary Dialect in Jamaican Creole," *Journal of Pidgin and Creole Languages* 21, no. 3 (2006): 45–96. In such studies the *literary* staging of "dialect" (Creoles, pidgins, and so on) is typically reduced to, at best, a sub-Barthesian "reality effect" and subordinated to an entirely empirical register. "Hinduized aborigines" is the typologization used in Risley's colonial anthropology to denote those Indians living on the cusp of the tribal and nontribal worlds. H. H. Risley, *The Tribes and Castes of Bengal: Ethnographic Glossary* (Calcutta: Bengal Secretariat, 1892).

85. Barbara Stoler Miller, *Theater of Memory: The Plays of Kalidasa* (New York: Columbia University Press, 1984); Sheldon Pollock, *The Language of the Gods in the World of Men*.

86. A selection of the original criticism can be found in Dhananjay Das, ed., *Marksbadi Sahitya-Bitarka* (Kolkata: Karuna Prakasani, 2003).

87. Verrier Elwin, *The Aboriginals* (London: Oxford University Press, 1943), 32.

88. David Hardiman, *Gandhi in His Time and Ours: The Global Legacy of His Ideas* (London: C. Hurst, 2003), 150–51.

89. G. S. Ghurye, *The Scheduled Tribes* (Bombay: Popular Prakashan, 1963), 11–20.

90. An appropriate collective name for the "untouchable" groups had been debated since the 1920s. The colonial administration's term was *Depressed Classes*, though *untouchable* was a popular term, even entering official discourse in 1909. Various less patronizing alternatives were proposed by Ambedkar and R. Srinivasan during the period of the Round Table Conferences in the late 1920s and early 1930s (e.g., "Non-caste Hindus" or even "Protestant Hindus"), but Gandhi then brought in the religious-popular term *Harijan*, which stuck. In the Indian Constitution of 1950 the term is *Scheduled Castes*, while the *adivasis* become *Scheduled Tribes*. For a more detailed examination of the emergence of these terms, see Marc Galanter, *Competing Equalities: Law and the Backward Classes in India* (Berkeley: University of California Press, 1984), 18–40. The Sanskritic *dalit* (downtrodden, oppressed), now widely adopted, was in use in the 1930s but did not gain more

general currency until the 1960s and 1970s. It was perhaps coined as a translation of the "depressed" in "depressed classes."

91. Partha Chatterjee, *The Nation and Its Fragments: Colonial and Postcolonial Histories* (New Delhi: Oxford University Press, 1993), 125.

92. Hundreds of nomadic or resistant rural groups were outlawed by the British during the nineteenth century as "born criminals" or "Criminal Tribes." These communities were subjected both to continual police surveillance and harassment and to anthropological classification. Christoph von Fürer-Haimendorf, *Tribal Populations and Cultures of the Indian Subcontinent* (Leiden: Brill, 1985); G. N. Devy, *A Nomad Called Thief: Reflections on Adivasi Silence* (New Delhi: Orient Longman, 2006).

93. Suniti Kumar Chatterjee, "Letter to Tarashankar Bandopadhyay," in *Prasanga Hansuli Banker Upakatha*, ed. Rabin Pal, Nimai Das, and Anil Ray (Kolkata: Chatterjee, 1996), 4, my translation.

94. Pareschandra Majumdar, "Tarashankar: Bhasajagat," in *Tarashankar: Desh, Kal, Sahitya*, ed. Ujjvalkumar Majumdar (Kolkata: Pustik Bipani, 1998), 218; Debesh Ray, *Upanibesher Samaj O Bangla Sangbadik Gadya* (Kolkata: Papyrus, 1990); Rabin Pal, Nimai Das, and Anil Ray, eds., *Prasanga Hansuli Banker Upakatha* (Kolkata: Chatterjee Publishers, 1996); Parthapratim Bandopadhyay, "Hansuli Banker Upakathar Jagat," in *Prasanga Hansuli Banker Upakatha*, 1–16; Purnendusekhar Mukhopadhyay, *Marksiya dristikone Tarashankarer upanyas* (Kolkata: Pustak Bipani, 1994); Ranjitkumar Mukhopadhyay, *Tarashankar o Rarh-Bangla* (Kolkata: Nabark, 1987).

95. V. N. Vološinov, *Marxism and the Philosophy of Language*, trans. Ladislav Matjeka and I. R. Titunik (Cambridge, MA: Harvard University Press, 1986), 137. Hereafter referenced parenthetically in the text as *Marxism*.

96. Vološinov, 144, original emphases. Vološinov's term for it (in the translation) is "quasi-direct discourse," defined as the "interferential merging of two differently oriented speech-acts" (137).

97. Vološinov regards the antagonistic voices as markers of social antagonisms, class struggles, not simply as reflections of already-secured class positions: "In the vicissitudes of the word are the vicissitudes of the society of word-users" (157). This must not be studied by only looking at language as the *"medium for ideological reflection of existence"* but in the enigmatic and more difficult project of a *"history of word in word"* (158, emphasis original).

98. The repetitive, refrain-like glossary device of *arthāt*, developed for this novel does not occur in other works by Tarashankar. A fuller history of the "standardization" of Bengali is too complex to enter into here. Modern "standard" Bengali developed in a tacit and fragmentary way during the nineteenth century and was primarily activated through and for literary production. Intimately linked to the response of the Bengali Hindu middle class to the colonial intervention, the changes wrought on the language had primarily to do with an attempt to excise its many Persian and Arabic lexical elements, as well as to regularize grammatical forms. The best accounts of this process to date are Anisuzzaman, *Muslim Manos O Bangla Sahitya* (Dhaka: Munir Chaudhuri, 1964); Sushil Kumar De, *Bengali Literature in the Nineteenth Century* (Calcutta: Firma K. L. M., 1962); Quasi Abdul Mannan, *Adhunik Bangla Sahitye Muslim Sadhana* (Dhaka: Student Ways, 1969); Mannan, *The Emergence and Development of Dobhasi Literature in Bengal* (Dhaka: University of Dhaka, 1966); Debesh Ray, *Upanibesher Samaj O Bangla Sangbadik Gadya* (Kolkata: Papyrus, 1990).

99. A comparative study would be worth undertaking. For example, Raja Rao's *Kanthapura* (1938, notes 1963), John Masters's *Night Runners of Bengal* (1951), and R. K. Narayan's *Malgudi Days* (1972) would each yield very different considerations of the relation of the glossary to the main textual body.

100. The earlier *Ananda Bazar* version is more explicit that it is the narrator "in person" who is addressed by Suchand. Bandyopadhyay, "Hansuli Banker Upakatha," *Ananda Bazar Patrika*, Puja number (1353 [1946]): 20–78, "Suchand told me this story . . .'If ya can, keep it in writin'," 78.

101. "To write is to produce a mark that will constitute a kind of machine that is in turn productive." Jacques Derrida, "Signature, Event, Context," in *Margins of Philosophy*, trans. Alan Bass (Hemel Hempstead: Harvester, 1982), 314.

102. Hardiman, *Gandhi*, 155.

103. Galanter, *Competing Equalities: Law and the Backward Classes in India*; Eleanor Zelliot, *From Untouchable to Dalit: Essays on the Ambedkar Movement* (New Delhi: Manohar, 1996).

104. See note 41.

105. Sanyal, "The Quit India Movement in Medinipur District," details participation of many *adivasi* and peasant groups in the uprisings of 1942 in Medinipur district, Bengal. The Congress established parallel "national administration" in many areas. For example, in Rampur Hat subdivision (northern Birbhum) "civil administration completely collapsed" (41), and there were comparable areas in which Congress controlled parallel government in Medinipur. It would perhaps be possible to ascribe the staging of distance from political militancy to Bandyopadhyay's own politics. Certainly, this kind of charge was made at the time *Hansuli Banker Upakatha* was published. Writing in the Marxist cultural journal *Marksbadi* in 1948, Bhowani Sen, secretary of the Bengal Committee of the Communist Party of India, described the novel as "reactionary literature" because "Tarashankarbabu, like Saratchandra, has only portrayed problems. It's not that he didn't give a solution, he did give one: that solution was for poor villagers to give up in the face of capitalism," cited in Ray, "Hansuli Banker Upakatha," *Ebang Musayera* 10, nos. 2–3 (2003): 67. Bandyopadhyay was jailed in 1930 for his work as a rural activist around his native Labhpur (Birbhum) within the nationalist movement. On release from prison in 1932 he disengaged from activism somewhat, pledging to engage with the political through literary means. Tarashakar's relationship with party Communism became much more antagonistic (on both sides) during the 1940s. See Bandyopadhyay, *Amar Sahitya Jiban*; Malini Bhattacharjya, "Tarashankarer Silpakriti O Fyasibirodhi Lekhaksilpisangha," *Janark* (Sraban-Paus 1390); Ashok Bandyopadhyay, "Gana andolane Tarashankar," *Sakhal Tumi*, Boisakh-Aswin Number (1405 B.S. [1998]); Sudhi Pradhan, ed., *Marxist Cultural Movement in India: Chronicles and Documents* (Calcutta: Santi Pradhan, 1979).

INDEX

movement and, 151, 163, 331*n*18;
Notebook of a Return to the Native Land, 96;
Sartre on, 157–58; *A Season in the Congo*,
151–52; on self, 143–45; Senghor and,
322*n*37; on struggle, 140, 143, 145; *The
Tragedy of King Christophe*, 151–52. *See also
Cahier d'un retour au pays natal* (Césaire)
Chakrabarty, Dipesh, 12–13
Chambers, Jessie, 342*n*7
Changeling, 67–68
Chatterjee, Bankim Chandra, 273
Chatterjee, Kalyan, 265–66
Chatterjee, Partha, 7–8, 279
Chatterjee, Suniti Kumar, 281
Chauri Chaura incident, 258–59, 354*n*39
Cheah, Pheng, 48
Chervel, André, 164–66, 168
Chesterton, G. K., 150
China, 211
Christianity, 248
Citizenship, 99–100, 103, 112–13, 117–18, 133,
136–38, 319*n*17
Civilizationism, 316*n*102, 327*n*84
Class, 218–20, 320*n*22
Classism, 218–19
Class struggle, 101, 252
Clifford, James, 158
Cohen, Hermann, 52–53
Cold War, 15–16, 150–51
Collectivity, 18–19, 204, 222, 260, 321*n*32
Colonial classroom, 168, 174–88
Colonial education, 16–17, 25, 95–138,
146–48, 150–88, 271–76
Colonial humanism, 98, 134, 320*n*19
Colonialism, 12–15, 51, 114, 121–22, 135,
224–25. *See also* Internal colonialism
Colonial Month, of Paris International
Exposition, 133–34
Colonial rape, 226–27
Colonial subject, 6, 233
Colonization, 118, 121–22, 217, 227, 325*n*68.
See also Decolonization
Colonizers, 257
Common education, 3, 23, 25, 31, 43, 272–76
Common school, 34
Communism, 37–38, 149, 195–96, 202,
211–12, 266

Communist International, 265
Communist Party of India, 211
Condorcet, 36, 300*n*70
Congress of Black Writers and Artists in
Paris, 325*n*68, 335*n*28
Congress of the League Against Imperial-
ism, of 1927, 293*n*1
Congress Party, 244, 260
Connolly, James, 345*n*42
Conrad, Joseph, 213, 215–17, 222, 225
Coppet, Marcel de, 138
Cortés, Hernan, 220
Cosmopolitanism, 202–3
Counterassimilation, 115, 118, 120
Craven, David, 227–28
Creole language, 166–67, 277, 281–87, 358*n*84
Critical philosophy, of education, 99–100
Critique of Judgment (Kant), 11
Critique of Postcolonial Reason, A (Spivak), 11
"Critique of Violence" (Benjamin), 251–53,
257
Cullen, Countee, 75
Cultural deficit, Lenin on, 38–39
Culture, 302*n*89; agriculture and, 120–21,
124; American, Locke on, 64, 67, 69;
assimilation and, 110; colonization into,
121; education and, 108–9, 111; episteme
of, 109; Franco-African, 135–36; Lenin
on, 38–39; literature and, 126–27;
Mesoamerican, 204; modern conception
of, 136; national, 48; Senghor on, 108–11,
114, 126–29, 133, 135–36
Curtius, Ernst Robert, 263
Cypess, Sandra Messinger, 226

Dakar, 117, 122–23, 135, 138
Damas, Léon-Gontran, 92, 94–96, 104,
128–32, 323*n*51
Dange, S. A., 243–46, 251–52, 267–68, 349*n*1
Dark Princess (Du Bois), 89
Davis, Gregson, 161–62
Death penalty, 110, 270
Debray, Régis, 208
Decolonization, 14–16, 150–54, 313*n*71
Delavignette, Maurice, 135
Delavignette, Robert, 100–1, 122, 326*n*75
De Man, Paul, 53

Modernist Latitudes

JESSICA BERMAN AND PAUL SAINT-AMOUR, EDITORS

Barry McCrea, *In the Company of Strangers: Family and Narrative in Dickens, Conan Doyle, Joyce, and Proust*, 2011

Jessica Berman, *Modernist Commitments: Ethics, Politics, and Transnational Modernism*, 2011

Jennifer Scappettone, *Killing the Moonlight: Modernism in Venice*, 2014

Nico Israel, *Spirals: The Whirled Image in Twentieth-Century Literature and Art*, 2015

Carrie Noland, *Voices of Negritude in Modernist Print: Aesthetic Subjectivity, Diaspora, and the Lyric Regime*, 2015

Susan Stanford Friedman, *Planetary Modernisms: Provocations on Modernity Across Time*, 2015

Steven S. Lee, *The Ethnic Avant-Garde: Minority Cultures and World Revolution*, 2015

Thomas S. Davis, *The Extinct Scene: Late Modernism and Everyday Life*, 2016

Carrie J. Preston, *Learning to Kneel: Noh, Modernism, and Journeys in Teaching*, 2016

Gayle Rogers, *Incomparable Empires: Modernism and the Translation of Spanish and American Literature*, 2016

Donal Harris, *On Company Time: American Modernism in the Big Magazines*, 2016

Celia Marshik, *At the Mercy of Their Clothes: Modernism, the Middlebrow, and British Garment Culture*, 2016

Christopher Reed, *Bachelor Japanists: Japanese Aesthetics and Western Masculinities*, 2016

Eric Hayot and Rebecca L. Walkowitz, eds., *A New Vocabulary for Global Modernism*, 2016

Eric Bulson, *Little Magazine, World Form*, 2016

Aarthi Vadde, *Chimeras of Form: Modernist Internationalism Beyond Europe, 1914–2014*, 2016